Development Administration in Latin America

Development Administration in Latin America

Edgardo Boeninger   Mark W. Cannon
Luigi R. Einaudi   Lawrence S. Graham
Roderick T. Groves   Alberto Guerreiro-Ramos
Helio Jaguaribe   Fred D. Levy, Jr.
Charles J. Parrish   James Frank Petras
John C. Shearer   Frank P. Sherwood
Gilbert B. Siegel   Clarence E. Thurber
William S. Tuohy   Jerry L. Weaver

Edited by Clarence E. Thurber
and Lawrence S. Graham

Published in cooperation with the Comparative Administration
Group of the American Society for Public Administration
Duke University Press, Durham, North Carolina 1973

L.C.C. card number 72–96986
I.S.B.N. 0–8223–0292–6

Printed in the United States of America
by Kingsport Press, Inc.

To

Fred W. Riggs

and to the memory of

Herbert Emmerich

Contributors

Edgardo Boeninger was born in Santiago, Chile, in 1925. He graduated in 1950 from the Catholic University of Chile with the degree of Civil Engineer, and in 1960 he received the degree of Commercial Engineer Economist from the University of Chile. Between 1948 and 1955 he served on the faculty of the Catholic University of Chile, first in the School of Engineering and then in the Faculty of Architecture. Between 1958 and 1969 he served successively as Professor of Economics, as Academic Coordinator for economics and for mathematics and statistics, and as Dean—all in the Faculty of Economics in the University of Chile. From 1969 to the present time he has been the Rector of the University. His government service includes work as Traffic Engineer for the City of Santiago, Director of the Budget in the Ministry of Finance, and member of the national advisory Economic Council for the years 1964–69. He has been a delegate to many international conferences sponsored by organizations such as the United Nations, the Organization of American States, the Council on Higher Education in the American Republics, and others, at which he has presented papers on such topics as administrative reform, the teaching of management in Latin American universities, and on various problems of education in Latin America.

Mark W. Cannon was born in Salt Lake City, Utah, in 1928. He received his bachelor's degree from the University of Utah and master's and doctor's degrees in political economy and government from Harvard University. He worked as administrative assistant to Congressman Henry Aldous Dixon and subsequently was chairman of the Political Science Department of Brigham Young University. He then directed, in Venezuela, an urban development technical assistance project of the Institute of Public Administration (IPA), New York, financed by the Ford Foundation. This project helped develop Fundacomun, the Foundation for Community Development and Municipal Improvement. As Director of International Programs of IPA, he supervised an advisory project in public administration training and governmental reorganization in Peru, assisted the Municipal League of the Dominican Republic and consulted with Insora at the University of Chile. He studied and worked in Argentina and Mexico. As Director of IPA, he has supervised projects in metropolitan reorganization and urban transportation as well as overseas development projects in Africa and Asia and Latin America. In 1972, he became Administrative Assistant to the Chief Justice of the U.S. Supreme Court. His books include *The Makers of Public Policy: American Power Groups and Their Ideologies* with R. Joseph Monsen (1965); *Partnership for Progress: Atlanta-Fulton County Consolidation* with others (1969); *Urban Government for Valencia* (forthcoming). His published papers include "The Role of Host Institutions in Increasing the Benefits from Technical Assistance Programs" (Inter-American Development Bank, 1966), and "Latin American Cultural Values as They Affect Decision Making and Program Implementation" (American Society for Public Administration, 1971).

Luigi R. Einaudi was born in Cambridge, Massachusetts, in 1936 and received his bachelor of arts and his Ph.D. degrees from Harvard University in 1957 and 1967, respectively. He now holds concurrent positions as a member of the Social Science Department of the Rand Corporation and as a member of the Department of Political Science at the University of California at Los Angeles. His publications include an essay *Changing Contexts of Revolution in Latin America* (1966), a co-authored monograph *An Annotated Bibliography of Latin American Military Journals,* and an article "University Autonomy and Academic Freedom in Latin America" (published in *Law and Contemporary Problems* in 1963). Recently he has published accounts in *U.S. Foreign Policy and Peru,* ed. Daniel A. Sharp, under the title "United States Relations with the Peruvian Military as Military and as Government," and a Rand document prepared jointly with Alfred C. Stepan III, *Latin American Institutional Development: Changing Military Perspectives in Peru and Brazil.*

Lawrence S. Graham was born in Daytona Beach, Florida, in 1936. He received his B.A. in Spanish from Duke University in 1958, his M. A. in Hispanic studies from the University of Wisconsin in 1961, and his Ph.D. in political science from the University of Florida in 1965. He is associate professor of Government, University of Texas (Austin), and he is currently chairman of the Latin American Development Administration Committee, a position which he assumed as of September 1970. His field work includes experience in Brazil,

Peru, Mexico, and Portugal. During 1967 and 1968 he held the position of Public Administration Adviser in Peru under contract with the Institute of Public Administration of New York and the U.S. Agency for International Development. His publications include *Civil Service Reform in Brazil: Principles versus Practice* (1968), *Politics in a Mexican Community* (1968), and *Mexican State Government: A Prefectural System in Action* (1971). His current research concerns public administration in Portugal, where he conducted field research during the latter half of 1971, on a grant from the Gulbenkian Foundation, and development administration in Latin America.

Roderick T. Groves was born in Madison, Wisconsin, in 1936 and received both the bachelor's degree (1958) and the doctor's degree (1965) in political science from the University of Wisconsin. He then joined the faculty of Northern Illinois University in 1965, where he is presently associate professor of political science. He has served as a visiting professor at the University of Indiana. His early Latin American field research was conducted in Venezuela and Mexico. He has contributed to various professional journals, including the *Public Administration Review,* particularly in the area of admnistrative reform. Currently he is involved in research on political development in Latin America, with particular reference to Colombia, where he did field research during 1970–71. During academic year 1971–72, he was on leave from his university in the position of Director of Higher Education for the Illinois Department of Education.

Alberto Guerreiro-Ramos was born in Brazil in 1915. He holds a degree in law from the University of Rio de Janeiro and a degree in social science from the National Faculty of Philosophy in Brazil. He was a member of the technical staff of the Civil Cabinet of the Presidency of the Republic of Brazil (1951–54), and was a delegate to the Sixteenth General Assembly of the United Nations. He was also a member of the Committee on Foreign Relations and of the Committee on the Judiciary while serving in the Brazilian National Congress and represented the House of Representatives at the 1963 Latin American Conference, preparatory to the World Conference on Commerce. He held a chair in sociology at the Brazilian School of Public Administration of the Getulio Vargas Foundation, 1952–70, and has taught sociology at the Superior Institute of Brazilian Studies and the Faculty of Sciences (Rural University of Brazil). He was also distinguished lecturer at the University of Paris (1955). Since 1966 he has been professor of public administration at the School of Public

Administration, University of Southern California. He is the author of *Industrial Sociology* (1952), *Sociology of Infant Mortality* (1955), *Critical Introduction to Brazilian Sociology* (1957), *Sociological Reduction* (1958; 2d ed., 1965), *The National Problem of Brazil* (1960), *The Crisis of Power in Brazil* (1961), *Myth and Truth of the Brazilian Revolution* (1963), and *Administration and Strategy of Development* (1966), all of which were published in Portuguese. He is presently preparing a book entitled *The Parenthetical Man: An Anthropological Approach to Organization Design,* to be published in the United States.

Helio Jaguaribe was born in Rio de Janeiro in 1923, where he received his diploma from the Law School of the Pontifical Catholic University in 1946. Since then, he has concentrated on political science and social theory with respect to problems of sociopolitical development and Brazilian and Latin American affairs. In 1952 he started, with a group of young economists, sociologists, and political scientists, a research and teaching project for the reformulation of the current understanding of Brazilian sociopolitical structure. This Itatiaia Group was the nucleus of the subsequently founded Brazilian Institute of Economics, Sociology and Politics, active in the 1950's. The Institute's journal, *Cadernos do Nosso Tempo,* acquired national influence and was a major source of Brazilian thinking in the social sciences concerning national development. In 1956 he played a leading role in the foundation, in the Ministry of Education and Culture, of the Superior Institute of Brazilian Studies (ISEB) which continued and developed the work of the previous institute. Head of the Department of Political Science of ISEB until 1959, he resigned as a consequence of the national controversy over his book *Nationalism in Brazil Today,* which opposed "etatists" to his development-oriented conception of nationalism. He has since then been engaged in teaching and research in Brazil and abroad and is currently professor of political science and fellow in the Instituto Universitario de Pesquisas of Rio de Janeiro. He has been visiting professor of political science at Harvard (1964–66), Stanford (1966–67), and M.I.T. (1968–69). He is also a member of the Committee of Direction of the Latin American Council of the Social Sciences (1972–76). Professor Jaguaribe's books include *Nationalism in Brazil Today* (Rio: ISEB, 1958); *Economic and Political Development* (Rio: Fundo de Cultura, 1962; English translation, Cambridge: Harvard University Press, 1968); *Problems of the Latin American Development* (Rio: Civilização Brasileira, 1967); and *Political Development* (New York: Harper and Row, 1971). He has published widely in leading professional journals.

Fred D. Levy, Jr., was born in Chicago in 1937. He did his undergraduate work at Purdue University and received his doctorate in economics from Yale University in 1966. He has been a member of the faculty of the Maxwell School of Public Affairs at Syracuse University since 1964, taking leave of absence from 1967 to 1969 to serve as economic adviser in the US AID mission to Brazil, and again from 1972 to the present to join the Treasury Department. He has also served as a consultant to AID, as well as to other public and private organizations. He is author of *Economic Planning in Venezuela* (1968), *Documentos para projetos de planejamento* (1971), and *Basic Economics: Analysis of Contemporary Problems and Policies* (1973, with Sidney C. Sufrin) in addition to papers on planning, technical assistance, and international relations.

Charles J. Parrish was born in Los Angeles in 1933. He obtained his bachelor's degree (1955) and his master's (1960)—both in political science—from the University of Florida. He served as a pilot in the U.S. Air Force, 1955 to 1959. He was awarded his Ph.D. from the University of North Carolina in 1964. He is currently chairman and professor in the Department of Political Science at Wayne State University and co-director of the Wayne State–University of Michigan Institute of Gerontology. He previously held positions as associate professor of government, University of Texas, Austin; Visiting Fulbright Professor, University of Chile, Santiago; and Visiting Senior Lecturer, University of Essex, England. He has published monographs and articles on Chilean politics and presented papers, lectures and seminars at a number of universities. A book on Chilean politics will be published in 1973.

James Frank Petras was born in Lynn, Massachusetts, in 1937. He received his B.A. from Boston University and his M.A. and Ph.D. from the University of California, Berkeley, in 1963 and 1967 respectively, where he was a fellowship recipient at the Institute of International Studies. In 1965–66, he conducted research in Chile on a Doherty Fellowship. In the summer of 1967, he was a visiting professor at the Center for the Study of Democratic Institutions at Santa Barbara. In September 1967 he joined the Pennsylvania State University political science faculty and was also director of Latin American Development Studies in the Institute of Public Administration, a project financed by the Ford Foundation. In 1970–71 he was on leave with a Ford Faculty Fellowship conducting research on agrarian reform and public administration in Peru and Chile. He is currently professor of sociology

at the State University of New York, Binghamton. He is the author of
Politics and Social Forces in Chilean Development (1969), *Politics
and Social Structure in Latin America* (1970), co-author of *Cultivat-
ing Revolution* (1971), co-editor of *Latin America: Reform or Revolution,* and *Fidel Castro Speaks,* co-author of *Peasants in Revolt* (1973)
and editor of *Latin American Dependence on Revolution* (1973). He
has contributed to numerous professional journals. He is currently
completing research on the industrial elite of Argentina.

John C. Shearer was born in Philadelphia in 1928. He received his
undergraduate training at Cornell University and was subsequently a
Fulbright fellow at the University of Manchester, England. After five
years with Union Carbide Corporation, he received the master's and
Ph.D. degrees in economics from Princeton University. He has been
assistant professor of economics in the Graduate School of Industrial
Administration, Carnegie Institute of Technology; professor-economist,
Latin American Institute of Economic and Social Planning (U.N.
Economic Commission for Latin America), Santiago, Chile; and
associate professor of economics at Pennsylvania State University. He
joined the faculty of Oklahoma State University in 1967, where he is
presently professor of economics and director, Manpower Research
and Training Center. He is a labor arbitrator and member of the
Southwest Regional Manpower Advisory Committee. He has served
as a consultant on manpower matters in Colombia, Venezuela, Peru,
and Chile for the Organization of American States, the Ford Foundation, the Council for International Progress in Management, and
Educational and World Affairs and has served as a consultant in the
United States for the United Nations and the Organization of American States. He was guest lecturer for several years at the International
Manpower Institute. His published works include *High-Level Manpower in Overseas Subsidiaries: Experience in Brazil and Mexico*
(1960), *La importación y la exportación de los recursos humanos*
(1964); and *Formación y utilización de los recursos humanos en
empleo* (1964). He is a co-author of *Los recursos humanos como parte
de los procesos economicos* (1963); *The Development and Utilization
of Human Resources: A Guide for Research* (1967); and *Employment
and Unemployment Trends in Colombia* (1969); and has been a contributing author to Solomon Barkin et al., eds., *International Labor*
(1967); Alfred Kamin, ed., *Western European Labor and the American Corporation* (1970); and James Heaphey, ed., *Spatial Dimensions
of Development Administration* (1971). He has contributed to a
variety of professional journals.

Frank P. Sherwood was born in Brunswick, Georgia, in 1920. He received his A.B. from Dartmouth College and his doctorate in political science from the University of Southern California in 1952. He was on the faculty of that institution from 1951 to 1968, during which time he served in overseas programs in Iran and Brazil. He was director of the Federal Executive Institute in Charlottesville, Virginia, from 1969 to 1973. At present he is Director of U.S.C. affairs in Washington, D.C. Previously he served as director of the School of Public Administration at the University of Southern California. He is a member of the National Academy of Public Administration, a former member of the National Council of the American Society for Public Administration, and a member of the board of trustees of the Inter-University Case Program. His books include *Institutionalizing the Grass Roots in Brazil: A Study in Comparative Local Government* (1967), *Administrative Organization,* with John M. Pfiffner (1960), and *California's System of Governments,* with Richard W. Gable (1968). He has been a contributor to other volumes in the Comparative Administration Series, notably *Frontiers of Development Administration,* ed. Fred W. Riggs.

Gilbert B. Siegel was born in Los Angeles in 1930. He received his bachelor's and master's degrees in public administration from the University of Southern California (1952, 1957) and his Ph.D. in political science from the University of Pittsburgh (1964). From 1954 to 1957 he held various management positions with the County of Los Angeles. He served in research, teaching, advisory, and administrative roles with the University of Southern California in Iran (1957–59) and Brazil (1961–63). He now is associate professor of public administration, School of Public Administration, University of Southern California. He has also held positions in the Graduate School of Public and International Affairs, University of Pittsburgh (1959–61) and has served as consultant to national, state, and international agencies in regard to local government. He was consultant to the Creole Foundation, Venezuela (1959), the Brazilian School of Public Administration and the U.S. Agency for International Development (1969), and the United Nations (1970–71). He is author of *The Vicissitudes of Governmental Reform: The Case of Brazil* (1966). He has contributed articles on Brazilian government and public administration to leading professional journals at home and abroad; his research interests include administrative reform, personnel, institution building, environmental quality, and gaming simulation.

Clarence E. Thurber was born in Nampa, Idaho, in 1921 and received both his B.A. and Ph.D. (1961) in political science from Stanford University. During World War II he was research analyst with the Department of State, and during the immediate postwar period served as secretary of the Interdepartmental Committee on Scientific and Cultural Cooperation, a forerunner of the Point IV Program, where his interest was aroused in Latin American affairs. From 1948–52 he was a research associate with the International Studies Group at The Brookings Institution. He has been consultant to The Public Administration Clearing House, to the Foreign Affairs Task Force of the Hoover Commission, and to the U.S. Agency for International Development. From 1952 until 1962, he was program associate in the international division of the Ford Foundation. In 1962 he joined the faculty of Pennsylvania State University as associate professor of political science and public administration. At this time, he became a member of the executive committee of the Comparative Administration Group, on which he served until 1971. From 1963 until 1970 he was founding chairman and executive director of Study Fellowships for International Development, a ten-university consortium for education in overseas development assistance, financed by the Ford Foundation. In 1964, he became the first chairman of the Latin American Development Administration Committee, a position he held until 1970. During this period, he visited Latin America on numerous research and educational missions. During November 1967 he was co-chairman of the Conference on Research and Education in Public Administration sponsored by LADAC and the Getulio Vargas Foundation. In 1968 he did field research on administration and agricultural development in Guatemala on a grant from the Ford Foundation administered by the University of Oregon. In 1966 he had assumed his present position of professor of public and international affairs at the University of Oregon, where he is also director of the Program in Public Affairs and Administration and deputy director of the Institute of International Studies. His publications include, as author or co-author, *Major Problems of United States Foreign Policy* (3 vols.) 1947–48, 1948–49, and 1949–50; *The Governmental Mechanism for the Conduct of U.S. Foreign Relations* (1949); *The Search for the Peace Settlements* (1951); *The Administration of Foreign Affairs and Overseas Operations* (1951); *Training for Specialized Mission Personnel* (1952);"Training Foreign Administrators," in the *International Development Review* (1964); and "The Professional School and World Affairs," a report on a regional conference (1967). His articles and reviews have appeared in such journals as the *American Political Science Review*, *Western Political Quarterly*, the *Annals*, and the *International Development Review*.

William S. Tuohy was born and raised in western New York State and graduated from Cornell University in 1961. In the same year, as part of an anthropology field project, he lived with Peruvian Indians in Vicos and subsequently entered graduate school at Stanford University. After working as a sociologist he resumed his graduate education and in 1966 conducted research in Mexico, receiving the Ph.D. in political science in 1967. Since then, in addition to Latin American studies, he has devoted considerable attention to culture and personality as related to politics and student behavior and has worked with various approaches in humanistic psychology. He is an assistant professor at the University of California at Davis and is co-author of the following publications: "Political Control and the Recruitment of Middle-Level Elites in Mexico: An Example from Agrarian Politics," *Western Political Quarterly*, vol. 22 (1969); *Mexican University Students in Politics: Rebels Without Allies?*, monograph no. 3, Monograph Series in World Affairs, vol. 3 (1970); and *Politics and Privilege in a Mexican City* (Stanford University Press, 1972).

Jerry L. Weaver is associate professor of political science at California State University, Long Beach. He is currently engaged with a study of the political economy of health care delivery in Guatemala and Panama. His concern with Guatemala goes back to a year (1965–66) spent as a Doherty Foundation Fellow in research there and is expressed in numerous journal articles dealing with Guatemalan military, political elite, and public administration. His interest in Latin society and politics has led him to research in the Mexican American community and he has published widely on Mexican American health care behavior and its implications for public policy. Professor Weaver holds degrees from Ohio University and the University of Pittsburgh (Ph.D.) and has been at the University of Texas at Austin, both in the Institute for Latin American Studies and more recently (1971–72) as visiting professor in the Government Department.

Acknowledgments

A great many people involved in LADAC have contributed to the efforts that made this volume possible. The editors would like to thank the following: Frederick N. Cleaveland, Co-Chairman of LADAC during 1964–66, who while on the staff of the Brookings Institution contributed much to the success of the Washington Discussion Group; Morton Tenzer, Vice-Chairman of LADAC, who chaired the Washington Discussion Group for the following two years and who, with John Honey, contributed greatly to the planning and conduct of the Rio Conference; Athyr Guimarães, Director of the Inter-American School of Public Administration, who contributed in a crucial manner to the Rio Conference; and to Ernest deProspo, Charles Goodsell, Robert Daland and Ivan Richardson, who, in addition to the above-named, served on the Executive Committee of LADAC. Arnaldo Pessoa of the Inter-American Development Bank has been a valued source of advice and cooperation. Julian Malnak and Francis K. Cholko served at various times as Secretary of LADAC. Several Washington meetings were organized by Roy Crawley in 1968–69, and by Richard Fehnel and Jack Hopkins in 1971, and by Rogério Pinto in 1973.

In addition, we would like to thank the following organizations: the Comparative Administration Group, which provided the basic financing for LADAC; the Brookings Institution and the Institute of Public Administration, for providing space for our Washington meetings; the Ford Foundation, the Inter-American Development Bank, and the Getúlio Vargas Foundation, for financial support of the Rio Conference on Education and Research in Public Administration held at the Palácio Itamaraty, 6–10 November 1967, and the Inter-American School of Public Administration and the Getúlio Vargas Foundation for acting as host institutions; and to the American Society for Public Administration, which has provided administrative support and assistance over the years.

Thanks are also due to the Graduate School of the University of Texas for its support of the Austin Conference, held 9–11 April 1970, and to the Lyndon Baines Johnson School of Public Affairs and its Dean John A. Gronouski, for providing assistance for typing the final manuscript. The Institute of International Studies and Overseas Administration of the University of Oregon has provided administrative support throughout the production of the volume. We wish also to thank the editors of *Yale Economic Essays* for permission to reprint the contribution of Fred D. Levy, Jr., which originally appeared in the spring 1967 issue of that publication. Levy had earlier presented his chapter as a paper to the Washington Discussion Group. To all these individuals and organizations we are grateful; none is, however, responsible for the views expressed in the book. Only the authors can be praised or blamed for them, as the case may be.

Contents

Development Administration in Latin America

Introduction

Clarence E. Thurber

The Latin American Development Administration Committee (LADAC), founded in January 1964 as the first subcommittee of the Comparative Administration Group (CAG), was formed by a small group of professors and administrators who believed that public administration in Latin America would have to be greatly strengthened if the ambitious social goals of the Alliance for Progress were to be even approximately achieved.[1]

"Development administration" in 1964 was a relatively new term. Although a precise definition was not available, clearly it meant that basic or structural changes are necessary in administration in order to achieve development goals. While the meaning of the term has not been greatly clarified over the intervening years, still a number of characteristics can be spelled out. It is future-oriented; it is interdisciplinary; it is concerned with the administration of national plans and with implementation of public policy in such areas as agriculture, education, health, and industrialization; and it is sensitive to the environmental factors which influence bureaucratic behavior.

The founders of LADAC hoped to establish a four-way continuing conversation that would involve both academic persons and government practitioners, and both North Americans and Latin Americans. Several forums have developed over the past years as vehicles for maintaining this dialogue. The Washington Discussion Group was the first of these, meeting periodically. Papers presented and discussed at the Washington semi-

1. The author of this Introduction was chairman of LADAC from 1964 to 1970.

nars were not commissioned in advance; instead, the seminars served as a preliminary testing ground for reports on research and projects undertaken through other auspices. Chapters 1 to 5 of the book were all originally papers presented to the Washington Discussion Group. No underlying intellectual schema is claimed for them, except that they share a concern with development administration and its applications in Latin America. As always, there are two sides to the focus on development administration: to see it as it is, and to determine how it can be improved.

In Chapter 1 the present writer sets forth the concept of "islands of development" as one approach to development administration, pointing to the crucial role of the bureaucratic entrepreneur in organizational innovation and structural change. His role in forging "organizational links" between the upper levels of the political system, on the one hand, and the grass-roots levels of the social system, on the other, is seen to be crucial to development.

In Chapters 2 and 3, attention shifts from institution-building strategies to the problem of how to engineer change in the public sector at the top of a governmental system. Here the authors look at the experience of Venezuela in two areas: government-wide attempts at administrative reform and the creation of a national planning system. These two chapters let us compare alternative organizational strategies within a single country and similar time periods. The experience of Venezuela's Public Administration Commission, a cross-cultural application of the Hoover Commission idea, is reviewed by Roderick Groves (Chapter 2) as an effort of great magnitude and as an example of the vicissitudes of an organization which attempts to tackle administrative reform head-on. When the original paper was presented at a Washington seminar, it provided a particularly lively interplay between scholar and practitioner. Present at that meeting was the late Herbert Emmerich, an early proponent of the scheme and sometime U.N. adviser to the commission. In Fred Levy's chapter (Chapter 3) on the role of the Venezuelan Planning Commission, we have an instructive account of the manifest and latent roles a national-level planning body can play. In its overt role as economic planner and priority setter, the commission could not be judged an unqualified success. But, in its secondary or latent role as a political staff arm to the president—as a source of nonpartisan economic expertise which could be utilized for a variety of political and administrative as well as economic and social purposes—the commission apparently achieved a striking success. Tracing the relationships between the Public Administration Commission and the Planning Commission, and between them and the President of Venezuela, results in a fascinating account of bureaucratic politics, Latin American style.

In Chapter 4 Helio Jaguaribe argues that national development must be self-generative and that foreign technical assistance —unless remarkably attuned to the values of the host country and its dynamic political processes—will be dissipated and have only an "enclave effect." In his chapter, this Brazilian political scientist not only outlines a problem that has bedeviled foreign-aid efforts from the beginning; he also provides a leitmotif for much of the discussion that follows in Part II.

Providing an introduction to the theme of Part II—Mobilizing Human Resources for the Administration of Development Programs—is the problem of scarce human resources. John Shearer points out in Chapter 5 that at the beginning of the major Venezuelan land reform, only two or three persons in that government had technical competence in the area of land economics— namely, competence in deciding how large a parcel of land is needed to support a family of average size in a particular region. Yet action had to be taken. Thus, one of the familiar vicious cycles of development emerges once again, this one in human resources. Increasingly, the modernization process has come to be viewed in human terms which recognize high-level human resources as the scarcest of all scarce capital resources. What is the scope and nature of these resources needed for modernizing a country and how are they to be produced? The question leads us back to the theme of Chapter 1. For obviously a country "begins" with what it has. And while Chapter 5 is mostly about education, it highlights another development problem: How will the prevailing social values held by national leaders affect the allocation of resources for public and private purposes? Here is a critical problem for all countries at all stages of development.

The Washington scene served as an ideal center for discussions on the theory and practice of development administration. The four audiences we hoped to reach all had major representation in and around Washington: the United States Government, especially the Agency for International Development (AID) and other agencies concerned with Latin American development; international organizations such as the World Bank (IBRD), the United Nations, the Inter-American Development Bank (IDB), and the Organization of American States (OAS); private consulting organizations, such as the Institute of Public Administration of New York (with its Washington office); and professors from various universities. However, beyond this group LADAC wished to reach a wider audience. Vehicles for this endeavor were the *LADAC Occasional Papers*—a series of working papers circulated prior to their formal publication as articles or chapters in books; the LADAC portion of the *CAG Newsletter;* and the panels organized for annual meetings, particularly those of the American Society for Public Administration. In addition, LADAC was active in the two national-level conferences supported by the Comparative Administration Group: the conference held at College Park, Maryland, in April 1966 and the one held at Syracuse University in April 1971.

The third forum utilized by LADAC for stimulating interest in development administration in Latin America was international in scope: the organization of an inter-American conference on public administration. Out of the Washington seminars awareness developed of the important role played by research and educational institutions and training centers in preparing civil servants for careers which would keep them active in the development process. In order to explore this potential role more fully, plans were made for an international conference on teaching and research in public administration in Latin America. The conference was held in Rio de Janeiro, 7–11 November 1967, under joint sponsorship of LADAC, the Getúlio Vargas Foundation (Rio), and the Inter-American School of Public Administration (Rio). Here, the state of the arts in public administration in Latin America, and the conceptual differences between public administration and development administration, were explored, while focusing on the central role of teaching and research.

Part II of this book contains three papers selected from those presented at the Rio conference (Chapters 6, 7, and 8). These concentrate on the status of teaching and research in Latin American institutes and schools of public administration, consider new techniques to be employed in preparing persons for public service careers, and evaluate the experience gained from utilizing external resources to build more effective training programs.

As 1970 approached it became clear to the Executive Committee of LADAC that some reappraisal of its role was in order. Already the hopeful early stages of the Alliance had faded into the background. A new phase was at hand. A new administration in Washington had established its own style and was searching for a redefinition of policy toward Latin America. A new generation of scholars, both north and south of the border, were making their views known. All of these developments impinged on LADAC. It was a time for taking stock. Hence, the creation of a fourth forum for dialogue on Latin American development administration. The Austin conference, held at the University of Texas, 9–11 April 1970, provided such a forum. Organized under the direction of Lawrence Graham, the conference not only provided a set of papers designed to increase our empirical knowledge of Latin American administrative systems; it also re-examined, in business sessions, the basic purposes of LADAC, the progress that had been made in six years, its failures by commission and omission, and prospects for the future. The conference faced up to the major question—whether LADAC should continue, and if so, how—now that the Ford grant funding the operation of the Comparative Administration Group as a whole was coming to an end.

Partly because the Austin conference was both stimulating and intellectually rewarding, perhaps as much as or more than any other in LADAC's brief existence, the members present unanimously decided to go forward with whatever resources they could command. No doubt this conclusion was due to the fact that no other seemed rational. The past decade had seen the emergence of a generation of younger scholars trained in politics, economics, and administration with a strong commitment to fieldwork in Latin America. Those present at the conference had been part of this movement. Indeed, one participant who had done bibliographic research in the field estimated that 80 to 90 percent of all North Americans who had done research on public administration in Latin America were present. To them it seemed that LADAC was needed more than before. It was a natural step, and one highly gratifying to the writer, that Lawrence Graham agreed to become the chairman of LADAC beginning in September 1970.

The papers presented at Austin constitute, in a way, a new assessment of the role and prospects for development administration in Latin America. In a striking presentation, Professor Guerreiro-Ramos forecast the need for a "new ideology" for development administrators, based on a concern for individuals as human beings and on the need for clientele orientations which extend beyond narrow, partisan interests. In Chapter 15, while he does not supply a road map to the administrative promised land, Ramos raises fundamental issues, calls attention to the failure of the "old" public administration in Latin America, and makes a plea that both the academician and practitioner recognize that the current ferment in U.S. public administration has cross-national implications whose eventual impact on the Latin American republics cannot be overlooked.

Luigi Einaudi's Chapter 12, when read with Guerreiro-Ramos' chapter, brings to mind the question whether the "new reality" is in any way compatible with the "new ideology." Nevertheless, Einaudi's chapter is hopeful to the extent that military administrators are shown to be susceptible to some, even if not all, of the pressures that affect civilian bureaucrats. Jerry L. Weaver, in Chapter 13, raises a similar question through his examination of a civilian bureaucracy of middle-class origin during a period of rapid change in Guatemala. The dominant bureaucratic attitudes and behavior identified indicate the degree to which it is less than fully responsive to the developmental needs of the country. "Compliance norms" are much more likely to be fulfilled than performance norms. The Guatemalan bureaucracy is said to violate the rational model which development theory posits, partly because major decisions are made so far above operational levels that organizational controls from the top down are not really effective.

The Chilean case provides further insight into this dilemma of how to create bureaucratic supports for development policies and change-oriented programs when the average middle-range and upper-level bureaucrat is the product of a dependent or status-oriented middle class. Charles Parrish in Chapter 9 explores the gap between intent and result in human affairs. Parrish explains why he thinks that Selznick's theory of cooptation is a powerful concept in explaining the failure of development plans. He goes on to compare this concept with Riggs's concept of the prismatic society and indicates that he believes the former has the greater explanatory power. As Parrish sees it, organization theory developed in the United States has a great, unexplored potential for the analysis of data concerning Latin American bureaucratic behavior.

The question posed by William Tuohy in Chapter 10 is whether the Mexican elites are chiefly concerned with system maintainance or are still devoted to revolutionary goals, as their ideology claims. He focuses on the behavior of middle- and low-level political elites in a state capital (Jalapa, Veracruz) associated with the government party (PRI) that rules Mexico. While these are not the top-level or ruling elites, the author believes that the interaction between them and their political and administrative superiors, and their respective publics, provides a valuable insight into the governmental processes between state and nation. Tuohy finds confirmation of Parrish's belief in the explanatory power of cooptation, for, he writes, "the Mexican government's elaborate measure of cooptation and control certainly give cause for scepticism about opportunities for political participation." In the behavioral realm, he continues, "public

officials are encouraged toward conservatism . . . in the sense
that maintenance of the existing political structures and the status quo . . . is the safest goal." In the process, which is variously
termed "authoritarian executivism" and "administered politics,"
administrative performance suffers. Meanwhile, the Mexican government exhibits a devaluation of professional expertise and
planning. In closing, Tuohy asks: Will the dominant elites move
toward a policy of accommodation with dissatisfied publics, especially workers and peasants whom the revolution was supposed to benefit, or will they increasingly confront dissatisfied
publics with additional controls?

Although Gilbert Siegel in Chapter 14 is concerned with quite
a different political-administrative culture, located in Brazil,
half a continent away, his questions and his answers are remarkably and distressingly similar. Siegel's data are taken from
three vignettes of Brazilian administration history: (i) a résumé
of the history and problems of the Administrative Department of
the Public Service (DASP), an innovative central staff agency
having its origins under President Vargas in 1937, (ii) a brief
review of the functions of central plan development and plan
implementation during the period of the Alliance for Progress,
and (iii) a study of the reform of tax administration, assisted by
the U.S. AID. The latter had as a side effect a decline in the relative importance of Brazilian municipal government. Siegel's conclusions show a rough congruence with Tuohy's and are equally
pessimistic on the prospects of broadened participation. With
respect to DASP, for example, Siegel writes that the selection of
a strategy of control led to the failure of administrative reform
itself and eventually to an emasculation of the organization when
the Vargas dictatorship fell. DASP's reform functions either could
not be effectively performed or became transformed into authoritarian controls. Operating within the context of a closed
governmental system, it saw its reform goals displaced by the
power-maintenance needs of the country's leader. Further, with
respect to national planning, Siegel writes, to have aimed programs toward achievement and performance rather than at
patronage would have struck at "the roots of the political balance

of power." In the area of municipal government, Siegel details how a new constitution removed from municipalities sources of taxation that had always been theirs and brought about, through a set of intricate political devices, a near-total dependency of the municipalities on the central government. And finally, as if to destroy any lingering doubts, Siegel sums up his conviction that at least so far as Brazil is concerned, the accomplishment of developmental goals and the maintenance of the political regime remain incompatible.

Chapter 11 by James Petras on Cuba is more overtly concerned than other chapters with domestic political processes. It documents the shift in attention of the Castro regime, beginning in the mid-1960's, away from revolutionary movements abroad and toward its present concern with economic problems at home. With respect to the bureaucracy, the author asserts—and describes as far as he can—the impressive bureaucratic innovations that underlie the redistribution of national resources in benefit of large numbers of people, primarily rural inhabitants. These changes in the bureaucracy have occurred regardless of the emigration of the very sectors from which a bureaucracy ordinarily draws its technically and professionally trained members. While it would be premature to draw any significant comparisons or contrasts between the Cuban political administrative style and that of other Latin American governments, it should be noted that Petras' chapter is the only one to advance a claim, with some documentation, that the lot of the poorest classes in the society under review has shown improvement, due to the policy and action of the government concerned.

No conclusion in the ordinary meaning of the term is possible in a book of this nature. Yet some patterns do emerge; the significance of development administration in Latin America in the years of the 1960s is a proper subject for scholarly speculation. Accordingly, Lawrence Graham has written a final conspectus.

It would be impossible to complete this introduction without paying respect to the intellectual leadership that Fred Riggs has exercised in all CAG enterprises. As a member of the CAG Executive Committee for some seven years I observed this leadership at close range. In this time of reformation of all things international, it is clear to me that his intellectual and personal contributions to the study of comparative administration will remain of the first order. Hence it is only fitting that he be one of the two persons to whom we dedicate this volume.

The other individual to whose memory we have dedicated the volume, the late Herbert Emmerich, made signal contributions to the art and science of public administration through a long and useful career in the public service. He was perhaps best known to his North American colleagues as Director of the Public Administration Clearing House, with headquarters in Chicago. From his office at "1313" he made signal contributions to the practice of government at all levels in the United States. But to Latin Americans—and to many others in all parts of the world—he was best known for his work as Special Consultant to the Public Administration Division in the United Nations Secretariat. Emmerich completed his professional career as a member of the faculty at the University of Virginia, where he remained until his death.

Part I

Strategies for Development Administration

Chapter 1

Islands of Development: A Political and Social Approach to Development Administration in Latin America

Clarence E. Thurber

There appear to be two classic approaches to inducing development. One of them is to identify *elements of strength* in a society, and try to build programs and projects around them. The other is to identify *the strategic obstacles* (gaps or weaknesses) that must be overcome if certain goals are to be reached, and try to overcome them. The two approaches are useful and complementary. They both imply some type of political and administrative system, related in some manner to the needs and desires of the society. The first approach (building on strength) impresses me as the framework congenial to political leaders and development administrators. It recognizes that development takes leadership, requires action, and is something that happens through people both individually and in groups (organizations). But this approach has not been spelled out by social scientists in terms of the needs of the development administrator.

Albert Waterston in his book *Development Planning* gives an illustration of this point. In the chapter "Administrative Obstacles to Planning" he adopts initially the second approach—that of identifying obstacles. But toward the end of his chapter he suggests that we cannot expect the administrative skills required for development planning and administration to grow up overnight. We should, he states, be alert to already existing nuclei of administrative skills.[1] There is much wisdom in this approach. It

1. Albert Waterston, *Development Planning: Lessons of Experience* (Baltimore: Johns Hopkins Press, 1965), pp. 285–87.

15

is a theme that has recurred from time to time in LADAC papers and discussions, but in a minor key. As I have tried to think through what I have read and seen about public administration in Latin America, I decided to try to confront this theme, which I call "islands of development," examine it, and see whether there may be elements of a basic approach in it.[2]

What is a "nucleus of strength" or an "island of development" in development administration? How does one recognize it? How can such nuclei or islands be encouraged to grow? How are the islands related to the political system, to the society, and to stages of development? These questions arise out of more fundamental ones: Who really wants development? Who really wants public administration reform? What is it specifically that they want and how can they get it?

Let us recall two very early doctrines in the core of technical assistance: (i) the technical consultant should start where the people actually are—at their level of understanding, skills, etc.; and (ii) the technical consultant should respond to the "felt needs" of the people. With respect to reform of public administration (or to development administration), these doctrines pose problems. Have North American public administrators in their technical assistance roles found the doctrines useful? How have the host countries in Latin America demonstrated their felt needs with respect to bureaucracy and to public administration? How much insight do North Americans have into the decision-making process in Latin America, either within the political-administrative system or the social system as a whole?

A major assumption of this paper is that pressure for the reform of public administration (or for development administration) rarely arises overtly in the political system. Demands for more efficiency in government operation, for the establishment of a merit system, for the establishment of civil service commissions, and the like seldom arise as overt political issues. They

2. In this context, the term "islands of development" is not used as it was used during the late 1950's in the ICA, the predecessor to AID. It was then used to identify certain especially promising developing nations, e.g., India, Colombia. It is used here to identify nuclei of strength which exhibit the development ideology and know-how wherever they may be found, whether in local communities, countries, or regional (supranational) groups.

are more often regarded as technical matters, not the dramatic stuff of political discussion. Instead, demands are made by interest groups (the merchants, the landlords, the church, the bureaucracy, the military, labor unions) for specific programs or goals which may actually require more effective public administration. However, this fact is only slowly perceived, and movements for the reform of public administration cannot expect startling breakthroughs. It is hard to envision an approach that will dramatically raise the level of administrative behavior in an entire society. This does not mean that progress cannot be made or that we should be pessimistic about likely results. But moderate expectations do have the benefit of surface validity, i.e., a reasonable relationship to known fact.

Let me illustrate islands of development by mentioning two examples from American life—the U.S. Bureau of the Budget and the Tennessee Valley Authority. The favorable influence that these two organizations have exerted on public administration in the United States has been tremendous. Neither one was made out of whole cloth, so to speak. Each grew out of a long background of American experience. Yet they were real institutional breakthroughs that have had wide implications for all of American public administration. They are islands of development in the public administration of our own society.

Islands of Development: Some Criteria

Every society and every administrative system has potentials for development. These potentials are likely to be widely separated, even scattered. The strategic questions are how to identify and locate them, how to energize, strengthen, and expand them, and if possible, how to relate them as islands of development so that they become the firm undergirdings of a modern society.

Minimum elements in the approach are (i) administrative leadership, the concept of "bureaucratic entrepreneurship"; (ii) "institution building" and "institutional transformation," or when to establish new organizations and when to transform old ones;

and finally (iii) interorganizational relationships for developmental purposes.

Bureaucratic Entrepreneurship

It has always surprised me that public administration, being concerned with action programs, has paid no more attention than it has to a vital aspect—leadership. There are, of course, the earlier studies of Barnard, Selznick, and Dimock, but on the whole, administrative leadership has not been a major subject of research and writing in this country. Josiah Stamp, the great English administrator, in discussing the importance of leadership, once wrote: "Atmosphere is everything!" The tradition of bureaucratic neutrality is no doubt responsible for this lack. While the discipline of sociology has the concept of the change agent, and economics has the concept of the entrepreneur, public administration gets along with the venerable POSDCORB. The acronym has in it a D for directing, but this is only a small part of the matter. The R does not stand for "responding" and "responsiveness," as everybody knows, which are a large part of the matter. Leadership and "followership" are the two sides of a coin. Surely, the theory of development administration will remain deficient as long as it fails to provide us with a better concept of organizational leadership.

The term *bureaucratic entrepreneur* appeals to me because it conveys the concept of the activist who *brings together* all the vital factors that make a development-oriented organization viable—the idea or the policy, respect and influence among policymakers, creative executive leadership, a wide following among able co-workers who staff the agency, an ability to instill public confidence, and the like. Above all, the bureaucratic entrepreneur is an outside man as much as an inside one. He does not stay at his desk or in the shop just to keep the wheels turning. He is not a technician. He is concerned with articulating the social purposes and values that his organization serves. He seeks to relate the organization to its environment as fully as possible. In Harlan Cleveland's terms, he has both "organizational skills" and a "sense for politics." In our terms, the bureaucratic entrepreneur is the irreducible unit. He could be called a one-man island. Without him, there is nothing to build with or to build on.

Thus far, we know very little in a scientific sense about the personality structures or the educational experiences that go into the making of such men, especially in a variety of cultures. That is, we are not certain that we can construct a reliable selection test or design a special training course that is reasonably certain to improve on natural ability.

To judge intuitively, however, it seems likely that Latin American culture will produce an interesting variant on this basic type, for the culture requires a dramatic flair (*personalismo?*), self-confidence (*dignidad?*), and good human relations (*muy simpático?*) as well as great executive skill. Many of us could name Latin American administrators who combine the qualities of the successful bureaucratic entrepreneur.

We may hypothesize that there is no evidence to suggest that any particular culture has a greater natural ability than others to produce such types. It is more likely that they spring up in response to need and opportunity. This raises the whole question of how to create the conditions in which such types can operate.

Institution Building

Another term originated by Harlan Cleveland—"institution building"—formed the subject of a large research program at the University of Pittsburgh and a related consortium. The consortium has added to our understanding of this complex process.

In terms of our theme, we see institution building in a somewhat new perspective. The organization is the basic unit. For development purposes, it is led by bureaucratic entrepreneur types and to a certain extent populated with them. The general doctrine of institution building is that major development activities require permanent organizational forms so that they will continue to perform as self-generating systems. The fundamental question, however, is at what point in the decision-making chain to make a commitment for the establishment of a new institution. It represents, obviously, a substantial drain on future governmental budgets and raises questions as to alternative opportunity costs. Moreover, the question may appear to have a different value in old and developing countries, like those of Latin America, than in the newer nations. Presumably, the latter will have fewer established institutions to rely on and may be called on to create many new services in a short time.

It may be all the more remarkable in this situation that one of the most notable features of Latin American governments is the propensity to establish autonomous institutes, government corporations, development corporations, and similar quasi-independent entities for carrying out new services. In a well-known article, Harold Seidman has commented on this tendency:

> More [government] corporations probably can be found in Latin America than in any other area of the world. The . . . corporation has been seized on as a panacea for inefficient or even corrupt government. . . . With the draining off of major government programs, the ministries in some countries have become hollow shells. In some parts of Latin America public corporations can be said literally to constitute a headless and irresponsible fourth branch of government.[3]

Seidman raises an important issue for the central theme of this paper. Government corporations, central banks, development corporations, and the like are a striking feature of Latin American administration. It is widely agreed that setting up autonomous institutes and government corporations is overdone. At the same time, some of the best-administered organizations are of this type (as well as some of the worst-administered). Suppose we look at some facts.

In 1960 there existed some thirty-five autonomous institutes or public corporations chartered by the government of Venezuela. Of these, seventeen were created between 1948 and 1958, many for the purpose of carrying out development programs. (Between 1928 and 1960, there had been many other autonomous agencies that did not survive.)

3. Harold Seidman, "The Theory of the Autonomous Government Corporation: A Critical Appraisal," *Public Administration Review* 12 (Spring 1952): 96.

Some of the concerns expressed by Seidman seem to be borne out in the case of Venezuela. Out of the total number of government employees in 1959 (146,302), over one-third (48,763) were employed by the autonomous institutes, and just under two-thirds (97,539) were employed by the ministries. For fiscal year 1959–60, out of a total budget of Bs 5,068,900,000, more than 22 percent, Bs 1,128,260,027, was appropriated in support of the autonomous agencies.

Particular cases bring out even more striking relationships. A single autonomous agency, the Venezuelan Institute of Petrochemicals, received 81 percent of the funds appropriated to its parent agency, the Ministry of Mines and Hydrocarbons. One ministry had six associated institutes, one had five, and several had four. In such circumstances, effective control by the central ministry is difficult or impossible to maintain.[4]

Nevertheless, some of the most promising work in Venezuelan development is carried out through autonomous institutes. The National Agrarian Institute (IAN), created in 1948 to administer the agrarian reform law, has turned in an exceptionally good performance in the opinion of qualified observers. So has its related institute, the Bank for Agriculture and Livestock.[5] President Betancourt took great pride in the state-owned airline, the Venezuelan Airmail Line (LAV), although in some eyes a privately owned line demonstrated greater advances. Betancourt is also said to have felt that the reorganization of the state-owned shipping industry under another institute, the Grancolumbiana Merchant Fleet, was a great success. This was carried out in cooperation with Colombia and Ecuador. Longer-term results were disappointing.[6]

The widespread use of the autonomous institute in Latin America indicates that it is peculiarly identified with the indigenous political culture. However, the autonomous form raises

4. I was allowed to examine an unpublished study by the Public Administration Service of Chicago in which these facts are developed. "Bs" are bolívars, units of the Venezuelan currency.

5. Robert J. Alexander, *The Venezuelan Democratic Revolution* (New Brunswick, N.J.: Rutgers Univ. Press, 1964), p. 31.

6. Edwin Lieuwen, *Venezuela* (New York: Oxford Univ. Press, 1961), p. 85; also, a letter from Frank Brandenburg in the author's files.

a problem of policy control. Can this problem be dealt with successfully? A study on Mexico seems to indicate that it can be. Anderson believes that the Mexican development banks are remarkably responsive to public policy. He goes so far as to view them as "instruments of political leadership." Such autonomy as they possess, he states, is derived from normal expectations concerning legitimate banking behavior. On the whole, these expectations "have led policy makers to devise financial techniques to reconcile demands for proper banking conduct with politically determined public policies." Thus, Anderson states that there is not much ground for considering "banks as private governments," since they are not "dominated by their clientele groups" as a North American political scientist would probably expect. They are used instead to encourage desirable performance by the clientele in terms of general economic policy.[7] No doubt the special political system the Mexicans have devised, under the "one-party democracy" of the official party (PRI), with its representation of various interest groups, would go a long way toward explaining this political inversion. For one thing, the large commercial interests are not formally represented in the party structure, whereas small industry and commerce, the general recipients of government credit, are represented there.[8]

Institutional Transformation

The concept of institution building naturally turns first to the establishment of new organizations and their control, but new development possibilities also arise as old institutions are transformed. Here some very tricky questions arise, illustrated in Latin America by two specific cases: the army (or the armed forces) and the church. Both have been conservative forces in the past, have supported the elites, and have been regarded as obstacles to development. Yet, for some time, modernizing elements have become evident in the armed forces, as the art of

7. William F. Glade and Charles W. Anderson, *The Political Economy of Mexico* (Madison: Univ. of Wisconsin Press, 1963), 165–68.
8. Brandenburg's analysis of banking performance throws some doubt on the above. Cf. Frank Brandenburg, *The Making of Modern Mexico* (New York: Praeger, 1960), pp. 343–44.

warfare becomes more technical and the officer corps more professionalized. This more or less coincides with the growth of the middle class or the middle groups, and as the armed forces increasingly provide a channel for men from the lower classes to achieve middle-class status. Some similar modernizing trends are evident in the clergy and the church.

Although earlier examples could be given, it was a group of younger and "upward mobile" army officers in Venezuela that was instrumental in bringing Acción Democrática and Betancourt to power in 1945. (The army also brought his regime down in 1948, when they thought it was going too fast in social reform and not giving army interests sufficient representation.) A former Colombian minister of defense called for systematic use of the army in projects for economic development—presumably for road building, housing, and the like. Unfortunately, this was interpreted by the president as a bid for political power, and the minister was forced to resign. To the extent that the suggestion was sincere, and not motivated by partisan politics, it represented a new mode of military thinking. Of course, there has of late been a spate of studies concerning the developmental role of the military.[9] The Peruvian government, dominated as it is by the military, has carried this trend to a new level, and there are signs that the Brazilian and Argentine governments will follow suit.

On its part, the church has shown signs of shedding its conservative image. In places, it has supported reform in agriculture, in politics, in its own educational system, and in the church-oriented elements of the labor movement. To its great credit, it openly participated in the overturn of the Pérez Jimenez dictatorship in Venezuela and of Rojas Pinilla in Colombia.[10]

It is too early to tell how fully committed these institutions are to modernization. The question of the extent of active government

9. Edwin Lieuwen, "Arms and Politics in Latin America," in *The Role of the Military in Under-Developed Countries*, ed. John J. Johnson (Princeton, N.J.: Princeton Univ. Press, 1962); John J. Johnson, *The Military and Society in Latin America* (Stanford, Calif.: Stanford Univ. Press, 1964); and Chapter 12 in the present volume, by Luigi Einaudi.
10. William V. D'Antonio and Frederick B. Pike, *Religion, Revolution, and Reform: New Forces for Change in Latin America* (New York: Praeger, 1964); also Frederick B. Pike, *The Conflict Between Church and State in Latin America* (New York: Knopf, 1964).

support and financing, especially of church-sponsored efforts, may be answered differently according to the traditions and political climate of each country. Yet any such efforts pose the issue of "institutional transformation" dramatically and may develop experience on this score that is transferable to other institutions. From this vantage point they are of great interest to development administration.

Identification of Focal Points

It is hard for a development administrator to determine where the crucial points for change are located. At just what points are strategic decisions going to be made? Where can the time and energies of development administrators and "bureaucratic entrepreneurs" be most usefully focused? Obviously this is an important determination. The time, energy, and opportunity costs of bureaucratic entrepreneurs, being limited, are a precious resource.

Since development administration implies change, and major change implies the need for political support, it is not surprising that development administrators and bureaucratic entrepreneurs tend to diagnose the possibilities close to the seats of power: the office of the president, an important minister, or the head of an agency. This tendency is especially notable in those who deal with the highly centralized, personalized regimes of Latin America. It provides the reason, of course, for proposals to attach national planning agencies to the office of the president or to the cabinet, or to relate them, at the very least, to a very powerful ministry, such as Finance. In order for a new service or organization, or a transforming old one, to be effective, however, there must be the awareness of need, at political levels, and continuing commitments of support by political elements.

As early as 1945 Ebenstein pointed out in a general survey of public administration in Mexico that there was some general awareness of the need for "economic planning" at the higher levels of Mexican administration. There was, as we might have expected, almost no awareness of the intricate interrelationships between economic planning and administrative statesmanship.

Public administration was conceived of as concerned exclusively with low-level operations. This administrative myopia was so pervasive that it was not even realized that the function of high-level administrative planning was already being performed, at least in part, in the office of the personal secretary to the president. It was performed there out of the sheer pressure of necessity, in an *ad hoc* fashion and without professional advice or assistance, because there was no way to escape it. It is just such situations as these that provide "focal points of change" for the bureaucratic entrepreneur. However, he has to be fortunate enough to have access to the right persons at the right times and be endowed with the ability to diagnose the situation.[11]

The tendency to seek "focal points" at the presidential or ministerial level brings many risks and may lead to frustration if political power is not wielded in the desired directions. The attempts of the Public Administration Commission in Venezuela to promote a civil service law and other major reforms in public administration have thus far met with qualified success. (This lack of successful articulation of a major administrative agency with the presidential or political power may be said to be fairly typical. In a sense, there is an undue separation, with respect to program administration, between the political and the administrative systems.) Although created as a presidential agency, on the model of the Hoover Commission, the Public Administration Commission never got Betancourt's full backing. This failure has been attributed to a variety of reasons. For one, the Commission was established prior to Betancourt's accession. His regime had other high-priority political commitments to keep. It was fighting for its political life during most of the 1962–64 period. He hesitated to back the proposal for a merit system because he did not want to give permanent posts to political enemies. Finally, he seemed to prefer to work through Cordiplan (the economic planning agency) for many essentially political purposes. The head of the Public Administration Commission was supposed to report to Betancourt through Cordiplan. But the director of the Com-

11. Ebenstein, "Public Administration in Mexico," *Public Administration Review* 5 (Spring 1945): 106–7.

mission felt this belittled his own independence and status with the president.[12]

Although each of these facts may tell part of the story, the real fact seems to be that the president, while an extremely successful politician of the old school, had no personal acquaintance with modern administration. He hesitated to upset the administrative applecart while pushing for agrarian reform and similar measures. To the president, the political cost of pushing for a civil service law in the congress apparently was not worth the anticipated benefits.[13]

Discussion of the issues in the Betancourt case among students of development administration has led to some interesting speculations. Did the president really have the power to push the proposed law through the congress? It was probable that he did, at least in his first year. If President Betancourt did not see the advantages, what is the underlying difficulty? There was no real demand on the president or the congress from the political system to take this step; ergo, no political advantage to be gained.

Basic reforms in government administration may thus have to come from the citizenry itself. Only when citizens are sufficiently aroused to organize pressure groups to accomplish the desired ends is fundamental action likely to be taken. But how likely is this in most Latin American countries? Here again, we observe the familiar vicious circle of development. Yet the intimate interconnection between the bureaucracy and the political system is a fact of developmental strategy, and the time scale of development progress may have to be adjusted to take it into account.

In this connection, I should like to quote from a letter from a colleague in LADAC:

> The question of finding islands of development is not one of levels of government, location at the *presidencia,* or superministerial level, but is one of identifying the more promising functions, programs, or missions carried on within a country, and encouraging and supporting them. It is not always a question of creating new institutions; bureaucratic entre-

12. Cf. Chapters 2 and 3 in this volume.
13. Ibid.

preneurship may be found within existing agencies and can be rewarded and supported through intelligent technical assistance.

I do not know how to identify the charisma in administration, or even if there is, despite Max Weber, a good definition of it. I refer you to Rex Tugwell's article on Robert Moses called "The Moses Effect." It provides at least the beginning of a handle on the subject. The comparative examination of T.V.A., Port Authority, Triborough Bridge, etc., along with the government corporations both here and in Latin America should provide some fruitful clues for pursuing the strategy of "islands of development."[14]

Before leaving the concept of "focal points" of change, it should be noted that development administrators also frequently face a decision as to whether to initiate projects at relatively low levels, and without any discernible political support. In-service training, secretarial training, and projects for the reorganization and installation of filing systems are frequently of this character. They are sometimes undertaken in the hope that they will have a demonstration effect and will lead to more ambitious undertakings in the future. Sometimes the islands of change are very small!

Organizational Links

The importance of interorganizational connections may be obvious from the outside, but this is the area where development programs suffer most. There is the obvious gap between the planning agency and the line departments; the gap between the political leaders and the bureaucracy; the gap between headquarters and the field agency; and the gap between the organization and the client system. These all have an apparent resemblance to some typical problems of coordination in industrialized countries, but there is a difference. In the developing countries there is the distinction between the modernizing elites and the traditional elites; there are "transitional" types who may be riding both horses in opposite directions; and the "conservative oligarchic"

14. Professor Morton Tenzer to Clarence E. Thurber, 6 April 1966.

types who may be riding the modernizing movements for selfish or traditional purposes.

The "development ideology" may thus be held by various groups and types and held in various degrees and for various purposes. The problem of creative organizational consensus and links thus becomes vastly more complicated than in the modern societies. It becomes in fact a quasi-political problem.[15]

Something more needs to be said, in fact, about the lack of adequate links between local governments (*municipios*) and the national governments. Unfortunately the distance between them seems to be growing. The lure of the "primate city," the single major metropolitan area which is the center of important cultural, financial, and political activities, seems to be greater in Latin America than almost anywhere else. Thus, the urban-rural gap harbors extremes of modernity-traditionality probably greater than elsewhere. Many of the pressing social-economic-political problems (land reform, agricultural production, rural education, etc.) in Latin America can be solved only by narrowing this gap. The bureaucratic performance—and the shortfall in reaching program goals—can be explained, in many cases, by the desire of the rising middle-class bureaucrat to stay in the city. It is clear that new links must be formed between rural and urban areas. This is a major step in which both political and bureaucratic entrepreneurship need to be brought into play.

Development Administration in Latin America

Macro Approaches vs. Micro Approaches

In Latin America we may distinguish "macro" and "micro" approaches to development. Macro approaches aim at nationwide or even continentwide improvements, under a long-range development scheme. This may be a single plan, a series of plans, or an overall grand strategy of international development. Macro

15. Albert Hirschman, *Journeys Toward Progress* (New York: Twentieth Century Fund, 1963) and *The Strategy of Economic Development* (New Haven, Conn.: Yale Univ. Press, 1958).

approaches characterize such program objectives as those of AID, the U.N., the OAS, and the Economic Commission for Latin America.

Micro approaches are related to improvements on a project-by-project basis, whether or not the projects are conceived of as part of a total strategy for national or continental development. The micro approach is utilized by the IBRD and the Inter-American Development Bank when they process loans for particular projects, and by such private agencies as the Rockefeller Foundation, the Ford Foundation, and a series of smaller agencies.

Under macro plans it is often quite difficult to respond flexibly and adequately to local needs and initiatives, i.e., to islands of development. For example, the Economic Commission for Latin America (ECLA), under the leadership of its former executive secretary Raul Prebisch, devoted itself to the establishment of national programing and planning organizations in various Latin American governments, including Planeación in Colombia and Cordiplan in Venezuela. Prebisch also stimulated the establishment of the Institute for National Economic and Social Planning (ILPES) in Santiago. Its particular operating doctrine has been "the Prebisch thesis," and macroeconomic planning, i.e., the establishment of investment goals and priorities based upon projections of gross national income, population growth, educational needs flowing from population growth, and the like. This approach has been criticized as fitting too easily and neatly into the tendency of "creating a dream-world and living within it." It also has some congruence with the view of public administration as public law, that is, as nonoperationally oriented. Prebisch himself urged national planning boards to concern themselves with the management and public administration aspects of planning, but by and large the hoped-for results have not been forthcoming.

The Alliance for Progress was the latest in a series of U.S.-sponsored aid programs in Latin America of the macro variety which began in 1939 and extend to the present. In 1938 the U.S. Interdepartmental Committee on Scientific and Cultural Cooperation began to provide U.S. technical assistance in Latin America, followed by the Institute of Inter-American Affairs, the Point Four

Program, and all its successors, down to AID. These were bilateral aid programs. The Alliance for Progress was intended to be a multilateral program, somewhat on the model of the Marshall Plan. Assistance to public administration "reform" has been available under most or all of these programs.[16]

Stefan Robock criticizes the effects of such macro approaches in his analysis of the effects of U.S. AID on the Northeast region of Brazil.[17] Simon Hanson also dwells on this theme. How can we be so sure, he asks, that "the briefcase brigade from AID, which, having identified the causes of Latin America's social and economic 'evils' and armed itself with a 'program' for overnight elimination of them, will be . . . successful?"[18] Moreover, Hanson continues, we have "the endless traffic of missions from North to South and from South to North happily learning what is already known. . . . Is it not time that we placed in proper proportion the emphasis on vast abstract plans so incapable of realization and so largely intended as a device to create the *image* of activity?"[19] The fact of the matter is that we sometimes seem to believe that there is a formula for "instant development." We are so used to thinking about machines and technologies that we sometimes seem to believe we can invent a "development machine." In a word, we are prone to forget the human, organizational, and political elements, because they are difficult to analyze and to express in formulas.

For examples of micro development projects, we might glance at some of the projects of Central Banks and Development Banks, projects in subject matter fields like health (e.g., the Special Services of Public Health, SESP, in Brazil), certain autonomous institutes (the National Institute for Agrarian Reform in Venezuela), and certain educational projects such as those at the University del Valle in Cali, Colombia.

16. Edward W. Weidner, *Technical Assistance in Public Administration Overseas: The Case for Development Administration* (Chicago: Public Administration Service, 1964).

17. Stefan H. Robock, *Brazil's Developing Northeast: A Study of Regional Planning and Foreign Aid* (Washington: Brookings Institution, 1963), pp. 4–17, 177–201.

18. Simon G. Hanson, "The Economic Difficulties of Social Reform in Latin America," in D'Antonio and Pike, p. 188.

19. Ibid., p. 196.

There is no magic to the micro or project approach, but it does have the advantage of being more comprehensible and more adaptable to an action orientation. It comes more quickly to terms with human and organizational problems, such questions as these: Are the necessary professional skills available? If not, can they be imported or developed? Is the necessary managerial know-how present? What is the standing of individuals concerned with the political and economic elites? etc. The fact is that the micro approach brings us to the individual organization unit where real administrative changes have to take root.

Efforts at Public Administration Improvement

Efforts to reform public administration and to encourage development administration have corresponded generally to successive phases of programs designed to stimulate national and regional development. The first phase seemed to be *personnel-oriented* and attempted to establish merit systems through the passage of civil service laws, to establish central personnel commissions, to create personnel classification schemes, and the like. A number of institutes of public administration and in-service training programs were established at this time which emphasized work in the personnel field.[20] The second phase, which seems to have occupied the period of the mid-1950's, gave emphasis to organization and management techniques, while not dropping the earlier attention to personnel. A third phase gave attention, admittedly indirect, to administrative problems in program fields, such as public health and agriculture, largely through the establishment of *services* in these fields and the introduction of administrative experts within them. The fourth phase, beginning approximately with the Alliance for Progress, focused on improving administration in revenue-producing areas (tax administration and customs), on the administrative problems of social develop-

20. Cf. Enrique Tejera París, "Observations on Personnel Management in Latin America," *Public Personnel Review* 17, no. 4 (Oct. 1956): 295–301. Tejera-París states that at the time of writing there were "fully developed" personnel systems in Argentina, Brazil, Chile, Costa Rica, and Mexico; cf. also Felix A. Nigro, "Personnel Administration in Latin America," *Personnel Administration* 20 (Nov.–Dec. 1957): 33–39. Nigro considered Puerto Rico's Office of Personnel an excellent example of a good personnel system.

ment (e.g., education, housing), and on administrative aspects of national planning as such.

Participation in these aspects of reform has led to certain diagnoses of "the public administration problem" in Latin America. One of the best of these analyses is "Administrative Roadblocks to Coordinated Development," which Herbert Emmerich wrote as he completed his long-term assignment as Senior Consultant in Public Administration at the United Nations. This article reflects the "removal of obstacles" approach that was identified at the beginning of this chapter. In his article Emmerich commented on the important new tasks of public administration if the development goals of Latin America were to be fulfilled. He then related public administration to the political environment and called for the establishment of political science in Latin American educational institutions. Under the general heading Adaptation of Personnel Systems to a National Culture, he recommended the establishment of an "administrative and professional corps" at a high level as an appropriate place to begin a merit system in such a way as not to interfere too much and too directly with the established pattern of things. He guessed, probably correctly, that if the higher-level positions could be established on a professional basis, it might favorably affect the entire administrative system.[21]

Emmerich pointed to "over-centralization as the major roadblock to Latin American development" and indicated that this is a result of the political and social environment. He doubted whether it is a problem susceptible of direct attack. If it is not, then it is unfortunate that most of the efforts at public administration reform in Latin America to date have been one or another variety of "direct attack" (i.e., proposed civil service laws, central personnel commissions, etc.). If Emmerich was right, a broader approach to development administration will be needed which will attempt to work through the political, educational, and social

21. Herbert Emmerich, "Administrative Roadblocks to Coordinated Development," prepared for the Expert Working Group on Social Aspects of Economic Development in Latin America, sponsored jointly by UNESCO, ECLA, and the U.N. and held in Mexico City in December 1960. U.N. Secretariat (ST/TAO/Conf. 6/L.C-4/Rev. 1, S.Am/Org/3(a)) (28 April 1961).

systems. This will obviously have to be done within a longer time perspective. The implication is inescapable: most technical assistance efforts in public administration in Latin America have been too optimistic as regards time perspectives.

Characteristics of Public Administration in Latin America: The Practitioner's View

Emmerich in his comments was typical of a number of North American commentators. Many of these have seen service in technical assistance programs in Latin America. Without attempting to give each one separate attention, we can compress these comments into a single list of main characteristics of Latin American public administration. The following points of emphasis emerge.

1. *Personalismo.* Dominance of *personalismo* (loyalty to a political boss) in public administration; of *amistad* (working through friends rather than through official channels); and of family and regional ties (loyalty to family and home-town groups).

2. *High turnover rates.* Frequent changes in government; even more frequent changes at the ministerial level, with the great uncertainty this causes throughout the ranks and the damping effects it has on initiative and continuity of effort.

3. *Corruption.* Widespread petty bribery at low levels and large-scale corruption at high levels. Ebenstein states that there are fifteen words for "graft" in Mexico. There is also a popular adage that "the thief who fails goes to jail; the thief who succeeds, to him all worldly goods." Mexicans are reputed to believe, however, that graft is more democratic—because it is more egalitarian—than in the United States.[22]

4. *Ministerial separatism.* The high and impenetrable walls that separate the ministries, making effective coordination difficult or impossible. Also, because of this, central personnel systems are difficult to install and even more difficult to administer.

22. Ebenstein, p. 102; cf. also Brandenburg, pp. 160–2.

5. *Bureaucracy and employment.* The use of the bureaucracy to relieve unemployment rather than to carry out programs;[23] the permissible practice of holding two or three jobs, so that no one of them gets more than cursory attention; and the prevalence of low pay scales.

6. *Humanistic tradition.* The predominance of the humanistic and the oral tradition—which is non-action-oriented—in the bureaucracy; the severe scarcity of professionally and technically trained manpower; the blurring of the difference between "facts" and "doctrines" and the difficulty of preparing fact-based memoranda leading to logical conclusions.[24]

7. *Lack of delegation and "responsibility."* The desire not to accept responsibility and to carry through on action without close supervision; the lack of delegation of authority.[25]

8. *Lack of a "civic culture."* The substitution of private concerns in place of "the public welfare."[26]

Most of the commentators from whom the above characteristics are taken thus use the method of pointing out "weaknesses," "obstacles," or "lacks," thus suggesting that their implicit model of administration is either the United States or western Europe. Are these perceptions culture-bound and are Latin American indigenous views different? Writings of Latin Americans on the subject do not differ materially from the criticisms summarized above.[27] A North American author, however, has verbalized a

23. This tendency has been called the "empleocracia" by C. A. M. Hennessy, "Shifting Forces in the Bolivian Revolution," *The World Today,* 20 (May 1964): 197–207.

24. These comments are based on interviews in Argentina, Jan. 1964.

25. Ibid.

26. This point and other related comments are developed in detail in such works as Philip Glick, *The Administration of Technical Assistance: Growth in the Americas* (Chicago: Univ. of Chicago Press, 1957); see Laurin L. Henry, "Some Characteristics of Public Administration in Latin America," in *Government and Politics in Latin America,* rev. ed., ed. Adolfo Gomez (New York: Random House, 1963), pp. 52–58; William W. Pierson and Federico G. Gil, *Governments of Latin America* (New York: McGraw-Hill, 1957), "The Executive," pp. 208–41; Martin C. Needler, ed., *Political Systems of Latin America* (Princeton, N.J.: Van Nostrand, 1964), pp. 18, 48–49, 134 passim; and Gabriel Almond and Sidney Verba, *The Civic Culture* (Princeton, N.J.: Princeton Univ. Press, 1963).

27. Cf., for example, *Rio Organization and Methods Workshop Development Administration Program, Public Administration Unit,* report of a conference in Rio de Janeiro, 6–10 May 1963 (Organization of American States, UP/G, 16/2, 4 Feb. 1964), pp. 21–22.

point that one frequently hears made orally by Latin Americans and which represents a widespread point of view:

> It is possible to argue that, in their present stage of develop-ment, a merit bureaucracy would not be functional in view of the needs of most Latin American states. From the point of view of the leader who has just come to power, for ex-ample, merit or seniority may be of secondary importance to loyalty as a consideration in making key appointments. This is certainly the case if a country has a tradition of violent change of government. . . . [Moreover] a spoils system of appointments might have advantages if it were used to create *enduring* parties [emphasis supplied] . . . security of tenure makes for complacency . . . whereas obstacles to social development in the Latin American states can be sur-mounted, if at all, only by individuals chosen for their devotion to the programs and goals of the government leaders.[28]

One is thus thrown back on the political and social system for the origins of what might be called the pathology of public ad-ministration in Latin America. Needler, in the quoted passage, appears to be describing another of the by now famous vicious circles of development. A particular set of administrative reforms, he seems to be saying, may well be characteristic of advanced Western countries. But if they are adopted in Latin America, they will only darken an already cloudy political-administrative picture. There may well be truth in this observation, but how does one break out of the vicious circle? Again, one is forced to con-sider more fully the relationship of public administration to the operation of the political and social systems.

Another Viewpoint

When the bureaucracy of Latin American governments is looked at in a longer-range historical and a broader political per-

28. Martin C. Needler, *Latin American Politics in Perspective* (Princeton, N.J.: Van Nostrand, 1963), p. 150.

spective, it may appear in a somewhat different light. The Mexican bureaucracy, for example, has reached a relatively advanced stage, at least as an interest group. According to Scott, the Mexican political process is centered in the machinery of the official party, so much so that the government bureaucracy is "one of the strongest elements in the popular sector of the official party." Its favored position is rewarded with low-cost housing, special commissary facilities, a special hospital, year-end bonuses, and other benefits. It is, however, the contribution to the political purposes of the official party, rather than the contribution to program and policy goals that leads to these extraordinary rewards.[29] However, it is not without significance that the support of the bureaucracy is so valuable to political leaders. And the favored economic position has led to some professionalization.

A well-known Mexican writer, Octavio Paz, introduces a new note when he states that with the coming of the Mexican revolution, "diplomacy, foreign trade, and public administration opened their doors to an intelligentsia which came from the *middle class* . . . thanks to the new *professional schools*."[30] Moreover, if staff members of the central Bank of Mexico, numerous development banks, and other decentralized agencies can be regarded as an assimilated part of the Mexican public administration, as Glade and Anderson believe they can, then it is clear that some sectors of the public bureaucracy in that country have reached an advanced, professional level.[31]

The very important relationship between the rise of the middle class and its effect on the professionalization of the bureaucracy and on decision making in Latin America suggests that the phenomena described above are not necessarily unique to Mexico. The political role of the "middle sectors" in five countries, Uruguay, Chile, Argentina, Mexico, and Brazil, when studied by Johnson, demonstrated a considerable impact from this source on the scope, operating style, and overall character of public ad-

29. Robert E. Scott, *Mexican Government in Transition* (Urbana: Univ. of Illinois Press, 1959), pp. 9, 81.
30. Octavio Paz, *El laberinto de la soledad,* rev. ed. (Mexico City: Fondo de Cultura Economica, 1959), p. 141, quoted in Glade and Anderson, p. 12.
31. "Bankers as Revolutionaries," esp. "Political Process and Policy Making," p. 143, and "Direct Administrative Control," p. 155, in Glade and Anderson.

ministration. The expansion of economic opportunities in these countries, he notes, has been an *urban* phenomenon. It has especially benefited the "middle groups" (Johnson wants to avoid the term "middle class"). These same middle groups coveted government posts for reasons of power, the opportunity to make money, social prestige, and the like. As economic growth proceeded, their influence expanded. Johnson even sees a "spill-over effect" from private business to government with regard to technical qualifications as a basis for employment: "The large corporate enterprises . . . which offer greatest opportunity for advancement, are inclined to consider individual qualifications more than family credentials. A similar condition is developing in government . . . nepotism has gradually given ground to civil service systems and professional bureaucracies.[32] Johnson writes in an historical perspective. His study covers the period from 1810 to the mid-1950's. And looking toward the future, he foresees an even more active role for government because "thousands of [high-level] bureaucrats [have been given] the prestige of being associated with the planning and management of industrial and commercial undertakings—a prestige that their own financial resources deny them."[33]

How can we explain the difference in the evaluation of the public bureaucracy by the two sets of observers whose opinions we have set forth in the above pages, the technical assistance types and the social science types? It is probably to be explained by the very different standpoints from which they write, the base line of expectations from which they operate. To the technical assistance types, what is important is not that progress has been made over the past hundred years, or that bureaucrats do, in certain countries, play an important role in the political process. It is rather that much greater progress needs to be made in the here and now and set in train for the future. In their eyes Latin American public administration is archaic, anarchic, and a roadblock to development. The social scientists, on the other hand, have

32. John J. Johnson, *Political Change in Latin America: The Emergence of the Middle Sectors* (Stanford, Calif.: Stanford Univ. Press, 1958), p. 11.
33. Ibid., pp. 193–94.

looked at bureaucracy in a broader political, social, and historical perspective. They do not necessarily feel a personal obligation for helping public administration to progress. To them, some parts of the bureaucracy look surprisingly good.

Who can say which group is closer to the truth? To some extent, the truth depends on what your purposes are. Perhaps we can simply say that each group provides a healthy corrective to the other.

Culture and History

It is time to face up to the most difficult question. If public-administrative behavior can be explained in relationship to cultural norms and political myths, what gives Latin America its own individuality? Here, we have to recognize that the majority of North American studies about development politics and development administration have reflected an Asian or an African orientation. It may be well to suggest certain major ways in which Latin American governments and societies differ from other less developed areas. This will serve to highlight certain major focal points of Latin American developmental problems.

The Latin American states are not really "new nations," a term that seems to have arisen largely out of African experience. The wars of independence by which most Central and South American countries established themselves as legally independent entities began around 1810 and were completed about 1825. Thus, the experience of independence for most Latin American countries is anywhere from 130 to 150 years old. The principal importance of this fact is that Latin American governments got over very quickly the first flush of optimism that accompanies the winning or the granting of independence. They learned quickly, and perhaps too soon, that legal independence is only a first step and that political integration and economic development do not automatically follow. This realism might be counted as a "good thing" if it were not for the fact that numerous coups d'état, palace revolts, and revolutions had made the lesson so painfully clear.

It is perhaps laboring the obvious to point out that colonial experience in Latin America, largely Spanish and Portuguese, has had a powerful effect on the institutional and the social-psychological development there.[34] Spain and Portugal were not highly developed politically in the pre-independence period, and their influence as models of development in either the political or economic realm perhaps left much to be desired, certainly in the eyes of anyone interested in prospects for democratic development. Thus, the Latin American states lacked a thriving model for development, and this is more important than we can appreciate.

Not all Latin American nations, however, are "lesser developed." If one uses the common definition of $500 per capita income as the dividing line, then Argentina, Costa Rica, and Venezuela are higher on the scale. However, if an equitable *distribution,* however defined, of economic, political, and social status is taken as the criterion, most of the countries would still be considered "lesser developed."

Moreover, not all Latin American countries are necessarily "non-Western" even if one equates "Western" with "modern," and "non-Western" with "underdeveloped." While many writers do just that, "white" Argentina, Uruguay, and Costa Rica would probably rate as Western nations on any scale. But there is much ambiguity in these terms as used. Vera Michelis Dean in *The Nature of the Non-Western World,* Robert Scott in *Mexican Government in Transition,* and George Blanksten in *The Politics of the Developing Areas,* all use "Latin American" and "non-Western" interchangeably. This usage seems unnecessarily confusing. I would readily agree that the Latin American countries in which there is a sizable Indian population (Guatemala, Bolivia, Ecuador, Peru) bear a sociological resemblance to certain non-Western countries such as India and Pakistan, especially in the mix of "Westerners" to natives. But Latin America is after all located in the Western Hemisphere. More important, the role of

34. Cf. Chapter 4 in the present volume. Jaguaribe there uses the terms "anallagmatic" and "synallagmatic" to characterize social attitudes toward equality and inequality in Latin and Anglo-Saxon cultures.

Spain and Portugal in colonizing the continent, and the role of the church in subsequent Latin American history, it seems to me, are sufficient grounds for classifying the areas as Western.

If "Western" is to be equated with "modern," how should we classify other western but lesser developed areas—Spain, Portugal, Southern Italy, Greece, Ireland? It seems preferable to use "Western" and "non-Western" primarily for geographic entities, and "developed" and "underdeveloped" as qualifiers. Thus, Latin American countries, with the exceptions noted, may be referred to as "Western, lesser developed countries." It was, of course, terms such as these with all their ambiguities that led Fred W. Riggs to discard them and to substitute instead the trilogy of "fused," "prismatic," and "refracted."[35]

It is almost impossible to discuss these terms without considering, at least in passing, the issue of the so-called Protestant ethic. Those who equate "Western" and "modern" may have implicitly in mind the role that the Calvinist tradition has played in the economic development of the Western industrialized nations. This notion was early articulated by Max Weber,[36] and it has become a truism to suggest that the process of development requires the "functional equivalent" of the Protestant ethic. Perhaps McClelland has discovered this functional equivalent in his closely related term "achievement motivation."[37] However, here we have another paradox in Latin America. How can a region which has been so heavily influenced by the church in its religious tradition develop this functional equivalent? Brandenburg maintains that Freemasonry has provided the equivalent both in Mexico and in some other Latin American countries. "If the Reformation ever reached Mexico," he writes, "it did so in the backhanded form of Freemasonry."[38]

There is a fourth consideration that tends to differentiate Latin

35. Fred W. Riggs, "Prismatic Society and Financial Administration," *Administrative Science Quarterly* 5 (1960): 1–46; also idem, *Administration in Developing Countries: The Theory of Prismatic Society* (Boston: Houghton Mifflin, 1964), pp. 27–38.

36. H. H. Gerth and C. Wright Mills, trans., *From Max Weber: Essays in Sociology* (New York, Oxford Univ. Press, 1946), pp. 63–65.

37. David C. McClelland, *The Achievement Motive* (New York: Appleton-Century-Crofts, 1953).

38. Brandenburg, p. 167.

America from other developing areas. Latin American nations have been subjected for many decades to a degree of U.S. influence which is uncharacteristic of Asian and African areas (except for the Philippines). The Latin American countries have grown up in the shadow of the North American colossus. At least since 1898 and the arrival of manifest destiny, this factor has colored mutual relationships with certain subtle aspects of colonialism. It seems that the United States has been a substitute colonial figure.

Whether these factors establish a qualitative difference in Latin America is a subject worthy of debate. Those who have lived both in Latin America and in other culture areas insist that Latin America *is* different. If there is a major qualitative difference, I suggest it probably arises from the history of independence of Latin American countries, their lack of a strong, culturally derived model of development, combined with a disappointing record with regard to political development. Here again there are exceptions—Chile, Uruguay, and Costa Rica. To borrow Eisenstadt's term, one may suggest that, with the exception of three or four countries, the history of Latin American political development has had more than its share of "breakdowns."[39]

Yet it is also uncontestable that Latin America *is* developing economically and socially. Meanwhile, the appearance of the New Nations in Asia and Africa, and the policy attention that has been paid to these developments by both the capitalist and communist nations, have given us new insight into the Latin American scene. The interplay between the "old" and the "new" developing areas is a fascinating aspect of international politics. The concern with development, and the study of the process in all its ramifications, have provided new concepts with which to view Latin American problems and new tools to work with. (We have to remember, of course, that Argentina was considered to be an advanced economy, with a relatively high per capita income, a railroad system, and the like, in the early 1900's.) However, in a certain sense, the advanced industrialized nations themselves

39. S. N. Eisenstadt, "Breakdowns of Modernization," *Economic Development and Cultural Change* 12 (July 1964): 345–67.

have just recently "discovered" development as a self-conscious process. Latin America within this framework emerges in a somewhat more hopeful light. Silvert's contention that Argentina "remains in a pre-national condition" illuminates all consideration of politics and administration both there and throughout the continent.[40]

Thus, we can perhaps characterize the Latin American countries as Western and "older nations," developing nations, influenced primarily by a Spanish or Portuguese heritage, having lived in the *Yanqui* shadow most of their lives, and now beginning to emerge in the light of their own genius. We can thus suggest ways in which Latin American history and development to date are distinct from Africa, the Near East, and Asia, and why this development is still dynamic and hopeful.

Social and Political Factors Bearing on the Conduct of Governmental Affairs

There is a remarkable degree of consensus about the major social and political factors that bear on the conduct of governmental affairs in Latin America. Politically, there is the factor of force. Force or the threat of force has played a role as a major arbiter in many Latin American nations. The legal tradition has failed to take deep roots in terms of government by consent and consensus. The principle of legitimacy, i.e., the transfer of power through nonviolent means, has also failed to develop deep roots, although there have been some encouraging signs. The military man in politics has been the rule rather than the exception. The legislatures and courts have been weaker than in Europe and in North America. The standard explanation only a generation ago was that the rule of force has so dominated politics that it has been difficult to develop any effective delegation of authority. Such delegation is of course central to the establishment of any effective, modern bureaucracy.[41]

40. Kalman H. Silvert, ed., *Expectant Peoples: Nationalism and Development* (New York: Random House, 1963), p. 353.
41. Frank Tannenbaum, "Personal Government in Mexico," in *The Evolution of Latin American Government* ed. Asher Norman Christensen (New York: Holt, 1951), pp. 423 ff.

The chief executive in many Latin nations was, until a generation ago, involved in a personalistic style of government that is only slowly passing out of existence. He was a benevolent authority figure who could reverse any decision made by any subordinate. He would theoretically be available to hear the case of an aggrieved party. The waiting rooms of the chief executives were filled with supplicants for favors and pleaders for causes of the most diverse and motley character. The chief executive was expected to hear them out. Worse: in the end, only he could make the decision. This could only lead further into the welter of *personalismo* and *ad hoc* decision making that would be the ruination of any sustained attempt at public administration reform.[42]

The tradition of democracy and of legitimate government in Latin America has been carried along partly as a literary tradition. Constitutions express noble sentiments, but are not expected to control behavior. The game of politics in Latin America for a hundred years after independence was a classic game, that of protecting the *status quo* interests of social elites established during the Colonial regime. Society was a two-class society, until shaken loose by war, depression, and "the revolution of expectations."

A case has frequently been made that Latin America has no natural talent for self-government and political development. The suspicion of ungovernability is said to have become an obsession with Bolívar. He is said to have searched "every nook and cranny of structure for proof" perhaps hoping that he might be wrong.[43] Bolívar blamed the Spanish Colonial heritage for this condition. Latin America was dominated by "the vices which were inevitably formed under the rule of a nation like Spain . . . noted for its fierceness, ambition, vengefulness, and greed." Racial heterogeneity, poverty, and personalism were obstacles to stability in Bolívar's political lexicon; but these were bitter fruits of the heritage from Spain.[44]

42. Ibid.
43. Arthur Whitaker, "Pathology of Democracy in Latin America: An Historian's Point of View," *American Political Review* 44, no. 1 (March 1950): 103.
44. Ibid.

In spite of this past, for some decades there have been truly impressive political gains in Costa Rica, Uruguay, and Chile and more recently in Venezuela. Nevertheless, a habit of trenchant social criticism was apparently inherited by Latin Americans. In *The Alliance for Progress,* Maritano and Obaid come close to identifying Don Quixote as a kind of "modal personality" of Spanish culture, pertaining also to Latin America. (Maritano is Latin American.) Maritano and Obaid list the following as some of the dominant Latin American personality traits: egocentrism, inability to work in a team, temperamentalism, doctrinaire thinking, lack of a civic consciousness, distaste for manual labor, and an ability to create an idealistic dreamworld and live within it. The "fetish" of self-criticism in Spanish culture is noted by the authors.[45]

Overall, we can see that slowly a change is being wrought. The middle groups are rising and bringing a broader civic consciousness with them. There is a higher degree of technical competence, a higher degree of professionalization within society as a whole. Educational opportunities are slowly spreading. Although not at flood tide, these movements are having their effects.

If this is the whole story, the prospects for political and economic growth in Latin America are rather unpromising. But how do we explain the exceptions? How do we account for the exceptional economic growth in countries like Mexico and Venezuela, and political development in countries like Costa Rica? Where, indeed, do we put Chile, and for that matter, Cuba, in this field of analysis?

Conclusions

It is one thing if a developing nation shows a massive commitment to developmental goals on the part of the political elite. It would also be fortunate if such a nation possessed a high degree of professional competence in a bureaucracy devoted to the goals

45. Nino Maritano and Antonio H. Obaid, *The Alliance for Progress: The Challenge and the Problem* (Minneapolis: Denison, 1963), pp. 37–38.

of development, an adequate economic and human resource base, a growing middle class, a political system favoring progressive national political integration and participation, and so on. But if these circumstances exist, the society is no longer "lesser developed."

It is quite another thing, however, if there is no massive commitment to the development ideology, where the political system does not produce growing participation and a consensus and where the patronage bureaucracy, by and large, takes precedence over the merit bureaucracy. If these circumstances prevail, another approach is needed. The "islands of development" approach has much to offer.

The merit in this approach is that it is openly but properly opportunistic. It recognizes that all development in the past has been, in the modern sense, accidental—that is, unplanned. We do not know enough about what has caused certain nations to develop and others to remain undeveloped. The concepts of development we use today may, in the future, seem as wrong as the racial concepts of Gobineau or as incomplete as the climatic theories of Huntington.

The approach I have called "islands of development" is, to be sure, a theory of sorts. It is personality-centered, insofar as the bureaucratic entrepreneur may exhibit certain model personality traits. It is organization-centered in that the bureaucratic entrepreneur must operate within appropriate institutional settings. Institutional development and institutional transformation are seen as the heart of the development process. Development change is basic or structural. Development administrators are those who, recognizing this, are able to move organized groups in the directions of desired structural change.

Thus, the "islands of development" approach looks for nuclei of strength, especially organizational strength, wherever they exist. The concept accepts the necessity for a certain degree of planning, to keep things moving generally in the same direction and to prevent the unwise and untimely proposal from being adopted. It puts more emphasis, however, on organizational development and management. It does not force things too much into predetermined categories (or sectors) but seeks to capitalize on and maximize the effectiveness of the elements that are forward-looking, energetic, and civic-minded.

Because of Latin America's history and cultural heritage, basic institutional transformation seems to be needed even more than new institutional development. This has both advantages and disadvantages. Latin nations do not have to learn everything about development because they have already come a part of the way. They have rich, complex, and varied histories. But there is also a good deal of history to "overcome." The political systems of Latin America have in most cases only recently been used to redefine "situations" (starvation, natural disasters, sickness and disease, waste food supplies, and the like), which have always been with us, into "problems" (public health, population control, housing, food storage systems, and the like) that organizations can do something about. Nor have they, until the recent past, been in the habit of turning "problems" over to the public administration with the honest expectation that something could and would be done about them.

At the heart of the difficulty is the fact that the Latin American system of political socialization has produced a weak "civic culture."[46] The institutions responsible for education (the family, the schools, the church, the military) have apparently all been deficient to varying degrees in the development of the civic culture—the role and obligations of citizenship, the broadening of the base of political participation, and the notion of the common good. Thus, in the long run, the most fundamental islands of development in Latin America are the aspects of education that can strengthen the civic culture.

46. Gabriel A. Almond and Sidney Verba, *The Civic Culture* (Princeton, N.J.: Princeton Univ. Press, 1963).

Chapter 2

The Venezuelan Administrative
Reform Movement, 1958–1963

Roderick T. Groves

Venezuela has long been reputed to have administrative problems as severe as those in any part of Latin America. The impact of centuries of poverty and despotic rule is apparent in many characteristic features of the public administration: the dominant influence of personalism, the weak tradition of public service, the strong tendency toward excessive centralization, the paucity of trained personnel. Yet Venezuela in recent decades has also become a land of aspiration and commitment to political liberty and economic and social progress. In 1958, in the surge of reform spirit that followed the fall of Pérez Jiménez, most recent of Venezuela's many dictators, these aspirations prompted a comprehensive, widely supported effort to reform the public administration. A decree of 27 June 1958 issued by the National Junta of Government formally initiated the reform by creating a commission, the Public Administration Commission of Venezuela, "to study the . . . Public Administration, . . . with the purpose of recommending reforms for the Public Administration of the country."[1] Six years later as the first democratic era of Venezuelan history came to a close, this organization could look back on a history of hard work and dedicated pursuit of administrative change. But as happens with most reform organizations, the role it played, the support it received, and the accomplishments it could claim differed considerably from what was initially anticipated and planned.

The Public Administration Commission (Comisión de Adminis-

1. Decree 287, article 1.

47

tración Pública, CAP) was not the first Venezuelan effort at administrative reform nor the first institution set up for the purpose. In 1947 a Commission for Financial and Administrative Studies (Comisión para Estudios Financieros y Administrativos, CEFA) had been created in the Ministry of Finance replacing an earlier Commission of Fiscal Studies. The new unit like its predecessor was planned largely as a research unit, but with a scope that contemplated administrative as well as financial investigation.[2] Even in 1946, administration was being recognized as a national problem, as attested by Tejera París's little book, *Los empleados públicos y la reforma administrativa.*[3] But concern was only beginning. CEFA was a pioneering venture that began very cautiously. Hardly had its work started when the military captured control of the government in 1948. Though the organization of the agency was left unaltered, its stature and resources were soon reduced. During the Pérez Jiménez dictatorship (1952–58) it was confined to performing "miscellaneous duties for which the Minister of Finance . . . could find no other logical depository."[4]

By 1958 CEFA was so weak and discredited that few considered it capable of mounting a high-level attack on the nation's administrative inadequacies, even if given resources and support. Apparently its leadership forthrightly recognized this and threw their weight behind the idea of a new reform agency. One observer has suggested that "CEFA's chief, Dr. Leopoldo J. Bello . . . [and] the knowledgeable Dr. Arturo Sosa, Minister of Finance, were the focal points for the administrative reform movement which gathered impetus in 1958."[5]

Most administrative reform work carried out in Venezuela prior to 1958 under the regime of General Pérez Jiménez was by contract with private foreign consultant companies or individual specialists. Since CEFA commanded neither prestige nor power, it was unable to centralize, coordinate, or program the reform work. Every unit of government operated strictly on its own.

2. Comisión de Administración Pública, 23 *Preguntas sobre reforma administrativa* (Caracas, 1963), p. 47.
3. Caracas: Tipografía Americana, 1945.
4. George Sugarman, "Analysis of Personnel Management in the Ministry of Agriculture of Venezuela," (Ph.D. diss., American University, 1960), p. 294.
5. Ibid., p. 295.

Money was abundant during the dictatorship, and that spent on improving the regime's image was never considered wasted. With few restrictions, ministries and institutes arranged for consultant companies or individuals to examine selected aspects of their agencies and to make recommendations.[6] Thus, small-scale and isolated studies occurred frequently during the dictatorship, but seldom with any commitment to implementation. Frequently recommendations were given only cursory consideration. Since the consultant companies knew this, they sometimes took advantage of the situation by charging high fees and placing ill-trained personnel on projects.[7]

There were exceptions. In the Ministry of Agriculture, a new minister in 1953 brought in three prominent experts to make a complete appraisal of organization and a few selected procedures in the ministry. Though unfamiliar with Venezuela and the Spanish language and though extremely limited in time (the longest study was one of two months), the advisors had no difficulty noting the chief problems of the ministry.[8] Further, the minister kept faith by acting forcefully to carry out many of the reforms, and a substantial number of obvious improvements were made.

Yet even in this case the gains, isolated and unpursued, were soon overcome by old habits and neglect. Sugarman notes that by 1958 the reform work was little known to the ministry functionaries.[9] Outside the ministry, even in the Public Administration Commission, the Ministry of Agriculture work was forgotten, and copies of the reports are today unavailable. With no attention to follow-up and no lasting awareness of the goals and thinking of the reformers, initial progress was short-lived.

That this was the case in the Ministry of Agriculture gives some idea of the fate of the other reform efforts of the period. Isolated, generally covering only a small area of administration,

6. As a partial enumeration of the firms involved, Sugarman (p. 303) lists the following: Cresap, McCormick and Paget; Griffenhagen and Associates; McKinsey and Co., Inc.; Booz, Allen, and Hamilton International Ltd.; Price, Waterhouse and Co., Inc.; and the George S. May Co.
7. See Sugarman, p. 303.
8. Ibid., p. 46.
9. Ibid.

and carried out in slipshod fashion and for nonadministrative ends, they were either ignored from the start or overcome by latent distrust and apathy within the government. By 1958 the every-agency-for-itself approach to reform had been thoroughly discredited as wasteful and ineffective. Yet the problem remained. The new Public Administration Commission was a new start, an attempt to elevate administrative reform to a governmentwide, even nationwide level, with a comprehensive program and unified leadership.

Government Policy Toward the Commission and Administrative Reform

In setting up the new commission, the 1958 Junta of Government showed strong support for the idea of administrative reform. More important, in the manner in which it went about its task it showed awareness of the need to avoid the pitfalls of past reform efforts. Particularly strategic in this regard was the need for prestige and stature if the work of the new agency was to be recognized and governmentwide administrative unity and reform consistency were to be achieved.

The administrative-reform campaign was dramatized publicly by calling on a senior member of the U.N. technical assistance staff, the internationally known authority Herbert Emmerich, to conduct an analysis of the Venezuelan administration and to make recommendations for its improvement. The prestige of Emmerich was such that his report commanded immediate and widespread support and agreement when issued on 5 May 1958.[10] In it he proposed that a commission of prominent persons be formed after the pattern of the U.S.'s Hoover Commission and the U.K.'s Haldane Commission to examine the nation's administration and make recommendations for its improvement.

10. Herbert Emmerich, "Informe sobre un estudio preliminar acerca de posibilidades de mejoras en la administración pública de Venezuela," mimeographed (Caracas: Administración de Asistencia Tecnica de las Naciones Unidas, 1958). For an abridged English version, see United Nations, Department of Economic and Social Affairs, *Public Administration in Venezuela* (TAO/VEN/13, 1 Nov. 1961) (New York: United Nations, 1961), pp. 1–9.

The junta moved promptly to implement the Emmerich report. In June it issued Decree 287, and by 15 July it had appointed the eight-member collegiate governing body, the "commission." Every effort was made to give the new institution an impressive send-off. The inauguration took place in a solemn ceremony at the presidential palace attended by all members of the junta, cabinet ministers, the armed forces high command, and other important figures.[11] The event was given national coverage by radio and television and the press.

The junta deliberately balanced the composition of the governing commission to win favor with the public and all groups on which the new agency might depend. All members were well-known and highly respected. Each of the major political parties was represented, as was the military and the business community, from which came the executive director, Dr. Carlos Lander Marquez. Lander had been instrumental from the first in stimulating junta interest in an administrative-reform movement. He had the advantages of an established family name and close ties with the business community, and he enjoyed the confidence and ear of the president of the junta, Vice-Admiral Wolfgang Larrazábal.

More important for the firm establishment of the commission during its first few months of existence preceding the national elections was the prestige it won by close association with the presidency. It was given more than a million dollars to begin its work.[12] Communications were frequent between it and the presidential palace, and it was facilitated at all points. The concept of a nonpartisan agency, independent of executive authority, was maintained, but the junta clearly bestowed favored treatment on the commission.

In certain respects, however, the commission was left in an uncertain status by the junta, though without any apparent intent to lessen its effectiveness and authority. In particular it was given strangely garbled lines of responsibility and authority. Articles

11. *El Universal* (Caracas), 16 July 1958, p. 1.
12. Decree 394, 22 Oct. 1958. The official exchange rate used to convert the figure to dollars is 3.35 bolívares to the dollar.

2 and 3 of Decree 287 stated: "The commission . . . will be the advisor of the Executive Power, and the Ministry of Finance will be the legal organ of coordination. . . . The expenses incurred by this commission will be charged to the budget of the Ministry of Finance." These provisions were at best ambiguous, but can be read as giving the Minister of Finance primary control over the new agency. But the President of the junta appointed the members of the governing commission, and the inauguration ceremony definitely gave the impression that CAP was a presidential dependency. Further, from the start the executive director conferred regularly with the President, and the Minister of Finance apparently was never even considered as a proper channel to higher authority. Finally, the concept of a "little Hoover Commission" favored a close tie between the commission and the Chief Executive.

The most probable explanation for the confusing provisions of the decree is that at the time it was issued, no precedent existed for establishing such a unit under the President. The Venezuelan concept of the Chief Executive had never included much direct attachment of staff and advisory officers. To some extent the Ministry of Finance had accumulated these functions instead, much as the Directions General had accumulated them, apart from the ministers in the various ministries. The national budget office was located in Finance as CEFA had been. In December 1958 a national planning agency, Cordiplan (Oficina Central de Coordinación y Planificación) was set up directly under the president, and later an autonomous institute[13] was even added to the presidential organization; but in June 1958 no such precedent existed.

The Ministry of Finance may also have exerted some pressure to have the commission placed under its direction. As an agency of administrative reform, CEFA had been reduced to insignificance by the creation of CAP, and the ministry may have argued that its function was a ministerial prerogative. The commission, on the other hand, convinced that its program would end within

13. Corporación Venezolana de Guayana.

a short time, could not have been greatly concerned about such niceties.

Finally, there is a possibility that operating funds for the commission were more easily and rapidly available to the Ministry of Finance than to the presidency. In an interview, Carlos Lander attributed considerable importance to this factor. Probably a combination of these elements was in truth responsible for the odd legal location of CAP in the governmental hierarchy.

Another uncertainty the junta left to the commission was the continued existence of CEFA. Decree 287 made no stipulation regarding CEFA, and no effort was made to alter or abolish it. Exactly what its role was to be was unclear, for obviously CAP was meant to take over all administrative reform functions. The Emmerich report suggested that within a year a permanent national organization and methods office ought to be set up by the commission, but made no mention of CEFA in this regard.[14] Nonetheless, CEFA was allowed to continue side by side with the commission.

The Larrazábal government showed both an understanding of and appreciation for the "little Hoover Commission" idea.[15] While in power, it worked closely with the Public Administration Commission and showed a willingness to support its recommendations. Before CAP had time to make any important recommendation, however, Vice-Admiral Larrazábal had resigned to campaign in the presidential elections. Shortly thereafter, Rómulo Betancourt was elected President.

With Betancourt as President, the commission found itself in far different circumstances. Not only did it soon lose its favored status; its work received no such personal presidential support as previously. The new presidential attitude was frequently attributed to the traditional opposition of Venezuelan leaders to the programs and achievements of predecessors and competitors. But Betancourt's position seemed to be less one of opposition than of measured support. His electioneering commitments prevented the

14. Emmerich, "Informe," p. 7.
15. The head of the governing junta of 1958 was Vice-Admiral Wolfgang Larrazábal, the leader of the military rebels that had overthrown the dictatorship in January 1958.

elimination of the commission, but they did not require his enthusiastic support. The reform effort had not been his idea nor the commission his creation, and he had not been consulted on its work and plans. He proceeded to treat the commission in much the same way that he treated the other standard agencies and programs he inherited, neither as one of the specially deserving nor as a pariah.

Later, lack of presidential support was explained by those sympathetic to the regime as a matter of priorities.[16] Highest priority belonged to sustaining constitutionalist government, and as hostility toward the regime changed into a wave of terror and violence, the President had no choice but to give his full attention to maintaining the system even if some less immediate concerns (such as administrative reform) had to suffer. There was obviously a good deal of truth in this explanation. Toward the end of his term Betancourt had all he could do to secure a democratic succession. But this explanation by itself is insufficient, for the president's position remained consistent throughout his term; it did not begin when the regime came under fire. In fact, the most important reform decisions arose well before the concerted campaign to prevent the election of 1963 began. And other matters, some not very unlike the administrative reform program, received attention and support throughout the period of greatest stress. Cordiplan, for example, never suffered from presidential neglect.

In fact, the president did not seem to be much interested in the reform, personally. He was a tough, old-school politician who had survived in Venezuelan politics on the strength of his courage, determination, and conviction. While the embodiment of a new political age, he was also a link to the past. His political habits were formed in the twilight of the age of *caudillos,* though his political thinking rejected its ideological bankruptcy. Like so many of his Latin American political contemporaries, he was a peculiar mixture of new idealism and *caudillismo;* governing and politicking instinctively along personalist lines, but for idealistic ends or subject to democratic limitations.

16. See Antonio Stemple París, "Venezuela y su reforma administrativa," *La República* (Caracas), 16 Sept. 1963, p. 6.

His attitude toward administrative reform was both a manifestation and a consequence of this incongruous combination. Intellectually he was a supporter of administrative reform and committed himself and his party to it publicly. In a speech during the electoral campaign of 1958, for example, he stated:

> The necessity of a reform of the Public Administration, that rusty and decrepit machinery that is the Venezuelan State, is apparent. It is necessary that the Public Administration be technified. It is necessary that a civil service law be passed. It is necessary that a system be created that prevents the public employee from being abused by political change and that gives him stability in his position.[17]

Yet in practice, Betancourt seems to have felt at home in personalistic government, where the sheer weight of personality (with which he was generously endowed) dominated, and where there were few rules that would not yield to audacity, courage, and capacity to influence. Face to face with administrative reform proposals he found them uninteresting, and this of course affected his view of their necessity.

Betancourt was far more interested in social and economic reform, and he sought to govern for a whole series of ends that had been largely ignored in Venezuela's political past. To accomplish this he had to rely on public administration and the cooperation of the national bureaucracy and its leaders. Any executive tends to measure change of administrative structure and practice by the degree to which it will upset the administrative programs he is responsible for. And where these programs are social and economic reforms, sought with a conviction born of years of political perseverance, the incentive for administrative reform will suffer. This seems to have been the case with Betancourt. It is ironic that social reformers often make poor administrative reformers.

Whatever the cause of the Betancourt attitude, and it was probably a combination of factors, it was not long in producing an effect. At the time of the power transition, the commission staff

17. Rómulo Betancourt, *Posición y doctrina* (Caracas: Editorial Cordillera, 1959), p. 288.

was completing proposals for a complete overhaul of the presidential offices. The new President and his assistants had been informed of the changes contemplated and had responded encouragingly. No extensive alterations had been proposed. Once the President was inaugurated, the atmosphere changed, and the reforms were found unacceptable in almost every major respect. Efforts were made to find grounds for compromise through an exchange of ideas and explanations of points of view, but with no success. Finally the dispute was brought to an end when the President simply offered his ideas to the commission for ratification and it refused on the ground that there was little similarity between these and any proposals it had made.

During this episode the first executive director, Carlos Lander, left the commission. He apparently had anticipated problems, for before the inauguration he had proposed a replacement for himself and the successor had been accepted by the incoming regime. Lander continued in an advisory capacity, however, until the dispute over the presidential offices exploded, and then he left precipitately.

Even though the new executive director, Benito Raúl Losada, was an "independent" supporter of the government party, Acción Democrática, the problems with the Chief Executive continued. Losada found it so difficult to see the President that virtually all lines of direct communication between the presidential palace and the commission were broken. The commission was left to conduct its affairs in isolation. Even when Losada was later replaced by a very important figure in Acción Democrática and a confidant of the President, the administrative reform continued on its own with no greater presidential support and sympathy than previously.

With the advent of the national austerity campaign in 1960, in which virtually all government agencies had their budgets reduced by a flat percentage, the commission fared like all the rest. Many persons in the administrative-reform movement felt that such action was myopic, that if given some high-level support instead of financial reductions, the efforts of administrative reform could have saved the government much more than it gained by cutting budgets. But this position received no sympathetic consideration.

The effect of the change in presidential attitude in 1959 was to throw the commission onto its own resources. Thus it was in time forced to abandon all efforts to achieve sweeping government-wide reform. Its role as special advisor to the President, the very heart of the Hoover Commission idea, was ended almost before begun. Instead the Public Administration Commission became, altogether unwillingly and without quite realizing it, a high-class pressure group within the government.

The Executive Directors

The persons who most influenced the formation and orientation of the commission were its four executive directors and Herbert Emmerich of the United Nations. It was Emmerich of course who had formulated the initial plan of the commission, nearly all the important aspects of which were followed by the junta. The four executive directors departed in varying degrees from the initial plan under pressure from unforeseen obstacles and lack of support.

The Emmerich scheme, as noted above, proposed the creation of a commission of investigation and recommendation with "the stature and prestige of the first Hoover Commission of the United States and Lord Haldane's Commission of the United Kingdom."[18] The commission was to carry out its investigations by means of task forces with U.N. technical assistance available where wanted, but it was to exist for a short time only. Emmerich estimated that all the evaluation and recommendation work and the most important implementation work could be completed in approximately one year.[19] At that time the commission would end, leaving behind two permanent national offices (one of personnel and another of organization and methods) to handle the remaining detail of implementation and reform work of the future.

The Emmerich proposal went on to lay out a schedule of work with which the commission was to concern itself. In the field of

18. Emmerich, "Informe," p. 5.
19. Ibid., pp. 5,6, and 8.

organization it was first to undertake a complete evaluation of the presidential offices and the Ministry of Finance. In a second stage it was to carry out studies of the ministerial level of government, the autonomous institute level, and intergovernmental relations. First priority in the personnel field was to be assigned to the creation by law of a modern merit system, the development of a classification scheme and remuneration plan, and the provisional incorporation of government personnel into the new system. As a second stage, Emmerich recommended that full adaptation to the new merit system be accomplished by holding examinations for all members of the public service and then placing them according to competence demonstrated. The Emmerich proposal also recommended that high priority be given to overhauling national financial procedures, particularly budgeting, accounting, and auditing. Government-wide studies on decentralization and delegation of authority were proposed as a third priority to be carried out after the other commission recommendations had been established.

The first executive director of the Public Administration Committee, Carlos Lander, adopted most of the Emmerich proposals as his plan of action. He found the idea of a little Hoover Commission so appealing that he spent a day conferring with Ex-President Hoover in his New York hotel suite. He worked tirelessly to build a close relationship between the commission and the presidency of Venezuela and resigned when he felt his presence threatened this relationship.

In organizing the commission, Lander established the two areas of reform Emmerich had suggested (personnel and organization) and added two of his own: systems and procedures, and training. The CAP personnel were divided into three "groups," each concerned with one of the first three divisions, while training was placed in the hands of the United Nations. As recommended, work was initiated in the presidential-offices study and a career service law (civil service law). All the groups began by carrying out brief panoramic preliminary surveys.

In some respects Lander departed from the Emmerich proposals, most importantly in securing outside assistance. Emmerich had suggested that Venezuelan personnel should be "capable of taking charge of all investigation necessary for the Commission to arrive at conclusions."[20] Yet it became clear to Lander that such personnel were not in 1958 available to the commission, and that the commissioners (who were expected to work part-time without compensation) needed a great deal more than a mere supply of information to make useful recommendations. Acting on this view, Lander took a course of action that had an enormous effect on the whole reform movement. He proposed that the commission contract with three private consultant firms from the United States to assist in the reform work for a period of two years, extendible to three. Subsequently the J. L. Jacobs Company of Chicago was hired to carry out work in personnel, the Public Administration Service of Chicago for work in organization, and Griffenhagen and Associates of New York for work in systems and procedures. The contracts specified that the number of experts employed could be varied by the commission to conform with the requirements of its programs.

Almost as an afterthought the Emmerich report had noted that there might arise occasions when it would be worthwhile for the proposed agency to hire private consultants.[21] But the report's words on relying on Venezuelan technical personnel clearly implied that consultants would not be necessary in the investigation work. Nonetheless CAP claimed the Emmerich proposals in its support on this score.[22] In fact, this was Lander's own contribution. In the course of three years the commission was to spend over $2 million for consultant services.[23] The consultant influence on the commission and its employees in turn was to be profound.

The immediate effect was to enlarge greatly the importance of the executive director. The work of the consultants had to be

20. Ibid., p. 6.
21. Ibid., p. 15.
22. Comisión de Administración Pública, *Memoria correspondiente al Ejercicio Anual 1959* (Caracas, 1960), p. 3.
23. $2,009,572.27 for total services: $860,042.25 to Griffenhagen and Associates; $653,738.74 to J. L. Jacobs & Co.; $495,746.28 to the Public Administration Service. Figures taken from accounting statistics of the Public Administration Commission, Caracas, and the Ministry of Finance, Caracas.

directed and coordinated, and the executive director was the
logical person to handle this. But as the importance of the day-to-
day direction grew, that of the executive commission (collegiate
directorate)[24] declined. The commissioners were working gratis
and part-time. As the presidential campaign drew near, the political members were drawn into partisan activity and seldom attended commission meetings. With Lander a member of the
executive commission, there was a tendency to take his views
as those of the commission, short-cutting thereby the increasingly
laborious task of gaining full commission approval. After the election many of the commissioners suspected that their position
and that of the commission would be changed for the worse
under the new presidential regime. With these handicaps, the
executive commission became less and less an integral part of
the working machinery of the new agency. After the election it
gradually fell into disuse, and by the time the second executive
director took over, it had for all practical purposes ceased to exist.

This occurred despite the fact that Lander devoted steadily
less time to his duties after the election of 1958. Disillusioned
over the outcome of the election and under mounting pressure to
devote more time to his business responsibilities, he spent only
a small part of his time directing the commission. This caused a
critical absence of leadership, especially since the commission
was in its formative stages. Programs had to be formulated and
agreed upon, and the three consultant companies required full-
time supervision. This absence of leadership, however, was filled
by technical experts sent to the commission by the United Nations, particularly the first, John B. Blandford. To Blandford be-
longs most of the credit for the commission's having started to
function smoothly. Under his supervision, a series of panoramic
surveys of Venezuelan administrative conditions were carried
out, and with this information the broad goals of the Emmerich
proposal were broken down into specific projects. By the time
Blandford left in April 1959 the commission was firmly oriented

24. The word "commission" when used in the text means the organization and
not its collegiate directorate—unless otherwise indicated, usually by the phrase
"executive commission."

and making impressive headway in its investigations. Blandford was succeeded by Dillon Myer, who continued where he had left off. Myer was instrumental in maintaining continuity during the period of adjustment under the second executive director. He was aided in this by a full team of U.N. technical assistance experts, specialists in most of the areas of commission concern.[25]

The second executive director was Benito Raul Losada. Losada was something of a protégé of Lander, but was also an Acción Democrática sympathizer and supporter of Rómulo Betancourt. Losada and Lander worked closely together to make the transition a smooth one. Losada kept the commission firmly oriented in the direction Lander had initiated. Work moved rapidly forward along the lines laid out in the Emmerich report in all three areas of investigation set up by Lander. The fourth training area, however, took on new impetus with the arrival in May 1959 of a U.N. expert on training. Prior to this time the only training activities within the commission were the indoctrination each consultant company decided to give the Venezuelan members of its staff. This haphazard arrangement had produced a planned program and integrated curriculum in only one case, that of the Jacobs company. Under the new direction, however, the consultant companies were required to set up a joint training program to be given to all the analysts. A library and documentation center were established in the commission, and a general survey on in-service training programs of other government agencies was conducted. Further, a series of seminars was launched to stimulate interest. Plans were also discussed for the establishment of a national institute of public administration.

This was a period of great activity within the commission. The consultants pressed on with investigation, aware of the Emmerich timetable, and impressive progress was made, particularly in organization and in classification of personnel positions. But as the priority reform projects were being pushed to completion, it was becoming increasingly clear that any implementation

25. All told, seven U.N. experts served in the commission during 1959, including Blandford and Myer. For further details see: *Public Administration in Venezuela, 1958–1961* (U.N. Report TAO/VEN 13).

would have to take place in an unpropitious political climate. The loose governing coalition between the party of the government and the other two major parties was beginning to fall apart. Schism and factionalism had weakened and were to further weaken the government party. Threats to take over the government by force were growing in number and intensity, and no one was sure, not even the leaders, of the government's capacity to weather such opposition.

On top of this there was no evidence of an improvement in the government's support for administrative reform. Instead of becoming convinced that this was an essential step in effectuating a larger program of reform, Betancourt seemed largely unconcerned with the matter. He left the commission and its leadership in semi-isolation, neither encouraging nor discouraging its work nor concerning himself with its orientation. No effort was made to pave the way for a massive program of change such as was being developed in the commission offices.

By the time the governmentwide organizational studies were finished it had become clear that their fate would once again be that of relegation to dusty shelves as "background studies," not utilization as a strategic rationale for a sweeping program of change. So remote was the likelihood of any action that the commission made only a token effort to gain their implementation. And by the summer of 1960 when Benito Raul Losada resigned as executive director to accept a high administrative position in the Ministry of Finance, the prospects for personnel reform were no better. In spite of a somewhat hesitant endorsement of the civil service law by the Council of Ministers, the national Congress, now seething with political intrigue and in-fighting, was unwilling to even give the measure serious consideration. Thus the administrative reform movement faced a major crisis. If it was to continue as an effective force it had to take a different tack. The first tentative steps of reorientation were being taken when the second executive director was replaced by the third.

Alberto López Gallegos, Losada's replacement, was a very prominent member of the government party, Acción Democrática, and a close acquaintance of Rómulo Betancourt. A lawyer by profession, he had long been interested in and associated with administrative reform, first as governor of Aragua state in 1945, next as president of the Municipal Council of the Venezuelan Federal District, and then for a time as chief of the Advanced School of Public Administration of Central America (San José, Costa Rica) while in exile from the Pérez Jiménez dictatorship. He had been the representative of Acción Democrática on the executive commission of the Public Administration Commission when it was first set up, but had had a falling out with the first executive director, Carlos Lander. Thereafter he had refused to cooperate with the commission leadership and had not attended commission meetings. Notwithstanding this, he was familiar with its programs and problems. He was to control the commission from the middle of 1960 to the middle of 1963, the longest term of any executive director.

López Gallegos gave the commission an orientation that could survive within the Betancourt environment.[26] He realistically assumed that very little was likely to come out of the initial governmentwide failure and took the position that this was always meant to be the case. The first stage of the reform, he suggested, had been merely a diagnosis of the country's administrative problems, preliminary studies to test the administrative conditions. This the commission had completed without any intent to turn these investigations into specific proposals for reform. Now it was time to turn to implementation. Emmerich had proposed that about this time the commission be disbanded in favor of a permanent central organization and methods office. Even if there had existed a willingness to take this step, the meager achievements of the reform would hardly have justified it. Instead, López Gallegos decided to reorganize the commission into two such offices, to serve as its major internal divisions.

In effect López Gallegos initiated a major departure from the Emmerich blueprint. The latter had emphasized implementation of what was now nearly impossible, governmentwide reform.

---

26. For a clear exposition of the López Gallegos philosophy see Comisión de Administración Pública, *Memoria correspondiente al Ejercicio Anual 1961* (Caracas, 1962), Introd.

López Gallegos meant to emphasize not implementation so much as the implementable. He wanted to be free of the dead weight of unacceptable reform and to start on something feasible.

The organization group of the commission had already initiated projects of a much more specific character in several ministries and government agencies, upon their request. López Gallegos gave these his full approval, but discontinued all work on the governmentwide organization studies. Many aspects of the broad systems-and-procedures program were terminated precipitately, and the group was directed to concentrate on a few, specific programs. In the personnel area the establishment and maintenance of a central personnel system in preparation for eventual passage of the career service law was downgraded, while the cultivation of separate ministry and institute personnel offices and systems was upgraded. The new agency-by-agency approach gave CAP a program flexibility that allowed López Gallegos to emphasize work in the government's high-priority policy areas.

The net effect of the changes made by López Gallegos was to transform the role of CAP from that of an advisory agency to that of an advocate. To strengthen this change the new director took and demanded other organizational actions consistent with it. First, he secured the termination of CEFA's administrative reform functions and the merger of a good share of its staff with the commission, including its director, who became executive secretary of the commission. Second, he dispensed with the executive commission of CAP. This institution had failed to operate since Carlos Lander had left and was for all intents and purposes already defunct. Finally, he insisted that the commission be able to communicate to the President directly, and not through any other agency or leader.

In particular he was adamant against having to communicate through Pérez Guerrero, head of Cordiplan, the national planning agency. Pérez Guerrero was very close to the President and was a strong supporter of administrative reform. He had previously acted as the commission's link with the President, and while this had produced no startling breakthroughs, there was a considerable feeling that it would eventually pay off. The effect of this relationship, however, was to informally make CAP a dependency of Cordiplan. López Gallegos objected to this and sought and obtained direct communications with the President.

In another major shift, López Gallegos decided to cut back on the role of the consultant companies. With the national program of austerity in 1960 serving as a convenient rationale, he immediately cut consultant staffs from an average of seven or eight to three persons, when he took over as executive director. His eventual goal, as noted in the *Memoria* of the commission of 1961, was to cut back the consultants to the point where they would be needed for only "periodic revisions and evaluations" of the work of the commission.[27] Likewise he sought to greatly reduce the role of the United Nations within the commission.

The cutback in consultant staffs gave the commission the resources to later undertake a new academic venture,[28] the creation of an institute of public administration. To do this López Gallegos sought to have the old Curso de Administración Pública, a legalistic training program of the Ministry of Finance, transferred to the commission. With this as the foundation, the new School of Public Administration was begun. Initially the school was limited to offering training programs useful for advance entry into or advancement in the public service, but broad future expansion was optimistically forecast. It was hampered, however, by a low budget and a dispute between those who wanted to gain prestige by greatly broadening its curriculum and activities and those who wanted to concentrate its resources on a more limited program of in-service and pre-service training.

The training of the commission's Venezuelan analysts had previously been largely a responsibility of the consultant companies. With the reduction of company staffs and programs, not much training help could be expected from this source. López Gallegos did not fill the gap, however, and left training an incidental activity. He did initiate a scholarship program for overseas study, substantially aided by the largess of the U.S. AID.

In reorienting the administrative reform program, López Gal-

27. Comisión, *Memoria 1961*, p. 489.
28. Ibid.

legos showed that he was well aware of the fact that the commission had reached a point where it would have to rely on its own resources. Such was the prestige and influence of the new executive director that he had no reason to fear such a prospect, but he nevertheless altered commission tradition in at least one important respect, with the idea of gaining even greater political leverage. Previously the commission had been quite possessive about its personnel. The analysts, many of them with several years of experience working under the consultants and participating in the major work of investigation, were among the greatest assets the commission had. It was reasoned that to squander this resource would be unwise. Occasionally analysts left the commission of their own free will for work in private industry or government, but never were they encouraged to take other positions. There was a high level of *esprit de corps* within the commission, and not infrequently experienced analysts would reject better jobs to stay in the commission.

López Gallegos, however, took the view that well-trained and dedicated analysts would be at least as valuable elsewhere in the public administration, for they would proselytize in behalf of reform and provide substantial internal support for commission work. Thus the executive director decided to accept most requests for commission-trained personnel and even to encourage them. The predictable consequence was that soon many of the best-trained and experienced analysts had left, and the process accelerated as the once strong bonds of professional association weakened. So rapid was the "dispersal" that new analysts with only two or three months' experience in the commission were pushed into tasks of great responsibility, often with poor results. Not infrequently, promising recruits would be "assigned" to government agencies to fill important posts before they had had even minimal training or experience in the commission.

There developed from this an inclination to look at the commission as a means of gaining admittance into prominent government positions. This could conceivably have compromised the ethical and technical objectivity of the commission, but this seems not to have happened. Nonetheless, it did have a damaging

effect on commission morale, an effect compounded by the low-
ness of CAP salaries. As part of the national austerity campaign,
in 1960 the new executive director lowered salaries within the
commission across the board and left them at the new level
throughout his three years with the commission. These lower
salary levels made it harder to get good people, and even harder
to hold them after they obtained initial training.

It is difficult to evaluate how successful the López Gallegos
policy of personnel distribution was, since there was really no
other period of implementation experience against which it can
be measured. No doubt it did facilitate and advance the process
of reform in a few specific cases. But on the whole, most commission appointees seem to have made their peace with the administrative status quo, going far in accepting the administrator
(as opposed to reformer) philosophy that existing conditions
must be altered only with great caution lest government programs
be upset. The initial impact of this personnel-transplant policy
must be considered a disappointment.

One final characteristic of the commission during this period
was the undeniable entrance and growth of partisanship. There
is no doubt that with López Gallegos at its head, the commission
took on a partisan image in the public mind. During part of this
time López Gallegos retained his position as a high official in
Acción Democrática. Far from being disturbed by this image,
he clearly felt that some partisan politics in administration was
a healthy and natural thing, and to cover it up or to bend over
backwards to disassociate oneself from it was dishonest and
hypocritical. But the fact that the commission leadership was so
clearly identified with a party inevitably encouraged a growth of
partisan activity within the commission. The decline of the consultant influence may also have removed an important obstacle
to this trend.

Thus, López Gallegos' new approach was not totally successful. In a few instances it is true that some significant
changes were effectuated, particularly in the area of reorganization. This was made possible primarily by cooperative leadership
within the agencies involved. Executive leadership turnover

rates were very high during this period, however, and in some instances initial reform accomplishments were jeopardized by later leadership changes. More important, though, was the failure to generate a substantial impact or reformist momentum throughout the government by the new effort to do on a piecemeal basis what could not be done earlier by central authority. Particularly frustrating in this regard was the attempt to secure personnel reform. López Gallegos managed to secure a civil service decree from the government when enactment of a law seemed dead, but with responsibility for implementation left wholly up to the commission. Working with several cooperative ministries, the commission sought to effectuate ministerial civil service systems, but the work of classification was done with such haste and superficiality that the effort had little enduring impact and made a more negative than positive impression elsewhere in the government.

In the summer of 1963 López Gallegos resigned as executive director of the commission for reasons of health. As his successor he recommended one of the two directors in the personnel wing of the commission, Hector Pujol, who was accepted and appointed as acting (*encargado*) executive director. Pujol's appointment caused some division within the commission because two other leaders within the agency with more seniority and higher or equal previous positions were passed over. One of these, Amadeo Araujo, had been the chief of CEFA before it was combined with the commission and had been second only to López Gallegos in authority. Pujol, young and ambitious and a member of Acción Democrática, had come to the commission only a few years earlier, but as a protégé of López Gallegos had risen rapidly. Placed in charge of the commission's implementation efforts in the personnel area, he had enjoyed much authority by virtue of the shift in emphasis brought about under López Gallegos' tenure.

Between his appointment and the transfer of presidential power, there was little opportunity for Pujol to make major contributions to the commission's character. His direction tended to follow the lines set by his predecessor. Politics increasingly permeated the commission, largely due no doubt to the imminence of the national elections. As a young man promoted from the ranks, Pujol found it difficult to restrain highly partisan members of the commission. Because of the period of transfer of power, perhaps, the new leadership of the commission began to reopen some questions of commission status and policy that had been "settled" by López Gallegos so as not to embarrass the Betancourt regime. The strategy behind this seemed to be one of building up pressure on the next president. For example, in order to stress the need for a new reform initiative, it was again suggested that all previous work of the commission had been an investigation stage and that implementation would only begin with the second five-year period. It is true that most of the significant work of the first five years of commission existence had been investigative, but this was hardly intentional. Again the question of governmentwide reform was raised, with the assertion of the new leadership that agency-by-agency reform would get nowhere without previous full-scale reform throughout the government, principally the establishment of a merit system and governmentwide reorganization. And once again the issue of the commission's position in the executive hierarchy was openly discussed. As a combined personnel office and organization and methods office, the commission again argued that it was entitled to a prominent position in the presidential staff organization, with direct access to the President.

With the election of the new President, however, hopes for a substantial change began to fade. In a variety of ways the President-elect, Raul Leoni, indicated that his attitude toward administrative reform differed little from that of his predecessor. His response to the plea that he give more attention to administrative reform, for example, was to set up a committee composed of the minister of finance, the chief of the state planning agency, and the acting executive director of the commission to inform the Council of Ministers of the nation's administrative reform needs.

Popular Support for Administrative Reform

When the administrative reform movement began in 1958, it received broad and enthusiastic support. The nation's newspapers gave it fine editorial backing and did much to publicize the new commission. The political parties in the 1958 electoral campaign agreed that administrative reform was important and that the commission should be given ample political and financial support. Further, large numbers of influential people gave their personal endorsement to administrative reform. Administrative reform did not elicit the popular enthusiasm that greets social reform programs (e.g., land reform), but this was not expected. Herbert Emmerich, then head of the U.N. technical assistance staff, noted in an interview that in all his experience in Latin America he had known of only one administrative reform movement that had been sustained by more initial enthusiasm than that of Venezuela.

Yet, impressive as the initial backing was, equally or more impressive was the rapidity with which it disintegrated after 1959. With the decline in presidential support for the reform, there occurred a simultaneous and precipitate decline of support from other sources. The press tended to take its cues from the presidential offices and had no interest in developing a campaign for administrative improvement on its own. No real tradition of interest-group activity and few substantial groups existed to channel and concentrate the backing of individuals. There were no influential schools of public administration to stimulate new interest in the reform. Advocates who were members of the government or of the official party tended to defer to the presidential viewpoint. This in particular was a great disappointment to the reformers, since many of these persons, while in exile, had worked for the United Nations and had been deeply involved in technical assistance and administrative reform. And the public, while it gave its general approval to the reform, as it had given it to all proposed change and improvement, showed very little interest in the detail of administrative reform, the sort of interest that could be turned to the advantage of the movement.

In truth, throughout most of the Betancourt period there existed widespread indifference to administrative reform. Only one post-1959 issue really caused a show of broad interest in the reform, that being the question of congressional approval of a merit-system personnel law. But even this issue failed to arouse much general public interest. While this is disappointing, in view of the initial support shown, such a response should not be surprising. Seldom in history has reform of governmental apparatus been a major popular concern. It has no direct effect on the public and is complex and difficult to understand. Further, it often must confront much cynicism and pessimism born of long years of administrative abuse and arrogance.

Evaluation of the Reform Impact

While this chapter has not paid detailed attention to the operational aspects of the Public Administration Commission, enough has been said to indicate that the commission fell far short of its expectations. Even within the commission this conclusion was not subject to much argument. The most sanguine have estimated that no more than 20 percent of the reforms proposed were implemented in the period under study. A more accurate appraisal would certainly come up with a figure far lower, and even then such an estimate would not take into account the importance the commission attributed to its various reforms. When placed against this standard, the achievements of the commission seem even less significant.

A number of factors joined to frustrate the commission, but in the last analysis the most important was the lack of leadership support. Venezuelan executives from the top down, with a few happy exceptions, were hesitant and indecisive in their response to the reform. Their reluctance did not stem from any hostility to reform or widespread disagreement over the need for improvement; the commission, for example, never suffered from lack of requests from interested agencies. Nor was it often based on serious disputes over reform proposals themselves; many reforms were "accepted," but then left uneffectuated.

In fact this unwillingness to exercise leadership was probably due more to unfamiliarity with the idea of reform and its consequences than to doubts about its necessity or effectuality. The reform idea is an "institutionalist" one, which conceives of public administration in large part as subject to institutional modifications, and not merely as an extension of personality or program. As such it is alien to both the *caudillo* view of administration as a patriarchal community and to the modern social reformer's almost exclusive emphasis on governmental programs of substantive reform. The Venezuelan administrator, long accustomed to the *caudillo* view yet increasingly influenced by the reformist attitude, found the institutionalist approach to administration different and unappealing in its strangeness.

Further, the reformist approach is based on the idea that administration is of sufficient importance to merit separate and specialized consideration. In the United States this view is widely accepted today, but only after many years of slow change. In Venezuela it is only now beginning to have an influence. Politics has traditionally ignored administration, the public has either sympathized with it or despised it but never admired it, and education has either treated it as an aspect of law or has considered it inconsequential. Even administrators have belittled its (and their) importance and have joined in abuse of it. The idea that it is of separate importance is new and by many still considered unrealistic.

Consequently there was nothing familiar, nothing engaging in the idea of administrative reform to Venezuelan administrators. At the same time, however, the traditional *caudillo* approach to administration had been discredited and found unacceptable, particularly since the fall of the Pérez Jiménez dictatorship. What resulted from this has been a leadership ambivalence, an interest in and recognition of the need for reform in the abstract, but an unwillingness to carry through on application in the specific.

The ambivalent attitude of political leadership to administrative reform was hardened by the fact that the consequences of reform were unknown and therefore were considered risky in the unsettled political conditions of Venezuela. In the United States reform grew gradually and was promoted by an abundance of devices and institutions available for experimentation. New ideas frequently arose or were popularized in university and academic circles, and thereafter were undertaken in one or another level or branch of government, in business, or in other institutions. Seldom did national government executives lack evidence on how new administrative ideas and techniques worked in practice. But in Venezuela no similar means of getting acquainted with new ideas was available. There had been little experimentation in the national government, and most past efforts at reform were ignored or dismissed as gimmicks. Neither state or local governments had the resources or inclination to make any contribution. The nation's businesses, with the exception of large foreign firms whose example was considered largely inapplicable by Venezuelans, practiced little of advanced management techniques and showed slight interest in new ideas. Most have been small and dominated by the patron pattern. The example of the United States was evident and well-known to many Venezuelan leaders, but they viewed it as even more inapplicable than that of the foreign firms. Prior to the advent of the commission's School of Public Administration, no advanced schools of public administration existed in Venezuela. The nation's universities had not made a significant contribution in the area of public administration either, and no important pressure groups dedicated to the better practice of government existed.

Thus, nothing had paved the way for reform. Government administrators were asked to act with consequences unknown. Under normal circumstances this would have been difficult, but under the political and economic conditions faced by the Venezuelan regime of Rómulo Betancourt it was especially difficult. At stake during much of the government's term was the very existence of democracy in Venezuela, and with the stakes so high, government administrators tended to be overcautious. Innovation was accepted only when no other alternative existed or when personal conviction ran very strong.

Since unfamiliarity and apprehension of unknown consequences were sources of the leaders' reluctance to install reforms, the real task of the Public Administration Commission was to build confidence in and familiarity with reform in concept and in practice. This meant that it had to substitute itself or find some other substitute for the diverse institutions and influences that stimulate administrative improvement in more highly developed countries. It was impossible for the commission, in the short time it had set for itself, to undertake to develop backing from the grass roots up. In the first place it was committed to a far more ambitious program and would undoubtedly have encountered considerable difficulty in gaining governmental support for an approach so diffuse and indirect. In the second place the country lacked the institutions, organizations, and attitudes existent in more advanced nations that make reform "from the bottom up" a short-range possibility.

The commission sought instead to establish reforms from the top down without waiting for support to develop below. To make this possible it predictably looked to the backing of the President of the Republic. This was the greatest source of prestige and influence available to the reform movement, one that was capable of overcoming administration cautiousness and resistance on a large scale by shifting the burden of responsibility for consequences from the shoulders of lesser officials and by building confidence in the reform concept. The President had the acknowledged right to make extensive changes in administrative forms and practices and had traditionally wielded the political power and prestige to command administrative and legislative backing for such decisions. More important, perhaps, his was an office of such influence that it could stimulate broad support and interest in reform throughout society.

The advocates and leaders of the administrative reform movement were at first highly successful in gaining the support of the nation's Executive, the junta of 1958, and its head, Vice-Admiral

Larrazábal. Further, the reform program adopted by the reformers clearly demonstrated their expectation that presidential support would continue. It proposed nothing less than a governmentwide, simultaneous overhaul of all aspects of administration. Reforms of this scope were possible only with the enthusiastic support and cooperation of the chief executive.

With the change of government in 1959, however, presidential support dropped sharply. Whether this could have been avoided is open to question. On the one hand, Betancourt's position derived substantially from his individual attitude toward reform and from political conditions within the country, matters beyond the control of the commission. On the other hand, the eagerness of the original backers of the reform movement may ironically have contributed to the President's coolness. The warm support of the junta of 1958 for the program provided an excellent opportunity to establish firmly the reform movement and reform agency, yet possibly at the price of the full support of the President that followed. Given the political traditions of Venezuela, any successor other than the candidate of the junta itself could have been expected to some degree to regard the administrative-reform program and the Public Administration Commission as the projects of a competitor and political opponent. There were of course, good reasons for taking the opportunity to establish the reform movement while it existed. Once in effect, it was likely that it would not be handicapped or eliminated by the following regime, because of the fear of incurring an antireform image. But it was also quite possible that it would not be enthusiastically supported. One cannot blame the original advocates of reform for deciding to seize the opportunity the junta provided, and some effort was made to cover political uncertainties by giving all partisan forces a voice on the executive commission. On the other hand such a rapid plunge was a gamble, and an alternative and more cautious policy might have been pursued, one that would not have linked the reform too closely with the junta. The commission might, for example, have moved less quickly to commit itself to a program and a timetable, and in particular might have delayed in hiring foreign consultants.

In retrospect it is evident that it was futile for the commission to attempt governmentwide reform without presidential backing. This was the key (though unspecified) ingredient in the reform program set up by the Emmerich report in 1958, and without it the large-scale reform approach was doomed. Budget outlays for the reform remained high; but without a full-scale commitment at the top, this alone could not produce reform success. The fact that such support did not accompany the sizable budget allocations for the commission has, incidentally, disproved the contention of many persons that the government would effectuate the reform proposals because it, not some other nation or institution, would be paying for their preparation.

Other prestige-gaining devices used by the commission failed to provide a substitute for active presidential support. The commission-of-distinguished-men device fell into disuse after mid-1959, in part because it reflected rather than compensated for the lack of presidential interest. Obviously its members had little belief in its efficacy as an independent source of prestige and status for the administrative reform. The contracting of foreign consultant firms likewise failed to compensate for the absence of presidential interest and backing. Despite the obvious boost this gave to the professional reputation and capacity of the commission, it was a handicap because of the attitude, widely held within the public administration, that non-Venezuelans are incapable of appreciating Venezuelan conditions and thinking.

In view of the failure of governmentwide reform, the question arises whether an administrative-reform agency like the commission can have any value in the absence of presidential support. This is an important question because, if history is any indication, popularly elected Presidents will more frequently reflect the Betancourt-type viewpoint than any genuine enthusiasm for administrative reform.

The Venezuelan case gives reason to believe, however, that even without top-level backing, administrative reform can make headway. As noted above, the key obstacle to reform has been the resistance of administrative leaders stemming from their unfamiliarity with the ideas and probable consequences of reform. While top-level pressure is a most effective way of overcoming this, it can also be attacked by the use of example. Though Venezuelan administrators have usually been unwilling to accept, on their own, examples from foreign nations or foreign firms, they have been willing to imitate new thinking and practice within the administration. Perhaps the clearest instance of this in Venezuelan public administration is the fashion in which the concept of the controller and of financial-control procedure and organization has been transplanted from the ministries (where it is required by law) to the autonomous institutes.

By concentrating on producing a few nuclei[29] of reform and exploiting their demonstration value an administrative reform agency may be able to make substantial headway in overcoming resistance and spreading improved practice. The difficulties of such a course, however, should not be minimized. The high rate of turnover in leadership makes it extremely difficult to plan a consistent strategy of reform and even more difficult to sustain reforms that have been installed. Frequently agencies that seem sincerely interested in reform renege on promises or procrastinate. Reforms that are only partially implemented often cause problems as great as those they seek to cure, and this increases resistance to reform. Yet while the difficulties of building confidence by example are great, progress would seem to be possible by concentrating resources.

The reform agency must maximize the resources it possesses and focus them on a few points in the administration. For the most part this means limiting reform efforts to specific administrative units, to institutes, ministries, or parts of these. It also means assuring that the reform work is of good quality. To this end the reform agency should develop a cadre of first-class technicians who have been trained in depth and who have been exposed to considerable practical experience.

To the credit of the third and to a small extent the second executive director of the Venezuelan Public Administration Com-

29. For development of this concept, which is taken from Albert Waterston, see his article, "Administrative Obstacles to Planning, "*Economía Latinoamericana* 1 (July 1964): 308–50.

mission, some adjustments of emphasis tending in the above
direction were made, after it had become obvious that the commission could expect very little presidential backing. Most important, beginning in 1960 the scope of the reform work was
reduced, and a decided emphasis was placed on agency-based
(as compared with governmentwide) reform. At this time the
commission's reputation was probably at its height. Its personnel were considered well-qualified, and it had carried out some
outstanding work of investigation. The third executive director
was a man who clearly wielded considerable influence within
government circles. The effect, given a concentration of effort
on several likely agencies, was in part a successful one. Gains
were made in the Worker's Bank (the national housing agency),
the Agricultural Bank, the Agrarian Institute, the Ministry of
Finance, the National Controller, and a few ministry personnel
programs.

But in other respects the commission's leadership adopted a
course that rapidly sapped its effectiveness. Most important in
this regard was the personnel policy. By first cutting salaries and
then encouraging the dispersal of commission technicians
throughout the government, the leadership eliminated most of
its trained talent. At the same time it compounded the problem by
reducing the consultant personnel and eliminating nearly all the
consultant training activities. This alone would not have been too
damaging, but combined with the departure of much of the seasoned staff, it left the commission poorly manned and with little
means of rejuvenation. The decline in the quality of commission
personnel probably contributed most to the steady decline of the
commission's effectiveness after 1961, a decline made more noticeable by the unwillingness of its leadership to limit the number of
projects undertaken.

As an agency intent on making use of the demonstration effect
of good administrative practice, the commission should have
sought to make itself a good example. Originally it did so, but
with the decline of its effectiveness after 1961 and particularly
as a result of the already noted decline in morale, the commission
lost much of its spirit of professionalism and gradually yielded

to some of the administrative malpractices characteristic of the rest of the government. The growing influence of partisanship was the most obvious of these.

The commission also made little effort to draw other government agencies into the campaign for administrative change in order to strengthen its influence and effectiveness. Most obvious in this regard was the refusal of the commission leadership after 1960 to coordinate its work closely with that of Cordiplan, the national planning agency. It is possible that by making a greater effort in this direction the commission could have succeeded in making reform a condition in given cases for investment of international or even national funds in agency programs. Certainly it could have increased attention given to administrative factors in the planning and investment process. This omission was particularly serious because the head of Cordiplan was a known advocate of administrative reform and had worked very closely with the commission under the second executive director.

The commission might also have made a greater effort to bring the national controller into the process of administrative reform. One of the commission's greatest successes, governmentwide adoption of encumbrance accounting, was secured largely by virtue of the fact that the national controller accepted the idea and directed the ministries promptly to put it in effect. It is true that the controller was suspicious that under the influence of modern accounting doctrine the commission was intent on removing much of its authority. For this reason it might have been necessary to considerably compromise reform principles to gain the controller's confidence and support. But in light of the fact that the controller had enough political strength to veto any changes of financial procedure it opposed, the commission had very little to lose by making the concessions needed to gain the controller's support. And as suggested, it might have gained considerably by that support.

One should not conclude this discussion of the commission's performance without noting that the Venezuelan administrative reform has undoubtedly had a greater impact than might be presumed by adding up its immediate, tangible accomplishments.

Though it failed for the most part to effect short-term reform, it nonetheless may well have made a significant contribution to long-term improvement. The School of Public Administration which it created and its work in training have begun to inculcate a new attitude toward administrative reform, as well as knowledge of modern administration. Its investigations and their inclusion in a commission library together with other reform documents have provided a lasting source of reform information, approaches, and ideas. And its steady pressure on government officials since its inception has increased understanding of reform and familiarity with it, has softened opposition and scepticism, has provided orientation, and has stimulated an interest in improvement. In many areas in which the commission conducted its work, progress occurred even when commission proposals were not acted upon. For example, the budget and the budget process have undeniably been improved in the intervening years, although the commission budget proposals themselves have not gotten very far. New budget offices, whether or not as proposed by the commission, have sprouted up everywhere; attention has been given to statistical compilation and to programming; and a few steps have even been taken toward evaluating and challenging ministerial budget requests, rather than "rubber-stamping" them in traditional fashion.

The form and substance of Venezuelan public administration will certainly change greatly in the future. Basic changes in national life and politics will be reflected in attitudes and behavior that will inevitably alter the character of public administration. The existence and the efforts of the Public Administration Commission, limited though its tangible accomplishments may have been, have undoubtedly strengthened currents of change and inclinations toward reform.

Chapter 3

Economic Planning in Venezuela

Fred D. Levy, Jr.

Much of the literature on economic development since the end of World War II has been devoted to the topic of economic planning. It is our contention that this literature, by concentrating on the development of techniques and criteria for formulating the plan document, has not only overstated the rationality inherent in any plan as such but has also neglected other important aspects of the planning process. By describing planning in Venezuela as it evolved in the years 1959–63, we hope to shed light on planning strategy and on the contributions that planning can make to economic development. We are interested particularly in the demands which implementation places on the planning process and the implications of these demands for the quality of decisions generated by the process.

Rather than attempt to judge the rationality of any particular decision, we focus on the process which generates decisions. It will be argued that in order to have significance as a real guide to decision making, the process of plan formulation has had to be quite different from that implied by planning theory, and furthermore, that planning theory does not offer appropriate criteria for evaluating planning's results. Our discussion of the impact of planning in Venezuela is followed by a review of current planning theory. Applying our empirical observations to the theory, we conclude the chapter with the proposition that not only are political considerations an inevitable part of the planning process (if the plan is to be implemented) but they also make a positive contribution to the objective rationality of public decision making.

Economic Planning in Venezuela

The Central Office of Coordination and Planning (Cordiplan) was created by decree of the provisional government on 30 December 1958. It was born in an atmosphere of extreme political and economic uncertainty. The newly elected government of Rómulo Betancourt was not seriously expected to survive its constitutional five-year term; indeed, no popularly elected Venezuelan government ever had. The fall of the Pérez Jiménez dictatorship in January 1958 coincided with a severe weakening of the world petroleum market which combined with the uncertain political situation to bring a decade of vigorous economic growth to an abrupt end.

The concept of planning embodied in the planning decree is at once limited and broad. It is limited in the amount of ultimate decision-making authority granted to the central planning office. The decree makes it explicitly clear that Cordiplan was created as an *aid* to the President of the Republic and the Council of Ministers, and that the ultimate responsibility for setting goals, selecting means, and planning and executing projects was to remain with the latter. Rather than creating a supreme central decision-making body, it was intended merely to introduce an additional participant into the decision-making process, a participant that would bring to bear a new, technical point of view on the long-run development needs of the economy. To quote from the report of the working group commissioned to draft the planning decree:

> It is not intended to create a new ministry or to erect a costly bureaucratic machine, but rather to forge a new attitude of foresight, of maintenance and cohesion of long-term policies. In other words, it is intended to introduce a new element of government opposed to improvisation, to the neglect of investment, and to the waste of resources.[1]

1. "Informe de la Comisión Preparatoria, El Sistema Nacional de Coordinación y Planificacíon," reprinted in Enrique Tejera París, *Dos elementos de gobierno* (Caracas, 1960), p. 339. All translations are mine.

In the fulfillment of this role, Cordiplan was charged with three primary functions: to conduct the basic economic studies necessary for analysis of the current state and trend of the economy; to formulate, on the basis of these studies and with the cooperation of the President, the operating agencies, and the advice of the private sector, a national development plan; and finally, to advise the President and the Council of Ministers on the execution of the plan.

The decree's concept of planning, on the other hand, was remarkably broad, for it was to be the enterprise not just of the central planning office, but of the entire public administration. What was visualized was a "national system of coordination and planning," in which the interrelated functions of data collection and analysis, program formulation, and implementation were carried out throughout the ministries and autonomous institutes, and all way down through regional, state, and municipal planning agencies. It was to be the responsibility of the central planning office to promote, guide, and coordinate these scattered planning efforts. Thus, what was being proposed was a drastic reform of the entire Venezuelan governmental apparatus. Not only was the decision-making process to be changed radically within the operating agencies, but the plan also called for the establishment of a mechanism by which the activities of the various public agencies could be coordinated to conform with the overall program.

The coming of a new regime, however, did not signal a break with past tradition for the society as a whole, or even for the public administration. Many public servants, particularly in technical positions, were holdovers from the previous regime and some were career men with up to twenty-five years of service. In addition, no small proportion of the new officeholders, including members of the President's own party, came in with a traditional view of their position. New attitudes and new procedures would have to be adopted if the new program was to be implemented effectively.

Traditionally, the various ministries and autonomous institutes were thought of and behaved as independent empires. Interference of one agency in the affairs of another was not tolerated.

Each ministry was responsible for defining and executing its own programs; consultation was kept to a minimum; collaboration was nonexistent. The autonomous institutes and public enterprises enjoyed the same independence, even from the ministries to which they were technically tied. Often the same autonomy existed between departments of the same ministry.

One of the most difficult problems to be faced in any attempt at administrative reform was the lack of "mystique" within the public administration. Those that did possess the will to serve were frustrated by their minority position and by the general absence of a notion as to what direction their efforts ought to take. In the allocation of public resources, there was no concept of priorities or consideration of alternatives. A project was judged on its engineering or political merits; economic criteria rarely entered into consideration. Consequently, a project was often undertaken more as a monument to its engineer, to its minister, or to the regime than as a contribution to national progress.

In sum, the planning agency was being fitted into a long-established administrative structure, which, like any other, had its vested interests that would resist change. The introduction of Cordiplan's influence into the process would necessarily mean a decline in the relative influence of other participants. Without the deep commitment and complete support of the President of the Republic, Cordiplan would have been doomed to early failure. That it had that support is amply reflected in the selection of Manuel Pérez Guerrero as Cordiplan's first chief. Pérez Guerrero was not only a respected economist with an international reputation but also, significantly, a close personal friend of Betancourt. Indeed, Betancourt had long demonstrated in his books and speeches a great enthusiasm for planning.[2] Even with the President's support, however, Cordiplan would depend heavily upon the voluntary cooperation and collaboration of the technical and implementing agencies. Erecting barriers of resentment would only complicate or even make impossible the entire effort.

The process of reform was seen, therefore, as a long-term battle not to be won in the first year or during the first five-year admin-

2. See, for example, Rómulo Betancourt, *Venezuela, política y petróleo* (Mexico City: Fondo de Cultura Económica, 1956).

istrative period. The strategy chosen was to lower resistance to change through persuasion and the creation of an image of objectivity and fairness, and only occasionally and gently to invoke the pressures of presidential authority.[3]

Pérez Guerrero and other top-level Cordiplanners met often with the ministers and high ministry officials. It was made clear that Cordiplan neither sought nor had the authority to take over ministry responsibilities. The administrators generally agreed on the overall lines of the President's economic policy and on the need for administrative reforms to carry it out. As expected, however, there was substantial resistance to the idea of a central agency forcing the speed or shape of that reform. Ministerial sovereignty was guarded jealously. This resistance has faded only gradually and has not progressed evenly in all sectors. At the time of our visit in 1963, relations with at least one important ministry, the Ministry of Agriculture, were still being described as cool.

Nevertheless, some basic elements of the planning apparatus had been established. Two interministerial commissions, the Economic Commission and the Social Commission, were formed and met weekly at Cordiplan to discuss broad issues of economic policy and budget priorities. In addition, the sectoral divisions of Cordiplan maintained constant contact with the technicians and budgetary officials of the ministries pertinent to their sector. In the attempt to center the budgetary and planning process within the ministries themselves, thus largely decentralizing the overall planning process, the strategy has been to set up little Cordiplans in each ministry. These agencies were supposed to assume the function of coordinating the planning and the budgeting of their own ministry programs and to act as liaisons with Cordiplan.

According to the planning decree, the planning process should include consultation with the private sector. With regard to the business community, this consultation was minimal during most of Cordiplan's first four years. Business was initially apprehensive of the Betancourt regime and interpreted planning to imply greater government incursions into the private sphere. On the other hand, Cordiplan believed that productive communication

3. For a detailed statement of this strategy see Tejera París, p. 8.

would not be possible, since none of the business leaders had been trained in economic planning or understood what planning meant. Furthermore, conflicts of interests within the business sector itself would make agreement on plan details difficult to achieve. These factors, the Cordiplanners argued, combined with what was seen as a basic difference in ideology between the public and private sectors, could only have made attempts at collaboration break down, creating more mutual bitterness than had there been no consultation at all. Thus it was decided, as specific strategy, to invite comments from the business sector on the development plan *after* it had been prepared within the public administration. Small modifications might then be made on the basis of these comments. This is not to say that there was no contact between Cordiplan and the business community during the preparation of the plan. The sectoral divisions of Cordiplan had established some informal contacts with certain segments of the community pertinent to their sectors as sources of data and information. But these relations were limited, and there was not the give-and-take discussion that existed within the halls of government. Other channels of private-sector influence that cannot be overlooked, however, were its effect on public opinion through the news media and its close ties with the Christian Democratic Party and the ministries controlled by them.

The Impact of Planning in Venezuela

By 1963 Cordiplan had become an effective participant in the decision-making process; the allocation of resources for the public sector was apparently being shaped at least in part by the planning office. But is the planning agency to be considered a success for proving itself politically adept and being able to carve itself a niche in the administrative bureaucracy?

Plan Fulfillment

One obvious way of measuring the effectiveness—but not necessarily the rationality—of planning is to examine the degree to which the plans' goals or targets are being achieved. Tables 3.1

through 3.5 review the performance of the first three Venezuelan plans.

As of 1962, when it was replaced by the Second Plan, the Plan de la Nación 1960–64 must be graded a marked failure according to this criterion. Gross domestic product, which was to have grown at better than 7 percent per annum over the period, barely achieved a 4 percent rate through 1962. Construction and mining activity continued to tailspin despite the plan's optimistic projections; growth in the manufacturing and agricultural sectors fell far short of projected rates, as it did also in most other sectors. Net investment, which was to average 22.7 percent of national income over the four years, in fact averaged only slightly more than 10 percent through the first two.[4] Net disinvestment occurred in the petroleum, construction, and commercial sectors. Only in agriculture, as a result of heavy government outlays, did investment keep pace with the plan. Housing construction, through 1962, was proceeding at only one-fifth the planned rate. With job opportunities failing to materialize, unemployment continued to rise. On the other hand, better-than-anticipated gains were made for the expansion of social overhead capital, particularly in education and highway development. By 1962 the goals in these sectors were well on the way to fulfillment.

Although petroleum output expanded sharply in 1962, prices continued to weaken, limiting the value of petroleum exports to a 6.6 percent gain over the 1960–62 period. One bright spot in the economic picture, however, was the return in 1962 to a surplus balance-of-payments position, owed largely to a slight reduction of imports after 1960 and some stemming of the flight of capital.

The performance of the 1962 Plan was not appreciably better. The upturn in the petroleum sector was greater than had been hoped, but did not provide the immediate stimulus expected. The major disappointment was in the construction industry, but agriculture and manufacturing again failed to meet even the reduced projections. Investment fell well below the planned figure, net investment amounting to only 8.6 percent of national income.

4. Venezuela, Banco Central, *Informe económico 1964* (Caracas, 1965), p. 314.

Fred D. Levy, Jr.

Table 3.1. *Target achievement, 1960–64 and 1962 development plans*

Sector	Targets, Plan I 1960–64	Targets, Plan II 1960–62	Achievement 1960–62
Growth of GDP (percent)	32.0	14.8	8.1
Petroleum and natural gas	17.0	6.0	12.5
Mining	46.4	−21.0	−32.8
Manufacturing	71.4	23.1	12.0
Construction	26.2	43.6	−19.9
Agriculture	33.5	15.2	9.5
Transport and communications	31.1 ⎫		1.8 ⎫
Commerce	21.6 ⎪		5.4 ⎪
Electricity and water	93.9 ⎬	13.8	32.7 ⎬ 9.1
Housing (rent and interest)	36.0 ⎪		9.4 ⎪
Services	28.5 ⎭		12.3 ⎭
Value of petroleum exports (percent growth)	17.0	6.0	6.6
Increase in number of persons employed (percent)	22.3	9.0	4.9
Unemployment rate in terminal year (percent of labor force)	5.8	8.9	13.9
Number of students enrolled in terminal year	1,723	—	1,611
Increase in output of electricity[a] (percent)	106.0	21.5	35.2
Road construction during period (kilometers)	1,921	—	1,496

Sources: Venezuela, Oficina Central de Coordinación y Planificación, *Plan de la Nación 1960–64, Plan de Desarrollo 1962* (Caracas: Venezuela Cordiplan 1960, 1962); Banco Central de Venezuela, *Memoria, 1960 Informe económico, 1962, 1963* (Caracas, 1961 through 1964); Ministerio de Obras Públicas, *Memoria, 1963* (Caracas, 1964).
a. Does not include production of private companies for own use.

The shortfall in gross fixed investment for the year was more than 35 percent. The pace of the agrarian reform slowed as coordination and execution of the multipronged attack on rural poverty reached the limits of administrative capacity. Housing construction again showed the greatest shortfall, and unemployment continued to mount. The 1962 Plan would seem, on balance, to score a slightly higher achievement rating than the preceding effort, but this may only reflect its reduced projections. To be sure, by the middle of 1962, there were signs of recovery in the Venezuelan economy. Recovery, however, was very much dependent upon the resumption of growth in the petroleum industry and of the con-

Table 3.2. *Net fixed investment, plan 1960–64 (millions of bo-lívares at 1958 prices)*

Sector	(1) Planned annual average 1960–64	(2) %	(3) Realized annual average 1960–61	(4) (3) ÷ (1)
Petroleum and natural gas	282	5.6	−106	—
Mining	132	2.6	68	0.52
Manufacturing	761	15.2	312	0.41
Construction	39	0.8	−52	—
Agriculture	362	7.3	394	1.09
Transport and communications	424	8.5	287	0.68
Commerce	198	4.0	−25	—
Electricity and water	387	7.8	180	0.47
Housing	1,106	22.2	229	0.21
Government and other services	1,302	26.1	182	0.14
Total	4,993	100.0	1,464	0.29

Sources: Venezuela, Oficina Central de Coordinación y Planificación, *Plan de la Nación 1960–64* (Caracas: Cordiplan, 1960); Banco Central de Venezuela, *Informe económico 1962* (Caracas, 1963).

Table 3.3. *Gross fixed investment, 1962 plan (millions of bolívares at 1960 prices)*

Sector	(1) Planned investment	(2) %	(3) Realized investment[a]	(4) %	(5) (3) ÷ (1)
Petroleum and natural gas	546	8.0	433	10.1	0.79
Mining	26	0.4	58	1.4	2.23
Manufacturing	1,000	14.7	625	14.6	0.62
Construction	100	1.5	34	0.8	0.34
Agriculture	1,110	16.3	774	18.1	0.70
Transport and communications	1,100	16.2	719	16.8	0.65
Commerce	300	4.4	159	3.7	0.53
Electricity and water	310	4.6	197	4.6	0.64
Housing (urban)	1,456	21.4	500	11.7	0.34
Other private services	300	4.6	240	5.6	0.80
Government	562	8.3	530	12.4	0.94
Total	6,810	100.0	4,269	100.0	0.63

Sources: Venezuela, Oficina Central de Coordinación y Planificación, *Plan de desarrollo económico y social para 1962* (Caracas: Cordiplan, 1962); Banco Central de Venezuela, *Informe económico 1964* (Caracas, 1965).
a. Original data given in 1957 prices. Conversion was made by sector on the basis of price data and breakdown of investment by type provided by the *Informe económico* for 1964.

Table 3.4. *Plan targets and achievement, 1963–66 plan*

	Target 1963–66	Realized 1963–64
Annual Growth of GDP (%)	8.0	5.8
Agriculture	8.0	6.8
Petroleum	4.0	3.0
Mining	10.0	7.2
Manufacturing	13.5	11.4
Construction	14.9	12.7
Electricity and water	18.0	14.9
Transport and communications	7.4	8.2
Commerce	5.4	5.8
Urban housing	6.8	3.0
Other private services	6.4 }	6.3
Government	7.9 }	

		Achievement	
	Target	1963	1964
Annual Growth of Employment (thousands of persons)	111.8	82.3	115.0
Agriculture	6.5	14.6	15.0
Petroleum	0.8	−0.9	−1.0
Mining	—	−0.4	−0.1
Manufacturing	20.5	14.8	22.7
Construction	27.5	19.9	17.7
Electricity and water	2.8	—	0.3
Transport and communications	6.5	2.6	4.5
Commerce	5.8	13.5	14.8
Other services	38.5	18.1	41.1
Agrarian reform (families settled per year)	50,000	9,656	10,250
Land irrigated, 1963–64 (hectares)	13,254	4,868	11,800
Highway construction (kilometers)	1,017		(1,090)
School construction (pupil spaces)	42,300		(43,884)

Sources: Venezuela, Oficina Central de Coordinación y Planificación, *Plan de la Nación 1963–1966* (Caracas: Cordiplan, 1963); Banco Central de Venezuela, *Informe económico 1964* (Caracas, 1965); Comité Interamericano para la Alianza para el Progreso, "El esfuerzo interno y las necesidades de financiamiento para el desarrollo de Venezuela," mimeographed (Washington, 24 July 1965), p. 53; Notas sobre el desarrollo sectorial de Venezuela," mimeographed (Washington, 9 Aug. 1965), p. 20.

fidence of private investors in the nation's political future. Neither of these crucial variables was much influenced by planning activity.

As demonstrated in Tables 3.4 and 3.5, recovery was becoming apparent in 1963 and 1964, and target achievement was, on the whole, far more successful through the first half of the third plan period than under the previous plans. GDP rose 8.0 percent in 1964 to match the programed rate and establish a 5.8 percent average growth rate through the 1963–64 period.[5] Unemployment was significantly reduced in 1964.[6]

Table 3.5. *Gross fixed investment, 1963–66 plan (millions of bolívares at 1960 prices)*

Sector	(1) Annual planned average investment 1963–66	(2) %	(3) Actual average annual investment 1963–64[a]	(4) %	(5) (3) ÷ (1)
Petroleum and mining	748.8	11.4	587.5	12.1	0.78
Manufacturing	1,283.5	19.6	595.0	12.2	0.46
Construction	98.5	1.5	70.5	1.4	0.72
Agriculture	670.2	10.2	798.0	16.4	1.19
Transport and communications	700.5	10.7	874.5	17.9	1.25
Commerce	525.8	8.0	195.0	4.0	0.37
Electricity and water	343.2	5.2	157.0	3.2	0.46
Housing (urban)	1,353.5	20.7	698.0	14.3	0.52
Other private services	225.0	3.4	277.0	5.7	1.23
Government	602.5	9.2	623.0	12.8	1.03
Total	6,551.5	100.0	4,875.5	100.0	0.74

Sources: Venezuela, Oficina Central de Coordinación y Planificación, *Plan de la Nación 1963–1966* (Caracas: Cordiplan, 1963); Banco Central de Venezuela, *Informe económico 1964* (Caracas, 1965).

a. Original data given in 1957 prices. Conversion was made by sector on the basis of price data and breakdown of investment by type provided by the *Informe económico* for 1964.

Measured against the rising trend being shown in all sectors, the only major shortfall was again in urban housing. Despite the seriousness of the housing shortage in Venezuela, this sector has continued to be held back by administrative bottlenecks.[7] Though agricultural output increased vigorously (up 8.6 percent in 1964),

5. Preliminary estimates of the Banco Central de Venezuela indicate a 7 percent increase in GDP in 1965. Reported in Bank of London and South America, Ltd., *Fortnightly Review*, 22 Jan. 1966.
6. In Caracas, unemployment fell 22 percent over the year. Economist Intelligence Unit, *Quarterly Economic Review: Venezuela* 26 Feb. 1965, p. 1.
7. See Comité Interamericano para la Alianza para el Progreso (CIAP), "El esfuerzo interno y las necesidades de financiamiento para el desarrollo de Venezuela," mimeographed (Washington: 24 July 1965), p. 53.

failures of administrative coordination and shortage of marketing facilities impeded progress in the agrarian reform program. In the face of a high rate of peasant desertion from distributed land parcels, an official shift in reform policy took place in 1964 in favor of providing necessary services to previously established settlements rather than creating new ones.[8]

Severe shortages of skilled labor were being felt in most sectors[9] by the end of 1964, pointing to increasing priority for expenditures on education and training. Public works construction in general was progressing as planned.

Gross domestic investment, which was targeted at 20.8 percent of GDP over the four-year plan period, averaged 18.3 percent of GDP in 1963–64. Gross fixed investment was falling about 25 percent short of the planned rate, with urban housing again showing the most serious shortfall in absolute terms. Despite its rapid growth of output, manufacturing fell more than 50 percent short of its investment target, demonstrating the high level of unused capacity existing in that sector. Agriculture again overfulfilled its investment target, as did the government sector, transport and communications, and "other private services."

A measure of effectiveness based only on target achievement is not very convincing, however. In the first place, the stated targets may be the result of nothing more than projections of what the economy is likely to do, even in the absence of planning, and thus represent policy in only a very passive sense; our criterion would then be a measure only of the quality of the projections. Furthermore, such a criterion assumes that the plan has been fully implemented, and that there is a significant cause-and-effect relationship between plan implementation and final results. Merely because of vagaries of chance, it is conceivable that the planned targets might be attained to a high degree, even though the policy prescribed by the plan was never put into effect. Quite different decisions may, in fact, have been made. Conversely, the plan may have been assiduously implemented, but unpredictable

8. CIAP, "Notas sobre el desarrollo sectorial de Venezuela," mimeographed (Washington, 9 Aug. 1965), p. 20.
9. CIAP, "Esfuerzo interno," p. 29.

exogenous factors, such as drought or political crisis or, in the Venezuelan case, a sudden disruption in the world petroleum market, could lead to major shortfalls from the targets. It is, moreover, impossible to know how economic performance would have differed, if at all, in the complete absence of a plan.

In any case, the target achievement criterion may be complemented by another designed to test the degree of implementation, the final index of effectiveness being a combination of the two. Two questions are important here. Did the planners or the process of planning significantly affect the overall emphasis or goals of government development policy? Did the planners or the planning process affect the specific allocations of resources within the overall policy outline?

To the question on policy goals, the answer in Venezuela apparently is no. The general emphasis of the plans on economic diversification and import substitution through development of domestic industry and agriculture, and on raising the standard of living of the masses through agrarian reform, education, and expanding employment opportunities, was identical with the long-espoused doctrine of Acción Democrática.[10] Plans for a major industrial complex for the Guayana region and for public promotion of steel and petrochemical industries were first laid during the short-lived AD government of 1945–48. Such would have been the stated government policy during the period under study with or without planning. A review of the various party platforms in both 1958 and 1963 shows, moreover, that there was very little political disagreement on these basic goals.

Table 3.6 compares the allocation of national government expenditures during the first 6½ years of the AD administration with the last four years under Pérez Jiménez.[11] Political and general administrative expenditures varied little, as a proportion of the total, over the decade. The share going to defense declined after

10. See *Acción Democrática, doctrina y programa* (Caracas: Secretaria Nacional de Propaganda, 1962). It is unlikely that Cordiplan ever seriously considered changing that outline. Several top Cordiplanners, after all, had also been influential in formulating the AD position.

11. We have eliminated amortization and interest on the public debt in order to remove the distortion of the large increase in these payments since 1959, engendered in large part by debts accumulated in earlier years.

Table 3.6. *Functional distribution of national government expenditures, 1954/55–1965 (annual averages—millions of bolívares)*[a]

	1954/55–57/58 Annual average	%	1959/60–62 Annual average	%	1963–65 Annual average	%
Political and administrative	639.8	16.2	889.8	14.8	1,057.5	16.3
General administration	50.0	1.3	79.0	1.3	135.2	2.1
Police and justice	141.3	3.6	170.3	2.8	182.4	2.8
National defense	416.7	10.5	579.4	9.6	691.7	10.7
Foreign relations	31.6	0.8	61.1	1.0	48.2	0.7
Economic and financial	2,001.9	50.6	2,759.0	45.8	2,581.5	39.8
Financial administration	293.7	7.4	488.8	8.1	374.9	5.8
Mining	34.6	0.9	44.3	0.7	39.3	0.6
Agriculture and water	326.4	8.3	624.2	10.4	726.4	11.2
Industry	217.6	5.5	325.6	5.4	324.2	5.0
Transport and communications	870.8	22.0	957.2	15.9	1,094.1	16.8
Tourism	57.2	1.4	10.1	0.2	7.4	0.1
Other[b]	201.6	5.1	308.9	5.1	15.3	0.2
Social and Cultural	904.0	22.9	1,627.4	27.0	1,906.9	29.4
Health and social assistance	323.6	8.2	573.8	9.5	667.8	10.3
Housing and urban development	317.4	8.0	354.9	5.9	372.7	5.7
Education and culture	242.8	6.1	674.0	11.2	839.8	12.9
Other	20.2	0.5	24.7	0.4	26.6	0.4
State and Local Government	405.8	10.3	740.4	12.3	941.8	14.5
Church	4.3	0.1	6.7	0.1	5.8	0.1
Total	3,955.7	100.0	6,023.3	100.0	6,493.5	100.0

Sources: Venezuela, Ministry of Finance, *Evolución de los gastos del Gobierno Nacional 1954/55–1958/59; Memoria 1962; Memoria 1963; Presupuesto por Programas 1962; Presupuesto por Programas 1964; Ley de Presupuesto 1963; Resumen del Proyecto de Presupuesto 1966* (Caracas, 1959 through 1965); Ministry of Public Works, *Memoria 1962* (Caracas, 1963); Banco Central de Venezuela, *Informe económico 1962* (Caracas, 1963).
 a. Excludes interest and amortization of the public debt.
 b. Includes public works expenditures which for lack of information we were unable to distribute among the other categories.

the fall of the dictatorship, but rose again in response to terrorist activity. The rise in general administration in the later period is due in large part to the expenses of the 1963 national election.

The major shift in relative budget shares occurred between the second and third categories, economic and social, the former declining and the latter rising sharply. Of the sectors composing the economic and financial expenditures, only agriculture increased its share of the budget over the decade. The largest sector in this category, and in the budget as a whole, continued to be transportation and communications, consisting almost entirely of road construction, but its relative share of government spending was reduced substantially. The most dramatic increase in government spending occurred in education, which more than doubled its share of the budget under the AD regime. Public-health expenditures also rose more rapidly than total spending, but expenditures on housing lost ground.

Although the picture is clouded by the varying degree of investment shortfall from sector to sector, government spending does seem to conform generally to the pattern outlined by the plans. It does not necessarily follow, however, that the plans were influential in determining the budget, since both budgets and plans should be expected to reflect the policy emphasis of the administration under which they are formulated. Moreover, the formulation of both documents was necessarily based heavily upon programs and projects already in various stages of execution or preparation.[12]

If the plans were indeed a meaningful expression of public policy, their poor record of target fulfillment would seem to indicate flaws in the plans themselves or a pronounced weakness of public policy in influencing the national economy. In fact, both elements are involved. In the first place, the planners grossly underestimated the depth of pessimism generated in the private sector by the weakening of the petroleum sector, the turbulent and uncertain political situation, and the high level of idle capacity. As a result, they greatly overestimated the government's ability to stimulate private investment through tariff and credit policies. Cordiplan's failure to establish communication with the private sector was a major cause of this miscalculation and may indeed have contributed to the private sector's uneasiness about the new regime's intentions.

On the other hand, the investment shortfall was even greater in

12. It was estimated that about 60 percent of the planned public investments under the 1960–64 Plan represented projects under way or in advanced stages of preparation prior to the planning exercise. Since costs were in most cases underestimated, and total investment overestimated, the share of old projects carried out under the plan was probably substantially higher.

the public sector. Since actual government revenues throughout the period under consideration closely approximated Cordiplan's projections, the unexpectedly low rate of public sector investment cannot be blamed on a scarcity of financial resources. The short-fall was rather the result of the government's inability to maintain the programed ratio of investment to total expenditures. Several explanations may be offered. Bureaucratic inertia and the diffi-culty of pruning heavily feathered public payrolls in the face of high private-sector unemployment were more severe restraints than anticipated in the drive for administrative efficiency. In ad-dition, investment was held back in a number of sectors by a shortage of projects and continuing difficulties in coordinating the execution of projects involving more than one government agency.

Another problem, as pointed out by CIAP, was the difficulty of obtaining data on important short-term economic indicators.[13] For the first plan in particular, the gravity of the unemployment problem was seriously underestimated, and as a result, no steps were planned to confront the situation directly.

Planning and Public Decision Making

Our evaluation of Venezuelan planning thus far has looked at the role of planning largely in terms of the plan document itself, as measured against economic performance for the 1960–64 period. The essence of planning, however, lies not in the prepara-tion of the paper plan, but in the entire decision-making process. It is to this dimension that we now turn our attention.

Although projects for the public sector are designed and im-plemented within the operating agencies, Cordiplan has had a direct effect on project selection and execution. Many projects have been altered and some stopped at Cordiplan's request. A few others have been initiated at Cordiplan's suggestion. The greatest impact of Cordiplan and the planning exercise, however, has been on the work done by the operating agencies themselves. By bringing the operating agencies into active participation in the planning process, and by gaining their accord with national development goals, the planning concept influences their own

13. CIAP, "Esfuerzo interno," p. 103.

processes and results in better project selection and elaboration at the starting point. In preparation for discussions pursuant to the formulation of the plan, the administrators are forced to think out, often for the first time, the problems of their sector and their relation to the rest of the economy and to the general policy goals. With information and insight thus increased and improved they have been better able to intelligently shape their own programs and policies. Similarly, they are forced to think about the projects that are to follow those currently in execution and on the drawing boards. The formulation of the plan, then, when carried out in the collaborative manner described, has a high educational value which can be expected to lead to better decision making.

Once established as a guide to the budget, the plan also has an incentive effect. During plan formulation, and again during budget formulation, each agency must, more convincingly than was formerly the case, justify to the other participants the allocations that it recommends. As a result, there is a positive motivation for each operating agency to work out its program more carefully and to step up and improve its formulation of new projects. To the extent that the evaluation of agency requests also takes into account past performance, there is additional incentive to improve administrative efficiency.[14]

After the plan has been formulated and given the stamp of executive approval, it represents a commitment on the part of the agencies that participated in its formulation. That commitment is supported, on the one hand, by the very fact that each agency had a voice in shaping the document and, on the other, by the plan's being used as a starting point in allocating the national budget.

In the other direction, the plan has also supplied the ministries with a partial shield against the interest-group pressures constantly acting upon them. Several representatives of interest

---

14. Abundant evidence to this effect can be found in the annual reports of the various ministries, which now include numerous references to the plans and the agencies' respective roles in them. See, for example, the statement by the minister of public works, Leopoldo Sucre Figarella, *Las obras públicas y el desarrollo integral* (Caracas: Oficina Central de Información, May 1965). The plans themselves have become progressively more detailed with regard to the components of the sector programs and the assignment of agency responsibilities for executing them.

groups with whom I spoke reported that their petitions to the government had been received politely, but that action would have to wait until other projects having higher priority *according to the plan* had been completed. They seemed satisfied, at least temporarily, with this answer. Interest-group leaders themselves may find relief behind the protective shield that the plan offers them when facing the various pressures of their own constituents.

Perhaps the most significant contribution that Cordiplan has yet made to public decision making is its success in achieving a high degree of coordination in the activities of the public sector. By promoting and playing host to interagency discussions and, in effect, bargaining sessions, Cordiplan has assisted in breaking down the traditional separate-empire concept of public administration and has encouraged the growth of a self-coordinating political marketplace. Individual agencies have been brought to realize the advantages of cooperating with other agencies in the pursuit of mutual goals, as well as the possibility of mutual benefits even when particular goals may differ. Cordiplan has acted the role of catalyst and mediator, keeping the discussions within the context of "national interest" and thus providing a basis for reconciliation of group rivalries.

Taking a still larger view of Cordiplan's role, it has been a major promoter and salesman of the development mystique. After almost four decades of accelerating petroleum boom, upper- and middle-class Venezuelans were not easily convinced of the immediate need to prepare for the day when the wells would run dry, and that such preparation might require a dramatic change in the structure of the economy. If a national effort was to be made, some degree of consensus on general goals had to be reached. This would require a real interchange of ideas concerning the nation's problems and their possible solutions.

By supplying a coherent, analytical argument and a bold statement of government policy, the plan has become a stimulator and center of public commentary and debate. Although private groups have not yet taken part to any great extent in the formulation of the plans, they have been influenced by them. Traditionally opposed groups, such as labor and management or government and business, had always talked past each other without a real interchange of ideas or genuine attempt to arrive at a mutual understanding. Now, by focusing on the plan, they have begun to discuss meaningfully and frankly the nation's economic and social problems and the direction of national development. This has great significance not only for the possibilities of implementing the development effort but also for realizing the potential of the political process.[15]

Cordiplan has increasingly made use of its carefully groomed image as a group of serious, objective experts to present its analyses of national economic needs and policies to the public, and there were signs in 1963—in party platforms, in public debate, in the pronouncements of the various conventions and seminars, etc.—of a growing national consensus centered upon these analyses. Hardly a day passed when the newspapers or television did not contain notice of some statement concerning economic policy issued by Cordiplan. When the newspapers, news magazines, or television presented a debate on economic issues— a frequent occurrence in 1963—Cordiplan was always represented. When private-interest groups brought petitions to the national Executive, they were more and more often directed to Cordiplan or told that the President would have to confer with Cordiplan before a decision could be reached. Cordiplan leaders became frequent guest participants at the meetings of business, trade, professional, and regional groups.

It is, of course, exceedingly difficult to gauge the planning office's success as a promoter of new values and attitudes. We were, however, much impressed by the many businessmen and labor leaders, as well as public administrators, who in conversations with us and statements in the newspapers used such expressions as "national development effort" or "national priorities." Not all were wholly in agreement with or perhaps even understood fully the meaning of these expressions, but it was evident that a change in outlook had begun. The economic development effort and the development plan were the central topics at numerous

15. A similar analysis is made by John Friedmann in his *National Planning in Venezuela: From Doctrine to Dialogue* (Syracuse, N.Y.: Syracuse Univ. Press, 1965).

association meetings and conventions, particularly within the business community. One important group of Venezuelan executives, for example, met for several days to discuss the role and *responsibility* of the businessman in the promotion of national economic and social development. The frequency with which Cordiplan views were being invited and publicized was itself evidence of their increasing importance and acceptance.

There were growing signs, then, of a development mystique in Venezuela. To be sure, this cannot be credited solely to the efforts of the planners. It was necessary for there already to exist important nuclei of persons ready to accept the new attitudes and lead other members of their group toward them. Undoubtedly, the shock of the severe recession, which awakened all Venezuelans to their economy's extreme vulnerability to world market conditions, and the disclosure of the monumental wastes of the preceding regime worked to weaken the old set of attitudes.[16] It is probably also important that the nature of Venezuela's wealth is such that no extraordinary sacrifices have to be asked of anyone. All things considered, however, the work of the planning office and the enlightened way in which it has gone about its task have made a major contribution to the success achieved. Clearly, public education in this sense has constituted one of Cordiplan's primary roles and one of the greatest benefits so far derived from the planning experience.

Our discussion of the planners' role in Venezuela seems a far cry from the familiar picture of the technician-planner found in the planning literature. He has been portrayed here as a teacher, a politician, and a diplomat, and indeed he has had to be all these things in Venezuela. But this has not meant that Cordiplan has abandoned its role as a center of economic analysis. Its success in the more political areas of decision making has been heavily dependent upon the maintenance of its image as an essentially technical body. Otherwise, Cordiplan would never have been acceptable in its mediator-educator role to the other participants in decision making.

16. Friedmann greatly credits the success and the form of planning in Venezuela to the social and economic crisis being experienced at its inception.

Cordiplan, of course, has been primarily a technical body, established by law and in fact as the top economic adviser to the President. Its role of clarifying the broad outlines and feasible limits of government policy goals, and of analyzing the structure and potential of the Venezuelan economy and the requirements for achieving that potential, depend directly upon its technical labors. If its educative function has contributed to rationality, it is because its technical work has generated new and better information and analysis, thus providing the other participants with an improved basis for calculating the national as well as their own individual interests. The point to be made is that it is not enough to generate new information and keen analytical insights. They must also be put to real use in the decision-making process. In Venezuela, this has required that the planning agency also play the nontechnical roles described.

That planning, like any social decision-making process, must contain political elements seems obvious. It is thus not surprising that Venezuelan planners have also had to be adept politicians and that politics have in part shaped the plans. Less obvious are the implications of this fact for the quality of the ensuing decisions.

The Dynamics of Planning

Until recently, the literature of economic planning concerned itself primarily with the elaboration of techniques for formulating national development plans. Planning was treated as a deductive process in which specific decisions flow logically and unambiguously from the evaluation, with regard to explicit goals, of the projected consequences of alternative means. The contributors to the planning literature obviously intended that the plans be implemented, but little attention was given to the practical problems of plan implementation.

Yet many countries have found these problems more difficult than the more mechanical process of plan formulation. Unless the "optimal" plan, as prepared by the planners, can be said to have chances for successful implementation at least as good as those of alternative plans, the problems of plan implementation become important factors in plan formulation. The task, therefore, is no longer to devise the best plan, in some abstract sense, but rather the best implementable plan. A plan's "implementability" depends upon the capability and willingness of the implementers to carry it out. Since there is no reason to expect the sectoral distribution of administrative abilities to coincide with the planners' concept of sectoral priorities, at least in the short run, it is belaboring the obvious to point out that it may be necessary to modify the "optimal" plan to correspond more closely to administrative realities.

The need to alter a plan in accordance with the capacity to implement is neither startling nor particularly alarming; it merely means tightening the definition of plan consistency. The need to gain cooperation—the willingness to implement—of the other government agencies, however, raises some sticky problems. It generally means bringing the other agencies into the planning process and giving them an important role in plan formulation as the price for obtaining a firm commitment to implement. Venezuelan plans, as we have seen, are formulated through a multilateral process of bargaining and compromise. In their analyses and policy recommendations, the planners represent a point of view and an approach that in varying degrees differ from those prevailing in other parts of the public administration. Very often, the planning agency must compromise its own position in order to gain agreement. In achieving implementability, then, the technical appreciations of the planners are diluted by political considerations, and consequently the decisions generated by the planning process are somewhat different from those that would be made by the planners if they were able to act unaffected by such political necessities.

The Political Dimensions of Planning

Economic theorists have long considered centralized decision making a substitute for or supplement to the market mechanism and compared the merits of the two systems for achieving social goals in general or with regard to particular kinds of decision problems. But, inevitably, governmental decisions also involve the play of political forces. To the extent that decisions are increasingly made according to the deductive prescriptions of a central plan, by implication less reliance is placed upon the political mechanism. Planning should also be discussed, therefore, with regard to its relative merits vis-à-vis politics. Economists have been obsessed for too long with the evils of political manipulation and not sufficiently appreciative of the contributions that the political process can offer economic rationality.[17]

In the first place, the political process is the primary source of information pertaining to the nature and relative intensities of social values. The aggregation and resolution of the diverse viewpoints of the society are the very essence of a democratic political process. In a system in which the top policymakers retain their positions only at the will of the electorate, one would expect that their policies would tend to be designed to please—i.e., promote the goals of—at least a majority of that electorate.[18] In his attempt to secure votes, the politician selects the policy alternatives which he believes reflect the preferences of the majority of voters. These preferences are made known to him through the activities of partisan "pressure groups" formed for that purpose. If we make the not wholly unreasonable assumption that citizens tend to exercise political pressures on each policy issue in proportion to the intensity of their feelings concerning that issue—that is, the degree to which they feel their own set of values affected—the politician can be visualized as a sort of social welfare machine or weathervane whose resultant attitude represents an "optimum" resolution or decision.[19] The important point is that the political process, unlike the central planning approach (taken in the strict sense of planning theory), permits and indeed forces the con-

17. For brilliant pioneering efforts to integrate the economics and politics of government decision making, see Anthony Downs, *An Economic Theory of Democracy* (New York: Harper, 1957). See also Robert Dahl and Charles E. Lindblom, *Politics, Economics, and Welfare* (New York: Harper, 1953); and Albert O. Hirschman, *Journeys Toward Progress* (New York: Twentieth Century Fund, 1963).
18. For an extended discussion of such a model, see Downs.
19. See Edward Banfield, *Political Influence* (New York: Free Press, 1961).

sideration of a great number of goals or values of the diverse elements of the society. Moreover, in the political process there is no necessity to force agreement in advance on a particular set of goals. Through the political process, men are able to agree on policies (often heartily) without prior, current, or eventual agreement on goals. Goal sets are not formulated and then rigidified, but are continually discovered and rediscovered in the light of each decision problem. They are allowed to shift as new information is received, much of this information being generated by the political process itself. The very inconsistency or apparent lack of goals that is found in the political process may in fact produce a degree of accuracy in social evaluation far beyond the capacity of the deductive approach.[20]

Related to its clarification of social values, the political process can provide important information with regard to the behavioral equations of the society. For example, the original plans for Las Majaguas, an agricultural settlement project in central Venezuela, provided for large farm units, to be operated cooperatively but state owned. (Ownership was to pass gradually to the cooperatives.) The hypothesis was that this form of land tenure would provide the most rapid rise in total production. The plans, under heavy pressure from the Campesino Federation, were later modified drastically to conform to the Venezuelan peasants' intense desire for independence and private ownership. Given the heavy handicap of peasant dissatisfaction that would have been suffered under the cooperative system, the production targets of the original plan were probably highly optimistic. On a more global level, we have already argued that greater political contact between the planners and the business community might have led to more accurate projections on the part of Cordiplan and perhaps to a higher level of private-sector investment as well.

20. It might be argued, on the other hand, that much of the above is irrelevant to most underdeveloped countries. The sacrifices demanded, if development is to be achieved, are so great and the degree of social cohesiveness so low that what is needed is a highly centralized and authoritative government to force the pace and direction of the development push. For a reply to this, see the remarks of Lucian W. Pye, "The Political Context of National Development," in *Development Administration: Concepts and Problems,* ed. Irving Swerdlow (Syracuse, N.Y.: Syracuse Univ. Press, 1963), pp. 41–42.

Most planning theorists, as we have seen, are more than willing to leave value judgments to the politicians. The job of the technician-planner is to clarify for the political authority the relative costs and benefits of alternative courses of action. But they overlook the fact that here, too, the political process has useful information to offer. Central planners everywhere are faced with an extreme paucity of fundamental, technical data upon which to base their estimates of cost and benefit. Keeping an ear sensitively tuned to the pressures of various regional interest groups may be a highly accurate and inexpensive way of determining a priority list for schools, rural access roads, aqueducts, etc., compared with making a comprehensive inventory of needs and availabilities and a highly tenuous cost-benefit analysis on each element of the difference. In a well-developed political process one finds a number of centers of analysis, each attacking an issue from its own partisan point of view, considering only those values which it deems important and, at the same time, examining only those alternatives and consequences it views as relevant. By not attempting to be comprehensive in scope, each analyst is able to cast a more searching eye over his limited area of interest. A system which allows a high degree of interaction between these partisan analysts, each attempting to shape the decision to his own liking, may well be expected to produce decisions based upon a higher level of relevant information as well as more sensitive to the values of the society.

Whether a given political system fulfills these roles is, of course, an empirical question. Many of the "imperfections" of the real world which upset the Pareto optimality of the economic market solution find their analogues in the political sphere. The distribution of political power, like that of economic power, is highly unequal in many underdeveloped countries; some sectors of society may go virtually unrepresented in national politics. Information is far from perfect. Moreover, if we look not at the quite different demands that each places upon the individual decisionmaker (or decision-making body), but at the decision-making system as a whole, both the centralized, deductive method and the political system sketched above require a high degree of comprehensiveness for success. Whereas each individual policymaker in the political system can neglect important alternatives and consequences, the system as a whole can ill afford to do so. Probably few underdeveloped countries can provide many "centers of analysis."

Similarly, a country possessing a well-diversified stock of specialized policy tools with which it can quickly and effectively offset undesired consequences as they arise can probably afford to rely upon the "disjointed incremental" approach described by Lindblom.[21] In most underdeveloped countries, on the other hand, the tool box is woefully small and the tools painfully blunt. It is natural that in such countries the few policy tools will come under centralized control, and that the political passions surrounding their use will be great. A certain amount of insulation from those passions may in fact become a necessity if any solutions are to be found to the more critical problems.

But if centralized decision making can be shown to be justified in cases where the markets—economic and political—are unable to arrive at an efficient solution, or inevitable when decisions are crucial and their consequences irreversible, it can equally be shown that the markets have positive contributions to make in the many aspects of problems that fall beyond the capacities of the central decisionmaker. Just as planners have recognized the convenience, if not the necessity, of leaving much of the information gathering and calculation involved in determining efficient allocation of resources to the economic marketplace, they ought also to recognize the advantages of heeding the signals of the political mechanism. It may be that improvements in the functioning of the latter would do more to raise the general level of decision making than any foreseeable refinements in the techniques of central planning. And returning to the central theme of the essay, it is quite possible that the political nature of plan formulation in Venezuela contributes not only to the plan's implementability but to its objective rationality as well.

21. See Braybrooke and Lindblom, *A Strategy of Decision* (New York: Free Press, 1963).

The Role of the Planner

Nothing that has been said is meant to imply that the technician-planner should be excluded from the decision-making process. Though his tools have been exposed as incapable of defining rationality (something he himself has probably long known), they still have important contributions to make. To understand the role of the technician-planner, however, it must be viewed in the context of an administrative process in which the planner is but one of the participants, and the specialized information he provides but one of the ingredients essential to rational decision making.

Seen in this broad context, the technician-planner has several indispensable functions to perform. In the first place, the specialized information and analysis which he provides enable the other participants in the process to develop a clearer idea of where their own interests lie and how various policy alternatives are likely to affect those interests. Being thus faced with more and better data relevant to their own interests—at least to the extent of pointing up the absurdities of their own prior analyses—they are given a more rational basis upon which to conduct their own activities.

By shifting the emphasis of discussion to the "national interest," the planner helps illuminate the broad range of common interests in social goals which otherwise might be obscured by ideological differences and partisan debate. The introduction of long-range considerations into public discussion may serve to further this sense of common cause. Industrialists, for example, can be shown how price and wage policies affect not only their immediate profits, but also, in possible conflict with the latter, the expansion of markets in the future. Similarly, labor union leaders can be brought to understand that higher wages may mean higher incomes to their members now but may inhibit future expansion of employment opportunities. In some cases, the society's political viability may depend upon the provision of such grounds for compromise among the various social groups. To the extent that the collaborative planning process creates a greater sense of national unity in the development enterprise, it may serve to mobilize greater effort in terms of labor productivity, investment rates, project preparation, and so forth.

In addition to focusing the discussion on national needs, the planner also serves to keep the discussion within the bounds of national resources. The other participants are forced to think in terms of opportunity costs, to be selective as to the needs to be satisfied and thrifty in the design of projects to satisfy them. By eliminating the clearly infeasible among the alternatives, the planner can at least help narrow the range of possible decision outcomes. By providing certain normative models of good decision making, such as factual analysis and objectivity, the planning agency is able to limit the influence of "bad" interests in the ultimate decisions.[22]

The planning office, in sum, serves not as a replacement for the political process of public decision making but rather as an agent for improving that process by improving the information and incentives of the other participants. The latter, in turn, can provide valuable information enabling the planners to perform their function more usefully. Integration of the planning process with the political process such as is occurring in Venezuela is necessary not only to insure that planning will in fact have an impact on decision making but also to give additional strength to the contention that that impact will be positive.[23]

22. For a fuller discussion of this point, see Nicholas Nicolaidis, *Policy Decision and Organization Theory* (Los Angeles: Univ. of Southern California, 1960), pp. 159–61.

23. A working draft of this chapter was delivered at a LADAC meeting in Washington, D.C. It was subsequently published in *Yale Economic Essays*, Spring 1967. The present chapter is an edited version of the published article, in which some material unrelated to Latin American development administration has been removed because it is now available elsewhere.

Chapter 4

Foreign Technical Assistance and National Development

Helio Jaguaribe

Image and Reality in Technical Assistance

Increasing Assistance and Optimism

There has been a tendency since the end of the Second World War to increase the facilities for technical assistance rendered by international and national sources to underdeveloped countries not only in the Western areas of influence but also among the socialist countries, although the specific forms of such assistance may vary. There is also something of a tendency to consider technical assistance as the most important factor in international efforts to overcome underdevelopment.

For the sake of simplicity, if one considers only technical assistance rendered by and to noncommunist countries, he is impressed by the scope such activities have attained. The United Nations had, as early as 1963, an allocation of $50 million for such purposes, supporting a staff of some 3,000 experts.[1] An additional $20 million was provided by the Special Fund for contracting with specialized agencies for 1,200 experts. Technical assistance was also provided by FAO, UNESCO, and other independent U.N. agencies.

In addition to this international source of technical assistance, there are the national sources. In the United States, out of a total budget of about $3.5 billion for foreign aid, about $300 million

1. This and the following data of this topic are extracted from an unpublished paper of Professor Robert W. Iversen, "Personnel for Technical Assistance" (Maxwell Graduate School of Citizenship and Public Affairs, Syracuse Univ., Feb. 1965).

was allocated for technical assistance in the fiscal year 1965, which was to be the highest appropriation for foreign aid in the next ten years. The Agency for International Development (AID), acting directly or through contractors, employs annually an average of 2,000 experts for foreign technical assistance. The Peace Corps has about 5,000 volunteers in the field. The U.S. Department of Agriculture has a Foreign Agricultural Service (FAS) with agricultural attachés in 61 posts, primarily concerned with the Food for Peace Program, and many other experts (240 full-timers in 1963) to provide specific technical assistance abroad. American universities are becoming increasingly involved in foreign assistance, although they concentrate mostly in helping the education and training of technical professors and teachers abroad (e.g., Cornell University and the State University of Virginia in Kenya; the University of Hawaii in Indonesia; Oklahoma State University in Ethiopia; Harvard in Pakistan). In addition to the universities and U.S. official agencies, the foundations are playing an extremely important role in this field. The Rockefeller Foundation has spent $20 million in the last twenty years in scientific and technical assistance for its Agricultural Science Program, endeavoring to increase the production and productivity of basic food. The Ford Foundation, which began its Overseas Development Program in 1951, has invested in it about $200 million, one-fourth of this in agriculture alone, and is devoting 20 percent of its total budget to that program.

Other nations, such as Great Britain, France, the Netherlands, Germany, Japan, are concentrating increasing efforts in overseas technical assistance. Great Britain, devoting an annual budget of $80 million to such purposes, has some 15,000 officials connected with technical assistance through the Overseas Aid Scheme, while France has about 10,000 officers, not including the 40,000 overseas French teachers. Both countries, in addition, are the major suppliers of experts to the U.N. technical assistance programs. The United States, although it is the major single contributor of funds for the program, has not supplied a large percentage of technicians to the U.N. program, partly because of the geographic quota, and partly, presumably, because the U.S. AID has been more persuasive in respect to the limited numbers of personnel available for such assignments.

Increasing Deterioration of Underdeveloped Countries

In spite of the increasing international technical assistance efforts which have taken place over the past twenty years, the overall picture among recipient countries shows that the underdeveloped countries have neither achieved self-sustained development nor even attained the stage of "takeoff." (There are some exceptions—Puerto Rico, Hawaii, now a U.S. state, Hong Kong, and a few others.) On the contrary, the gap between developed and underdeveloped countries has become, in many respects, much larger, while internal conditions, for development within a democratic context, have steadily deteriorated.

In Latin America, between 1945–49 and 1955–60, the gross national product increased from $35,230,000 to $56,970,000, an increase of 61.7 percent.[2] The United States from 1945 to 1960[3] increased GNP from $213.6 billion to $502.6 billion, an increase of 135.2 percent. The comparative effect of this difference in growth rate is even larger. The per capita meaning is more accentuated in the United States than in Latin America, since the United States has only a mild demographic growth while Latin America is experiencing an explosive one. Also, the increase of American income is a displacement from wealth to affluence, while in Latin America the income continues to be very near the mere subsistence level. Thus, in per capita terms, Latin American average income increased from $243 dollars in the 1945–49 period to $296 for the 1955–60 period. In the United States on the other hand, the increase was from $1,512 per capita in 1945 to $2,782 in 1960.[4] Thus, the Latin American increase, per capita, has been 21.8 percent, while the American one has been 83.9 percent.

It could be said that although the trend is obviously unfavorable, in historical terms, the shortness of the period considered

2. "El desarrollo económico de América Latina en la Postguerra," *Quadro* 5, E/CN.12/659, 7 April 1963. Figures are in terms of 1950 dollars.
3. *Statistical Abstract of the United States 1964–65*, table 433.
4. Same sources as nn. 2 and 3.

still leaves open the possibility that the cumulative effects of increased efforts in foreign technical assistance will bear fruit in the next decades. Such a hope, however, is dampened by the historical examples of the takeoff process in other countries which indicate that such processes have usually occurred in an average period of twenty years. Slightly rounding the dates given by Rostow[5] in his classic study on the stages of economic growth, one sees that the takeoff of the major developed countries occurred in a basic two-decennial period:

Great Britain	1780–1800
France	1840–1860
U.S.A.	1840–1860
Germany	1850–1870
Sweden	1870–1890
Japan	1880–1900
Canada	1900–1920
U.S.S.R.[6]	1928–1938

Thus, although many of the preconditions for takeoff have existed for a long time in Latin America and elsewhere, there is no indication that the socioeconomic processes of such nations are being brought to any form of continued and self-sustained growth, in spite of the increasing foreign technical assistance and other forms of overseas aid.

The Triple Fallacy of Foreign Technical Assistance

There are three principal fallacies of foreign aid and technical assistance—the skill fallacy, the geographic fallacy, and the topical fallacy. To be sure, each of these fallacies or assumptions

5. Rostow's own dates are these: Great Britain, 1783–1802; France, 1830–60; U.S.A., 1843–60; Germany, 1850–73; Sweden, 1868–90; Japan, 1878–1900; Canada, 1896–1914; Russia, 1890–1914. Cf. *The Stages of Economic Growth* (Cambridge: Cambridge Univ. Press, 1964), p. 38.
6. In this study, the Russian takeoff is attributed to the two initial five-year plans. Rostow's proposed period (1890–1914) is here considered to represent only a regional and isolated industrial development around St. Petersburg and Moscow, which did not change the still essentially agrarian Russian economy.

contains within itself a partial truth. Nevertheless, to treat them as anything more than superficial symptoms leads to a program bias and an overemphasis in technical assistance efforts which deflect attention from the real or underlying causes of underdevelopment.

The Skill Fallacy

The first general fallacy of present and past foreign technical assistance is the underlying assumption that economic underdevelopment is primarily due to the deficiency in quantity and quality of some essential skills. Because such skills are not available to them, underdeveloped countries are not able to take better advantage of their natural resources which are, in the majority of cases, fairly sufficient for their needs. As a consequence, according to this reasoning, such countries are neither capable of accumulating investable surpluses nor able to administer adequately their existing wealth. Following from such assumptions is the belief that the best that can be done to help the developmental process of backward countries is to give them technical assistance in order to supplement, by foreign advice, their missing know-how. Technical assistance, according to this line of thought, should lead to appropriate use of the existing possibilities and, in the end, promote development.

The Geographic Fallacy

The second general fallacy of current technical assistance is another of its assumptions which I shall call the geographic fallacy. Underdevelopment (understood as primarily due to lack of skills) is considered to be a subutilization of actual or potential available factors in a given area. The use of these factors must be maximized. The purpose is to attain the maximum possible increase of total and per capita GNP, irrespective of considerations about who controls what.

The Topical Fallacy

The third general fallacy of past and current technical assistance, the topical fallacy, is of an operational nature and related to the two preceding assumptions. The topical fallacy consists in maximizing the facilities and opportunities for advisory help for all relevant activities of the recipient country. Besides deriving from the preceding assumptions, the topical fallacy tends to be the natural result of the multiplicity of foreign agencies, people, and purposes proposed from abroad to help underdeveloped countries. Even within such countries there is a multiplicity of agencies, peoples, and projects oriented for economic development which often compete among themselves in an uncoordinated fashion.

General Remarks

These three fallacies contain partial truths. It is obvious that the lack of skills is both a manifest feature of socioeconomic underdevelopment and its immediate cause. It is equally obvious that any process of economic development must, somehow, lead to an increase of the GNP. It is also true that to achieve any economic result the minimum required skills must be present and that foreign technical assistance may serve to improve and supplement local deficiencies. What must be taken into consideration, however, is that the lack of skills, itself, is determined by other causes. Why have some countries been able to develop and improve the skills of their own people, while other countries remain, in each successive generation, with a serious lack of skills? How can national socioeconomic development be considered irrespective of the degree to which the nation is its subject and not merely its object? In other words, although the GNP might be continuously increasing, how can a community attain socioeconomic development if its major activities are controlled by outsiders—outsiders who own the factories and farms and the systems of transport and communication, and who control the process of investment, distribution, research, and invention? What is the meaning, finally, of a multiplicity of projects and people supplying technical assistance from abroad, if the new generations are unable to staff the countries' own technical requirements?

The Causes of Underdevelopment

With few exceptions, underdevelopment is a social fact determined in Latin America especially by three interconnected but independent causes each representing a particular kind of sociohistorical alienation: cultural alienation, societal alienation, and national alienation.

Cultural Alienation

Cultural alienation consists in the inadequacy of the cultural system or of some of its patterns of behavior to lead to functional forms of social relationship, to a rational (scientific-technological) approach to nature, and therefore to the use of natural forces and resources. The most typical example of such alienation is the one given by the nonrational cultures. As long as such a culture is surrounded by other nonrational cultures, its cultural alienation is only a minor limitation, since all the societies interacting on each other are equally nonrational. Such is the case of a primitive people before they face an encounter with rational civilizations, or the case of ancient magic civilizations. Once faced with the presence and influence of rational cultures, the nonrational ones become impotent in any confrontation and unable to achieve any socioeconomic development without a thoroughgoing cultural change.

This extreme hypothesis, however, is applicable only to the remaining primitives of our time. The general case of cultural alienation today is not the one presented by nonrational cultures, but by societies whose cultural systems are perfectly rational since they are either direct descendants of western European civilization or have been deeply westernized. Such societies, however, in spite of that, bear some patterns of behavior incompatible with or at least not conducive to functional forms of social relationship. This dysfunctional quality must not be confused with similar factors existing in any society, such as crime and other forms of social or individual pathological behavior. Neither should it be confused with the derived forms of dysfunctionality, although sometimes it may be difficult, in specific cases, to determine whether some dysfunctionalities are derived forms or come directly from dysfunctional patterns of behavior peculiar to the social culture. Most of the features incompatible with, or nonconducive to the functional forms of social behavior that foreign Western observers tend to point out in the cultural patterns of Latin American countries, such as the *mañana* solution, the *jeito*,[7] the lack of response to economic stimuli, etc., are themselves a result of the preexisting situation of underdevelopment. Take, for example, the contrasts analyzed by Louis Hartz[8] between the egalitarian-minded and contractualistic spirit of the North American culture and the aristocratic and statutorial spirit of the Latin American culture. These are not the *results* of successful economic development of the U.S. as compared to the persistent underdevelopment of Latin America. On the contrary, they are one of the basic original *causes* of the different economic achievements.

The impact of the mother societies developed an egalitarian spirit in the Northern colonies and an aristocratic spirit in the Southern ones. In addition, a previous cultural pattern existing in the originating societies motivated different behavior in each. This pattern was the "synallagmatic" view of the condition of man-in-society peculiar to British culture, on the one hand, and the "anallagmatic" view peculiar to Iberian culture, on the other. The synallagmatic view led to the belief that differences of social condition, function, and fortune were external to man. His intrinsic equality was thereby unaffected by such differences. A belief in the intrinsic rights and obligations of social behavior, and in the same rules for every man, thus developed in British culture at home and in North America. The anallagmatic view led to the intrinsic magnification of the grandees and inferiorization of the peasantry both in Spain and Portugal and in Latin America, creating between the two strata relations of a master-serf nature, subject to essentially different moral values.

7. *Jeito* is a Brazilian term meaning "improvisation"; *dar un jeito* is "to find a solution."

8. Louis Hartz, *The Founding of New Societies* (New York: Harcourt, Brace and World, 1964).

The synallagmatic pattern of the North American civilization provided a built-in stimulus for political and social democracy, creating institutional and psychological conditions for a dynamic, innovating, self-enriching, and at the same time law-abiding society. The anallagmatic pattern in Latin American civilization has provided an equally intrinsic stimulus for a politically and socially aristocratic society, static, conservative, more statutorial (or ascriptive) than acquisitive, and inclined to different regimes of social behavior according to the social strata.

Societal Alienation

Societal alienation consists in the prevalence of social forms of domination—political, economic, and statutorial—based on the oligopolization of power, which leads to a dysfunctional relationship between the mass and elite. It also is dependent upon the continued maintenance of the status quo. The main feature of the dysfunctional mass-elite relationship is the fact that social leadership is not compatible with a general maximization of social welfare. Therefore, leadership is accepted in a passive traditional form or is imposed in nonconsensual coercive ways.

Societal alienation is related to cultural alienation, but not reducible to it. The former tends to be more frequent in societies affected by the latter, but also appears independently. Sometimes societies with anallagmatic patterns of culture do not reflect any societal alienation, an example being early twentieth-century Uruguay. Great Britain, on the other hand, whose synallagmatic cultural patterns were already clearly shaped by the end of the Middle Ages, underwent long periods of political, economic, and societal alienation before the consolidation of the parliamentary system. Societal alienation, in the economic field, has been equally relevant in North America from the second half of the nineteenth century to the New Deal, and continues even today.

Societal alienation leads to the preservation of the status quo and is incompatible with any effective process of socioeconomic development. Moreover, inevitably the masses start the struggle for equality and participation in social benefits. Then elites, founded on the oligopolization of power, become dependent on foreign support in order to control their own masses. They are thus driven to trade national independence and autonomy for external help.

National Alienation

National alienation occurs when there is a dissolution of the national structure of a society as a result of external pressures and internal disruptive effects. This is brought on it by the dominant society in whose area of influence the former is situated. There is no substitution of the affected structure by alternative ones.

National alienation occurs more frequently in societies affected by societal alienation, but, again, is not reducible to it. Germany, Italy, and Japan in the period preceding and leading to the Second World War were profoundly affected by societal alienation. But they were able, through the use of diverse forms of fascism, to keep their masses under control without having to give up their own independence and autonomy. Canada, on the other hand, with a rather functional elite, has suffered from national alienation vis-à-vis the United States. Canada has been able neither to prevent this nor to shape, in its relations with the United States, any alternative structure.

The combined effect of external pressure and internal disruptive effects is particularly clear in the relations between the United States and the Latin American underdeveloped countries. The U.S. government in the pursuit of its own conception of American strategic interests, or under the political compulsion of powerful internal pressure groups, exerts on underdeveloped countries whatever pressure it deems required to reach its goals. This is done in ways which vary from the usual diplomatic and economic pressures to the employment of commercial and financial coercion or the use of physical violence. The latter includes both military force and the use of internal subversion against foreign governments which dare to resist the milder forms of persuasion. At the same time, deliberately and undeliberately, by action of all kind of individuals and groups,[9] from private businessmen to the best-intentioned missionaries, the United States as a country and as a civilization, as a complex of interests as well as a mode of life, produces a devastating impact on the structures of the underdeveloped countries, not from outside but from inside, by the laws of imitation and the demonstration effect. The combined result of external pressure, going as far as military intervention or subversive mobilization of *coups*, with the all-pervading influence of American interests and values, disrupts the national structure of the affected underdeveloped country, without providing it with an alternative system of reorganizing its own people in a socially and spiritually meaningful way.

The worst effect of the disruption of underdeveloped countries is the distortion of the mass-elite relationship, depriving it of all its dynamism. The masses no longer expect guidance from their own elite. They realize only its impotence and become aware that foreigners, not the native elite, are calling the tune. The elites, on the other hand, realize that they have little to gain and much to lose if they maintain the right to represent the interests of their own masses. They therefore become divided about their own role. The intellectuals, faced by the contradiction between the two functions they usually perform—the cultural pursuit of knowledge and truth and the social dissemination and orientation of values—do one of two things. Either they emigrate, looking for a new cultural metropolis, or they are led to underground revolutionary action. The professionals and businessmen, deprived of the support of national structures, are inclined to displace their interests in a way compatible with that of the foreigners. They become their brokers and attorneys. In this process, the country loses its self-centeredness and becomes an overseas appendix of the dominating foreign power. It serves as a supplier of primary products and cheap labor and a market for exports. Meanwhile the increasing deterioration in internal socioeconomic conditions drives the masses and the radical intellectuals toward a revolutionary process.

9. Harlan Cleveland, Gerrard J. Mangone, and John Clarke Adams, *The Overseas Americans* (New York: McGraw-Hill, 1960).

U.S. Foreign Action

U.S. Foreign Assistance

The assumptions and practices of U.S. foreign aid, except under President Kennedy, were characterized by the three fallacies already analyzed in this study, with its corresponding limitations. Under the Kennedy administration, however, foreign aid, including the Alliance for Progress with its emphasis on economic and social development, was characterized by an increasing consciousness of the limitations of the conventional forms of foreign aid and technical assistance. This was buttressed by an incipient understanding, by some of the intellectuals surrounding the president, of the real nature of underdevelopment. This short period, however, abruptly terminated by the assassination of the leader, did not succeed in changing the actual practice of U.S. foreign aid. Because of the resistance of existing routines and habits to a new philosophy and style, the emerging Kennedy formulation did not have time to be practically implemented, except in some isolated cases.

The present phase of U.S. foreign assistance, it seems to me, represents a partial return to pre-Kennedy techniques and spirit. It is an aggravated awareness of the possibilities of deliberate manipulation of the socioeconomic context of underdeveloped countries, to conform closely to U.S. political, military, and economic interests. This has led to a change in emphasis from the promotion of development to the maintenance of stability.

This U.S. emphasis on stability in underdeveloped countries, however, in reality reinforces the status quo, contributes to societal alienation, and aggravates national alienation. The effects of these alienations have already been described. The internal mass-elite dynamism is distorted, dividing the elites at the extremes between collaborationists of foreign interests, on the one hand, and radical revolutionists, on the other. All the while the persistent and aggravated underdevelopment drives the country toward a revolutionary process.

Possible Alternative Courses

While Western and particularly U.S. influence in the developing countries is overwhelming, especially in Latin America, neither the present orientation of U.S. foreign action nor its effects and meaning are the only or the best possible courses of action in view of the circumstances. Without attempting to analyze the reasons of post-Kennedian U.S. foreign action, it might be pointed out that it represents an overemphasis on the concept of national defense at the expense of other equally essential U.S. interests, biased by a predominantly militaristic approach.

The basic fact is the national alienating effect on underdeveloped countries that is brought about by U.S. pressures and influence. Clearly confronted with that effect, the United States can act either to accentuate it or to remedy it. While the overwhelming influence of the United States, as a complex of interests and values, is an inescapable fact of our times, it is not equally necessary that all the other national structures, among the underdeveloped countries, be driven to dissolution by the American influence. In that respect, the United States faces clear alternatives, one leading to the preservation and reinforcement of the national structures of the underdeveloped countries, although not in their present form and limits, and the other leading to their suppression.

The preservation and reinforcement of the national structures of the underdeveloped countries imply, at the same time, the promotion of their socioeconomic development. This would necessitate the removal of the three sociohistorical alienations, already analyzed in this study, and, in their place, the reshaping of national structures. One of the fundamental conditions for the latter is their integration—already a necessity for the developed countries of Europe. It is even more indispensable for underdeveloped countries, including those in Latin America.

A second alternative which confronts the United States, and which must be faced, is the annihilation, either knowingly or unknowingly, of the national structures of the underdeveloped world. The Latin American countries, which are the most exposed to the United States, more by their cultural than by their geographic proximity to it, are particularly vulnerable to this eventuality. Such countries may simply become a geographical and ethnographical open space for the unchecked exercise of American predatory activities.

The first alternative, the preservation and reinforcement of national structures, was the one adopted by the Kennedy administration, and it continues to have the warm support of American liberals. It offers many long-term advantages, both to the United States and to the underdeveloped countries. But there are also many short-term difficulties. These difficulties arise from the fact that this alternative embodies a completely new vision of and approach to American foreign interests and action. And so it is opposed, in the United States as well as in the underdeveloped countries, by the combined resistance of routine inertia and vested interests.

The second alternative, the annihilation of national structures, presents, theoretically, these two possibilities: the case of positive suppression of the national structures of underdeveloped countries, through some incorporation of their people in the American institutional structure, and the present trend to the annihilation of the national structures of underdeveloped countries without providing any alternative form of organizing and protecting their people.

The incorporation into the American national commonwealth of the present underdeveloped countries—which would have an effect something like that of the Edict of Caracalla in the history of the Roman Empire—seems in general to be a less viable and likely occurrence. Neither the underdeveloped countries nor the American people would welcome such a measure, under present conditions. The majority of the people in underdeveloped countries do not yet realize the extent to which their own national structures are collapsing. Among the few who are becoming aware of this, the largest number are, unquestionably and more than anything else, interested in preserving the status quo.

The American public, at large, is absolutely unknowing of such a phenomenon and unprepared to act accordingly. For these and many other reasons, it is more probable that, in practice, the only possible choice for U.S. foreign action will be between the first alternative—preserving and helping the national structures of underdeveloped countries, combining their appropriate reshaping with an all-out effort for socioeconomic development—and the second possibility, leading to the annihilation of the national structures. The latter case is the one which, tragically, is somehow already spontaneously occurring. If it continues, its inevitable outcome will be the increasing pauperization of the underdeveloped countries. There will be a corresponding increase in the scope and intensity of their revolutionary processes.[10]

Whether these revolutionary processes will, ultimately, lead to the effective seizure of power by the revolutionary forces and whether these new revolutionary governments will or will not be able to achieve their special purposes, are questions open to discussion. An important remark, however, should here be made. "Wars of national liberation" in our times have acquired a new, double dimension. The first and most visible is their inevitable internationalization. The second new dimension, though not yet so visible, is no less real. This is what Sartre has noted in his analysis of the French military reaction against the independence of Algeria. It is the boomerang effect on the dominant country resulting from the buildup and the operation of a gigantic military apparatus, sufficiently powerful and flexible to deal with the wars of national liberation abroad. This boomerang effect brings in its wake the inevitable destruction of political democracy and social and cultural freedoms of the imperialist country. This is a process which, under conditions prevailing at the time, had its effect on Greek civilization and in turn on Roman civilization.

---

10. As has been observed by others, Marx's forecast of the increasing pauperization of the proletariat, leading to the final socialist revolution, has not been confirmed by the course of events in the developed countries, because, among other reasons, of social reforms. The revolutionary potentialities of pauperization, however, tend to be more likely in the international relations between developed and underdeveloped countries.

The Consequences of Present
Technical Assistance

Affected by the fallacies indicated in the beginning of this study, and carried on in the context of the three alienations which are the basic causes of socioeconomic underdevelopment, the present forms of foreign technical assistance tend to have either limited results or even negative ones.

Limited Results

One of the typical limited effects of the present forms of technical assistance is the "enclave result." To be efficient and lasting, technical assistance is generally concentrated on a specific project, considered to be a pilot one, on whose model many others are supposed to be fashioned later on. It is soon realized that for maximum effect, the showcase should be intensively planned, designed, projected, and operated by the technical assistance agency. The final result is the development of a foreign enclave, surrounded by circumstances and conditions which are incompatible with adoption by other concerns and projects. The original project tends, in order to maintain its level of performance, to formulate a continuing link with the founding foreign agency, which adds to the artificiality of the matter.

Another form of the limited, although positive, effect of present foreign technical assistance is its circumscription to a specific and isolated sector of the recipient country. Less likely than the "enclave result," the "sectoral result" is also detectable. A limited system of activities—say the extermination of certain diseases, the collecting of certain taxes, the use of appropriate forms for handling and packing products, mostly for export—has been conveniently and durably introduced by foreign technical assistance. Such sectoral results, however, are neither transferable to other sectors nor likely to occur in a sector where complex activities require a large interconnection between the specific sector and the country as a whole. Meanwhile, the determinant causes of underdevelopment—the cultural, the societal and the national alienations—far from being suppressed, tend to be aggravated. The best and most extended efforts of technical assistance are barely able at best to achieve limited enclave and sectoral results. They are impotent to introduce any durable structural changes in the underdeveloped country.

Negative Results

Even when manipulative purposes are not behind it, foreign technical assistance may have extremely negative results either directly or indirectly. Among direct effects, the most notorious is the reinforcement of the means of coercion and oppression of reactionary governments and forces. This has been a general result, in Latin America and other areas, of technical assistance, when supplemented by aid in material and equipment provided to armies and police forces. As long as the armies and police forces of underdeveloped countries are kept within the country's average limits of material and operational capability, such forces have to take into account the claims of public opinion, the expectations and rights of labor unions, and the ideas of intellectuals. Accordingly, a certain level of freedom is preserved and a certain area is kept open for social change, conducive to socioeconomic development. As soon as the equipment and techniques of action put at the disposal of those forces surpass the nation's operational capability, the military apparatus takes control. It does this either under the leadership and for the benefit of the traditional oligarchies or by its own initiative and for its own purposes. In the name of stability, morality, and anticommunism, an iron hand keeps subject to military dictatorship, ostensible or covert, all the activities of the country and suppresses every manifestation of freedom and all possibilities of social change.

A second variety of negative effect which may be brought about by foreign technical assistance is the "mirage result." This effect, of an indirect nature, is the creation of an illusion that massive foreign technical assistance, given the limitations referred to in this study, would be able to promote the national development of a country. The most forceful example, up to now, of such a "mirage effect," has been the Porfirio Díaz govern-

ment in Mexico, overthrown in 1911. During the Díaz administration all the relevant activities of Mexico were controlled by
foreign experts and interests. This led to the Mexican Revolution.
Some recent Latin American conservative governments furnish
examples of the mirage result. In addition to its denationalizing
effects, the mirage result leads underdeveloped countries to accentuate any propensities toward paternalism and other dysfunctional features of their cultural patterns. The final consequence
is an aggravation instead of an improvement of their socioeconomic conditions.

Conditions of Validity for Foreign
Technical Assistance

Basic Requirements

According to the analysis presented thus far, it can be seen that
the worth of any attempt at foreign technical assistance depends
upon the extent to which, first, the three fallacies (skill, geographic, and topical) are overcome and, second, the measure in
which the three alienations (cultural, societal, and national) that
cause underdevelopment are also overcome.

The fulfillment of these conditions implies two basic requirements, one concerning the recipient and the other the donor of
foreign technical assistance. Concerning the recipient country,
technical assistance is only valuable, in a meaningful and lasting
form, if it is a part, though an important part, of a general national effort for structural change. Foreign technical assistance
by itself cannot contribute to effective and lasting socioeconomic
development if it is merely superimposed on the routines linked
to the preservation of the status quo.

Concerning the donor country or agency, foreign technical
assistance is valuable and meaningful when it is based on respect
for the national structures of the recipient country. The aim must
be to develop these structures either nationally, as such, or in
the larger and more viable context of the regional system in
which the country is to be integrated. The preservation and re-

inforcement of national independence and autonomy permit the processing of mass-elite internal dynamics, which is the socio-historical force driving societies to their own socioeconomic development.

Operational Requirements

Accordingly, successful foreign technical assistance will adapt its purposes and means to the basic requirements herein mentioned, keeping in mind pertinent local conditions. Two specific exigencies should be pointed out. The first refers to an absolute priority that must be given to the education and training of native cadres. Because socioeconomic development is an inward process, oriented to increasing forms of social integration and self-determination, the best and most urgent help foreign experts can give to a country is to accelerate and improve the formation of a new functional elite. The influence of the new elite will not depend upon coercive spoliation, but upon effective services rendered to and demanded by the society. Education and training, at all levels, are the real goal of foreign technical assistance. The most important result to be achieved is to teach teachers, to teach people who can teach other people, so that the process of imparting, disseminating, and improving skills becomes more and more self-sustained.

The second important operational requirement of foreign technical assistance is the liberty of choice of the recipient country. It is not enough that foreign assistance be not inspired by manipulative purposes. It must also be freely demanded and selected by the recipient countries. This is so even if they commit, as they certainly do, many faults of judgment and of decision in their selection of assistance. One of the most important forms of aid adopted by some international financing agencies is the provision of loans for the free and competitive contracting of foreign experts. Only in this fashion are technical assistance programs likely to be linked to the internal efforts for promoting social change. And only so, in practical terms, can foreign assistance be shorn of its usual manipulative content.

The Role of Young Professionals

The role of young professionals in foreign technical assistance differs according as it is viewed from the standpoint of the donors or from that of the recipients. For the former, the relevant questions are the relationship to be established between younger and older experts and between the new recruits or volunteers and the agencies in charge of overseas technical help. This leads to such problems as the convenience of creating fixed careers, of developing a system of rotation between domestic and overseas posts, or in stable permanence abroad, etc. From the standpoint of the recipient countries, what is important is the education, training, and employment of their own youth. Foreign technical assistance, whatever be the age of the visiting experts, must concentrate on improving the educational and training facilities of the recipient country, in order to make its new generations capable of autonomous technical performance.

In addition to the fallacies which have been analyzed in this chapter, the natural egocentric bias of donor countries leads them to focus this question on the best employment of their own youth, forgetting the necessity of preparing the native youth for a better technical role. This is typical, for instance, in some of the most well-intentioned efforts of foreign technical assistance, e.g., the Peace Corps. Giving due tribute to the generous and patriotic impulses that drive, each year, thousands of young Americans to the most backward areas of the world, to live in precarious, often unsafe, conditions, we still need to appreciate the extent to which this effort is meaningful for the recipient countries.[11] The skill fallacy and a propensity to an anthropological approach toward underdeveloped societies, treating them as if they were a kind of advanced savagery, incline people to believe that it is very helpful to teach villagers in the hinterland

11. Lawrence H. Fuchs, Brandeis University, ex-director of the Peace Corps in the Philippines (July 1961 to June 1963), in a paper prepared for the International Development Institute, East-West Center, 17 Aug. to 11 Sept. 1964, entitled "Acceptance and Change by Peace Corps Volunteers in the Barrios of the Philippines," states that the influence of Peace Corps Volunteers was practically limited to interpersonal relationships.

of Colombia or the Philippines how to filter water or how to
breed chickens. Although such skills, like any others, have obvious advantages, it is never considered that the existing Colombian
or Philippine society, as a whole, determines the miserable conditions in the villages. Only a few individuals given such help
(even were the Peace Corps to have millions of volunteers instead of thousands) are able to take advantage of this kind of
assistance. Similarly in former times, the charitable and well-
intentioned alms given to the poor were never enough to suppress poverty or even to reduce it to any socially measurable
extent.

Conclusions

Underdevelopment is a global social fact, and only as such
may it be considered in an intelligent form and attacked in an
efficient way. What must be done in underdeveloped countries
is to create a new functional elite whose interests are compatible
with and dependent on an increase in the general welfare. Underdeveloped countries of Western or westernized cultures, like the
majority of societies, are not underdeveloped because they cannot master the appropriate skills. They are underdeveloped because their own elites want it that way. In order to maintain
their privileges, they are dependent on the perpetuation of the
status quo. Teaching villagers isolated skills is of little or no use
without a major change in the socioeconomic context. What is
important is to "force" social change by giving new qualifications
to the new generation, especially where they are and will become
more influential; also by helping the progressive forces to get rid
of oligarchical and military oppression which only perpetuates
the status quo. This last role is unquestionably the role of the
native youth.

Part II

Mobilizing Human Resources for the Administration of Development Programs

Chapter 5

High-Level Human Resources in Latin American Economic Development

John C. Shearer

The term "high-level human resources" represents those human beings who by virtue of educational or occupational attainment embody much greater than average knowledge or skills. They are the people at the apex of the educational or occupational pyramid. They include the leading thinkers, innovators, planners, administrators, adapters, and appliers of modern techniques and technology—in short, the organizers and combiners of all other factors of production. High-level human resources play the key roles in economic and social development. They are the individuals whose knowledge and skills give direction and meaning to any nation's efforts to improve the well-being of its people. The ability of any society to progress depends largely upon the quantity and quality of its high-level human resources, and the nation's ability to develop and utilize them. This ability is indispensable to the attainment of *any* of a nation's goals, cultural, political, social, or economic. If a country cannot develop its high-level human resources, it cannot develop at all. The efficient use of all resources depends on the nature and efficiency of a country's high-level human resources.

For example, consider Venezuela, which has for several years been heavily involved in a land-reform program of crucial importance to its future. When this program was well under way, the Venezuelan official who was its coordinator mentioned in my presence how important certain high-level human resources were to its success. He had discovered, after the program was in high gear, that there were only two men in the country who were able to make rational decisions on how to break up the latifundia into plots which would adequately support individual families. Poor decisions due to lack of trained personnel might in this vital matter seriously jeopardize the program and the national interest. Yet it proved impossible to recruit any other skilled decision-makers, and to train others would entail a long delay.

Another example comes from India, a country with considerable experience in comprehensive national economic planning. The first Five Year Plan had no specific human resources content. It soon developed that scarcities of key human resources in the steel industry and other heavy industries were seriously impeding the attainment of plan goals. With foreign help the country was building four modern steel mills which it was unable to staff effectively. Subsequent plans incorporated estimates of human resources needs and made specific provisions for the increased development of high-level human resources that national growth would require. Many other countries, whether or not they have engaged in national planning, have had similar experiences in which inadequate provision of high-level skills has seriously impeded progress.

The Development and Utilization of High-Level Human Resources

Useful definitions of what constitutes a high-level human resource vary roughly with levels of development. As a general guide for many developing countries, high-level human resources may be characterized as persons who have attained education beyond the secondary level or whose occupations require an equivalent level of knowledge or skill gained through experience. We often speak of "investments" in human resources and of "education" as the main means of increasing the population's stock of knowledge and skills. We should emphasize, however, that these usages do not imply that such investments are made solely to enhance the capacities of human beings as producers of goods and services. Educational investments have many noneconomic goals, but they are also the principal means for increasing the potential of humans as producers. Education is, therefore, among many other things, the developer of human resources. The term "education" as used here encompasses all means, formal or informal, for developing knowledge and skills. "Formal education" can be characterized as that related to regular school and university systems, and "informal education" covers all other significant ways in which human potential is increased.

For high-level human resources, formal education is probably the most important means of investment and is more susceptible to measurement than are other forms of education. Measures of formal educational attainment, that is, of level and nature of training, often constitute good approximations of the stock of human resources in a given population. The output, in quality as well as quantity, of a nation's system of higher education is probably the most significant determinant of the future goals of that nation. If a nation's universities, technical institutes, and professional schools cannot produce enough well-trained men and women in appropriate fields, development will be impeded or impossible.

Unfortunately, many universities in developing countries are not fulfilling their proper roles as the main producers of high-level human resources. Too often they persist in patterns and techniques inherited from Europe at a time when university education was more concerned with preparing the young elite for leisure than with training the most talented young people for productive careers. Many universities have been slow in relating their programs to the needs of their nations. They often place too little emphasis on programs in the physical sciences, engineering, management, and agriculture, for example, and too much on law and humanities. For example, in Argentina, a country heavily dependent on agriculture, only about 2 percent of university graduates are trained in any agricultural field. In this large and reasonably wealthy country the field of agricultural economics did not exist until it was recently developed through U.S. initiative.

The universities which best serve their nation's needs are usually those which have created the strongest ties with their communities. Most of them regularly involve leaders in government, business, labor, and agriculture in the formulation and evaluation of curricula so that their graduates will be well trained to fill community needs. Among the Latin American universities which have emphasized this type of relevance are the Universidad del Valle in Cali, Colombia, and the Instituto Tecnológico y de Estudios Superiores de Monterrey, Mexico.

Probably the most critical and persistent shortages of high-level human resources in most underdeveloped countries are in the fields of administration and management, and in these fields universities have thus far made very little contribution to national needs. High levels of competence are necessary to build, motivate, and utilize efficiently all sorts of organizations, both in the private and the public sectors. Experience in advanced countries demonstrates that administrative and managerial skills of a high order can be taught at the university level. Nevertheless, university training in either business administration or in public administration is very rare in developing countries despite the critical need for such competence.

Despite the obvious importance of the roles which universities play or should play in developing high-level human resources, there are other forms of investment in them. Perhaps the most important are those in which employers, public or private, use various means to upgrade selected employees for increased responsibilities. Many employers go to considerable expense to conduct training programs, seminars, special courses, and systems of "rotational training," that is, where a promising man is assigned to a sequence of positions of increasing responsibility in order to develop his competence for the top positions in the organization. Such investments by employers are often more efficient than are similar efforts by universities because of the necessarily close relationships between employer needs and the investments which are made in response to them. Nevertheless, the effectiveness of such employer investments will depend on the value of the educational bases provided by the universities upon which the employers can build.

The Development of Subprofessional Manpower

In sharp contrast to the general inadequacy of the universities in most Latin American countries in providing necessary high-level manpower is the extensive experience in Latin America with the training of middle-level or subprofessional manpower. In any country the effectiveness of most categories of high-level manpower is heavily dependent upon the availability and efficiency of auxiliary personnel. For example, it is generally estimated that each engineer must be augmented by an average of three or four subprofessionals in order for that engineer to work at maximum efficiency. The overall effectiveness of a physician depends heavily upon the availability and effectiveness of a wide range of other health-services personnel—nurses, medical technicians, therapists, etc. In the United States nonphysician health personnel outnumber physicians by approximately fifteen to one. It is clear then that the potential contributions of high-level human resources to economic and social development are heavily dependent on the adequate provision of subprofessional supportive personnel. Shortages of such manpower have seriously impeded the efficient utilization of high-level manpower and hence have seriously impeded the development of most underdeveloped countries.

Of all of the underdeveloped areas of the world, Latin America has made the greatest progress in training subprofessional and technical manpower. Several major Latin American countries have developed extensive systems for such training which are contributing substantially to their development. A most important common feature of these systems is that they are outside and independent of the regular systems of public-supported education in their countries.

The first such national system was originated in Brazil during World War II on Brazilian initiative, in response to the rapidly growing needs for trained personnel as a result of the war-induced surge of industrialization. The success of this system, which now encompasses the SENAI and SENAC organizations, prompted the International Labor Organization to support similar systems in other parts of Latin America, with technical assistance from Brazil and elsewhere. Among the most important such systems which have evolved elsewhere in Latin America are SENA in Colombia, INCE in Venezuela, SENATI in Peru, and INACAP in Chile. These and similar institutions elsewhere in Latin America generally offer training for the industrial, commercial, and agricultural sectors. Although the emphasis in most of these systems is on training in the manual skills needed in modernization, they are also the major trainers of technicians and other subprofessionals and some of the systems train significant numbers of supervisors.

SENA (Colombia) and INCE (Venezuela) are two of the oldest and most comprehensive systems. Both are supported by taxes on employers' total wage and salary payments—2 percent in Colombia and 1 percent in Venezuela. Although similar in purpose and in types of training, these two systems differ significantly in how they organize and train. SENA's training is mainly conducted in its own large modern training facilities located throughout Colombia. INCE's emphasis is on training on the employer's premises and with his equipment during idle shifts. In both systems there is considerable cooperation between employers and the training systems in order to assure that the training relates closely to actual needs.

Foreign Training

Many underdeveloped countries depend heavily on overseas training for the development of their high-level human resources. For example, the Indian government to help solve its critical shortages of high-level human resources in its vastly expanding steel industry utilized foreign training in the United States, Germany, and the Soviet Union. The largest of these programs involved private and public organizations in the United States in Project Instep (Indian Steel Education Program). Over a period of five years some 600 Indian engineers and managers worked and studied in U.S. steel mills and universities for periods of about nine months. They spent four days each week learning specific high-level positions in U.S. mills equivalent to those to which they would return in India. They spent one day each week in university courses in metallurgy, economics, and management.

The United States is a major trainer of university students from other countries. The annual census for the years 1969–70 of the Institute of International Education enumerated 134,959 foreign students regularly enrolled in colleges and universities in the United States.[1] The total numbers of foreign students in the United States reported by the IIE annual censuses has increased some 10 percent each year since 1946–47, the first year for which comparable overall figures are available. Approximately three-fourths of all the foreign students come from underdeveloped nations. Of the thirty-one countries each with more than 1,000 foreign students studying in the United States in 1969–70, twenty-three are generally considered underdeveloped. About 19 percent of all foreign students come from Latin America, which has had the second highest proportion (behind the Far East) of any geographic area for the past fifteen years. Foreign graduate students constitute approximately 44 percent of the 1969–70 total, compared with about 36 percent fifteen years ago. Almost one-third of all foreign graduate students are Ph.D. candidates, and this proportion is about the same both for advanced and for underdeveloped areas.

In a study of the impact of university training in the United States on the economic and social development of Latin American countries,[2] I attempt to assess the relevance of this training for the high-level human resources needs of these countries, that is, how such training relates or fails to relate to the development and utilization of those human resources of greatest importance to national development. The study at present is concerned only with graduate education, which is still rare in almost any field anywhere in Latin America. If a Latin American is to pursue education beyond the often inadequate level of undergraduate

1. *Open Doors 1970* (New York: Institute of International Education, 1970), table 1, pp. 22–23. Subsequent data on foreign students come also from *Open Doors 1967*, *Open Doors 1968*, and *Open Doors 1969*.
2. This work has been supported mainly by a grant from the Carnegie Corporation of New York through the Comparative Education Center, University of Chicago, and by the Research Foundation, Oklahoma State University.

training available in his country, he must usually go abroad. For most Latin American countries progress in many fields will depend heavily on foreign and especially U.S. graduate training, at least until those countries develop sufficient graduate programs of their own. This development is usually also heavily dependent on the overseas training of faculty at the graduate level.

More than a decade of involvement in Latin American manpower affairs has convinced me that foreign-student operations can offer invaluable opportunities to strengthen the human resources bases of these underdeveloped countries and thereby their prospects for development. This is especially the case through the contributions of foreign-trained professionals to institution building and to nation building. I have worked in Spanish with numerous persons in various types of Latin American institutions who, drawing directly on their U.S. university experience, were innovating and building to the considerable benefit of their nations in innumerable major and minor ways. For example, I have personal knowledge of profound changes for the better in the quality of Colombia's largest university, the National University, as a direct result of the knowledge and skills acquired by a relatively few faculty members who had recently returned from advanced studies in the United States. I cite but a few of these specific innovations: the initiation of a central university library as an alternative to thin and scattered collections in each of the largely isolated faculties (colleges); the institution by the physics department of basic courses to serve other departments by replacing a plethora of inferior basic courses formerly taught by each; the institution of periodic course examinations to test student progress rather than the former complete reliance on a final examination; the establishment of the office of Dean of Students; and the growth to excellence of a few faculties which emphasized quality teaching and research related to pressing national needs. It was quite clear in this and in many other situations in which I have worked that foreign-trained (mostly U.S.) young professionals can vastly improve important institutions, academic and other, as a direct result of what they learned abroad. On the other hand, I know of many instances of serious frustration and waste of talent and training among foreign students when they return home.

Successful utilization of foreign training operations depends mainly on the *relevance* for home country needs both in the selection of students and of the university programs they pursue in the United States. The student who is most likely to return to his home country after foreign training and most likely to make contributions to its development is the student whose overseas studies are vital to his country and for whom attractive opportunities exist at home. The likelihood that his foreign studies will make significant contributions to the development of his country is greatly increased if the student knows in advance that his satisfactory completion of appropriate overseas studies will provide him specific opportunities not otherwise available. Unfortunately, such ideal circumstances are not characteristic of training of Latin American students in the United States, even of those who are sponsored by agencies such as their own governments or the U.S. government whose purposes are precisely to encourage national development. My field investigations with decisionmakers in public and private agencies and in universities, here and abroad, persuade me that the selection of students often has little relevance to domestic needs. In many instances, the selection of students by sponsor groups is based on their families' influence with home-country decisionmakers. Even where decisionmakers apply objective criteria, rational use of the system is often impeded by lack of knowledge of specific university programs in the United States and how they relate to home-country needs.

The data for Latin American graduate students in the United States strongly suggest that very few countries are using efficiently this valuable opportunity to help overcome critical shortages of high-level human resources.[3] For example, despite

---

3. For detailed discussions of my analytic techniques and results see John C. Shearer, "International Migration of Talent and the Foreign Student," *Proceedings of the Twenty-Second Annual Meeting of the Industrial Relations Research Association* (Madison, Wis., 1970), pp. 258–69, and my "Intra- and International Movements of High-Level Human Resources," *Spatial Dimensions of Development Administration*, ed. James J. Heaphey (Durham, N.C.: Duke Univ. Press, 1971).

the crucial importance of agriculture for their development, most Latin American countries have given very little emphasis to foreign training in any agricultural specialty. For Argentina, Horowitz's studies[4] reveal that the most significant scarcities are of people in agriculture and especially of veterinarians and agronomists. Nevertheless, of approximately 500 Argentine graduate students who came to the United States in recent years, not one was in veterinary medicine and only two were in agronomy! Very few were in any other agricultural specialty. This dismal picture is characteristic of the generally poor utilization of foreign training to help satisfy urgent manpower needs. Among other vital areas getting very little emphasis is the field of public administration, despite its crucial importance and the fact that there is almost no university training available in this field outside a few advanced countries and especially the United States.

Movement of High-Level Human Resources

High-level human resources have much greater geographic mobility than do human resources of other types. This phenomenon, both within a country and internationally, has considerable significance for development. (i) Richer areas (that is, richer countries or richer areas within a given country) act as magnets which attract human resources, and especially high-level human resources, from poorer areas. (ii) These movements of human resources, in themselves, constitute major *subsidies* to the rich areas by the poorer areas. (iii) The costs to many poor areas of such movements constitute significant offsets to any aid (which may be in the form of high-level human resources) provided to these poor areas by rich areas. (iv) The movements of high-level human resources may to a great extent account for the persisting and often widening gaps between rich and poor areas.

4. Morris A. Horowitz, "High-Level Manpower in the Economic Development of Argentina," p. 35. This is chap. 1 in Frederick Harbison and Charles A. Myers, *Manpower, Education, and Economic Growth* (New York: McGraw-Hill, 1965).

Intranational Movements

Populations of the capital cities of most underdeveloped countries are growing much more rapidly (often more than twice as fast) than are those of their countries. This results mainly from large-scale migration of people from rural areas to provincial cities and to the capitals. A recent study in Chile revealed that 37 percent of the population and 53 percent of the labor force of Greater Santiago had been born elsewhere.[5]

Profound economic, social, and political effects result from the movement of people to the wealthiest cities. A major effect largely ignored by scholars is that in many countries this movement constitutes a heavy subsidy of the richest by the poorer areas of the country. Migrations invariably contain very high proportions of young people near the beginning of their most productive years. The natal area bears the costs of the birth, upbringing, and education and the direct costs of the migration of persons who choose to employ their abilities elsewhere. Thus, the capital city, already the richest area, obtains the benefits of the investments made in human resources by the poorer areas. The magnitude of these subsidies by the poor to the rich areas varies with the proportion of migrants who are high-level human resources, for they bring with them the highest levels of investment. High-level human resources are already highly concentrated in the advanced areas of any country and especially in the capitals of most countries. In Mexico, for example, the Federal District had almost four times the national proportion of population with secondary education. In 1960 the Federal District had less than 14 percent of the national population, but 53 percent of all Mexicans with secondary education and more than 56 percent of all Mexicans with university education lived there.[6]

The concentration of human resources in capital cities results

5. Bruce H. Herrick, *Urban Migration and Economic Development in Chile* (Cambridge, Mass.: M.I.T. Press, 1965), p. 46.
6. Charles Nash Myers, *Education and National Development in Mexico* (Princeton, N.J.: Industrial Relations Section, Princeton Univ., 1965), pp. 111–12.

from two major causes: the higher concentration of educational opportunities there, and the fact that in most countries migrant groups bring with them disproportionately large components of high-level human resources. For example, in terms of education and occupation, the high-level component of migration to Santiago has been much greater than the corresponding component of the populations from which the migrants came and is generally even greater than the corresponding components of the native Santiago population.[7] In other words, the Chilean data reveal that the migrant group from poorer areas, where high-level human resources were already in relatively poor supply, brought to the capital, already comparatively rich in human resources, a *higher* component of high-level human resources than that enjoyed by the capital's own population. The evidence strongly suggests that these movements are both caused by and contribute to the great and increasing disparities in wealth and opportunities between the capitals and the poorer areas.

International Movements

Emigration. The richest countries of the world attract high-level human resources from poor countries, just as the richest areas within any country attract them from the poorer areas within that country. The United States is a particularly strong magnet, especially for the scarcest skills in developing countries. During the thirteen years 1949–61, approximately 33,000 engineers and 10,000 scientists, a combined average of more than 3,300 per year, emigrated to the United States. The South American countries have been losing engineers to the United States at a rate of more than 300 per year.[8] Although the absolute numbers of high-level human resources who emigrate to the United States from underdeveloped countries are small compared with the widely publicized "brain drain" from more advanced countries such as Great Britain and Germany, they have very serious consequences for the less-developed countries, with their rela-

7. Herrick, table 6.4, p. 78; table 6.5, p. 80; and table 6.9, p. 86.
8. Based on data from Charles V. Kidd, "The Growth of Science and the Distribution of Scientists Among Nations," in *Impact of Science on Society* (Paris: UNESCO, 1964) 14, no. 1: 5–18.

tively small numbers of high-level human resources. Recent data on emigration to the United States from all South American countries shows that almost 25 percent of those reporting an occupation were in the important category "professional, technical and kindred workers."[9] This was more than 2½ times the proportion of the U.S. labor force in this category. The proportions of emigrants to the United States in other high-level occupational categories were also usually higher than the corresponding proportions for the U.S. labor force. This heavy flow of highly skilled people constitutes a major "reverse flow of foreign aid" from these poor countries to the world's richest country.

Importation of foreigners by foreign companies. A major inflow of high-level human resources to underdeveloped areas is represented by the importation of foreigners by foreign companies. Despite the potential benefits to underdeveloped countries, a study by the writer has revealed considerable evidence that these inflows are often of little real benefit to the host country. In fact, they may seriously *impede* the development of national high-level human resources. This study[10] deals with high-level manpower policies and practices in Latin America of fifty-two representative U.S. firms and casts considerable doubt upon the efficacy of this inflow either for the host countries or for the firms themselves. Home-office executives in the United States invariably stated that their company policy was to employ the "maximum possible number of nationals" in order to adapt their foreign operations more easily to the overseas environments and to avoid the very high costs of employing North Americans abroad. The direct costs of merely sending a U.S. family abroad usually exceeded $15,000 for Mexico and $30,000 for Brazil. In addition, there are great costs related to learning the language and methods of operation in a new environment. The salaries paid to North Americans abroad are very high. Base salaries are usually 20 to 25 percent higher than for comparable posts in the

9. Calculated from *Annual Report of the U.S. Immigration and Naturalization Service* (Washington, 1962), tables 8 and 8A, pp. 31–32.

10. John C. Shearer, *High-Level Manpower in Overseas Subsidiaries: Experience in Brazil and Mexico* (Princeton, N.J.: Industrial Relations Section, Princeton University, 1960).

United States. To this are added a multitude of special overseas allowances for children's education, housing, home leaves, etc. The writer conservatively estimated that on the average the direct recurrent costs (salary and allowances only) of employing North Americans in high-level posts abroad were approximately four times the average costs of employing comparable nationals in the same posts.

In spite of these high costs the great majority of companies studied depended heavily on North Americans. Although they constituted a small proportion of total employment, they dominated most subsidiaries because they occupied most of the highest posts. In some large and well-established subsidiaries the highest national was outranked and overwhelmed by dozens of North Americans. In the subsidiaries of nineteen companies operating in both countries, Brazilians occupied only fourteen percent and Mexicans only nine percent of the five highest posts in each subsidiary. In recent years the heavy dependence on North Americans has generally been increasing despite the claims of most home-office executives to the contrary.

The justification for the employment of more than 85 percent of the 501 North Americans covered in this study was the alleged inability of the firms to recruit, develop, and retain qualified nationals. However, there is a more fundamental problem: the characteristic ineptness of the subsidiaries in recruiting, developing, motivating, utilizing, and retaining competent nationals. This ineptness results largely from the difficulty most U.S. firms have in securing high-quality North Americans for overseas service and from their usual practice of assigning "second stringers" abroad on a career basis under the fallacious assumption that almost any second-rate North American will be more valuable than any available national, and that this will hold true indefinitely. This assumption blinds firms to the likelihood that heavy dependence on North Americans may harm rather than improve the efficiency of their subsidiaries, especially through its strong negative effects on the development, utilization, and retention of competent nationals.

There is a strong disposition by most overseas North Americans to protect their jobs at any cost. Job protection is a natural consequence of the assignment, on a career basis, of "second stringers" to better jobs abroad than they could generally hold in the United States. It is natural that they stubbornly refuse to implement the stated home-office policy of the "maximum possible use of nationals." The North Americans make little effort to recruit or develop nationals for (their) top posts. The low ceilings on opportunities for nationals with the consequent stifling effects on their motivation, morale, and effectiveness act as strong impediments to the efficient development, utilization, and retention of high-level nationals by most U.S. companies. The findings of this study strongly suggest that although inflows of high-level manpower which accompany U.S. investments in Latin America bring in important skills, they do so only at very high costs to the firms and to the host countries and that these inflows seriously impede the efficient development and utilization of national high-level human resources.

In summary, movements of high-level human resources both within and between countries have serious consequences for the development of underdeveloped areas. To the extent that a country wishes to reduce the great and increasing economic and social differences between areas within a country and among countries it must concern itself with these movements, for they seriously impede the prospects for more balanced development.

Chapter 6

Interactive Training Techniques for Improving Public Service in Latin America

Mark W. Cannon

The theme of this inquiry can be summarized as follows.[1] The training of Latin American public administrators should rely increasingly on research, development, and experimentation with participatory methods, i.e., those which emphasize relevant and meaningful student involvement.[2]

An emphasis on new techniques does not mean that lectures, which convey theory and information to help students to conceptualize, should be generally replaced. In fact, lectures can become more valuable if they summarize more research findings about Latin American public administration and behavior, much of which is available in doctoral dissertations and analytical reports read thus far by only a few teachers and researchers. Even with lectures at their best, however, training methods which simulate real life experience can be a critical complement.

Knowledge is only one factor influencing behavior. Conse-

1. The author expresses appreciation to many Latin American friends and associates whose observations stimulated this article and to IPA associates and others for comments and suggestions, particularly Laurence Birns, Laura de Coppet, Maria Maldonado, Jordan Schreiber, and Allan Austin, as well as to his patient and painstaking secretary, Karen Robertson.

2. For recent elaborate review of newer training techniques and diverse experience with them, see U.N. Institute for Training and Research, *Newer Techniques of Training Managers Concepts and Perspectives* (1971). The manuscript for chap. 1, "U.S.A. Experience with the Newer Training Techniques," by Sidney Mailick and Nancy Bord, was supplied to the author and was helpful on certain points. Other chapters of the UNITAR volume deal with experience in the developing countries and with specific countries or regions. There is no chapter explicitly devoted to Latin America. In addition to this volume, Occasional Papers are also being prepared for UNITAR on the management learning process.

quently, training programs should use techniques which affect the goals and values, motivations, analytical and decision-making skills, operational abilities, and self-confidence of the participants. A wide range of simulation techniques may reproduce in selective and condensed form the beneficial attributes of direct experience.

Training programs should include case studies, which require students to recommend and defend administrative and policy decisions generated by a concrete set of circumstances; supervised internships in well-organized agencies; role playing, where students carry out administrative practices; and human relations laboratories where small groups of participants explore each other's values and attitudes, hopefully learning to better understand and work with people whose values and motivations differ from their own and to recognize that the image each projects to others is often very different from the way he sees himself. Before discussing the characteristics and applications of specific techniques it is important to understand the needs they are intended to satisfy.

The Demand for Better-Trained Personnel

There is a critical relationship between education and national development. It is increasingly recognized that satisfactory development is related more closely to the production of skilled managers, technicians, and workers than to the construction of dams, roads, and the like. This trend in development strategies is characterized by Brown and Harbison as a "shift in demand from the product of ideas to the essential source of ideas."[3]

Education and training are especially important in the creation of high governmental competence in the low-income countries. Early enthusiasts for global administrative reforms came to recognize that structural changes often fail or produce only minimal benefits in the face of unchanged behavior patterns. In many in-

3. Douglas Brown and Frederick Harbison, *High Talent Manpower for Science and Industry* (Princeton, N.J.: Princeton Univ. Press, 1957), pp. 4–5.

stances, laws and systems are already theoretically adequate but have never been implemented at the operational level.

As an illustration of the problem, the need for the creation of more skilled managers is suggested by the results of a carefully constructed programing model for educational planning in Argentina. Depending upon which of a number of desirable economic goals was chosen, this model indicated that the supply of high-level manpower was either the only binding labor constraint in the economy or far more important than other types of labor. The optimal educational strategy indicated by the model was to produce as many university-trained managers and professionals as possible, even at the expense of simplifying the secondary-school system and deemphasizing commercial and vocational schools.[4]

Illustrative of low output due to managerial inadequacy, one old-line national housing agency, with an administrative overhead of more than 1400 employees and ample funds, not long ago completed in a single year fewer than 1400 dwelling units—all of them built by contractors. In the same country a more aggressively managed new agency with only 65 employees completed in the same year more new dwelling units than the other agency with 21 times as many employees. Owing to administrative complexities, an education ministry with a phenomenal 8,000 payroll clerks for 80,000 employees still required supplemental staff to make out payrolls; even then new employees had to wait months before their paychecks commenced, and old employees might wait up to a year after they had retired to receive retirement checks.

Recognition of the importance of training an expanded generation of administrative talents is reflected by the number of participants in the training programs of two institutions created in the early sixties with which the Institute of Public Administration (IPA), New York, has collaborated. The Peruvian National Office of Rationalization and Training in Public Administration (ONRAP) offered classes to 3,370 students between 1963 and 1968. Its successor, the School for Advanced Public Administra-

---

4. Irma Adelman and E. Thorbeck, eds., *The Theory and Design of Economic Development* (Washington: Johns Hopkins Press, 1966).

tion Studies (ESAP) has improved the quality and programing of its courses and projects a figure of 610 students from middle and top management in 1972 as well as a larger number through its extension program. The Foundation for Community Development and Municipal Improvement (Fundacomun) in Venezuela has provided training seminars for more than six thousand municipal officials. An older institution, the Brazilian School of Public Administration (EBAP), founded in 1952, has the remarkable record of having provided a four-year public-administration program for more than 1,000 students and having provided short courses to more than 3,000 civil servants.[5]

Need for Reassessing Traditional Methods of Preparation for the Public Service

Do traditional education and training generate confidence among leadership that increased productivity in public agencies is the result? The answer appears negative, regardless of whether the education and training of Latin American public administrators were conducted in the United States or in Latin American universities and institutes.

As the new Latin American nationalism advances, regimes which feel increasingly compelled to show results, may grow increasingly critical of bureaucracies recruited, oriented, organized and trained by traditional methods. This is illustrated by Peru, where President Velasco Alvarado frequently attacks the bureaucracy as self-serving, indifferent to public needs, and unproductive.[6]

Why is there skepticism concerning the efficacy of higher education in developing administrative ability? To begin with, there is no doubt that North American universities offer Latin students a broadening intercultural experience, valuable information, and disciplinary tools to analyze administrative problems

5. Information from EBAP Dean Kleber Nascimento through Arnaldo Pessoa, Deputy Director, Division of Training, Inter-American Development Bank.
6. Such attacks were reported in the Peruvian press 3 October 1970 and other times.

and their social and political context. Nevertheless, almost no U.S. universities have yet developed specific courses in Latin American development administration, and it is difficult to relate course work to Latin American administrative reality. A significant but little recognized factor in public-administration training for citizens of the United States is the widespread utilization of model managers who provide early in-service training. For example, a student who studies budgeting, municipal problems, or organization theory while at the university is not equipped by his studies to perform as a budget analyst, city manager, or management consultant upon graduation; nor is this expected of him. He is normally placed under a competent administrator, from whom he learns the techniques of practical application of concepts he studied in the classroom. The widespread existence of model administrators who supervise the experience of recent university graduates is implicit in the U.S. training programs but is rare in developing countries. Foreign participant trainees who study administration in U.S. universities are generally expected to perform on the job as soon as they return to Latin America. There are not many model administrators in their systems to whom they can turn for assistance in making the transition from academia to reality. The result is that young professionals learn to function within a context of traditional methods—a world largely removed from that of their training.

Secondly, in Latin America, universities do not emphasize the production of skills and professions which stimulate development, but emphasize traditional prestigious professions such as law, medicine, and architecture. In Mexico there are some 5,000 architecture students, although many trained architects are unemployed or working in other fields.

An education task force of the OAS contended:

> The university has failed to keep pace with the social and economic evolution of the Latin-American countries, and has made little effort to promote the "new" provisions needed for accelerating development. Although there is a critical shortage of trained, high-level manpower, Latin-American universities continue to emphasize the traditional professions, many

of which are neutral to development and have failed to train enough persons capable of leadership or to contribute to the mobility of societies.[7]

A study by Richard Fehnel discovered that national and regional planning on manpower needs in Chile had little discernible impact on university student admission policies, curriculum revision, and program development.[8]

Many universities and institutes have only part-time faculties and use outdated lecture-memorization methods which do not encourage students to deal critically with the materials given them. Classroom hours in universities and institutes are too often not complemented by relevant observation and outside reading. Classes in the area of government and public administration, when available, are likely to be highly legalistic and normative, with little opportunity for the student to gain an insight into the actual functioning of government in the society. Administrative training methods convey formalistic descriptions rather than realistic appraisals of administrative behavior and methods of improving performance.[9]

Teaching techniques are not developing in the students the analytical, organizational, and managerial skills which characterize effective administrators.

The Case for Participatory Methods

The major premise underlying the case for participatory training is self-evident and compelling: skills and behavior patterns cannot be learned entirely from listening but must come also from experience. The "transfer space law" suggests that the amount of learning transferred from a training to a working environment is related to the similarity of the two situations.[10] None of us would

7. OAS Education Task Force, as cited by Gabriel Betancur-Mejia, "Education: Backbone of the Alliance for Progress," *Americas*, Sept. 1963, p. 4.

8. Conclusions of a Ph.D. dissertation, Cornell University, 1972.

9. Fred W. Riggs, *Administration in Developing Countries* (Boston: Houghton-Mifflin, 1966), p. 10.

10. Carl Williams, "One to One Training of Top Management," *Training and Development Journal* 24, no. 8 (Aug. 1970): 40.

permit a surgeon to remove a brain tumor if the surgeon had only heard lectures on the appropriate techniques. Few people would ride with a chauffeur who had heard lectures on the process of driving, but had never actually driven. No inundation of depositors should be expected in a bank whose staff had only heard lectures on how to make sound loans and operate a bank. In fields such as development administration, where it is desired that executives improve upon traditional methods and techniques, the establishment of new work habits can be encouraged by simulation exercises geared to the culture, yet providing experience in a model decision-making environment.

Another unavoidable premise is that people are likely to learn when they enjoy what they are doing. They are happier and more productive in their work when they are participating and feel involved. Thus, students can be expected to be satisfied and receptive when they participate, whereas heavy use of nonparticipatory methods can leave students dulled, unhappy, and frustrated. The validity of these premises is reinforced by the felt needs of students. This was brought forcibly to the attention of the author several years ago when five Latin Americans, enrolled in master's degree programs at the University of Puerto Rico, pleaded for extensions of their fellowships in order to have internships in Puerto Rican agencies corresponding to their specialties. Their course work had provided useful background, but the students did not feel they knew how to function with confidence as budget analysts, personnel officers, etc., as they would be called upon to do when they returned home. The demands of these students for practical experience have been replicated by many other students attending varied institutions, not only in this hemisphere but in other regions.[11]

Other evidence for the validity of these premises is the success of postgraduate business-administration programs. Schools with such programs have widely concluded that lectures on prin-

11. As an illustration of this point, the author was invited to conduct a discussion of training techniques with a new class of more than fifty mid-career Egyptian students at their Institute of Public Administration. After considerable discussion they voted a unanimous preference for shifting to the case study method, with more than one-third of class time devoted to case analysis if good materials were available.

ciples of organization and administration are insufficient to convert students into dynamic entrepreneurs. The schools have developed and use techniques which force the student to cope with the challenges of the business world in the classroom. They recognize that theoretical explanations cannot assure the development within a person of the values, experience, and behavior patterns necessary for effective functioning. Drawing on techniques of the psychologist and sociologist, together with analyses of the dynamics of different work habitats, schools of business administration have created case studies and human relations laboratories and continue to develop new techniques to simulate working conditions in their courses and thus prepare their students to assume managerial responsibilities. Since businessmen typically have a hardheaded attitude toward training, it is noteworthy that students with postgraduate training of this type are in high demand by successful business enterprises and rise rapidly to the top, not only in the United States but also in Latin America and other regions of the world.

Surely training programs which require students continuously to make independent decisions in lifelike situations and defend them on the basis of fact and logic are most likely to produce what President Howard Johnson of M.I.T. called "the willingness to take responsibility and to be judged by results . . . [which] really distinguishes the concept of management from the muffled impersonal response of a bureaucracy."[12] This statement reflects Peter Drucker's notions of management by objectives which have had a wide influence on business practices.

The Challenge to Latin America

The challenge of experimentation and research with participatory techniques is complicated; yet it has a potential for valuable results for a number of reasons. (i) Unlike most other transitional societies, the countries of Latin America do not have modern ad-

12. Address to the Council for International Progress in Management, Montreal, 21 June 1967, entitled "The Challenge of Management Training and Development."

ministrative systems installed by colonial powers, since most won independence approximately a century and a half ago. Thus their need for public administrative improvement is more intense than in some economically less developed countries. (ii) In spite of some efforts to experiment with newer training techniques, there continues to be an overwhelming reliance on lectures (as revealed by a conference of twenty-five Latin American administrative-training executives sponsored by the Inter-American Development Bank in March 1970), so that there is widespread opportunity for pedagogical reform. (iii) Social and economic changes taking place in contemporary Latin America may be increasing the demand for reforming unproductive traditional bureaucratic practices. Illustrative of these changes is the rapidly expanding number of people with high school and university education, the restless, growing middle class, the growing number of foreign-trained people moving into leadership positions, the gradual expansion of the industrial sector, the demand for equality under the law,[13] the wave of national insistence on economic independence, and the movement of immigrants and their children, as well as of indigenous people, into leadership. Most of these groups have different values from the traditional perception of a government job as an escape from work, a product of favoritism, an opportunity to live in an imaginary world rather than a practical world of application and implementation, and as a setting where one can indulge excess pride of the kind that inhibits communication and objective evaluation of performance.

If the time is ripe for change in Latin America and if resources can be made available for major experimentation with new approaches to training, the results could provide insights into many questions concerning training effectiveness, could freshly illuminate comparative administration, and could provide useful leadership for other transitional societies, many of whose problems are similar.

13. According to an interview with Kalman Silvert, as yet unpublished survey research revealed that all of nineteen socioeconomic groups in Mexico selected equality before the law as the top priority of five social goals (interview, April 1971). This suggests at minimum ambivalence and at maximum hostility to the favoritism of public agencies.

Even in the United States, where novel training methods are widely used, hard data are limited on the substantive impact of various types of executive development programs. Relatively little is known, for example, about how participants in different programs change the allocation of the only resource which they cannot expand—their time; about the methods they use to identify and solve major problems; about their choices among types of men to fill vacancies; about their relations with subordinates and with other executives; and about the effects of these changes on the communication of important information, employee productivity, and organizational morale.[14] Although it would require enormous will and investment, Latin American countries could be among the first areas to produce consequential answers to such questions as well as to other hard questions, such as how to retrain old-line trainers from traditional to newer techniques.

The slowness of Latin American agencies to adopt the Weberian elements of continuity, stability, and a disciplined, supervised, and integrated system of division of labor is partly due to the culturally antithetical loss of dignity, seeming enslavement, and impersonalism that they perceive in advanced bureaucracies. Yet this traditional exaltation of the person in Latin America could contribute creatively to the development of what Erich Fromm refers to as a desirable new "non-bureaucratic humanist management."[15] Small-group training methods could well be utilized as laboratories in the effort to achieve such an experimental evolution.

Although many basic answers must come from research, some major apparent advantages and disadvantages of various training techniques are identified below with illustrations of their use and comments that relate specific methods to typical Hispanic American cultural characteristics.

14. A less complex method: testing of attitudes before and after an executive development program using different small-group techniques revealed a noticeable reduction in authoritarian outlook as a result of the seminar. Kendall O. Price and Kent Lloyd, *Improving Police-Community Relations Through Leadership Training: A Behavioral Science Approach* (Creative Management Research and D:velopment, 1967), pp. 30–36.
15. Erich Fromm, "Thoughts on Bureaucracy," *Management Science* 16, no. 12 (Aug. 1970): 699–705.

Lecture Method

The traditional lecture method enjoys the advantage of being familiar and comfortable to educators, largely protecting them from confrontation or criticism. Particularly with the aural and personalist traditions in Latin America, lectures may be more emphatic and persuasive than written materials. When trainees are light readers, good lectures can summarize considerable professional literature. When there are large groups to be trained, the lecture method can be cheap because classes can be large. The cost of training materials and facilities and necessary preparation time may be kept at a minimum.

The beneficial impact of lectures would be greatly enhanced if the rare Latin American lecturers who can meaningfully summarize and relate the findings of research and analysis of Latin American public administration could have their lectures more widely disseminated. Among other techniques, this could be done by a major expansion development and use of the now scant supply of educational films and television.

There are, however, objections to sole reliance upon the lecture system:

(1) It is not action-oriented. It does not afford the practice essential to the learning of new skills.

(2) It is a low-keyed approach which does not necessarily stimulate the attentiveness nor continuously activate the involvement of the audience.

(3) It generally reinforces a memorization tradition in Latin America, whereas the formulation of a much stronger analytic tradition is needed.

(4) Training classes in Latin America are usually of intermediate or small size. Therefore, the efficiency of the lecture method in handling large groups often goes unrealized.

(5) The lecture system normally requires little of the students by way of advance preparation and involvement. A student may selectively turn on or off the flow of information.

(6) Heavy reliance on lectures establishes an essentially one-

way communication system which prevents the lectures themselves from being enriched by the stimulus of students, unlike techniques involving their interaction.

(7) The authoritarian lecturer reinforces the tradition of the authoritarian administrator whose style is to make decisions with little interaction with his subordinates.

The lecture method alone, therefore, is not the best training system for decisionmakers and administrators, who need supplementary training designed to develop decision making and managerial skills, even though lectures combined with reading assignments can provide necessary background information and conceptual frameworks and could usefully occupy a substantial part of the training time.

Discussions and Workshops

A committee meeting in Latin America is likely to turn into a monologue of some authority figure, or if it utilizes discussion, to evolve into a prolonged, somewhat random set of opportunities for individual expression rather than a serious and interrelated progressive elaboration of relevant data and analysis leading to a rational decision.

A major goal of discussions and workshops in training, consequently, should be to teach the methods and value of group participation in decision making. A technique used to accomplish this by RCA's in-house management-training program is to provide a set of problems for which there are explicit answers. Both individual and group consensus responses are obtained, the latter proving to be more accurate than the average of individual responses.[16]

To achieve the goal of making discussion an expeditious and useful part of decision making, training discussions should be based upon high-quality lectures (and/or carefully selected reading assignments), appropriately selected groups, and clear goals that should stress written end products. A major problem is

16. Michael C. Jensen, "Multimedia Class," *New York Times,* 17 Jan. 1971.

the scarcity of trained or natural leaders who can avoid creativity-quelling authoritarianism and guide discussions so that obscure points are clarified, multifaceted aspects of problems are put into perspective, and the quality and clarity of expression are improved.

Consider the Executive Conference Program of the United Arab Republic, founded less than a decade ago. This was greeted with skepticism by executives because it suggested that they needed training. However, the program centered on the discussion and formulation of recommendations on the importance of national policy and administrative issues. The quality of preparatory work, conference techniques, and staff was such that there were soon several candidacies for each opening. The program took root and ultimately affected—typically in six-week seminars —some three to four hundred government ministers, undersecretaries, directors general, and top public-corporation executives annually. Few developing countries now have as many high officials who have been through such stimulating developmental programs, programs that provide unique insights into national and personal executive problems.[17]

One reason why the UAR was able to carry out this high-quality program was the staff base which had been previously built up. They could select the best of dozens of staff with doctorates in administrative sciences from British and American universities. In contrast, until recently there have been virtually no natives from Hispanic-American countries with doctorates in public administration working in Hispanic-American countries. Ildemaro Martinez, with a doctorate from Syracuse and now working at IESA in Venezuela, is among the first of a small new group.

Brazil, which has more foreign graduate-trained professors in public administration (as a result of the University of Southern California/AID program) than the Hispanic countries, uses practical problem-solving discussion techniques at the Brazilian School of Public Administration (EBAP) and the Inter-American

17. Based on a review of ECP for the Ford Foundation, by the author, June 1969.

School of Public Administration (EIAP) of the Getúlio Vargas Foundation. A solution-oriented workshop approach is also used by the Inter-American Development Bank for training seminars in industrial project preparation.

A special form of discussion group in use as a training technique is the well-known syndicate method developed at the Administrative Staff College, Henley-on-Thames, England, and used in executive development programs in areas as distant as the University of the Philippines. The method is of value in quickly training experienced administrators, not in theory, but in improved practice. Training participants are men with ten to fifteen years of experience who usually have diverse academic backgrounds. Groups or syndicates of nine or ten members are formed and assigned to specific tasks. The group membership is deliberately selected so as to constitute a heterogeneous mix of talents, background, and specialized experience.

The college makes its staff, publications resources, and facilities available to the syndicates. Periodic progress reports are made to the faculty and course participants, and free interchanges take place. The principal of the Administrative Staff College underscores the importance of the teaching method when he says the curriculum is adapted to the method rather than the reverse.

The Case Study Method

Following World War I, the Harvard Business School shifted from discussions of principles of business administration to analyses of specific cases. This decision was influenced by the shift of law schools from teaching the principles of jurisprudence to the examination and analysis of legal cases, and a similar change to case analysis in medical training. The case approach spread. It has become a basic training tool in American business schools, and since World War II has been adopted in quality business schools around the world.

A case study may be defined as "an administrative experience based on actual circumstances and recorded either in writing or presented verbally for study and for which there is more than one possible outcome. The study requires the assessment of all factors involved and provides scope for the student to suggest an approach and solution even where these may differ from the ones actually taken in the circumstances recorded."[18] Students must be prepared to defend the decisions they recommend against the critical onslaughts of fellow students. The faculty discussion leader plays a nonauthoritarian role and avoids interposing his preferred solutions. He raises questions when necessary, and guides discussion. Students come to see the weaknesses of their proposals and consequently learn to deal more thoroughly and skillfully with the interrelated parts of a decision matrix. In discussions, participants bring to bear various experiences, thereby helping individual students develop interdisciplinary approaches. By simulating the making of a greater variety of complicated decisions than a successful executive is likely to make in his entire life, students gain not only analytical finesse but also self-confidence, which helps assure their success in the real world.

The case study method involves a fairly radical shift in methods in Latin America; the attitudes of students and faculty members will need adjustment if the method is to work. Several members of the Harvard Business School faculty found when they were leading case discussions at the Central American Institute of Business Administration (INCAE) in Managua, Nicaragua, that the reactions to case study by Latin students differed from those of their North American counterparts. The Central American students were more restrained and less spontaneous. To question the judgment of their professor or, publicly, their fellow students was felt to be a breach of etiquette. Nor did they wish to expose themselves to possible ridicule by going out on a limb in taking a position on a case problem. Another professor who experimented with public-administration cases in Colombia noted that the typical student reactions sometimes led to a superficial unanimity of the class based on factors extraneous to a thorough exploration of facts and their implications. Henry Gomez, Aca-

18. M. Bennion, "The Teaching Function," in *Institutes of Public Administration in the Commonwealth, 1963* (London: Royal Institute of Public Administration, 1963), p. 34.

demic Dean of the Instituto de Estudios Superiores de Administración (IESA) notes that culture shock is also observed in Venezuelan students when they enter IESA in Venezuela. Those from the cosmopolitan upper class adjust more quickly and readily than those coming from the rising middle class.

To counter this outlook, one Harvard professor at INCAE altered his usual case study procedure. He instituted a "shock treatment" in which several faculty members joined a case discussion and in front of the students argued against their colleagues' viewpoints. It was allowed to sink in for the students that the participants retained their congeniality after the heated exchange. After this episode, the case discussions among students were more animated and more productive.

In fact, case studies supplemented by human relations laboratories and games occupy an estimated 85 percent of teaching activity, and after students overcome their disconcertedness they relish cases and demand skillful professorial performance, according to INCAE rector Dr. Ernesto Cruz.[19] Since its founding in 1963, INCAE has given some 400 executives a six-week advanced management training program. The third graduating class from the two-year master of business administration program in June 1971 was expected to add forty-five to the forty-seven graduates from the two preceding classes. Strong selling efforts plus the effectiveness of the program demonstrated by its alumni have resulted in growing support for INCAE and growing demand for its graduates, particularly on the part of international corporations. The sufficiency of local backing will be tested following the termination of AID support, expected in 1972. An estimated 10 to 15 percent of the graduates go into the public sector, which is fewer than come from public employment. However, there is an increasing student interest in government work, which can be harvested if future salaries can be made more attractive.[20]

The Advanced School of Business Administration (ESAN) in Lima, with which the Stanford Business School worked from 1963 through 1970, has also succeeded in using cases as a domi-

19. Dr. Ernesto Cruz, interview, May 1971.
20. Ibid.

nant teaching method. This school gives an eleven-month program and a "magister," or master's degree, to some sixty-five graduates annually. There has been high demand for the graduates, and many have risen rapidly in their corporations. Government corporations are also stepping up their demand for ESAN-trained managers. Corporate top executives generally feel that ESAN products have problem-solving and decision-making ability and a willingness to try based on their self-confidence, far exceeding in these qualities their competitors who lack the case-oriented business-school approach.[21] Associate Dean Thomas Graves, of the Harvard Business School, believes that modern case-study-oriented business schools of Latin America, which are now established in all of the large countries except Argentina,[22] are beginning to strengthen many Latin American firms by providing competent middle management to fill a void which often existed between brilliant and urbane business elites and the workers below.[23] It is not clear, however, that the analytical skills are matched by superior ability to motivate and inspire subordinates. In some cases, pride over new skills and a glamorous degree may have widened the gulf separating business-school graduates from subordinates.

In spite of major adjustment problems encountered by both students and professors, the experience with the case method in Latin American business schools demonstrates both its feasibility and effectiveness for the following reasons.

(1) Students are forced to get involved with practical problems rather than allowed to avoid them, and they become emotionally committed to producing good solutions.

(2) Students become widely acquainted with different industries, product lines, and problems and their resolution in different circumstances; this array of experience can then be focused on any specific situation.

(3) Students learn how to cope with uncertainty so as to reduce the margin of error.

21. Interview with Sterling Sessions, former Chief of Party of the Stanford team in Lima and presently faculty member at the Stanford Business School, May 1971.
22. An executive development program in Argentina (IDEA) may soon expand into a business school.
23. Associate Dean Thomas Graves, interview, May 1971.

(4) The case method helps identify and screen out students unsuited for managerial careers.

(5) As they observe the improvement in their own analytical abilities during the course of their experience with cases, students gain a confidence which creates an enthusiasm for contending with real problems on the job. By contrast, others may seek to avoid problems for fear that they will appear inadequate because of their inability to solve them. Considering typical Latin American pride, such concern can produce escapism. The importance of confidence, and the related enthusiasm to deal with problems, cannot be overstressed.

(6) The case method requires that faculty members earn respect, and this demand stimulates them continually to sharpen their abilities and improve the program.

The experience of business schools suggests that traditional culture is not an insuperable obstacle to the case method, and that similar commitment could probably result in successful adoption of the case method in public administration training. Not only Latin American, but also U.S. public administration programs tend to use cases only peripherally, and then often as descriptive material rather than as exercises in decision making. Consequently, Latin American students from the region would have to enroll in U.S. business-school programs to learn the technique. There is no evidence that this has commenced to happen. The Harvard International Teachers Program, which trains foreign professors in the case technique, has records of some 69 Latin Americans of a total of 240 who have attended since its inception in 1958. Not one was sponsored by a Latin American public-administration training program, in contrast to some other regions.[24] A less thorough inquiry at Stanford University, which operates the International Center for the Advancement of Management Education (ICAME), similarly failed to identify graduates teaching in Latin American public-administration programs.

24. Information supplied by Michael Passage, Assistant Administrative Director, International Teachers Program, May 1971. The sixty-nine students came from institutions in fifteen countries. The following were the principal suppliers: Nicaragua, 16; Brazil, 14; Chile, 12; Venezuela, 5; and Mexico, 4. The ITP formerly offered an eleven-month course at Harvard. Since 1970 they have offered a nine-week summer program in Europe followed by an optional semester of independent study at Harvard.

A start has been made, however, by ESAP in Lima, two of whose professors are graduates of ESAN and employ the case study method in their own teaching.[25] Thus, although skillful teaching of cases requires a major specialized effort at faculty development, there is little evidence that Latin American public-administration centers have seriously commenced this.

Another need, if the case method or any other training method is to be effective in Latin America, is professors with practical experience in improving government administration who could help students bridge the gap between their limited experience and the intimate understanding of the details of agency problems. Dean Stephen Bailey, of the Maxwell School of Syracuse, underscores the value of professorial field experience when he says that "the practical experiences we acquire have important effects upon our students. We not only help to motivate them as we practice what we preach; we bring at least flashes of social wisdom—what Woodrow Wilson called the 'air of affairs'—into the classroom."[26] A problem in Latin America has been that while many professors have a wealth of experience in politics, few have had high-quality government consulting experience which has helped achieve administrative modernization. However, in institutions such as Insora at the University of Chile, and the School of Public Administration of the University of Minas Gerais, professors blend consulting experience with teaching. This is also true of some governmental training agencies such as the Central Office of Organization and Methods (OCOM) in Chile.

Another problem in developing the case approach in Latin America is a lack of published public administration cases. A bibliography of cases relevant to Latin America published in 1966 identified 260 cases from Latin America and 343 others which might be of interest in Latin America, many of which had been translated into Spanish or Portuguese.[27] However, virtually all of

25. These are Lt. Colonel Samuel Ureña and Engineer Felipe Diez.
26. Stephen Kemp Bailey, "The Social Sciences and Public Affairs," in *Public Affairs Education and the University*, ed. Gerard J. Mangone (Syracuse, N.Y.: Maxwell Graduate School, Syracuse University, 1963), p. 10.
27. Harvard University Graduate School of Business Administration, *Bibliography: Cases and Other Materials for the Teaching of Business Administration in Developing Countries: Latin America* (Boston: Harvard Univ. Oct. 1966).

these were business cases, few of which were directly relevant to government training. With a considerable output of new cases, particularly by ESAN and INCAE, the number of Latin American cases had undoubtedly more than doubled by 1971. In Brazil EBAP published some cases—e.g., Frank Sherwood, *O aumento do preço do aço da C.S.N.* (1966), and Danin Logo, *Estudos de organização—dois casos* (1965). These cases deal with such topics as a rise in steel prices, reorganization of local government, and a new system of administrative analysis for the federal railways.[28] Apparently the first major book of fairly specific Latin American cases will be edited by Dean E. Mann and Franklin Tugwell and is entitled *Politics and Economic Policy in Venezuela: Cases in the Management of Change.*[29] Numerous cases could be ferreted out of scattered doctoral dissertations on Latin America, and other possible short-run sources of supply for cases are translations and adaptations of selected public administration cases in the U.S. and developing countries.[30]

In view of cultural and governmental differences, such approaches could only be short-run; for the longer run, only skilled writers working with local cases can supply the needs. Developing the specialized skill of case writing, as with case teaching, may require sending people to top U.S. business schools, or possibly transferring experts from Latin American business schools to public-administration institutes.

Writers of cases in many development-administration situations would do well to delineate the four key elements suggested by

The principal countries with which Latin American cases dealt were Brazil, 92; Mexico, 76; Chile, 26; Peru, 15; Colombia, 8; Venezuela, 6; and Panama, 6.

28. More than a hundred volumes have been published by EBAP.

29. The cases were completed in 1971 and publication was expected in 1972, although the publisher had not been agreed upon by mid-1971.

30. Illustrative of cases available, the first book of Nigerian cases is D. J. Murray, *The Work of Administration in Nigeria* (London: Hutchinson, 1969). Samuel Humes and D. J. Murray expect a book of local government cases in Nigeria to be published by the University of Alabama Press in 1972. The interest of the Royal Institute of Public Administration in cases has resulted in two books of British cases in F. M. G. Willson and Gerald Rhodes, *Administrators in Action* (London: George Allen, 1961, 1965), vols. I, II. A third book of African cases has also been published through RIPA. Other cases have been prepared in Ghana and agricultural project evaluation and management cases (some of which show an extraordinarily high benefit-to-cost ratio) are being prepared by Earl Kulp through an IPA/New York contract with AID in Uganda. Numerous U.S. cases are available through the Inter-University Case Study Program.

Garth Jones after reviewing 190 case studies. These essentials are an agent of change, a client system, a goal and the evidence of tactics, and strategies used to affect change.[31]

One method of developing cases fairly quickly, though somewhat amateurishly, is to require the writing of cases by competent students with government experience, under supervision of a skilled professor. In Latin America, such cases might normally have to deal with previous administrations (which would make the search for data less threatening to incumbent high executives) or be disguised. Another approach would be to develop fictitious cases dealing with well-known problems and prepared by authors highly knowledgeable of the local scene. Though efficient, this lacks the advantage of unearthing new information which may produce fresh insights and assure greater validity.

The case study method has other limitations aside from the scarcity of effective class leaders and the shortage of suitable material. The most significant of these limitations is that decisions are easier to make when one does not have to bear the consequences and when most of the relevant data has been collated. Discussion of written cases is not a complete substitute for real experience. Another problem is that students may overgeneralize from a few cases. The case technique, of necessity, slights the theoretical grounding which is a basic underpinning of expertise, in order to focus upon action-oriented decision making in complex situations.[32] Accordingly, it is important to sustain a simultaneous theory flow through reading and lectures which put cases in a perspective.

The case study method has been explored in some detail because its potential impact appears high and business-school experience now gives evidence that cultural constraints can be overcome. Nevertheless, it must also be recognized that a major development investment is needed and will probably require

31. Garth N. Jones, *Planned Organizational Change: A Set of Working Documents* (Los Angeles: Univ. of Southern California, 1964).
32. An interesting discussion of the case method approach in public administration is found in Edwin A. Bock, James W. Fesler, Harold Stein, and Dwight Waldo, eds., *Essays on the Case Method in Public Administration*, The Inter-University Case Program (International Institute of Administrative Sciences, 1962).

organization and financing on a regional basis, with numerous institutes committed to the program, if beneficial use of cases is to spread very far.

A variation of the case study method has been developed which has potential for overcoming some limitations of the conventional approach and which might reduce cultural problems. This is the "incident process" developed by Paul and Faith Pigors of the Massachusetts Institute of Technology.[33] In contrast to the usual case method, only a "bare incident is reported to the group." Other information is known only to the discussion leader.[34] Further information is made available only as requested by individual group members and is given in the form of handouts to the entire group. This is the fact-finding stage. Next comes the pinpointing of the main problem and subproblem. Then written solutions are prepared by each member, followed by group discussion and the airing of differing viewpoints. The incident-process approach may be particularly relevant to Latin American training needs. It places the student in a realistically simulated situation in which he must determine what facts are needed and practicably obtainable. This can closely approximate the on-the-job situation, where he must generate the facts himself. The incident process may also reduce the importance of cultural values which block participative training. It includes diverse means of expression (direct questioning, written analysis, verbal presentation). For a given participant, one form of communication may be freer from restraint than another. Also, because the material is so unadorned with peripheral matter, adaptation to the Latin American setting may be easily accomplished.

Another approach, which also has the benefits of the incident process in asking students to simulate fact gathering as well as analysis, is to bring special witnesses in to respond to students' inquiries.

A technique suggested by the Royal Institute is the utilization

33. For a description of this and other techniques see *Guidelines for the Training of Professional and Technical Personnel in the Administration and Management of Development Functions* (New York: U.N. Public Administration Division, 1971).
34. *Developing Managerial Competence: Changing Concepts—Emerging Practices* (New York: National Industrial Conference Board, Inc., 1964), p. 80.

of both sound and unsound cases of decision making. The focus on mistakes can often be at least as instructive as examples of success.[35] Other variations of the case method include the use of short concise problems and the use of tapes, cassettes, and records, as well as a variety of visual presentations, to heighten realism.

In a somewhat related area, the American Management Association has recently revised its basic management training programs for personnel of private U.S. corporations to include current educational techniques. The new in-company course makes use of the "visual case study," not to solve problems, but to portray them. Eight filmed dramatizations illustrate how the basic principles of management can solve day-to-day operational difficulties.[36]

Role Playing

Role playing is a technique which has come into vogue since World War II. Group members act out prescribed and commonly assumed reverse roles; that is, a subordinate may play the role of a supervisor, and vice versa. The intent is to dramatize to onlookers as well as to the actors themselves, in a deeply felt way, the emotional frame of reference as well as the intellectual horizon of a person in a specified position. Human relations problems are central to this technique.

The Harvard Business School professor referred to earlier indicated that during his tour in Managua, he intervened in role-playing verbal interchanges more frequently than at Harvard. He continually felt the need to soften critical remarks by role players which he perceived were blows to their Latin pride. The need for this softening influence of a discussion leader was similarly displayed by the results of an incident in which an IPA staff member organized a role-playing situation. Several Latin Americans were asked to assume the roles of garbage-truck drivers, each of whom wanted to be assigned one of a few newly purchased trucks. Each argued his own merits on the basis of a different rationale—the

---

35. Bennion.
36. Ferdinand Setaro, interview, American Management Association, Inc.

best safety record, the longest tenure in the sanitation department, and so on. The interesting result of this experiment was that these Latin Americans turned out to be more combative than North Americans put into similar situations. The emotional involvement was so intense that the hostility generated prevented some participants from speaking to fellow players for weeks afterward. One must not overlook the inherent danger of such a result; too much extraneous emotion could compromise the original learning purpose.

Another question to be explored, in areas where leadership is accepted on such traditional grounds as family ties, common geographic backgrounds, personal style, wealth, and social status, is the effect of reversing roles. Can this produce emotional reactions? Are role-playing statements by other actors likely to be perceived as personal attacks? Evaluation of such experiences may contribute to adapting training techniques to cultural values. This does not mean that training technique must be the prisoner of traditional values. These values are undergoing major alterations in all transitional societies. Much-needed societal research in Latin America can help distinguish between the values to which the training design should be submissive and the values for which training should accelerate processes of change, already under way or needed, that contribute to development.[37]

In-basket tests are a type of administrative role playing which may be useful in training, but which could also be used as a research method to understand cultural influences on management. Participants are given a job title and a description of a setting. They then are given the typical contents of an in-basket for that position. Within a prescribed time they must act upon the contents. Their performance is later analyzed and evaluated. Understandably this procedure requires instructors qualified to supervise the game and evaluate the results. It is most easily carried out when participants are experienced administrators rather than young students.

Norman Frederiksen, of the Research Division of Educational

37. Mark W. Cannon, "Program Implementation in Latin America: The Impact of Cultural Factors," presented at National Conference of American Society for Public Administration, Denver, 19 April 1971.

Testing Service, described and analyzed this approach in a study of performance in educational administration.[38] In this test 232 participants separately played the role of a new principal of a school. Enough information about this school and community was provided that subjects could reasonably be expected to take action on the administrative problems presented to them. After orientation, the test, which consisted of facsimiles of letters, memoranda, and the other typical material found in administrators' desks, was begun. A certain number of problems were included in the in-basket material. Upon completion (after a specified time period) each subject left an envelope full of memos, letters, reminders, instructions to his secretary, appointments calendar, and the like. The different modes of behavior and performance were then analyzed and related to differences of sex, age, educational level, and years of experience. Factor analyses were made and scores were correlated. Factors included such aspects as discussing before acting, maintaining organizational relationships, directing the work of others, responding to outsiders.

A test approach of this type, in addition to its use as a training method, may provide a means to identify the weight of cultural factors upon the administrative function. Subjects could include subgroups of Latins and North Americans. The same factor-analysis technique could be used to determine how different cultural systems relate to different factors of administrative performance. The values, as identified, might in turn aid in determining the adaptations needed in transferring training methods to the Latin American cultural setting. The approach could be particularly useful if research is done on the men whom evidence shows to be highly effective in their respective cultural milieus, in order to show how model administrators in different countries function. Further in-basket tests could serve to evaluate the adaptations which appeared to be recommended.

38. Norman Frederiksen, "In-Basket Tests and Factors in Administrative Performance," *Simulation in Social Science: Readings,* ed. Harold Guetzkow (Englewood Cliffs, N.J.: Prentice-Hall, 1962).

Human Relations Laboratories

A sense of exalted status accompanying a position of authority, a mistrust for peers and subordinates outside one's circle of personal influence, a sense of the inviolability of one's personal dignity, a readiness to take offense, a formalism emphasizing appearances—all these contribute to deference to authority and politeness which inhibit open communication of real feelings in Latin America. These features also contribute to lack of skillful supervision which might help develop employees and mobilize their energy, skills, and commitment to institutional goals. Instead, supervisory situations sometimes become anarchic, partly because confrontation is avoided, or they become one-way authoritarian command relationships.

Expanding the openness of communication, increasing awareness of other people's feelings, and expanding trust and cooperation are characteristic goals of human relations laboratories. Such laboratories typically take the form of sensitivity training in which people are removed from familiar organizational arrangements and social relationships and examine themselves and their interactions.[39] Thus, this technique emphasizes human relations processes rather than the substance of decision making.

Laboratories encourage participants to express and probe feelings and attitudes of themselves and other members of the training group (T-group). Candid discussions of such questions as how and why a person impresses others as being shy or aggressive, polite or discourteous, friendly or detached, sympathetic or arrogant, industrious or lazy, help the persons being discussed understand better their own underlying assumptions and the impact of their behavior on others. It also helps participants become more aware of the wide variety of values of others.

Objectives vary with the trainer and the situation. Robert Golembiewski emphasizes three levels of learning from the laboratory approach—self-understanding, transfer of this learn-

39. Mailick and Bord.

ing to improve working relations, and restructuring an organization into a more rewarding one for its members.[40]

Mailick and Bord recently observed that there has been a shift in emphasis away from the dynamics of the group—how participation and leadership styles contributed to a hindered group progress. In its twenty years of development the technique has come to focus more on personal feelings, styles of relating to others, and achievement of insight into oneself by being open to what others say about their reactions to him.[41] A cardinal goal of the movement is to help trainees realize that mutual trust is the foundation of team effort, and that dealing openly with conflict helps establish trust. The laboratory movement stems from positive assumptions about human beings. Douglas McGregor contrasts these—theory X—with the perceptions of man characteristic of traditional authoritarian administration—theory Y. According to theory Y, the average human prefers security and direction to responsibility and independence. He dislikes and avoids work and therefore must be coerced into putting out adequate effort for organizational objectives. According to theory X, physical and mental effort in work is as natural as play and rest, and there are many achievement satisfactions and rewards beyond the fear of punishment which induce commitment to objectives and labor.[42]

There are limitations to the evaluation of laboratory training, due to lack of empirical theory, insufficient research, and design limitations. However, scientists increasingly recognize the importance of overcoming obstacles to objective research which isolates the effect of the training variable and identifies the long-range consequences on the work environment.

After some initial frustration, most participants enjoy the training and find it revealing. Executives tend to be better liked in their organizations after returning from human relations laboratories. One careful study concluded that laboratory-trained exec-

40. Robert Golembiewski, "The Laboratory Approach to Organization Change: Schema of a Method," *Public Administration Review* Sept. 1967.
41. Mailick and Bord.
42. Douglas McGregor, *The Human Side of Enterprise* (New York: McGraw-Hill, 1960).

utives were viewed as having become substantially more open, receptive, and tolerant than non-laboratory-trained controls. The laboratory-trained people were also thought to have developed more operational skill in human relations and improved understanding of self, others, and group processes. Little increase, however, was noted in initiative and assertiveness.[43]

One review of research on the effectiveness of sensitivity training published in a British journal concludes:

> There is a high agreement among observers in the kind and direction of change reported: improved skills in diagnosing individual and group behavior, clearer communication, greater tolerance and consideration, and greater action skill and flexibility. . . . Finally, changes noted in these studies were found to last for some time after training, though there are conflicting reports of fade-out after 10–20 months.[44]

Experimentation with sensitivity training in Latin America is limited and suggests the need for careful planning and great finesse and a stronger role for the trainer. Enrique Peñalosa, executive director of the Inter-American Development Bank and former director of the National Colombian Institute for Agrarian Reform (Incora), concluded that laboratory training strengthened group relationships and effectiveness. Consequently, he budgeted to bring in foreign laboratory trainers regularly. Rogério Pinto, a public-administration specialist with the OAS noted that emotional difficulties, resentment over the invasion of privacy, and strained human relations characterized some students in a behavioral course using sensitivity training in EBAP.[45] Sensitivity training has recently been removed from the EBAP undergraduate program as part of a curriculum overhaul. Similarly, Alberto Torrentes Viera, chief of the Public Administration Unit at OAS, experimented with sensitivity training at the Inter-

43. See Douglas Bunker, "The Effect of Laboratory Training Upon Individual Behavior," in *Personal and Organizational Change Through Group Methods*, ed. Edgar M. Schein and Warren G. Bennis (New York: Wiley, 1965), 255–67.
44. Ian Mangham and Cary L. Cooper, "The Impact of T-Groups on Managerial Behavior," *Journal of Management Studies* 6 (Feb. 1969): 72.
45. Interview, May 1970. Another source of Brazilian experience with human relations training is found in Sela Moscovici, *Laboratório de sensibilidade* (Rio de Janeiro: EBAP, 1965).

American School of Public Administration (EIAP) in Rio de Janeiro. The experiment was conducted in 1966 through an American contract team when Viera was coordinator of courses at EIAP. After a generally negative emotional reaction from students who felt they were engaged in kids' play and disliked foreign cultural intrusion, the experiments were discontinued.[46] On the other hand, Dean Cruz at INCAE in Managua believes that the laboratory training they offer as part of the master's program contributes to more effective group relationships.

Professor Joseph C. Bentley, of the University of Utah and a resident of Latin America for thirteen years, is one of the few North American trainers who has conducted human relations laboratories with several Latin American groups, including two groups of urban corporate presidents and vice-presidents in Venezuela in 1970 and 1971. He reports that because Latin Americans who have not studied abroad are unfamiliar with the behavioral-science concepts of interpersonal and organizational relationships, there is a need for considerable preparatory effort. Yet he concludes that differences between Latin and North Americans are of degree rather than kind. He is optimistic that the laboratory approach can reduce the suspiciousness, fear of reprisals, masked hostility, and lack of sanctioned methods of expressing criticism in Latin American organizations as, he believes, it has helped to do this in the United States.

Bentley suggests the following as goals of T-group interchanges: supervision should be shared, not preemptive; supervisors and subordinates should be open with information on their feelings about their own and each other's performances, so each can benefit and subordinates are not left with uncertainties and doubts; the methods of problem solving and decision making should be clarified, and the processes should be particularized; a climate of freedom and openness should be developed. He finds Latin American officials to be in agreement on the human relations needs which he believes can be supplied through laboratory training. He finds that a passive role for the trainer so violates the Latin American concept of leadership that it is disconcerting,

46. Interview, May 1970.

and participants displace their early frustration onto him for not teaching them more. He also finds the need to mute excessive harshness. Consequently, he plays a more active and directive role than in the United States, where he can be more facilitative, supportive, and reactive.

This review suggests that little experimentation and research have been done on laboratory training in Latin America. Apparently, sensitivity training if done with adequate preparation and skillful bicultural leadership, may be useful in modifying some organizational values and behavior which resist organization. On the other hand, if poorly done, sensitivity training risks unleashing cruelty that leaves scars and producing alienation rather than trust and teamwork.

Games

Games through which participants simulate intricate real-world situations have been used for some years in training lawyers (moot court), military leaders (war games), and more recently businessmen (decision-making games). The expenditure by the U.S. Navy of over $7 million to construct a gaming computer to train officers in the use of weaponry suggests the level of sophistication of games that simultaneously deal with numerous variables. Training through games has shown that simulations are effective as analytic and research devices, as well as involving the trainee more actively in the learning process.

A game relevant to public administration is Metropolis, created by Professor Richard D. Duke, of the University of Michigan. In this game a hypothetical community is created in which three groups of players operate: the administrator and his staff, the politicians, and a group of real estate speculators. Each group has its own goals vis-à-vis a proposed local capital improvement program. Each group is given the facts of the situation and a definition of the characters and their objectives (e.g., speculators—to make money; politicians—to hold political power; administrators —to seek ego satisfaction that comes from a sense of achievement in their jobs). The interaction that occurs as each participant pursues his goals not only teaches the student how to act out a role but tests his ingenuity and flexibility. It forces him to anticipate the interests and plans of the other players, teaches him to reorient his course of action as new variables (such as a sudden flood) are interjected, and encourages him not only to capitalize on his personal and professional power but also to mobilize support in the larger community. In contrast with business-management games, this game is essentially noncompetitive. In fact, it is designed to demonstrate that only through creative cooperation, tempered by concern for one's individual rewards, can a solution with substantially higher payoffs for each group be achieved. This type of game could be important in reducing the frequent mistrust and noncooperation encountered in Latin America among people associated with different informal chains of friendship and influence.

Professor Richard Meier, of the University of California at Berkeley, sees as a major advantage of this type of game the helping of students to overcome certain difficulties in understanding how it is that complex organizations actually work. The experience of playing a game can achieve what neither written nor verbal explanations can for students without previous relevant experience.[47] Meier has pointed out that this type of game "conveys a sense of system dynamics, including both the routines in choice-making at the decision center and the crises that punctuate these routines. If a mistake is made in calculation or in judgment . . . the decision is one that must be lived with; the costs must be mitigated by subsequent adjustments."[48] He contends that the technique is particularly effective not only for what it teaches but for how it teaches.

Duke reports that Metropolis has been played by thousands of players, including many government officials and students, at a large number of the major North American universities. Among that number there was an almost universal appreciation of the game's value. Faculty members report many students are "turned

47. Interview, Oct. 1967.
48. Richard D. Duke, *Gaming Simulations in Urban Research* (Institute for Community Development and Services, Continuing Education Service, Michigan State Univ., 1964), p. iv.

on" by playing the game and pursue their studies with greater enthusiasm.[49] The rapid growth in variations of the game technique illustrates its continued success as a teaching method. In 1970 the University of Michigan's Environmental Simulation Laboratory offered such a variation in the form of a short course in urban gaming simulation for urban and regional problems.[50] It is noteworthy that an interdisciplinary team of social scientists has ranked gaming as one of the five top innovations in education.[51]

The principal difficulty with gaming is to obtain sufficient data and knowledge of underlying processes to make a game a meaningful approximation of reality. This suggests the major difficulty of using games interculturally. If a nation does not have extensive and reliable statistical and behavioral research in the field for which a game is to be established, the game could be poorly constructed and thus misleading to students. Nevertheless, as meaningful games are established, games which do reflect various operational systems, they can help make explicit the differences among national systems and contribute to intercultural research and understanding. For example, thirty German mayors who played Metropolis in Berlin have adapted the game to reflect German conditions for the training of German municipal officials.[52]

Programed Instruction

Programed instruction involves breaking a subject down into a series of very small instructional steps. This process leads students

49. Interview, Oct. 1967.
50. In a similar vein, an in-house urban relations program produced in 1971 by a Western Electric team led by Bernard McElhone, with the assistance of the Institute of Public Administration, stressed games as a key training aid.
51. Werner Hirsh and Sidney Sonenblum, *Selecting Regional Information for Government Planning and Decision Making* (New York: Praeger, 1970).
52. The need to adapt games to various cultural systems is shown by the fact that foreign students playing Metropolis with North Americans have proved to be at a disadvantage, unless they were highly cosmopolitan, because the North American players do not react according to foreigners' expectations. Much of the information on the use of games for administrative training has come from the work of, and discussions with, Professor and Mrs. Paul Nickel of New York University.

logically and gradually from elementary to advanced concepts and data. The learner must answer questions after each passage of reading. He is then shown the correct answers at each step so he knows whether he has understood correctly before proceeding to the next frame.

The programs of instruction are most commonly presented in book form. In larger facilities they may include the use of computerized "teaching machines" as a vehicle for presentation. Such machines can be programed to respond to incorrect answers of students by repeating in greater detail and clarity the material they did not understand.

As a learning device, programed instruction provides numerous advantages—individualization of scheduling, speed of training, and the immediate feedback of correct information after each question. Important to the training goal that we have defined is the fact that the student is actively, not passively, involved in the learning process. This form of easily understood self-study can be used with correspondence courses or other training devices which permit a trainee to learn without leaving his post of duty. They can be particularly useful in providing basic background knowledge required for advanced courses of study.

To achieve maximum training benefits the American Management Association includes the techniques of programed instruction in one of its recently revised supervisory management courses. The materials come in booklet form, and sections of it are distributed at the end of each unit to be used in preparing for the next level.[53]

Where the subject material consists of concept formation, analyses, and frequent complex and ambiguous problems—as in the administrative field—development of instructional programs is a complex undertaking. It is costly to develop instructional programs and it can be done efficiently only if large numbers of students will utilize it. This is why the applications to date have been in fields with mass markets, e.g., the game of bridge, rather than in fields with few students, like written Chinese. Although

53. Interview with Ferdinand Setaro, staff member, the American Management Association Inc., Jan. 1971.

there is a large potential audience for the study of public administration in Latin America, its members are widely scattered and only loosely associated with numerous uncoordinated and geographically dispersed training centers that have differing perspectives of their needs. This presents an uninviting market, particularly in the absence of a technical assistance agency with relations throughout the hemisphere which is committed to developing such new teaching materials.

In spite of current obstacles, programed instruction is a probable future method with which to train Latin public administrators. It represents an area of training where Latin Americans may pioneer. Since the development cost is high, it would be most efficient to spread the cost among many training centers by a jointly supported program, if they could be organized for this purpose—probably with the inducement of significant financial support from an international institution.

Kepner-Tregor Problem-Solving Programs

A commercial training program which merits attention is the Kepner-Tregor program. It is based on a systematic approach to problem solving, decision making, and the identification and analysis of potential problems in managerial situations.[54] Its focus is upon the problem not the problem solver, and accordingly it attempts to avoid the subjectivity of introspective techniques.

A Kepner-Tregor program involves a tripartite training method developed in class seminars: (i) a study of concepts basic to problem solving, (ii) practice of the concepts in a simulated business situation, and (iii) feedback sessions in which participants discuss the actions and decisions made with the course leader. The one-week training sessions are intensive and focus on the reeducation of managerial thinking. A six-month management-development program is offered as a follow-up course.

In assessing the effectiveness of the Kepner-Tregor program, critics of the rational approach have pointed to the lack of flexi-

54. For a more elaborate discussion, see Mailick and Bord.

bility in its scope of use. The counterargument, however, stresses the fact that this approach to problem solving is not designed to include "nonrational" or subjective elements. This very exclusion of personal relationships and values in the design of the program provides at least two advantages: the risks involved in dealing with human behavior in anxiety-producing situations are avoided, and as the tangible aspects of managerial training are emphasized, results are more visible. Considering the complications of utilizing methods dealing with interpersonal relations in Latin America, this type of approach may have the additional advantage of improving needed analytical aspects of decision making in a relatively uncomplicated environment. As skills and confidence are improved through such techniques, students may be better equipped for group interactions involved in cases, games, and the like.

The Managerial Grid

Another widely utilized commercial program is managerial grid training. This encompasses both individual behavior and group dynamics and is part of a new field of growing popularity called organizational development. The approach attempts to integrate management training into the larger goal of organizational effectiveness. The managerial grid defines a manager's role as two-dimensional—concerned with both production and people. Like the Kepner-Tregor technique, it is the first phase of a more comprehensive program. Phase I is a seven-day seminar for managerial personnel in which both group and individual behavior are studied. It differs from the Kepner-Tregor method by being more inclusive: both interpersonal relationships and the decision-making process may be incorporated in its design, and whereas both training methods focus upon "thinking" versus "feeling" components, the managerial grid is larger in scope.

To assess the effectiveness of the managerial grid: one fault may be that time and cost are beyond the range of many smaller organizations. A second criticism applies to the Kepner-Tregor method as well: both depend on a particular conceptual framework and highly elaborate design. With both means and desired ends specified by the techniques themselves, these training methods are less open-ended.

Supporters of the managerial grid technique, however, point to its built-in conceptual framework as a major asset. They assert the global usefulness of the technique, since it has been widely tested "throughout the world and found to be useful in varying degrees despite language barriers and cultural differences."[55]

Supervised Experience

Supervised internships provide yet another approach in planning programs for participatory training in the public service. This effort to integrate intellectual interaction with direct experience was displayed in the successful program which marked the inception of IPA originally as the New York Bureau of Municipal Research in 1906.[56] In that program students designed and performed applied research on the major problems of administration and operations of New York City government. The training included experimentation with trial installation of proposed reforms. The field experience was combined with seminars in which students made reports and were assisted in improving their methodology, analysis, and strategy by their professors and fellow students.[57] It is not surprising that subsequently many prominent and effective administrators and analysts came from these learner-centered programs.

A more recent example is to be found in the Development Administration Training Program (DATP) at the University of Connecticut. A 1969 review of DATP-sponsored training of more than 700 administrators from developing countries observed

55. Ibid., p. 69.
56. For additional information see Jane S. Dahlberg, *The New York Bureau of Municipal Research: Pioneer in Government Administration* (New York: New York Univ. Press, 1966); George Graham, *Education for Public Administration: Graduate Preparation in the Social Sciences at American Universities* (Chicago: Public Administration Service, 1941).
57. Charles A. Beard, *Efficient Citizenship* (Bureau of Municipal Research, 18 March 1914).

student difficulty in understanding classroom presentations. To correct this situation DATP arranged for internships in selected agencies and found that the internships increased considerably the benefits that the trainees received from classwork.[58]

Another example of learning through doing under supervision is provided by the formation of a competent cadre of municipal analysts by Fundacomun in Venezuela. Many of these people were recent university graduates hired strictly on the basis of technical qualification after being carefully screened by multinational committees set up by Fundacomun. Some were given short courses in municipal administration at the Brazilian Institute of Municipal Administration (IBAM) and in North American institutions such as the University of Southern California. With this as a background, it was found that the hard process of professional growth emerged on the job. The approach was assisted by the work of specialist-tutors, such as Ramiro Cabezas, who developed a variety of municipal manuals based upon Venezuelan needs. Instead of resting unused on library shelves, these manual drafts became the working guides for budding analysts in helping municipal governments install modern accounting and budget systems. As the students encountered both human and technical problems, they discussed solutions at headquarters and then proceeded to work them out in the field. Such discussions not only helped the analysts but also provided feedback which contributed to the rewriting and clarification of parts of the manuals.

Concern for the preparation of a new generation of Latin American administrators is not limited to this hemisphere. The unique Manchester Course begun in 1963 in Britain is designed for public administrators nominated by British embassies in Latin America. The group-study project consists of two modified forms of supervised experience: visits to public agencies and Latin American centers where each administrator's own problems can be seen against a comparative, wider background; and

---

58. Vinton Fisher, "Education for the Public Service: A Comparative View," *Connecticut Government* (Institute of Public Service, Univ. of Connecticut) 23, no. 1 (Fall 1969).

practical study internships, which increase understanding of the processes of institutional reform. By 1969 there had been sixty participants.[59]

Another illustration of supervised experience is the professor-assistant system of the School of Economics and Administration at the University of Chile. The approach starts with the presumption that students will generally study no harder than is necessary to complete their major objective, the earning of a degree. Professors, on the other hand, it is presumed, have to be experts in their specialization and are highly motivated to maintain their expertise through intensive study by the need to be able to answer questions and demonstrate their expertise in class. As a means to motivate selected students to study specialized subject areas intensively, they are given appointments as "professor-assistants," with some teaching duties. The "professor-assistants" are thereupon imbued with the same stronger motivation to study as are other faculty members.[60]

While supervised experience can be a most potent learning method, it cannot be productive without resourceful students and qualified supervisors. It is also a costly one-to-one teacher-to-student method, and scheduling has to economize the time of the teacher.

Recommendations

There is a crucial need to develop creative public managers at both high and intermediate levels, leaders who can mobilize available resources to attain key objectives. A research base is needed to define the problems so as to help design future administrative training programs. One core problem, evident without the need for further research, however, is that too few public employees are taught good work habits and methods on the job

59. W. Wood, "The Manchester Course," *Bank of London and South American Review* 3, no. 32 (Aug. 1969).
60. Andres J. Jeanneret and Oscar Johansen, "Teaching Administration: Methods Used at the School of Economics and Administration, University of Chile," in *Education in Public Administration,* ed. Donald G. Stone (Brussels: International Institute of Administrative Sciences, 1963).

because of the prime shortage of model administrator-trainers. Consequently, formal training methods should make use of participatory training methods which, in part, substitute for on-the-job model supervisors.

Major steps toward higher effectiveness of training programs include the following.

(1) *Establish long-range and short-range goals on the basis of administrative and societal research.* Goals should reflect needs identified through research. This approach may be illustrated by the effort of the Central Office of Organization and Methods (OCOM) in Chile to design a course for personnel administrators by using interviews of personnel administrators to identify their needs. Societal research is needed to create models of administrative, political, and cultural systems of a country, to show their interactions, and to place them in historical perspective. Such an effort encounters monumental difficulties. Efforts to do societal research and analysis can illuminate the focal points where training efforts are most needed and put them in perspective.

(2) *Assess the impact of present programs.* Detailed feedback on the strengths and weaknesses of current programs can be obtained by questionnaire and interview research of graduates. Appraisal of the objectives of present programs in relation to objectives determined through previous steps can help identify the new directions desired for existing programs.

(3) *Raise the quality of students.* Validated objective tests measuring administrative achievement potential and not unnecessarily prejudiced in favor of academic knowledge should be developed to screen students in many administrative courses.

(4) *Gather existing materials.* Some excellent administrative libraries have been built in Brazil, Peru, and elsewhere. Nevertheless, building a library requires assiduous efforts, particularly since many good materials are mimeographed or, though published, are not widely disseminated.

(5) *Develop new materials.* Clearly the best training materials for each country will be derived from that country itself. In addition to identifying the best current materials from foreign countries, new national materials should be created.

(6) *Develop new skills among staff.* The development of re-

search and the use of participatory training methods and the creation of new materials depend upon highly qualified staff. One suggestion, particularly to advance research goals, is the training of many Ph.D.'s in public administration and related fields. This is a degree that normally provides valuable training in research methodology. For the development of skills in the use of the participatory training methods described herein, graduate degrees in public administration and related areas can be helpful, particularly if students write papers and theses and themselves participate in training programs which build their understanding of these methods. Nevertheless, other types of observation and experience are essential. Observation of executive development programs and business school methods should be utilized, including the programs at Harvard and Stanford Business Schools that instruct foreign teachers in the case method. Sending students to participate in human relations laboratories may also be a useful supplement to graduate degrees in the behavioral sciences.

(7) *Relate administration to specialized fields.* Inevitably, courses in administration must at present be generalized in their presentation, drawing people from varied fields. An aim should be to develop materials highly relevant to the officials in a specific field such as public works administration, educational administration, health administration, and agricultural administration. To a degree the OAS-supported Inter-American Center for Training in Public Administration did this with specialized seminars for tax administrators.

(8) *Create clearing house.* Create at least one international clearing house to identify potentially valuable research and training materials and distribute them to all training centers for the public service in Latin America. This would help each center take advantage of the work of other centers, rather than unknowingly duplicate it.

(9) *Utilize a central organization to promote the use of new training techniques.* Most new techniques require heavy front-end investment and require extensive utilization to be cost-effective. This argues for regionwide strategies stimulated by a central organization—probably a multilateral one—such as the OAS.

Chapter 7

The Role of the University in the Training of Personnel for Public Administration: A Latin American Perspective

Edgardo Boeninger

The potential wealth of any country is based on its material and human resources, and if it is to attain its potential, an intelligent force must direct and coordinate them. Productivity today rests fundamentally in the coordinated action of individuals— on organization. In today's world with its complex social relations, the only visible way to develop rests in the possibility of attaining a better system of training and education and a better system of human organization.

The developing countries usually have strong traditions which affect administration. The public service, for example, is often the traditional shelter for persons who receive compensation from government for personal services, based on family relations and friendship. Public administration has also suffered from sudden attacks of political patronage. Employment in the public service is often a typical manifestation of the phenomenon called "disguised unemployment." It has also resulted in a large bureaucracy with negative attitudes toward the people and an inadequate level of education among staff. People regard it as a huge organization, weighted down in its movements, difficult to orient, devoted only to paperwork, and without a clear sense of purpose— an obstacle to the achievement of goals. Thus, it has not been common to think of public administration as an agent or factor that can enhance development.

Nonetheless, in Latin America the preponderant governmental role in the process of development is frequently observed. It would be redundant to emphasize the mounting public expense, the increasing public work force employed, or the weight it carries within the public finances of the developing countries. How can we obtain an administration consistent with developmental purposes? This is the challenge in motivation to the procedures and structures prevalent in Latin America.

The human potential in Latin American countries, which is relatively rich and abundant, requires education, training and orientation if the desired results are to be obtained. Without the education—technical, professional, or academic—it is impossible to expect increases in productivity. Education is recognized as one of the fundamental factors of development.

The university is not only a center where basic problems are researched and general ideas and disciplines studied but is also an entity for professional training. In these functions, university education must be integrated with the national realities and must participate in the problems that trouble the nation.

Human Resources in Public Administration

Public administration needs the contributions of three types of people in order to function: (i) *professionals,* who perform technical functions appropriate to their occupation either inside or outside of government; usually these professionals belong to the upper levels of the government departments and form a separate group from the other "functionaries," (ii) *career bureaucrats,* who carry on administrative functions and make a lifetime career in public administration, starting at the lower levels without any promise of moving up to executive positions; and (iii) *career executives,* who form the connection between the political levels of the government and the rest of the organization.

The career executive is the bridge between the policymaker and the rest of the organization. He is the one who has both a clear vision of policy and a precise understanding of the bureaucracy. This helps the career executive to adjust bureaucracy to the environment in which it evolves. In other words, he is the one responsible for the proper functioning of the organization in a way which is generally dynamic and permanently in the process of change.

The training of career executives for public administration is without doubt the direct responsibility of the university. The national functions which are expected to be carried out and the manner of conduct which should be observed require an intensive, high-level, and systematic educational process. Within such a process, there will be found basic disciplines like sociology, political science, economics, and public administration with its auxiliary technologies.

One will not find in the career public administration professional sociologists, political scientists, or economists as such. Rather one finds professionals who possess knowledge to understand a social complex with its structures and dynamics. Specifically they must understand how to play various socioeconomic and political roles within the development process. A professional person, then, must take responsibility for the successful functioning of a large organization within a rapidly changing society. Part of his education pertains to his role in the organization of these processes; also his role in orienting the efforts of his collaborators, thus enabling him to be an effective agent of development in the organization and in society.

The Role of the University

The university's function is to receive and transmit knowledge on the human cultural situation and to enlarge knowledge through research. The growth of the university has been inorganic and by aggregation—the same as the structures of public administration in many countries of Latin America. This has happened in response to daily needs and not within an integral context or organizing concept.[1]

In order for the university to play a dynamic role—especially

1. David Stitchkin "The Structure of the University Community," conference held in the Center of Culture, Alameda University, Santiago, Oct. 1967; original in Spanish.

in Latin America—it must meet first the challenge of developing an organic structure in accordance with its objectives, resources, and its functioning within the social sphere. The university cannot close itself off from society, in isolation, as it occasionally proposes. It must interact with its environment. Its responsibilities in research and diffusion of knowledge help to develop awareness and to shape its priorities in order to shed light on the discussion of the problems which preoccupy the citizenry. While we allow for the need for such changes, the following responsibilities fall to the university.

(1) Education or training of professionals or technicians of the first level;

(2) Training of middle-level careerists;

(3) Postgraduate education;

(4) Research; and

(5) Extension or diffusion of knowledge within the community.

Within this context, the university has a special role to fill in public administration training.

(1) As already stressed, the university must have exclusive responsibility for the training of career executives—those who fill the highest executive positions. These necessarily should attain the highest level of training in specific professions. At the same time, the university has the responsibility of making professional training more specifically relevant to the needs of the public service.

(2) The university should also have responsibility, at least supplementary, in the training of middle-level executives, by providing technical training as a preparation for these careers. In this connection, it should initiate collaboration within the rest of the educational system to secure the necessary coordination and continuity between the diverse levels of education and training.

(3) The university should also undertake collaboration with the public-sector entities which have undertaken training responsibilities. In this area the university can make valuable contributions by recommending priorities, by providing for the par-

ticipation of university professors, and by placing research results at the disposal of departments of government.

(4) The university needs to reorient research in order to give greater priority to the problems of public administration within disciplines like economics, law, political science, sociology, and administration. It would suffice to mention such problems as alternative methods of state organization in the ministries, the Office of Planning, and national, regional, and local institutes; how to improve public accounting, budgetary techniques, and personnel management; and the motivations of bureaucrats and their attitudes toward change, especially in the realm of administrative reform and fiscal administration. Each of the social sciences should be conscious that public administration shows peculiar characteristics which require specialized research without prejudice to the existence of valid principles for all types of organization.

(5) The university needs to promote a better understanding on the part of the community in general, about the role and functioning of public administration. The objective is to contribute to an awareness of the subject, and to eliminate prejudices about a "nonproductive bureaucracy."

A Case Study

As an example of university action related to public administration, the author's personal experience may be referred to in the Faculty of Economic Sciences of the University of Chile. There are two main entities, the School of Economics and the Institute of Administration, directly concerned with these problems. The former fulfills a responsibility for education and training in the fields of economics and administration, the latter a responsibility for research and for "extension of knowledge." It also shares some teaching responsibilities with the School of Economics.

The Institute of Administration (Insora) carries on research which is dedicated to an interdisciplinary search for Chilean reality in public administration. Previous research helps in the teaching process which is carried on in the School of Economics and in the Graduate Administration Program of Insora. There is also a special program, Public Administration, in the School of Economics which provides education for students who hope to work in the future as career public executives. These studies are oriented toward producing professional executives who will participate in policy making.

The type of education given at the School of Economics requires continuous and close contacts between the school and Insora. There is a special Department of Education in Insora; the programs for teaching in the School of Administration are prepared there.

In its Department of Public Administration, Insora exercises a three-way responsibility: (i) to increase the amount of knowledge about public administration as an academic discipline; (ii) to develop a clearer recognition of both a Chilean and Latin American reality in this field; and (iii) to develop an educational program destined to produce a significant group of career public executives. The emphasis here is on research. This is carried out both independently by Insora and also in conjunction with governmental departments.

The Department of Public Administration has set a group of standards that must be met by all research projects. These standards can briefly be summed up in terms of the relevance of topics to be studied or investigated; the application of a strict scientific methodology and research in depth; the requirement that research results must be usable for furthering education; and finally, the necessity of independent work to insure greater objectivity and independence of thought in the studies undertaken.

In other departments of the Faculty of Economic Sciences (the Institute of Economics, the Center for Social Studies, the Center for Mathematical and Statistical Studies) much importance is also given to public administration problems. This fact is attested to by the number of research projects and investigations which directly relate to the government and to public administration. But even with all this experimentation, we are not at all sure we have come up with the right answers, either in academic organization, in observable effects on the public service itself, or in community understanding. The point is, however, that the university can have and should have an important role in improving public administration in Latin America.

A concluding note: much in the foregoing paragraphs was put in final form in 1966. Allowance must be made today for the considerable changes that have taken place since then in the university organization, its academic structure, and its relationship with the national community.

Chapter 8

Technical Assistance for Education in Public Administration: Lessons of Experience

Frank P. Sherwood

The title of this paper may be somewhat pretentious. Nevertheless the time has come to begin to look rather hard at what we
have been trying to do in technical assistance for the past two
decades. Because such a venture involves self-assessment, the
"I" on the keyboard should be respectable in this kind of effort.
Of course, an endeavor of this sort means that the reader should
expect not a panoramic exposure but rather one that is constrained by individual experience.

Brazil has been my beat.

The arrival of Juscelino Kubitschek on the presidential scene
in 1956 signaled a new thrust forward for Brazil. By 1958 the U.S.
technical assistance program was undergoing significant expansion. One important outgrowth of that expansion was the creation
of a so-called consortium of Michigan State University and the
University of Southern California to provide technical assistance
in the development of university-level programs in the fields of
business administration and public administration. Planned for
a six-year period (1959–65), these programs probably represented an outlay of about $4 million. This experience provides
the basis for my evaluation of technical assistance in public-
administration education.

Assumptions and a Critique of the U.S.C. Project

Like every technical-assistance effort, the U.S.C./Michigan
State venture contained certain assumptions. The first is implicit

in the idea of the consortium. The linking of the two universities in a common project agreement seemed to recognize "administration" as a generic process. More than that, institutional arrangements were pushed on the Brazilians in two universities that called for both M.S.U. and U.S.C. to provide technical-assistance support to the same organization. As might be expected, this marriage of convenience posed very serious problems. Here we may simply note that the consortium was based on an important theoretical premise, namely that administration *is* a generic process and that the differences between business administration and public administration are essentially at the margins. The experience in Brazil with the marriage is a matter for broad consideration. Quite frankly, we encountered some problems in these respects in Brazil.

Public and Business Administration

There were different attitudes toward educational preparation, with economics and accounting holding less importance for us than for the business people. Conversely, political science, sociology and anthropology were regarded as central to the development of the public administrator.

The brutal facts are that it is difficult for public administration to compete against a business program for students. The conditions of employment in the public service are far from attractive to the average Brazilian student. For the professor, the opportunities in business for consultation far outweigh those in the public sector. The same goes for the things a school may do. It may increase appreciably its resources by running a special training program for businessmen, who are quite willing to pay for such services. In the case of the government, they are often provided free. Throughout my experience in Brazil, we had problems in the state of Bahia with admissions. There was a common entrance exam, with only the highest scorers admitted. There were no quotas to assure a balance for the public and the private sectors. On one occasion, I recall that only five of the thirty entrants recorded their expectation of entering the public service. It happens that public administration managed to hold its own; but I have never been able to see that anything was gained by the forced association. In fact, I would argue that definite harm resulted.

If a common program is to be undertaken, I would suggest that it should indeed be common. The business/public distinction should be completely washed out. While such an approach would obviously result in less focus on specific problem areas and somewhat less concern about environmental variables, it avoids the necessity of making a choice and then structuring the educational experience in terms of that choice. When 80 percent of the students have opted for business administration, it becomes difficult to argue against a course in marketing. When, however, the ultimate goal of the education is less determinate, the course in marketing takes its place among a variety of ways in which the organization searches its environments and makes its outputs relevant.

A National Program

A second orienting premise of the U.S.C. project was the conceptualization of the program as national. While seemingly innocuous, the thrust to build a "national" effort produced two problems. The first was to distribute the targets of technical assistance support broadly across the Brazilian landscape. It meant that we sought to give assistance to an institution in one case which had absolutely no background or tradition of interest in public administration. In two cases (the universities of Minas Gerais and Pernambuco), the problems were so great that the anticipated collaboration never did occur. Thus the public-administration portion of the program eventually operated in three places: Rio de Janeiro, Salvador da Bahia, and Pôrto Alegre.

Even though the program was thus truncated, the symbolism of a national effort continued. We were troubled throughout the project that our geographical spread was not larger. Most of us suspected that we were regarded as something of a failure because of our lessened scale. Beyond this, we suffered mightily in the first third of our contract in the state of Bahia. Yet the success in Bahia has been spectacular, and I believe one man made the difference. Without him, I fear, we would look with little pride at Bahia today. The lesson is another simple but important one. Without an ongoing institution and some demonstrated capability, the risks involved in launching any technical assistance program are high and the venture foolhardy. Bahia can be so regarded. But here a second lesson is evident. When in a jam, concentrate on leadership. That is what the U.S. public-administration adviser, Ray Jolly, did. He earned his two years of pay in a few short months, when he "courted" José de Senna and negotiated a seemingly unattainable two-year contract for him.

The fixation on the national projection was troublesome in another way. Inevitably, the idea of a national program brought into play the need for a center for that program. Inevitably, too, such a center was established in the Brazilian School of Public Administration (EBAP) in the Rio headquarters of the Getúlio Vargas Foundation. In fact, however, EBAP was in no condition to play the role of national center. It was undergoing an important leadership change in 1959, was experiencing extremely serious financial strains, and was consequently very short on human resources. Furthermore, these were problem areas where U.S. "self-help" concepts of technical assistance prohibited any form of support. But it was more than a problem of resources. The concept of the national center tended to create the notion of one first-class citizen and a couple of second-class ones. In fact, it reinforced provincial hostility toward the center of the Brazilian universe, Rio de Janeiro. It was bad enough that everyone knew Rio was the nerve center. It did not have to be formalized in the project agreement.

In my judgment the concept of the national center was a serious strategic mistake. It set up aspirations that were not and perhaps could not be met. It reinforced hostilities that were already present. It suggested a dependent relationship among the institutions that was not acceptable to all parties. And it blocked communications that might have been possible with a less-structured relationship. In many U.S. technical-assistance programs we have had a need for symmetrical tidiness. We have wanted the arrangements spelled out. My observation is that such arrangements are often premature and are as likely to be as harmful as helpful. In this case, looseness and ambiguity would have been preferable to structure and clarity.

Institution Building

A third assumption pertained to the building of institutions of public administration at the university level. The phrase, "at the university level," is used because the national center EBAP was not itself a part of a university. The Getúlio Vargas Foundation, its parent, conducts programs of higher education in public administration, business administration, and economics. However, it is not properly a university. In the beginning of the technical-assistance project, the distinction was extremely important. The public-administration degree was not recognized by the Ministry of Education. This had obvious implications for EBAP's credentials to lead an effort to build university capabilities in public administration. While the EBAP degree was recognized in the early 1960's and differences were therefore somewhat minimized, it seems fair to say that the institutional setting of the university continued to pose problems that were appreciably different from those in the Foundation.

More important than these legal-formal aspects, however, was an assumption about institution building itself.[1] The kind of institution to which I refer is an organization which has come to occupy such an important place in its society that its extinction is unthinkable. It is "infused with value," in the sense that people inside and outside prize its continuity and give it support. Such an "institutionalized" organization typically has the independence and the resources to engage in activities which its sensors tell it are appropriate to its broad mandate and which, instrumentally, will enable it to retain its bases of support.

1. Supported by the Inter-University Program in Institution-Building (Pittsburgh, Syracuse, Michigan State, and Indiana universities), we have had a particular opportunity at U.S.C. to study the organizational development of the Brazilian School of Public Administration (EBAP) and the Brazilian Institute of Municipal Administration (EBAM). Professor Jose Silva de Carvalho did the study of EBAP; and Professor Aluizio Pinto of the Brazilian Institute of Municipal Administration. Professor Wesley Bjur, of U.S.C., made a study of the technical assistance involvement of U.S.C. in Brazil, using the institution-building model as his frame of reference and looking particularly at the way in which an outside change agent participates in such efforts.

In these terms, the building of an institution is a touchy, difficult matter. It is more than putting a name on a door, building a fine new edifice, and inserting people into a new organizational milieu. Most of all, it is different from building a program. The development of an institution involves the long term, and it assumes the capability of that institution to retain its relevance to its society. It puts its emphasis on the organization-providing inducements that will make membership attractive, on building linkages in the environment, and on establishing a set of goals that will be neither confining nor ambiguous.

Such a theory suggests that the timing of the birth of an organization is critical. Insofar as possible, certain preconditions—such as the existence of supports in the environment, leadership capability, and human resources—should be satisfied in order to reduce risks of failure. There is a particular danger when the organization is regarded only as a vehicle for the achievement of a desired program or project. The interests of the organization and the achievement of a specified project may collide in a number of ways, most generally in the temporal dimension. Projects tend to involve targets and termination. Institutions are characterized by shifting goals and continuity.

Program vs. Organization

In the case of the U.S.C. technical-assistance program in Brazil, the distinction between program and organization was not always clear. There were certain goals sought, particularly the development of undergraduate education in public administration, and an organization structure was therefore created. It is to be observed that all the entities were established before the technical-assistance program began. EBAP had been launched in 1952. At the University of Rio Grande do Sul, an Institute of Administration was created in the Faculty of Economic Sciences. At the University of Bahia, a separate School of Administration was created. Presumably, a technical-assistance program is difficult or impossible without an organizational unit to assist. But it is also clear that there was a high risk involved in making these early commitments to build institutions in what turned out to be either a hostile or a barren environment.

Despite the general commitment to institution building, the targets of the technical-assistance effort were markedly programmatic. In the case of Bahia and Rio Grande do Sul, the new undergraduate programs in public administration were to be launched. Never mind that government employment had probably fallen to its lowest repute in Brazil since 1930. And never mind that in Rio Grande do Sul the undergraduate program was to be launched in a faculty which generally felt it was already teaching through economics the essential elements of governmental management. In Rio Grande it took the entire six years to get the undergraduate public-administration program approved. In Bahia, things got under way much earlier, but with almost no students. In my judgment these program commitments caused a considerable distortion in the use of technical-assistance resources and energies. We were constantly reminded by the U.S. AID people that success of the institution-building venture was to be judged in terms of a single program criterion. This tendency to evaluate the extent of development of an institution by such a program benchmark can, in the long run, be extremely dysfunctional.

Much the same confusion of program and institution could be seen at EBAP, where the target was the development of a graduate program in public administration. As the contract began, the EBAP director resigned. He was replaced by an eminent academician, whose basic obligation was that of gaining legitimation for the undergraduate EBAP degree by the Ministry of Education. As can be understood, this was a critical matter for the increasing number of EBAP graduates. It was believed that a man in good standing with the ministry would have the best chance of securing approval. Yet when this effort was going on, in 1959–61, the thrust of the U.S.C. technical advisers was toward the graduate program, which the contract obligated us to support. Ironically, the ministry's action sanctioning the public-administration degree came only shortly before a law was passed virtually eliminating graduate work in the field. The graduate program had been constructed on the premise that bachelor's holders from other disciplines—law, economics, and education—would be permitted to matriculate. Under the new law, only the bona fide holders of an undergraduate degree could do graduate work in the same field. The old program has lived on as an extension effort. But it again illustrates the point that program commitments can turn out to be quite incompatible with environmental demands and institutional needs.

To summarize, my interest has been to subject three assumptions about the technical-assistance venture in Brazil to scrutiny. (i) Is it true that administration is a generic process, in which environmental factors are important only at the margins? (ii) Is it true that an extensive approach is better than an intensive one, i.e., that the development of public administration should be on a coordinated, national scale? And (iii) is it true that institutions derive naturally from formally established organizations with specific program goals, which should generally form the basis for assistance support?

I have singled out only the assumptions that seemed to me to be most troublesome and from which we might learn. Further, each assumption tends to be common enough in technical assistance that it deserves most careful consideration and reporting of experience.

The Brazilian University Setting

The selection of a university to provide technical assistance in itself represents an assumption. Certainly there was an assumption in the U.S.C. project that universities have a responsibility to contribute to the public service. Yet we all know that this is not a totally shared view. And even if it is accepted that the university does bear a responsibility, there are further questions about means and capabilities. In George Homans' terms, this is the problem of the "given." That is, the decision to work toward the improvement of the public service within the university framework imposes certain constraints. The expectations toward a program for public administration must be generally congruent with those directed toward the university.

From the standpoint of public policy, it is important to recognize that the intervention of various funding elements can, over time, have highly significant implications for the university. For example, the rapid injection of federal money into the U.S. university system produced changes across the country that may be far more profound than realized; and then, the rapid reduction in such funds caused similar adjustment problems. For example, some schools of medicine are becoming little more than agencies of the U.S. Public Health Service. U.S. technical-assistance missions, without consciously seeking to do so, may have affected the allocation of resources in Latin American universities in a somewhat similar manner. Decisions to promote education for administration are made generally in terms of perceived needs for improved administration in the society, not in terms of the broad need for institutional development of the universities. U.S. AID money has supported programs in engineering, agriculture, education, and certain of the sciences, without particular regard for the lack of balance that may result for the university's own distribution of its resources. We should not forget that the university is highly important in its own right; it is much more than an instrument for the performance of certain publicly determined tasks.

These concerns have, of course, undergirded much of the opposition to professional education within the universities, both in Brazil and the United States. There are strongly held convictions that the activist, societally responsive orientations of the professional school do not mix with the contemplative detachment required of the university, in the long view.

It is not my intention to discuss this issue at length, but it is important to observe that a truce of some sort operates in the U.S. university. In Brazil, on the other hand, I think the forces of opposition clearly have the upper hand. The pity is that such detachment in Brazil has not generally produced contemplation. It has in many respects facilitated irresponsible behavior, in which the material and nonmaterial rewards to the professor far outweigh his contributions. Separation has also brought about a pattern of protection that makes it abnormally difficult to summon the resources of the university toward the pursuit of any

societal objective, whether better teaching, curriculum improvement, or a community service activity. With relatively few exceptions, one finds little of the "land grant" philosophy or psychology present in the Brazilian university system.

Further, the structure of the Brazilian university makes it relatively difficult for the president of the institution to have a substantial influence on the situation. The independence of the
faculties and the system of tenure both tend to reduce any leverage the president may have over his resources. I can well remember receiving enthusiastic expressions of support for our program
from university presidents. Somehow, their morale-boosting
statements had little consequence for the solution of our problems. In this respect, the bureaucracy within a Brazilian university can be frightful. At one of the institutions, our people
were consistently blocked by the ways in which a zealous accounting mind—who may, for all I know, have had prejudices
against our program—interpreted a maze of federal legislation
and administrative decrees. There was even a question raised as
to whether the university could receive and spend a grant from
the Ford Foundation.

The organizational pattern of the Brazilian university in some
respects has presented a particularly crucial problem for the
teaching of public administration. Here we must remember that
public administration is a problem-oriented and clientele-
oriented field. There is virtually no subject matter that is completely and exclusively its own. As a consequence, inputs must
come from many disciplines. However, the structure of the Brazilian university makes it virtually impossible for a student of
the Faculty of Administration to take a course in the Faculty of
Economics. No matter what the subject—Portuguese, sociology,
statistics—the individual school must offer its own classes and
therefore maintain its own professional staff. As can easily be
seen, this leads to serious strains upon resources. More than that,
it typically means the utilization of a considerable number of
part-time professors with attendant problems of quality and
standards. As a result, the organizational options available for
the teaching of public administration in the Brazilian university

are sharply reduced. A program such as that of the Institute of Public Administration at the University of Michigan, which relies heavily on other units of the university for instruction, would be impossible.

At first blush it may seem that these are problems which require only a little tinkering. In fact, they go to the roots of the university system; the professorial chair is the building block of the university's organization. The chairs are, of course, located in the individual faculties. For obvious reasons there are incentives to increase the number of chairs. In contrast, there are no rewards for interfaculty cooperation. Thus any diminution in the pivotal roles of the faculties in the university structure would involve a threat to professorial status and security.

A related structural factor also has profound implications for undergraduate education in Brazil, though it is seldom remarked. Academic positions in the university are structured on the basis of undergraduate teaching needs. Throughout the six years of our association with the Institute of Administration at the University of Rio Grande do Sul, no one was given tenure in the Faculty of Economic Sciences as a professor of public administration. The reason was simple: there was no undergraduate program in public administration. Thus the push to secure the adoption of the undergraduate curriculum was not merely to achieve an AID contract objective. On the Brazilian side, it meant the only way in which there could be assurance of a permanent relationship with the university.

Hence the U.S. observer who looks askance at the teaching of public administration at the undergraduate level in Brazil fails to appreciate the organizational imperatives which operate. This is an important point because one of my colleagues in Brazil, reflecting his own experience in the United States, felt very strongly that the U.S.C. party should sponsor only graduate education in public administration.

Again, we have to look at the total context. I have mentioned one variable, the university structure. In addition, however, there is some failure to appreciate the tremendous difference in education levels between the U.S. and Brazil. This is bound to be re-

flected in the expectations toward undergraduate education. We
can only begin to think of graduate education when we have a
substantial supply of baccalaureate holders. For example, the
first two decades in the history of the U.S.C. School of Public
Administration (roughly 1929–49) witnessed an overwhelming
enrollment at the undergraduate level. About 1950 that mix began to change. Today the great majority are graduate students.
At the same time, about 50 percent of college-age students in
California are actually attending a college. In Brazil the picture
is quite different. Relatively few even get out of high school.
Further, those who do are generally felt to have had a more substantial training in the classics and humanities than is true in the
United States. As a result, the Brazilian is expected to be a "whole
man" when he graduates from secondary school and a professional upon receipt of his bachelor's degree. While some may
disagree with this pattern, I find it quite understandable and a
general expression of the needs of the Brazilian society at this
stage of development.

I can illustrate the problems that ensue from the attempt to
introduce change into a situation where the content, the university structure, and educational perspective are in some degree
incongruent. One of the more venturesome ideas at the University of Bahia, borrowed from our experience at U.S.C., was to
create a certificate program, enabling certain mature government
officials to attend the regular undergraduate classes.

The entrance examinations to the School of Administration at
Bahia were quite difficult, with the result that many people holding important government jobs had little chance of matriculating
for the degree. Also because of the stiff entrance exams, the
classes in public administration were extremely small. Our proposal therefore called for the admission of a select group of government officials to these classes. Over a three-year period, it was
anticipated that they would complete one year of regular course
work and receive a certificate in public administration. The plan
was approved and operated for one year. Although we had a
group of twenty people who were generally regarded as having
performed ably in the classes, the certificate program was

dropped. I never fully understood what happened, but I certainly surmise that it was too radical a departure from the elitist notions that appear to underlie university education in Brazil.

I report this experience not only because it supports the theoretical argument that programs cannot outdistance the environmental givens, but because it suggests some practical limitations on the extent to which we can expect some of the useful forms of collaboration between the university and the community to emerge. I am thinking particularly of the tremendous amount of part-time education in public administration that exists in the U.S. While I am critical of Brazilian universities for their failure to become fully relevant partners in the development enterprise, it is also clear that what they do in this respect must be compatible with their own responsibility to seek, safeguard, and transmit knowledge. There is a need for change in the Brazilian university but it must be in context with this traditional mission.

The Spirit of Inquiry: Reflections on the Research Role of the Universities

The creation of a spirit of inquiry is a problem throughout Brazilian society. Why do we worry about such a spirit? Because it is becoming increasingly clear that behavioral change must be preceded by a basic interest in knowing, a willingness to expose oneself and to receive feedback.

Ideally, universities are in the business of creating change. They do this by promoting the reexamination of values, sharpening the skills of inquiry, and providing added increments to substantive knowledge. At the societal level, there is the urgent need to remove the taboos in the developing nations and to look objectively at the condition of things—latent as well as manifest goals and instrumental capabilities. Dialogue is not enough; it must ensue from an informed data base. Both the data base and the incentives for dialogues are, in my judgment, serious lacks in the Brazilian university, as well as more generally.

Library and Publications Program

Let us start with the data base, which obviously involves the acquisition and orderly maintenance of such experience as has been recorded—in short, an adequate library facility. Yet this economical and expeditious means of building at least a minimum data base has received little attention. We had the unsettling experience in the U.S.C. project of building a collection of quite adequate U.S. materials at the same time that virtually nothing was being done to secure Brazilian books and documents. Pitifully small budgets in *cruzeiro* amounts were provided for acquisitions and for personnel.

The "library problem," of course, is compounded by many factors. The Brazilian publishing industry itself is chaotic, is underfinanced, and generally manufactures products of poor quality. Editions are small; purchases must be made immediately or the book becomes unobtainable. The poor stock, paper covers, and wretched bindings provide little incentive to build a collection for the long term. There are also serious difficulties in keeping track of what has been published, reflecting again the great communications problems that exist in Brazil. An interested professor at the University of Bahia, for example, finds it impossible to know what is being published in his own country. It is easier for him to keep in touch with materials published in the United States and western Europe. Thus, even the experiences that someone has taken the pains to record are not known to many people.

In addition, there are few incentives to engage in the recording. The level of illiteracy and disinclination on the part of many to spend money for books make the writing of a volume economically uninteresting. Despite the growth of public administration as an academic discipline, for example, there is no Brazilian textbook in the field. The reason is simple; it would have a small sale and would return little to press and author for a great investment of energy and time. The only real university press in Brazil is at the Getúlio Vargas Foundation, which has done a remarkable job of publishing materials in public administration.

Yet a look at that experience suggests the profundity of the problems involved in such a venture. Partly because of inflation but also because of growth, there is a continuing problem of capital and, to a considerable extent, the foundation must apply commercial criteria in developing its list. For a variety of reasons, its books take an inordinately long time to produce. In one case, an author worked long hours to bring his book absolutely up to date as it went to press. The last time I knew, it had been in the process of production for eighteen months.

While I realize that none of these problems can be solved quickly, it seems to me that the creation of a data base can be most economically advanced by increased attention to the library and publishing activities. It is particularly discouraging to think of the many fine works that have been published and which have received relatively little attention in the universities of Brazil. One of the best programs in which we were involved in Brazil sought to give support to the university press concept of publishing. In this effort, U.S. AID, through the work of James Asper, bought a thousand copies of the books in public administration which were published by the Getúlio Vargas Foundation. In this fashion, the foundation received some money immediately, could be assured of recovering a considerable share of the costs of production, and actually had a subsidy for the several hundred books it would probably have had to distribute free in any case. The books were generally distributed to universities and libraries and were typically in hard covers, to emphasize the concept of permanence.

Under Asper's tutelage, AID also supported a translation program at EBAP that was innovative and should result in long-term support to the university press concept. This is a series of translations in the field of development administration. In this case, AID paid the full costs of producing the books, with the condition that all proceeds beyond direct selling costs would go toward the translation and production of additional books in the series. If I am not mistaken, thirteen books have been published in that series—including works by Simon and Riggs—for a total

AID outlay of less than $50,000. Also, any inspection of those books will reveal a much higher quality, not only in the products themselves but in the translations.

Original Research

While an effective library and publications program is an essential first step, it is obvious that an adequate data base relies on the generation of new knowledge as well. This is the point at which the translations are forgotten and the society seeks knowledge about itself. The absence of research about Brazilian problems, of course, makes the professor much more vulnerable to the charge that he is out of touch with his own reality and only a transmitter of foreign ideas. To the extent that a scholar finds little that is conceptually new in his own society, it is likely that he will look outside. This is a dependency relationship that we must all strive very hard to eliminate. There is no reason why a few societies should be the monopolists of new ideas in any field, and certainly not in public administration.

It is, of course, easy to say that research is a requirement for the effective university program in public administration. As in the United States, however, it is difficult to get a research movement under way that is really an integral part of the education program. I make this point because it is not unusual for an institution to display a showpiece research project that is typically funded separately and quite removed from the classroom. In an intensive study of university bureaus of public administration in the United States several years ago, Amin Alimard found that the problem of such separatism was critical. He concluded that the most effective bureaus were those whose research was performed by professors with regular teaching appointments. Where the bureaus were set up independently and functioned with a non-academic staff, the contribution to the teaching program was minimal.

One of the most interesting efforts to make research an integral part of the teaching activity was undertaken at the University of Bahia with important help from the Ford Foundation. The program started from the premise I mentioned earlier—that learning requires a data base. All too often in the developing countries, public administration had been taught as an abstraction. It has been a cataloguing of the procedures for handling personnel, money, and property; in many cases this has occurred because neither the professor nor the students knew anything in a systematic way of the administration of which they were a part. This was the case in Bahia. Very little had been recorded about the nature of the state's administrative operations. Under the new effort, the theory was that meaningful learning would occur only in a here-and-now setting—what it is like in Bahia—and not in a then-and-there world, to use the language of group dynamics.

There was another problem that Professor Senna of Bahia hoped to handle with a research emphasis in the classroom. Teaching public administration as an abstraction obviously tends toward the triumph of technique over purpose; and it was his position that this had been very much the problem in Brazil. In the studies undertaken, therefore, the emphasis was on inquiry into the way specific functions were handled, such as health, law enforcement, and social services.

The teaching-research venture got under way in a special postgraduate seminar for government officials, representing a number of the agencies of the state. Each participant then took on the task of studying his operations, writing up such analyses, and reporting to the group. This effort was later extended to the undergraduate classes.

The result was a wealth of documentation on the government of Bahia. Further, the teaching-training goals were enhanced. My observation was that the students really got off the then-and-there pedestal and got engaged in their own problems. Certainly the extensiveness of the reports suggests the degree of motivation and effort of the participants. It might be said that this was also good strategy for securing resources. Public administration became "relevant" in Bahia.

A contrast is worth noting between the approach at Bahia and at EBAP. As the premier institution of public-administration education in Brazil, it was only natural that EBAP should rather early have felt the obligation to expand the data base. A research

center was established about 1959, but it did not really become
active until a Ford Foundation grant in 1964 gave it resources
and a mission. In considerable degree the research effort at EBAP
occurred in the research-methodology classes. My feeling is that
research at EBAP was regarded as something separate. That is a
point upon which it is worthwhile reflecting. In an institution that
is well underway with defined disciplines, it is much more difficult to work a revolution in teaching approaches. Yet that was
what really occurred in Bahia: the teaching theory was premised
on creating an openness to learning, providing opportunities for
the exhilaration of discovery, and engaging in dialogue about
which there was no question of relevance. In making these comments, I do not mean to criticize EBAP. In my judgment the
EBAP leadership has been very sensitive to these dimensions;
indeed, one can point to numerous strategies used to build the
data base upon which students and professor may interact. The
special research course, the revitalized research center, the large
publications program, and the use of Ford funds for professorial
support are, it seems to me, all efforts toward data-based teaching.

Often, professors have a tendency to look for reasons *not* to do
research. There are claims that conditions are not right, that
anything important is too sensitive politically, that there are too
many teaching demands, and that it has been impossible to keep
up with the latest quantitative methods in the United States. My
experience with case studies is perhaps illustrative.

Public Administration Cases

Early in the U.S.C. project, in 1959, we concluded that one of
the best ways to encourage data-based teaching was to use the
case method. As a result, we spent considerable amounts of
money developing a catalogue of cases in the United States and
we put together a rather extended manual on the preparation and
teaching of cases. When I went to Brazil in 1962, however, I
found that virtually nothing had been accomplished in the preparation of indigenous cases. I was given many of the familiar
reasons why such a project was impossible. Here again the question of quality was at hand. If our standard was to be the Inter-

University Case Program in the United States, the claim was quite true. If, however, we settled for a reasonably honest recording of experience in the Brazilian situation, the goal was not impossible. When I proposed that we get our cases from a detailed clipping of the newspapers, I encountered almost total resistance. Newspapers in Brazil were biased. They distorted the news. At the time, however, there were about sixteen daily newspapers in Rio, more than one of which could be read to account for the various slants.

Though I found very little support for the project, I began to clip five newspapers, with the case-writing project in mind. As a result, I wrote three cases, two of which were published in the Caderno series by the Getúlio Vargas Foundation. Two other cases written by Brazilian professors were published by the foundation, written almost entirely on the basis of my clippings. Finally, a case describing a plebiscite on the establishment of municipalities in the state of Guanabara in 1963 was prepared from clippings and has appeared in a book on Brazilian local government. While I do not claim these cases are of the highest quality, it has been interesting to me that they have gone through rather intensive review, including use in certain classes, and there has been relatively little criticism of their basic authenticity. For a study of the freezing of prices in the national steel mill, I used nothing but clippings and secondary sources. When it was reviewed for publication, it was sent to the sales manager, the official in the steel plant most critical to the decision; he found no appreciable inaccuracies. As a matter of fact, he was quite complimentary, noting that he held this attitude in spite of the fact that the author was a North American.

Today in Brazil it is probably fair to say that research in public administration has achieved new recognition, thanks particularly to the activities of the Ford Foundation. The effect of the Ford grants, particularly at EBAP has been to create a capability which should find support from a variety of sources, not the least of them the government of Brazil. But much will depend on having a reliable research strategy.

Instead of speculating on what it would be nice to know about and therefore study, there must be a tougher-minded examination of what *needs* to be known to advance the society. Inquiry into the power structure of a community or the way in which political socialization occurs may be justified on the basis of scholarly interest. A more fundamental test, it seems to me, involves the specification of the way in which additional data can contribute directly to societal development. In suggesting this type of test, I am not taking issue with the desirability of knowing for the sake of knowing. Nor am I denying that the profound understanding of structure and process will in the long run be rewarding. It is a problem of time and circumstance. Further, it seems quite obvious that funding will become more available as the relationship of the research to the satisfaction of social needs becomes clear.

A Research Strategy

These considerations suggest to me two types of research strategy for today's Brazilian university setting: (i) expansion of the data base for policy development; and (ii) action research which posits the manipulation of a presumably crucial variable and the measurement of the effects of such a change.

As Brazil seeks to optimize its scarce resources and to respond to expanding expectations, the problem of what to do becomes increasingly important. The universities and related institutions will have an enlarged role in identifying emerging problems of public policy, of probing their dimensions, and of evaluating alternative strategies. This type of activity, for example, is a major objective in the creation of an urban research center in the Brazilian Institute of Municipal Administrations. A good example of the kind of policy research that we should expect to see increasingly in Brazil was an AID-commissioned study of strategies of technical assistance to urban development by a professor of the University of Minas Gerais, Dr. Paulo Neves de Carvalho. Not only was AID concerned about what it might do with its own limited resources, but it was also hopeful that the Carvalho study would provide some useful guidelines for other donors, as well as the Brazilian government.

Action research seems to me to be a particularly useful concept in the developing society. In Brazil, for example, the postal service is a special kind of problem. It affects economic growth, makes tax collection more difficult, and generally hampers development of a complex society. What types of changes can make a difference in the postal service? Further, how can we be sure that the variables we manipulate really are the ones that make the difference? Studies that take a real, live problem and seek to manipulate seemingly critical components in the system endow research with a special kind of reality. They take it out of the ivory tower. But there is no sacrifice of rigor. If one is to claim a variable is really crucial, he must be able to prove it. In a sense, action research represents the best of all worlds. It demands rigor, but at the same time its relevance should be clear to even the most reluctant granter of funds.

In the last analysis, change behavior is based on the capability to receive and process information about a situation. If unpleasant data can be handled and examined in terms of their implications for desired ends, presumably the possible responses will be canvassed more broadly. Fewer strategies will lie beyond the limits of consideration. Change itself will be more acceptable. Thus the notion of a data base seems crucial. It is particularly important in education, largely because the inculcation of a problem-solving approach can have value far beyond the resolution of any particular, immediate problem. Since a problem-solving approach requires data, I come back to the fundamental point that research and publications are absolutely essential parts of the development of education in public administration. They are not separable from the learning process.

Training and the University

I would now like to apply some of these notions to the training situation. In recent years in the United States, there has been increasing recognition that most of the conventional training has been only marginally effective. If one were psychologically ready to learn a new way to tie a knot, our typical training would probably be useful in describing the new method. A lecture-demonstration, for example, may be quite appropriate to the provision of such cognitive inputs. In most cases, however, the real task is to create the readiness to receive new inputs.

Often we put the cart before the horse. We assume the readiness for change, and we spend our training time providing cognitive data about what the good leader does, how he prepares his budget, how he manages his time, and so forth. You will note that this is a highly nonthreatening situation for everyone. The instructor usually adheres fairly faithfully to the gospel and is recognized as the prophet. By sticking to the high road, he avoids real engagement and therefore threat. The participants need not expose themselves, get little feedback, operate at the intellective and not the emotional level, and typically depart feeling very good about the experience and with little incentive to change.

Roughly the same thing happens in the educational situation. Students go through a series of routines preparatory to receipt of a symbol of completion, namely, a degree, indicating that they have successfully negotiated the procedural hurdles.

Theoretically, learning is an individual experience. It requires a willingness to receive inputs, but it does not stop there. Each individual has to work his own way through the inputs he receives, in terms of his definition of the situation, in terms of his own needs, and in terms of his own processing skills. But the building of a data base is not a passive thing. Learning involves anxiety, insecurity that one does not know enough, and willingness to risk exposure of ignorance to reduce such tensions.

Perhaps the concept in training that comes closest to providing a simple handle for dealing with the complexities of learning is problem solving. At first this may seem hardly like an earth-shattering statement. Ask yourself, however, how often in training sessions the problem becomes the focus, as compared with rules of behavior. It often seems that the problem must be found to fit the prescription. A specific illustration may help to get the point across.

One consulting project in Brazil involved a federal agency whose executive was regarded as having real leadership deficiencies. The executive personally initiated the consulting arrangements to "prove" that he was doing all the right things, e.g., his organization chart was in order. A good deal of consulting time and money was spent in going through the motions of examining processes and organization relationships, even though it was general knowledge that these were not the key problems at all. No one wanted to face the real issue. Such situations are not restricted to Brazil. They abound in the United States. Increasingly, however, we are recognizing that we cannot sweep the unpleasant things under the table. If the problem is a human one, it has to be confronted. To the extent we can, we must build processes that enable the participants in a situation to get the data out in the open. We need to do this not only to solve the immediate problem at hand but also to promote learning. The reluctance to face up to problems simply means that the same old failures are repeated over and over again.

In the case above, the problem was not a technological one. There is no mechanical model of the organization that can account for the variances in leadership behavior. Rather, the issue is one of providing feedback to the leader, of confronting the difficulties that may emerge, of enlarging the arena of information upon which the participants can agree, and of honestly contriving solutions that are as compatible with the articulation of needs as it is possible. Again, the problem-solving process becomes the more meaningful as there is commitment to superordinate goals, as there is willingness to risk the unpleasantness of interpersonal encounter, and as there is recognition that growth and new learning must be the product of tension and uneasiness.

To put it bluntly, the traditional "O and M" people are not ever going to do very much about the real problems in Brazilian organizations. Bear in mind that the executive in our case above found it to his political interest to support an inquiry whose restraints were such as to avoid the raising of the real problem. "O and M" work as currently practiced in Brazil and elsewhere is often a psychological crutch upon which inaction and resistance to change can be supported. The unsuspecting or unknowing person may be mesmerized by the charts and the evidences of tech-

nological neutrality. But I think it is high time that those who do
have sophistication and concern take a very hard look at the contribution of "O and M" to management improvement.

Now let us take a look at what I consider to be the worst of all
worlds. It is the case where an agency, for varying ritualistic
reasons, wants to appear concerned about improvement. It does
this by sending one of its people to a course in "O and M" offered,
perhaps, by a university well removed from the agency's scene of
operations. There are several reasons why such a course can be
guaranteed to produce no change in the organization.

First, the traditional subject matter of "O and M," which I
confess to having taught for a number of years, simply does not
have much to offer the administrator who honestly seeks change.

Secondly, such a course is typically taught on a cognitive,
prescriptive basis. Highly mechanistic strategies are suggested in
lectures that are processed in differing ways by participants. To
the extent that there is class interaction, it is around the technological issue of how to make a flow chart, rather than how to
create acceptance in a new situation.

Thirdly, the set of rules has been communicated only to the
administrator who went to school. The situation in the organization has not changed; and the fellow who took the course comes
back with ideas about how the situation ought to be, rather than
skills in defining problems and helping others to see the need for
change.

Thus, in a very real way, many of the same types of "O and M"
assumptions have characterized a long and tortuous effort in
Brazil over some twenty years to bring about national administrative improvement. The failure to do something about these problems may have been the most critical factor in the downfall of one
president. Yet the reform approaches have been mechanistic and
superficial. They have tended to assume that one can command
rational behavior—which is a particularly outrageous assumption
in Brazil. They have tended to rely on ad hoc arrangements external to the operating units, such as special commissions or
extraordinary ministries; and the effort has been largely devoted
to concocting new organization charts.

Essentially, the basic issue raised here involves the failure (i) to see training as a behavioral event, rather than an intellective one, (ii) to recognize the centrality of problem solving as a focus for change-oriented training, and (iii) to accept the significance of training as a basic strategy for administrative reform. Such propositions, of course, are not new to many Brazilian scholars. There have been encouraging efforts to get at some of these needs in all of the institutions with which I have been associated. However, to twist an old Frederick Taylor term, what is involved is a "mental revolution." In contrast to Taylor's mechanistic orientations, this revolution is behavioral and, more specifically, problem-centered.

For those concerned with the development of training capabilities in Latin American institutions, I think the propositions I have advanced in the preceding paragraphs should be carefully weighed for their significance in evaluating programs where nationals are sent abroad for training. The time spent away from the job is costly and can be crucial to the enhancement of institutional capability. These experiences should be planned in terms of future needs, not past ones. In general, I think most out-of-country experiences have been hit or miss. To the extent that there has been a theory about the kind of experience sought, it has tended to look backward toward the conventional disciplines. There has been relatively little effort made to know in depth foreign institutions and their programs.

In this respect, I think a word should be said about the contract arrangement whereby a single foreign institution assumes a special responsibility. As I look back on the U.S.C. experience, I take most pride in the aggressive efforts we made to induce the most able people to go abroad and in the care we gave to the total experience in the United States and to the continuing relationships that ensued from this undertaking. It should be noted that this approach tends to force a fairly coherent development of personnel, essentially by the organizational device of entrusting the responsibility to a single entity. In this respect, I would not deny that at U.S.C. we sought to construct experiences in the United States that were congruent with our intellectual understandings of public administration, our values, and our commitments.

Obviously, a counterargument can be raised that this locks the Latin American institution into a single frame of reference. Further, when the students go to one university, as they did under our project, these tendencies are even more pronounced. In some degree, the notion of an intellectual community as one in which there is a ferment of conflicting ideas is certainly affected.

This is an issue that has to be confronted far more honestly and straightforwardly than it has been in the past. Though I have seen no AID document that specifically criticizes the U.S.C. approach of relying primarily on its own resources to construct the training experience, there have been informal statements that we were wrong in doing this. Brazilians, too, have made this criticism. It has been particularly irritating that some people have implied our behavior was dictated by self-interest. As an administrator in the school, I realize to an even greater degree how far tuition falls short in paying the full costs of graduate education. From the point of view of self-interest, it would have been far more economical for us to ask other universities to take on the task of providing the education.

The real issue, it seems to me, involves (i) assumptions about appropriate institutional arrangements for training and education in public administration, and (ii) the evaluation of the current level of such institutional development.

With regard to the first point, at U.S.C. we have an activist view of the role of higher education in public administration. It is perhaps most symbolized by our status as a professional school, as contrasted with a place in the liberal arts college. Though the majority of our faculty may be labeled political scientists, we are somewhat less closely tied to this discipline than are most of the programs in the United States. Psychologists, sociologists, psychiatrists, educationists, and economists all hold professional appointments in our school. Rather than having a special methodology or a special category of knowledge, we define ourselves as problem-oriented, with an overriding value commitment to the public interest as contrasted with a professional, parochial, or private interest. These orientations have led us toward a some-what different set of commitments within the university world. Instead of looking inward only, we are forced consistently to check our reality orientations. We do this by keeping a foot in the world of affairs. Further, our commitments include service to the community, in the sense that the intellectual today can no longer be passive in societal problem solving, but must be actively involved.

While I do not suggest that we at U.S.C. alone hold these values, I do think they represent a total commitment that differs appreciably from the orientations of many other institutions offering programs in public administration. It must also be recognized that these positions have matured over a period of nearly forty years, a long time in the history of education for public administration.

Rightly or wrongly, it is our conviction that the values and structure of the U.S.C. school are more congruent with emerging needs in training and education for public administration than most others. Therefore, when we contract to take on a task, it seems only consistent that we should pursue our value orientations and that we should take advantage of our considerable resources.

These, then, are some of the basic assumptions which a Latin American institution must confront. To what extent does it seek to emulate this model? To what extent does it desire to confine itself to the more traditional concerns of higher education? What about its role in community service? In training? In consulting? In action research? The point here is that an institution must make some basic choices about what it wants to be. At one extreme, there is perhaps the model of the special, professional school with specifically articulated commitments, and at the other extreme the academic department as an assembly point for individual scholars. That kind of analysis should provide an appropriate starting point for the forming of a fruitful relationship with institutions abroad.

There is also the problem of timing. While I see the professional school as having more sharply focused values and commitments, the very nature of the professional society requires that there be a healthy amount of conflict, discord, and even hostility. However, the question is just when such healthy antecedents to creativity and innovation should be fed into the fledgling organization. It was U.S.C.'s position that Brazil is a pluralist society and that the cathartic effects of conflict are apt to be present in any case. That may not be true in other countries. As a result, I think we felt free to pursue immediate organizational interests which seemed to lie in consensus and commitment. Put another way, we wanted to promote belief in the organization and its purpose, rather than to promote a debate that might destroy it.

There is also another point that we did not fully recognize at the time. This has to do with the creation of sympathy and comradeship within institutions, and among them. The sharing of a common experience creates a bond that will overcome many communications barriers. Just having been in the United States or England, for example, can form the basis of a relationship. Having gone to the same institution is a further strengthening force. Having gone to that institution together is an even greater reinforcement of the relationship. There is absolutely no question in my mind that a lot of the good things that have happened in the institutions with which we were associated are a direct result of the personal associations that were developed in the United States.

There are obviously liabilities in the single institution approach. As I have indicated, there is the ultimate need to build diversity into any educational system. There is also the problem of elitism. Beyond a certain point, the conflicts between the "ins"—defined as those attending the "right" institution—and the "outs" can sow bothersome seeds of discord. In my opinion, there must now be a mix in the development of new people at the three institutions with which the U.S.C. project was concerned. The ties of the past should not be forgotten; and a few students should continue to go to U.S.C. However, the time has also come to expand the participating foreign universities. An important step, it seems to me, is the emerging relationship between the University of North Carolina's Department of Political Science and EBAP, Bahia, and Rio Grande do Sul.

In considering the general problem of making the experience abroad as rich and as supportive of the Latin American institution's goals as possible, it should be pointed out that the environment at home must be accepting of changed behaviors. This, of course, is a restatement of an old lesson. We know quite a bit about changing individuals. However, when they get back to home territory, they find that they are the ones who have changed the most. Everything else remains. In some cases the new incentives for change are replaced by an accentuated reversion to past practices; some valuable people simply depart, and a few try to buck the system.

Perhaps the most serious problem faced by the returning professional is the traditional expectation of what a professor is supposed to do. He is expected to convey a body of knowledge, not manage a learning experience. Thus the fix is on the lecture method. Only minimal demands are to be made on the student; most particularly, he is not to be asked to expose himself. When the returnee increases the student workload and seeks to secure inputs from the class members, he finds himself in some serious trouble. One obvious reason is that university learning in Brazil has traditionally occurred in the classroom, 20–22 hours per week, while only 7–10 hours per week are devoted to education outside. Further, while students claim they want to participate, my experience is they find it threatening and demanding. Only the very good students are willing to incur the penalties to receive the rewards.

These are very long-run problems that handicap the transfer of the educational experience across cultures. And they are not restricted to Brazil. We face the same kinds of difficulties in the United States. In any case, it must be realized that the improvement of professorial performance involves more than the professor.

To the extent that the professor can help to create change in the system by bettering his performance, it is likely that his participation in training and research activities will be crucial. In other words, I do not believe one sets out to create a "better" professor through the consideration of better classroom techniques, the employment of audiovisual techniques, and improved bibliographies.

In the case of the U.S.C. project, I think we had an impact largely because of our emphasis on training. Those who had a true training engagement seem to me to have performed outstandingly in the classroom in Brazil. There is a simple reason for this. The trainee learns to be sensitive to the needs of his group. If he is a good trainer, he continually seeks feedback on the degree to which the designed inputs are meeting needs. He is interested in two-way communication. In the degree to which that fundamental insight into the training process has been learned, I think we can anticipate better performance in the classroom. Frankly, however, I do not feel that our educational program at U.S.C. was sufficiently geared to exploit this path toward better teaching. We were not systematic about getting our participants into training experiences. As a result, a number of people have gone back to Brazil little changed from the previous orientations.

Research as a basis for better teaching has been relatively little exploited. To some extent, the seminar experience in the United States forces the participant into making a contribution to the data base; but in general, research as a teaching tool has been underutilized. We have argued with some justification that U.S.C.'s location in a large metropolitan complex with relatively good governments has given us an edge in designing research experiences. However, I do not think we have been systematic enough in utilizing these opportunities. With the exception of the few who have received the doctoral degree, I think we did not succeed in carrying the research enterprise far enough in the United States to help our participants to feel secure about their competence. The conduct of a joint research project does require real leadership on the part of the professor. Somehow, it has to come out a success; and the risk is therefore high. Yet such encounters with the real world are obviously central to a total experience. One of the best ventures in which I have participated occurred in Brazil, as a purely extracurricular activity, organized by Professor Jorge Gustavo. Before an important plebiscite on the

Guanabara constitution, a well-designed attitude study was run in one of the suburban communities. The students developed a large investment of time in that study; there was a great deal of interaction about the issues raised; and the quality of the data was sufficiently high that a dinner was held, at which the results were given to the regional administrator for the area involved. It represented, in my mind, a rich learning experience.

Conclusions

In the opening lines of this chapter, I warned that these "lessons of experience" in technical assistance are my own. Hence there has been no reluctance to use the personal pronoun and to refer repeatedly to my own institution. Similarly, I have dealt with my "beat," Brazil, and the three institutions of higher education with which I have had a close association.

If an anecdotal essay has any utility, it is because the variables that affect technical assistance are so numerous as to make it difficult to develop a set of propositions with any confidence. Professor Carvalho's study of the institutional development of EBAP[2] contributes to this humility. It emphasizes the degree to which seemingly primary goals have had to undergo change in EBAP's fifteen years. With the displacement of goals have come differing emphases on leadership, on resource needs, and on relationships within the larger system.

I am fearful that old impressions about public administration may get in the way of new understandings. For example, I have found it difficult to talk to some of my old and dear friends about a discipline in which we once shared common values. We no longer speak the same language. Frames of reference have particularly changed. Unfortunately, experience is often not used for learning and continuing growth but rather to restrict and confine such processes. In the last few years, it has become abundantly clear that the United States has much to learn from its

2. This study was part of the Inter-University Program in Institution-Building. See n. 1 above.

experience, not only in providing technical assistance to the other countries but also in solving its own problems. The difficulty lies, of course, in our inability to look freshly and openly at what has happened. Hopefully, this report has been honest enough and introspective enough to suggest the value of a more conscious effort to use our experience to learn for the future.

Part III

Bureaucratic Responses to Change

Chapter 9

Bureaucracy, Democracy, and Development: Some Considerations Based on the Chilean Case

Charles J. Parrish

The gap between intention and result in human conduct is always troubling, and it has become a considerable preoccupation in recent years for those who study comparative administration. Underdeveloped countries are littered with the remains of well-intentioned development projects which went awry. Fred Riggs' work stands out as the major catalytic force in the generation of comparative administrative studies which attempt to explain the role of bureaucratic factors in these failures.[1] Riggs employs a conceptual framework which involves the need to assess the level of development of entire political systems. He suggests that there are characteristics of bureaucracy peculiar to political systems which are at different levels of political development. It is here suggested that there are weaknesses in this approach and that it would be more fruitful to look to organization theory rather than to political-development theory in the comparative study of public bureaucracy.

A major reason for this position is to be found in the many difficulties presented by political-development theory. The teleological nature of much of this sort of analysis is apparent. More-

1. For basic statements of Riggs' point of view, the reader should consult the following works by him: *Administration in Developing Countries* (Boston: Houghton Mifflin, 1964); "Bureaucrats and Political Development," in *Bureaucracy and Political Development,* ed. J. LaPalombara (Princeton, N.J.: Princeton Univ. Press, 1963), pp. 120–67; "The Structures of Government and Administrative Reform," in *Political and Administrative Development,* ed. R. Braibanti (Durham, N.C.: Duke Univ. Press, 1969), pp. 220–324; and "Bureaucratic Politics in Comparative Perspective," *Journal of Comparative Administration* 1, no. 1 (May 1969): 5–38.

over, the ethnocentric models employed by many of those studying political development have colored their work with normative biases which are rarely stated explicitly.[2] Support for this contention can be provided by briefly turning to the work of Riggs.

The assumptions on which many bureaucratic reforms in the underdeveloped world have been based are questioned by Riggs. He accurately points out that while many of these reforms were intended to increase efficiency and rationality, they often strengthened the capacity of the national bureaucracies to dominate their environments. This allowed them to set their own goals independently of the structures constitutionally charged with responsibility for goal selection. The activities of reform-oriented foreign advisory groups from the industrialized world abetted this process. Riggs deplores this situation, arguing that where it occurred it discouraged "political" development.[3] In this sense, Riggs identifies political development with the capacity of political structures to dominate administrative structures.

His argument is based on the politics/administration dichotomy. Since the literature which has questioned the analytic utility of this concept is voluminous,[4] one would seem to need a

2. Gabriel Almond's work is as illustrative of this point as it is influential. His earlier statements on political development, e.g., "Introduction," in *The Politics of Developing Areas,* ed. Gabriel A. Almond and James S. Coleman (Princeton, N.J.: Princeton Univ. Press, 1960), pp. 3–64, are more clearly ethnocentric than are his more recent ones, e.g., Gabriel A. Almond and G. Bingham Powell, *Comparative Politics: A Developmental Approach* (Boston: Little Brown, 1966). In his later writings, Almond has attempted to make his model more dynamic, to account more adequately for change, and more general, to avoid the charge of an ethnocentric view of the development process. He does better on the former count than on the latter, for he still bases his model of a developed polity on his conception of the structures and operation of the Western democracies, specifically, the United States and the United Kingdom.

3. Time has changed Riggs' ideas about political development somewhat since his first fairly complete statement of them (Riggs, *Administration in Developing Countries*). However, his most recent conceptualization still depends on an acceptance of the theoretic utility of the politics/administration dichotomy. Now, however, he speaks of the "constitutive" system, rather than of politics, and the "bureaucratic" system, rather than administration. Riggs, "The Structure of Government and Administrative Reform." For a telling criticism, see Martin Landau, "Political and Administrative Development: General Commentary," in *Political and Administrative Development,* ed. Braibanti, pp. 325–53.

4. Scholars have long been disturbed about the utility of this idea. For an early example of this questioning, see Carl J. Friedrich, "Public Policy and the Nature of Administrative Responsibility," in *Public Policy,* ed. Carl J. Friedrich and E. S. Mason (Cambridge: Harvard Univ. Press, 1940), pp. 2–34. Other

particularly strong argument in its behalf if one is to base an analysis on such a slippery concept. Riggs does not provide a compelling justification of the utility of the dichotomy in any of his work. Usually, he merely assumes its worth and then proceeds in his analysis to cloak any number of shrewd observations about the operation of bureaucracy in underdeveloped countries in a series of obtuse neologisms. Moreover, a commitment to liberal democracy adds a further ethnocentric dimension to his work. It may be this use of the politics/administration dichotomy which often makes him seem to be a modern-day counterpart of those scholar-reformers who labored long and hard to bring the fruits of efficiency and rationality to public life in the United States. They worked to bring an end to the spoils system through the adoption of merit systems, budget reforms, and similar measures, with the aim of saving administration from pernicious politics. Although the rich obscurity of Riggs' writings does not always make it apparent, he seems to be laboring away in the underdeveloped world on the other side of the same workbench. Only his aim is to save politics from pernicious administration. Perhaps the lesson to be learned is that no matter how complex and abstract the theoretical constructs, they are of little value if they fail to address properly the relevant questions.

In devising theoretical formulations to clarify the analyses of public bureaucracies in economically underdeveloped countries, it is argued here that organization theory affords more fruitful avenues to explore for ideas than does the well-trod route of political development theory.

An organization is here defined as any set of "consciously coordinated activities of two or more persons."[5] A formal organization is one which has been established with the explicit purpose of achieving some stated goal.[6] A public bureaucracy is a par-

---

writers criticizing the idea are Emmette S. Redford, *Administration of National Economic Control* (New York: Macmillan, 1952), chap. 1; Paul Appleby, *Policy and Administration* (University: Univ. of Alabama Press, 1949), p. 15; and H. A. Simon, D. W. Smithburg, and V. A. Thompson, *Public Administration* (New York: Knopf, 1950), pp. 381–401.

5. C. I. Barnard, *The Functions of the Executive* (Cambridge: Harvard Univ. Press, 1938), p. 73.

6. Peter M. Blau and W. Richard Scott, *Formal Organizations* (San Francisco: Chandler, 1962), p. 5.

ticular type of formal organization. Precise definition in this
matter is not likely to avoid some of the ambiguities that one finds
in the real world. As Dahl and Lindblom have pointed out, there
are organizations in existence that defy ready classification as
either public or private, no matter what your definition.[7] However that may be, here a public bureaucracy is viewed as a formal
organization whose principal activities are the achievement of
publicly defined goals selected in the name of the political community in which it exists and whose existence is defended primarily in terms of its responsibility as an agent of that community.
The process through which a public bureaucracy defines its goals
is viewed here as dynamic. It encompasses both the organizing
and giving of direction to a bureaucracy by a legislative act or an
executive order and the process through which the initial goals
are defined and redefined in the subsequent operation of that
bureaucracy. Goal selection in public bureaucracies is a complicated process. The conventional view, in which "the ends of a
governmental agency were assumed to be determined by legislative enactment or executive order,"[8] has been tellingly criticized
by Lindblom and others as not squaring with the empirical
evidence. As suggested earlier, the simple dichotomy between
politics and administration, or even between policy making, program, and implementation, seems too narrowly conceived to be
adequate to explain the realities of bureaucracy. The purpose of
this chapter is to explore some aspects of the relationship between
the operation of public bureaucracy and the selection and achievement of development goals in the Chilean setting, which is both
economically underdeveloped and democratic.

That Chile is economically underdeveloped is not likely to be
questioned, but some may have doubts about its claim to be

    7. Robert Dahl and Charles E. Lindblom, *Politics, Economics and Welfare*
(New York: Harper, 1953).
    8. Robert L. Peabody and Francis E. Rourke, "Public Bureaucracies," in
Handbook of Organizations, ed. James G. March (Chicago: Rand McNally, 1965),
p. 805; see also Charles E. Lindblom, *The Intelligence of Democracy* (New York:
Free Press, 1965), and A. O. Hirschman and Charles E. Lindblom, "Economic
Development, Research and Development Policy Making: Some Converging
Views," *Behavioral Science* 7 (1962): 211–22, as reprinted in *A Sociological
Reader on Complex Organizations*, ed. A. Etzioni (New York: Holt, Rinehart and
Winston, 1969), pp. 87–103.

democratic. Chile can be accurately said to have had a democratic political system since the early 1930's, if one is precise about the meaning of democracy in this context. Democracy here means only that there are periodic elections in which different candidates compete for the votes of the citizenry for public offices and candidates who win the larger number of votes are elected and occupy the offices until the next regular election.[9] This definition is limited to the procedures through which those who fill public offices are selected and, it should be noted, is empirical and not normative. It makes no judgment about the degree of social or economic justice which is present in a system. The utility of such an approach is illustrated by Neubauer's study which undermines the contention of those such as Lipset and Cutright[10] who saw a strong correlation between economic development and the incidence of democratic practices.[11] This approach is particularly relevant here in that we are centrally concerned with bureaucratic aspects of the problem of achieving development goals within a democratic setting.

Defining Development Goals: Comprehensive Planning or Incrementalism?

Devising comprehensive development plans in Latin America is a well-established practice. There are important national and international agencies which are concerned with furthering such activities. A major purpose of the Alliance for Progress was to achieve a balanced economic and social development in the area through multilateral cooperation. In its efforts to do so, the

9. Anthony Downs, *An Economic Theory of Democracy* (New York: Harper, 1957); Robert A. Dahl, *Modern Political Analysis,* rev. ed. (Englewood Cliffs, N.J.: Prentice-Hall, 1970); Deane Neubauer, "Some Conditions of Democracy," *American Political Science Review* 61, no. 4 (Dec. 1967): 1002–9; and Deane Neubauer and Charles Cnudde, eds., *Empirical Democratic Theory* (Chicago: Markham, 1969).

10. S. M. Lipset, "Some Social Requisites of Democracy," *American Political Science Review* 53 (1959): 69–105; and Phillips Cutright, "National Political Development: Some Economic Correlates," in *Politics and Social Life: An Introduction to Political Behavior,* ed. Nelson Polsby et al. (Boston: Houghton Mifflin, 1963), pp. 569–81.

11. Neubauer, "Some Conditions of Democracy."

Alliance "has accelerated the trend toward comprehensive national planning in Latin America."[12] Despite the general trend toward national planning there are some who raise serious objections to the entire effort.

Charles Lindblom, for example, has suggested that comprehensive national planning in the selection of public goals is not a particularly fruitful enterprise for several reasons,[13] emphasizing complexity of the problems faced and the inevitable limitation on the availability of relevant information needed for planning on a broad scale. Lindblom argues that the actual behavior of bureaucrats inevitably subverts initial organizational goals. The bureaucrat proceeds from decision to decision in a pragmatic manner. The key variable in his decision in a particular case is much more likely to be his prior decisions in similar cases than the legally defined goal of the organization established by legislative enactment or executive order. Lindblom criticizes the "root" approach to administration which emphasizes the proper role of public bureaucracies as being largely determined by such enactments or orders, because its assumptions do not square with the facts of bureaucratic behavior.[14] Rather than being disturbed by the gap between the behavior of bureaucrats and the manifest objectives of public bureaucracies, Lindblom suggests that a properly run bureaucracy allows for such behavior. He does not imply that bureaucrats should be allowed to define their goals wholly without constraints, however. Such an extreme position is untenable, for one cannot both be committed to pluralistic democracy, as Lindblom is, and advocate the existence of an unfettered bureaucracy. He avoids this problem by arguing that bureaucracies should be controlled through the operation of various kinds of "partisan mutual adjustment among the large number of in-

12. *Partners in Development: Report of the Commission on International Development*, Lester B. Pearson, chairman (New York: Praeger, 1969), p. 245.
13. Hirschman and Lindblom. For an understanding of the philosophy underlying Lindblom's position, consult his *Intelligence of Democracy*; "Economic Development"; "Policy Analysis," *American Economic Review* 48 (1958): 298–312; and "The Science of 'Muddling Through,'" *Public Administration Review* 29, no. 2 (1959): 79–88.
14. Lindblom, "Science of 'Muddling Through.'"

dividuals and groups among which analysis and policy making is fragmented."[15] He summarizes his support for a "disjointed incrementalism" in the making of public policy in trying to

> show how the specific characteristics of disjointed incrementalism, taken in conjunction with mechanisms for partisan mutual adjustment, meet each of the difficulties that beset syntopic [comprehensive] policy making: value conflicts, information inadequacies, and general complexity beyond man's intellectual capacities. His [Lindblom's] line of argument shows the influence of pluralistic thinkers on political theory, but he departs from their interest in the control of power and rather focuses on the level of rationality required or appropriate for decision making.[16]

Virtually every student of organizations recognizes the disparity between the actual behavior of a bureaucracy and the goals that it was established to achieve. However, few have gone so far as Lindblom in raising the disparity to the level of a virtue. Every bureaucracy evidences characteristics of "disjointed incrementalism" and an important key to the operation of any organization must be how it behaves in this aspect. As Bennis states:

> Organizations are complex, goals-seeking social units. In addition to the penultimate task of realizing goals, they must undertake two related tasks if they are to survive: (1) they must maintain the internal system and coordinate the "human side," and (2) they must adapt to and shape the external environment.[17]

For public bureaucracy, the "mechanisms for mutual partisan adjustment" which interact with it constitute its relevant environment. The pattern of policy output of a public bureaucracy will depend largely on its style of carrying out what Argyris terms the

15. Hirschman and Lindblom, p. 93.
16. Ibid., p. 94.
17. Warren G. Bennis, "Organizational Developments and the Fate of Bureaucracy," in *Readings in Organizational Behavior and Human Performance,* ed. L. L. Cummings and W. E. Scott (Homewood, Ill.: Irwin and Dorsey Press, 1969), p. 434.

core activities of any organization.[18] These are (i) achieving objectives, (ii) maintaining the internal system, and (iii) adapting to the environment.

As Thompson and McEwen have pointed out, "the setting of goals is a problem of defining desired relationships between an organization and its environment."[19] The nature of the process of "defining desired relationships" between a public bureaucracy and its environment is at issue in Lindblom's formulation. This is of particular pertinence to problems of development because there is a strong national and international bias toward comprehensive planning for development goals. Questions on the role that a public bureaucracy will play in defining and achieving development objectives must then center on the relationship between its internal system and the process of adapting to its environment. In terms of Lindblom's formulation, the relevant questions would be these: What sort of mechanisms for mutual partisan adjustment exist? What is the nature and range of interests they represent? What is the nature and degree of conflict between those interests? What is the manner in which these are brought to the attention of the bureaucracy? In addition, it is useful to ask if comprehensive planning has a role to play in shaping the nature of these mechanisms.

Formal Governmental Structures

In this and the following sections we examine the Chilean experience for an example of how development goals and bureaucratic behavior are likely to be related in a democratic setting. Now, the data on the Chilean bureaucracy are very thin. Most studies of it which exist are legalistic and give us little information on the actual manner in which the informal systems within the bureaucracy operate. As a result, the utility of this chapter

18. Chris Argyris, *Integrating the Individual and the Organization* (New York: Wiley, 1964), pp. 119 ff.
19. James D. Thompson and William J. McEwen, "Organizational Goals and Environment," *American Sociological Review* 23 (1958): 23–31.

must be sought in its suggestions for research into these matters in Chile and elsewhere.

The present governmental arrangement is set in basic outline by the provisions of the Constitution of 1925. Since 1833, Chile has had but two constitutions, a remarkable record for Latin America. The Constitution of 1925 provided for a unitary republic under a presidential system of government. The model followed, in general, was that of the U.S. Constitution, with its provisions for separation of powers and checks and balances. However, the 1925 Constitution was adopted in a period of reaction to the political chaos and policy immobilism of the Parliamentary Era (1895–1924), during which the congress assumed the dominant position in Chilean politics.[20] As a result, the president was given wide formal powers which projected the office again to the center of the political stage, a position it had held from Independence until the defeat of President José Manuel Balmaceda in the civil war of 1891. It was this struggle which brought on the period of congressional dominance.

However, the extensive constitutional powers granted the president must be assessed within the context of the realities of Chilean politics. The ability of the president to develop and implement policy is dependent upon factors well beyond the letter of the Constitution.

The period of congressional dominance prior to 1925 left a strong tradition of congressional autonomy in the Chilean political system.[21] While the formal powers of the congress may seem to be slight in comparison with those of the president, the actual operation of politics gives considerable weight to the congress. However, the effective power of the congress does not lie in the area of the initiation of legislation. Rather, it is essentially a power

20. For accounts of the "Parliamentary Era," see Manuel Rivas Vicuña, *Historia política y parliamentaria de Chile*, 3 vols. (Santiago: Ediciones de la Biblioteca Nacional, 1964); Luís Valencia Avaria, ed., *Anales de la República: textos constitucionales de Chile y registro de los ciudadanos que han integrado los poderes ejecutivo y legislativos desde 1810* (Santiago: Imprenta Universitaria, 1957); and Federico G. Gil, *Genesis and Modernization of Political Parties in Chile* (Gainesville: Univ. of Florida Press, 1962), and *The Political System of Chile* (Boston: Houghton Mifflin, 1966).

21. Gil, *Political System of Chile*, pp. 106–22.

which counterpoints the policy initiatives of the president. The multiparty situation in the congress is a major source of power for those opposed to the policies of the president, for he is unable to count on having in both chambers a majority from his party. When he has a majority of one chamber, he still has to face the need for a coalition with other parties in the other chamber. No president in modern times has had control of both chambers at the same time. The result of this situation is that the president must always depend on multiparty coalitions for the passage of his program. This has proved to be difficult for most chief executives. Even the presidential power to designate a bill as urgent, in order to force congressional action, is limited in its effectiveness. As Weston Agor points out, the public-housing measure proposed by President Frei in 1965 was designated as urgent four times.[22] Each time, as the thirty-day limit on debate approached, the president retired the urgency designation to avoid having the congress reject the measure out of hand. Some ten months elapsed before a much-modified bill could be pushed through for presidential signature. In this case, as in many others, the president had been forced to agree beforehand not to use his power of the additive veto to alter the bill.[23]

The strong sense of tradition felt by members of the congress to the institution is supported by an intricate web of informal norms. This intense institutional loyalty, felt most strongly by senators, adds in many ways to the difficulties of the president in getting his program through the congress. Strong presidential pressure on the congress brings sharp counterattacks from opponents to the chief executive's program occupying very diverse positions on the political spectrum. It is ironic to read some of the defenses of the Chilean senate made by Salvador Allende, the president of the body elected in 1965, against executive attacks on congressional delays. Allende was the opponent of President Frei in the 1964 presidential election and is a dedicated Marxian socialist who, if one believes his statements, advocates revolu-

22. "The Chilean Senate—Internal Distribution of Influence" (diss., Univ. of Wisconsin, 1969), p. 27.
23. Ibid.

tionary changes in Chilean political institutions, including, one must suppose, the congress. Allende's revolutionary stances did not prevent him from filling the role of president of the senate in a manner which has shown great respect for the traditions, internal norms, and formal rules of that body. When Allende became president (after winning the 1970 election), the shoe was on the other foot, and it was he who found the congress recalcitrant.

The National Bureaucracy

The structure of the Chilean government can be said to be both highly centralized and highly decentralized. Geographically, the administration of the country is dominated at the center by the president, who appoints all major officials having the responsibility over particular geographic units. This includes the appointment of mayors of all cities over 10,000 in population.

While the geographic administration of the Chilean government is highly centralized, this is not the case with the national bureaucracy. The central bureaucracy is organized into a series of ministries, which are comparable to those to be found in most countries. There are some fourteen ministries, each headed by a minister appointed by the president and directly responsible to him. An important segment of the public bureaucracy is made up of "institutionally decentralized" agencies. These agencies are numerous and have the responsibility for the regulation of wide areas of national life and are particularly relevant to development policy. In recent years around 35 percent of the national budget was allocated to these decentralized agencies.[24] Even this figure considerably understates their importance. For example, one of them, the social security agency, sees an amount of money flow through it annually which has been recently equal to over 90 percent of the total national budget.[25] This figure included con-

24. Jorge Guzmán Dinator, "Commentario," in *Nueva sociedad, vieja constitución*, ed. J. Guzmán Dinator (Santiago: Orbe, 1964), p. 123.
25. Charles J. Parrish and Jorge Tapia-Videla, "Welfare Policy and Administration in Chile." *Journal of Comparative Administration* 1, no. 3 (1970): 467.

tributions to it as well as budgetary and other allocations. Another example of an important institutionally decentralized agency is the Chilean Development Corporation (Corfo). It was established in 1939 to encourage industrial expansion and was the first of such institutions to appear in Latin America.[26] Corfo's involvement in national industrial life is considerable, for no new industries may be established or plant expansions occur without its approval. The sorts of activities which are encompassed by these semiautonomous agencies can be illustrated by the following examples: the University of Chile and the Technical State University, the Central Bank, the National Council of Foreign Trade (which controls all import and export authorizations), the National Health Service, and most other social services agencies, the Public Housing Corporation, and the Corporation for Agrarian Reform. There are many others which could also be cited.

The basic governing arrangement for these organizations is a composite directorate usually made up of representatives of the President of the Republic and the various interests concerned with the policy area in which the particular agency is involved. Sometimes the president appoints all the directors, but he usually must take a number of his appointments from short lists presented by the various interests directly affected by the policy of the agency. The process involved is usually both complicated and subtle and certainly not well understood in the Chilean public. Gil describes the appointment process to the board of directors of the State Bank of Chile in the following way.

> [It] is composed of seven persons appointed freely by the President . . . five members representing agriculture, industry, commerce, and mining appointed by the chief executive from lists submitted by the organization representing those fields; and two other members chosen by the Chilean president from nominating lists submitted by white-collar workers [*empleados*] and manual workers, respectively.[27]

26. Corporación de Fomento de la Producción, Fundación Pedro Aguirre Cerda, *Geografía económica de Chile*, vol. 3 (Santiago: Talleres Gráficos La Nación, 1962), p. 171.
27. Gil, *Political System of Chile*, p. 137.

The range of activities of the institutionally decentralized agencies related to development is very wide. The social welfare activities of the government, the educational activities, the industrial and agricultural policy areas are all largely overseen by decentralized bureaucracies. It is indeed unfortunate that there is little scholarly attention devoted to these bureaucracies which does not focus on their legalistic characteristics.

The Chilean public bureaucracy employs over 10 percent of the work force, and its total personnel number around 300,000. Its growth in the last thirty years has been rapid. Since 1940, the number of public employees has grown nearly 400 percent, while the population generally has increased only about 35 percent in the same period. The bureaucrats are a varied lot, reflecting many of the characteristics to be found in the population as a whole. However, there are limits to the extent to which the bureaucracy is representative of the Chilean population. For one thing, bureaucrats are better educated, better paid, and generally of higher social status than the average Chilean. Civil service regulations require that certain educational standards be met before one can become a civil servant. These regulations vary with the job to be done, but in order to become a white-collar government employee, the Administrative Statute, which governs public personnel matters, requires that one be eighteen years old or older and in good health and have completed four years of secondary school. Candidates for middle-level offices must hold a secondary-school diploma. These requirements mean that the bureaucracy will overwhelmingly be of higher social status than the general population. Further evidence of this is provided by James Petras, who found that the great majority of Chilean bureaucrats identified with the middle class. This was also true of the lower strata of the bureaucracy whose jobs are primarily menial. Since it is estimated that only some 15 percent of the Chilean population can lay claim to middle-class status[28] a gap of substantial proportions can be assumed to exist between the social status of the bureaucrats and the average Chilean.

One source of protection for bureaucrats against the vicissitudes

28. Ibid., p. 23.

of political life in Chile has been the civil service reforms introduced since 1930, when the first body of general rules governing public service were adopted. By 1960 a set of regulations had been legislated which provided a considerable measure of job security for bureaucrats. These reforms, rationalized as attempts to make the bureaucracy more efficient, served to protect the jobs of many of those added to the bureaucracy during the rapid expansion of the "Radical years" (1938–52).[29] One of the ironies of the reforms that were ostensibly designed to combat a spoils system was that they provided job security for those who originally obtained their positions through the operation of the political patronage system, which developed into a high art under the Radical presidents.

In many respects the operation of the recruitment system of the public service in Chile is characterized by what Riggs refers to as "attainment" criteria; that is, personnel are recruited on partially ascriptive and partially achievement bases. In many cases, the recruitment process is dominated by personal, social, or political considerations. The educational requirements limit at the outset the social-status background of those who have access to most public positions, particularly the higher posts. The oversupply of qualified manpower for jobs available in private life has created a strong pressure for the expansion of public positions to provide jobs for the middle class. Political patronage is important in the recruitment system for the public bureaucracy, with politicians acting as employment agents in many cases.[30]

Once an official is duly appointed he cannot be removed except for reasons covered by law. (This provision does not apply to those political appointees listed above.) Promotion rules combine two concepts: merit and seniority. Evaluation of an employee's merit is made by his superior. The decision on his promotion, however, is made by a qualifying board (*junta calificadora*) on

29. For examinations of the Radical Party, see Germán Urzua Valenzuela, *El Partido Radical: su evolución política* (Santiago: Imprenta Los Andes, 1961); Luís Palma Zúñiga, *Historia del Partido Radical* (Santiago: Editorial Andrés Bello, 1967) and Gil, *Genesis and Modernization of Political Parties in Chile* and *Political System of Chile.*

30. Osvaldo Sunkel, "Change and Frustration in Chile," in *Obstacles to Change in Latin America*, ed. C. Veliz (London: Oxford Univ. Press, 1963), pp. 116–44.

which the employees have one representative. The employee may appeal an adverse decision to the head of the agency. The final appeal and decision, however, are made by the General Comptroller's Office (Contraloría General de la República). In cases where two or more candidates have the same "merit" qualifications, the employee with seniority is promoted.

Some indication of how these rules are actually administered is provided us by Petras. He found a widespread belief that the most important basis for promotion in the bureaucracy was favoritism, not professional standards. There was a disparity between the attitudes of the technicians and professionals and the other ranks, but even among these bureaucrats some 32 percent saw favoritism as playing a large part in promotions. Among other strata of the bureaucracy, 43 percent of the middle-level semiprofessionals saw favoritism as important.[31] Petras further states: "If we examine the basis of favoritism among the bureaucracy we find that among all strata except the lowest, the majority ascribe favoritism to personal, family, or political contacts or pull (*cuña*)."[32] This evidence would point to the existence of a highly politicized informal system operating within the boundaries of the formal system. Moreover, this system would seem to operate in opposition to the formal intentions of the civil service reforms that have been adopted during the last forty years in Chile.

Presidential Controls

While the president of Chile is the chief executive and all administrative personnel in the executive branch are legally responsible to him, the realities are somewhat different than the legal provisions. The president has two major powers which he can employ in attempting to get bureaucrats to comply with his policy intentions. They are his appointment power and his budgetary power. The appointment power of the president is

31. James Petras, *Politics and Social Forces in Chilean Development* (Berkeley: Univ. of California Press, 1969), p. 307.
32. Ibid.

very important in the early stages of his administration when the higher political positions are being filled and there is considerable reshuffling and administrative reorganization. The incoming president is granted special administrative powers to reorganize the public bureaucracy. However, when President Frei took office in 1964 he came under strong political attack from the opposition political parties when he asked the congress for additional powers to introduce reforms which could increase the efficiency of the bureaucracy. The opposition saw the move as an attempt by the Christian Democratic government to gain control over the sprawling bureaucracy which was filled with officeholders whose political loyalties were, likely as not, to the Radical Party through which many of them had obtained their positions. The vigor and effectiveness of the attacks on Frei's plans in this area forced him to state that the reorganization would be carried out in such a way that "it will not signify loss of personnel nor of their salaries; on the contrary, it will mean the coordination of services and functions, with benefits for the public employees, the efficient running of the country, the state and all society."[33] The congress was not mollified by such pronouncements, and Frei did not get the powers for which he had asked. While Frei was able to get many of his partisans into the bureaucracy, it was done at considerable expense. Often, there were created new offices alongside the old ones, and while the incumbent official retained his position and salary, his powers were given to a new official appointed by the president. Where officials were forced out of their positions through reorganization, many were eligible for substantial involuntary retirement benefits. These alone would have proved very costly if the government had attempted to reorganize on a sweeping scale.

The presidential legal powers over the budget are, again, considerable, but this tool of executive control has its limitations. The budget must be passed through the congress and there is considerable resistance in that body to any serious attempts to cut the funds of agencies. The source of this resistance is twofold:

33. Leonard Gross, *The Last Best Hope: Eduardo Frei and Chilean Democracy* (New York: Random House, 1967), p. 134.

(i) the opposition parties fear that in giving in to initiatives aimed at increasing executive control of the bureaucracy they will reap the consequences in future elections in which presidential successes may be translated into votes for the government party or coalition; and (ii), given the tradition of the clientele style of politics, there is a natural resistance to executive efforts which could result in the loss of jobs by political supporters. Usually, a presidential initiative which envisions the creation of a new agency (and incidentally creates new job opportunities) has more chance of success than one which might involve the loss of jobs by present officials.

Cartorial Politics

In analyzing the political evolution of Brazil, Helio Jaguaribe has suggested that it has resulted in a "cartorial state." He describes it in the following way:

> The essence of the Cartorial State is found in the fact that the State is, in the first place, the maintainer or guarantor of the status quo. . . . [It] is a product of clientele politics and, at the same time, the instrument that utilizes and perpetuates it. . . . [In this system] public employment is not in actuality directed toward the rendering of any public service, but only toward the more or less indirect subsidization of clienteles in exchange for electoral support. This function, separated from social reality, unrelated to the need for rendering effective public service, results in an infinite pyramid of positions where innocuous papers are circulated and where the only activity exercised is the feeding of itself through self-benefiting practices. . . . Its objective is not the rendering of public services, but [instead] the provision for a marginal middle class, which, since it has little to do, becomes the predominant force in public opinion— an illustrious force which votes and orients itself within the mechanism of an indirect subsidy. The dominant class indirectly subsidizes the leisure and the marginality of the

middle class, giving it a place within the Cartorial State, and [the middle class] pays a tax which the [State] returns in the form of favors for the maintenance of clientele politics and a semicolonial and semifeudal structure.[34]

The political style of the Radical Party in Chile is clearly representative of cartorial politics. The party's strength has always been its ability to build support on the basis of patronage. During the years that the Radicals were in the presidency (1938–52), jobs were provided for the party faithful through a rapid expansion of the public bureaucracy. The party won the support of business through the distribution of government contracts and credit, the imposition of protective tariffs, and similar measures. The urban masses were also appealed to through an expansion of the welfare system (the actual operation of which was of dubious benefit to them). The efforts of the Radicals and their imitators in other parties severely overtaxed the resources of the system. The budgetary deficits which resulted from governmental attempts to play cartorial politics added considerable impetus to the high rate of inflation already characteristic of the Chilean economy.[35]

The argument might be advanced that the inability of the governmental resources to support cartorial politics of the Radical years paved the way for an increased reliance on the populistic appeals which have dominated executive politics since the end of the Radical years. Carlos Ibáñez' successful campaign in 1952 was based on a rejection of the political parties, and he appealed to national pride in terms which had made him the darling of the Chilean *nacista* political groups fifteen years earlier. As a reaction to the ineptitudes of the Ibáñez administration, political support in the 1958 campaign was divided three ways between the victor, the upright conservative Jorge Alessandri, the Marxist Salvador Allende, and the Christian Democrat

34. Helio Jaguaribe, *Condições institucionais do desenvolvimento.* (Rio de Janeiro: Ministério de Educação e Cultura, Instituto Superior de Estudos Brasileiros, 1958), pp. 22–23, as cited by Lawrence S. Graham, *Civil Service Reform in Brazil* (Austin: Univ. of Texas Press, 1968), p. 95.

35. A very useful summary of the Chilean inflation is to be found in A. O. Hirschman, *Journeys Toward Progress* (New York: Twentieth Century Fund, 1961).

Eduardo Frei. In 1964 Frei won election to the presidency over Allende in a campaign which was based on an emotional anti-Communism and an emphasis on the need for a "Revolution in Liberty."

The increase in populistic politics has created tension in the operation of the cartorial aspects of Chilean government. The expectations of the voting public are regularly raised beyond the capacity of the government to meet them. The result of the cartorial style in Brazil was the present military regime, which stepped in when the middle class became as fearful as the upper social and economic stratum that the Goulart government was going to establish a leftist government. The differences between the cartorial politics of Brazil and those of Chile are profound. Chilean politics have never reached the stage where the cartorial elements overwhelmed other aspects as happened in Brazil. However, even if the strain on national resources stemming from the cartorial politics of the past does not bring a similar fate to Chile, it is a legacy of dubious value for a political system attempting to generate social and economic development in the reality of today.

Defining Development Goals: Legislation

In the process of adopting development reforms, the Chilean congress has not assumed a position of leadership. Given the nature of the relationship between the president and the congress, this is not surprising. While it is the most independent legislative body in Latin America, still the congress acts more as a check on executive initiatives in legislation than the other way around. The president's extensive legislative powers involve him deeply with the congress, and it is largely his actions which set the initial terms for debate on most issues.

It should not be assumed, however, that he is able to have his way regularly with the congress. In many ways the failures that plagued the Frei government from 1964 to 1970 were due to opposition focused in the congress. However, the reforms adopted got through primarily because of pressure brought on the congress by President Frei and thanks to his capacity in the role which A. O. Hirschman has termed the "reformmonger."

In understanding the process of adopting reforms in the Chilean congress, it is instructive to examine the reformmongering model developed by Hirschman in his provocative book, *Journeys Toward Progress*. The parallel between his theoretic formulation and the Chilean congress is remarkable. Moreover, if his model has any practical applicability, it is for reform in a democratic setting such as that of Chile. Reformmongering is the policy strategy which pragmatically attempts to achieve limited development reforms rather than approval all at once for wideranging reform measures. Hirschman begins by assuming that a parliament in an underdeveloped country faces three basic issues. The three issues are assigned symbols and defined in the following way:

a for a moderate reform which is being proposed to Parliament;

$\bar{a}$ or non-a, for the status quo; and

B for the sweeping reform that would result from revolution (Hirschman, p. 275).

The parliament is divided into two broad groupings which can be characterized as progressives and conservatives. The order of preference on the three issues for each group is set forth in Table 9.1. On the basis of the preference order, there seems little

Table 9.1

Progressives	Conservatives
B	$\bar{a}$
a	a
$\bar{a}$	B

chance for much agreement to take place, "if one works . . . with the usual assumption in voting in collective choice models: namely, that only two alternatives are pitted one against the other at any one point of time" (p. 275). Hirschman points out, however, that if a reformmonger is able to confuse the particular issue so that on a particular vote the members of the two groups think that they are voting on different things, he may be able to carry the day for the reform. In other words, if the conservatives can be made to think that they are choosing between a and B and the progressives between a and $\bar{a}$, then "unanimous agreement on 'a' will be the result." In passing, it will be noted that a situation of this sort would be difficult to engineer in real life. To convince the status quo groups that revolution is imminent while convincing the revolutionaries, who are in close proximity to the first groups, that strong opposition to the status quo would not have any chance of success would seem a formidable task.

Hirschman, however, makes his model more realistic through the introduction of a number of divisions within the two groups making up his parliament. The progressives were split into three broad groups: (1) Staunch Progressives and Revolutionaries, (2) Reformers, of which there are two types, and (3) Revolutionaries. The conservatives also divide into three groups: (4) Staunch conservatives, (5) Reformers and Diehards, and (6) Diehards (pp. 281–83).

Table 9.2. *Hirschman reformmongering model*

	Progressives				Conservatives		
(1) Staunch progressives and revolutionaries, R^2	(2) Reformers		(3) Revolutionaries, R^1	(4) Staunch conservatives	(5) Reformers and diehards, D^2	(6) Diehards, D^1
	(i)	(ii)				
B	a	a	B	ā	a	ā
a	B	ā	ā	a	ā	B
ā	ā	B	a	B	B	a

Source: A. O. Hirschman, *Journeys Toward Progress* (New York: Twentieth Century Fund, 1963). p. 282.

Group (1), Staunch Progressives and Revolutionaries, are sincerely dedicated to the idea of sweeping revolution, but if this is seen as an unattainable goal, they will accept a moderate reform over the status quo; the Revolutionaries will accept it in hopes that a more complete reform will follow. Reformers, group (2), prefer reform to the status quo, but some prefer revolution over the status quo as their second choice, while a second group choose the status quo as their second alternative. The Revolutionaries of group (3) are all out for revolution and prefer to see the status quo remain in effect rather than support a piecemeal reform, in hopes that it will lead to revolution. Group (4), the Staunch Conservatives, want to preserve the status quo, but they are willing to accept a moderate reform in order to avoid revolution. The Reformers of group (5) are grudgingly for reform so that they can avoid the chaos that they feel may come without reform, and the Staunch Conservatives of this group are for reform because they anticipate that either it will not work or that they will be able to subvert it once it is on the books. The Diehards of group (6) are those who prefer the status quo and are willing to fight for it; thus they would prefer to see a revolution come rather than accede to a moderate reform (p. 284).

A perusal of the variation in preference order of the groups in the Hirschman model quickly reveals that there is a considerable basis upon which to put together a coalition behind the moderate reform. Members of groups (1), (2), (4), and (5) rate *a* as either their first or second choice. Hirschman analyzes the reformist coalition that could be put together in the parliament and concludes that it cannot be said that in this situation "the smaller the number of . . . extremists [the] better."

> For it is only the presence of the revolutionaries that makes it possible to obtain support for alpha [*a*] among conservatives along the lines explored above, and the progressives are similarly induced to settle for alpha by the presence of a solid group of staunch conservatives and diehards who are unwilling to yield anything. Any elimination of these groups may render agreement between progressives and conservatives impossible [p. 284].

In viewing Chilean history from Hirschman's vantage point, one must wonder why more important reforms have not taken place before this late date. The Chilean congress has had representatives of groups similar to the ones described in the above model for a long time, yet until recently the reforms introduced have not seemed to offer much hope for alleviating the continuing economic problems of Chile. One of the reasons for this may be that in the past the measures that would be put into category *a* by both conservatives and some progressives in Chile, have often not been really reforms, but rather policies in the interest of some specific groups. One example of this during the Ibáñez government was an attempt to reform the agricultural situation. Two main problems presented themselves: the lack of agricultural credit for capital improvements, and the absence of predictable market conditions.[36] The market situation was due primarily to the price controls which the government exercised over agricultural goods. Few could wisely invest in agriculture, for no one could accurately figure out what sorts of profits could be made because the government's policy on prices was very erratic and was as responsive to political considerations as economic factors. When the reform was presented to the congress, only part of it was adopted—not surprisingly, the proposal for expanding credit in the agricultural sector rather than the one for reforming the pricing situation. As was pointed out in another context earlier, the result was that from 1956 to 1960 the largest single sector receiving credit was agriculture.[37] Needless to say, since the market structure was not reformed, the credit which went into agriculture did not stay long, but was invested in other ways which promised a more favorable return. The result was that what paraded as a development reform was in fact special-interest legislation in behalf of the large landowners who benefited most from the newly available credit. Middle-class groups were willing to go along with the plan because it protected their interests in that it did not attack the government's system of price control over food products.

The adoption of reforms in a democratic setting seems inevitably to involve some form of reformmongering. While the last two Chilean governments have been committed to comprehensive

---

36. *The Agricultural Economy of Chile: A Report of the Mission Organized by the International Bank for Reconstruction and Development and the Food and Agricultural Organization of the United Nations* (New York: United Nations, 1952).
37. Corporación de Fomento, *Geografía*, 3:171.

national planning for development, the actual process of legis-
latively adopting development goals is indubitably incremen-
talist. The actual process of democratic politics makes it so.
Moreover, any reforms passed into legislation often have to be
purchased through the granting of special concessions to one or
another effectively organized group.

Defining Developing Goals: The Bureaucracy

As has been suggested earlier, the process of setting goals in
public bureaucracies is dynamic and is based on the interaction
of the internal system which it generates in its activities and the
relationship of this system with the environment. In devising
organizational goals in Chile, the environment of a development
bureaucracy is not often a stable one, and reappraisal of goals
. . . appears to be a recurrent problem for large organizations,
albeit a more central problem in an unstable environment than in
a stable one."[38] For a development bureaucracy in Chile, the
relevant environment would include the presidency, the congress,
clientele groups, and other groups and organizations, including
public ones, interested in its operations. In the words of Lindblom, these are the relevant "mechanisms for partisan mutual
adjustment" which influence goal selection within the bureaucracy. Organizational strategies for dealing with the environment
can be classified as competitive or cooperative,[39] and any large
bureaucracy's strategy for interacting with its environment is
bound to show evidence of both. It must compete for resources,
powers, sometimes clients, and other valued things with other
organizations. Sometimes its purposes are controversial, and it
can be subjected to strong attacks from its environment which
ultimately cause a reappraisal of these purposes; and in order to
survive, the bureaucracy may redefine its goals in ways that reduce the threats to it. An example of such a situation in Chile is
afforded by James Petras' brief description of the two organiza-

38. Thompson and McEwen, p. 23.
39. Ibid., p. 26; and James Thompson, *Organizations in Action* (New York:
McGraw-Hill, 1967), pp. 32–36.

tions established to manage agrarian reform.[40] The two agencies
are the Institute of Agrarian Development (INDAP) and the
Agrarian Reform Corporation (CORA). When the Frei government took office in 1964 much was made of its intentions to carry
out a vigorous program of agrarian reform, and one of the leading young reformers of the Christian Democratic Party, Jacques
Chonchol, was appointed executive vice-president of INDAP.
Petras found that there was a strong support for social change
among the many officials who came into INDAP and CORA in
this period. For the first three years of the Frei government the
two organizations operated under the mild agrarian reform law
which had been passed in 1962 by the conservative government
of Jorge Alessandri. The program under this law moved slowly
in three directions: the establishment of *assentamientos* (cooperatives) on expropriated *fundos* (farms), unionization of
peasants, and providing credit facilities and technical assistance
for small farmers. The passage of the 1967 agrarian reform law,
which provided a stronger legal basis for expropriation, "did not
accelerate implementation of agrarian reform. Lacking political
and financial support for expropriation and distribution of land to
landless peasants, INDAP and CORA's operations proceeded at
a snail's pace."[41] As of the date of the study by Petras, it could be
seen that there was a shift in the goals being pursued by the
agrarian reform bureaucracies.

President Frei, while maintaining a verbal commitment to the
goals of agrarian reform, had been forced by political considerations to limit his support for the program, and the congress,
which had passed the stronger 1967 law in a typical reformmongering situation, did not show sufficient support for the
agrarian-reform objectives to provide adequate financing for the
more stringent aspects of the program of expropriation. Those on
the left in the congress, who verbally support harsh expropriation programs, were reluctant for political reasons to give much
support to the Christian Democratic efforts to carry out a successful agrarian-reform program. Their recalcitrance coupled with the

40. Petras, pp. 239 ff.
41. Ibid., p. 240.

open opposition of their conservative colleagues to produce a situation which might be characterized as "status quo monger-ing." The situation led to the gradual shift in goals of INDAP and CORA from expropriation (very controversial) toward unionization of peasants (controversial, but less so).

A development bureaucracy, then, is likely to pursue a com-petitive strategy where (i) its goals are controversial and gen-erate conflict, (ii) its internal system operates in support of these goals, and (iii) there are strong organizations in its environment which support the goals. In the case of INDAP and CORA, the first and second elements were present and the third seemed to exist at first in the support generated by the presidential office. As presidential support proved to be more verbal than substan-tive, the goals of the organizations began to shift toward the less controversial goal of unionization, which could also be seen as an attempt to shape the environment through the creation of a po-tential source of support.

Of the range of cooperative strategies that might be followed by a development bureaucracy,[42] one is of particular interest here: cooptation. Cooptation comes about partly because of the struc-ture of the governing bodies of development agencies, which are of a corporative composition, in which representatives of con-cerned groups are given policy roles. Cooptation, following Selznik, "is the process of absorbing new elements into the leadership structure or policy-determining structure of an organi-zation as a means of averting threats to its stability or existence."[43] Selznik, in his much cited study, documented the shift in goals by the TVA as local interest groups were incorporated into the decision-making structure in order to gain acceptance for the organization.[44] In the case of the "institutionally decentralized" Chilean agencies, a degree of cooptation is provided for by law. It must be expected that in the development-policy areas this

42. Other strategies that also could be explored are bargaining and coalition, Thompson and McEwen, p. 25, and Thompson, *Organizations in Action* chap. 3.

43. Philip Selznick, "Foundations of Organization Theory," *American Sociologi-cal Review* 13 (Feb. 1948): 25–35, as reprinted in *Organizations: Structure and Behavior*, ed. J. Litterer (New York: Wiley, 1963), p. 288.

44. Philip Selznick, *TVA and the Grass Roots* (Berkeley: Univ. of California Press, 1949).

fact will inevitably affect the nature of the goal-achievement function of public bureaucracies.

Little is known about the operation of the internal systems of bureaucracies in relation to development policy making in Chile. However, Petras has provided us with data which give us some insight into the Chilean bureaucratic world. While most Chilean bureaucrats support the idea of social change in the abstract, they evidence a weaker commitment to issues which might threaten to result in rapid alternations of existing social and economic patterns. The issue which they rate as most important is educational reform, a fairly noncontroversial issue which does not have strong opposition from any quarter (Petras, p. 325). The reform of the formerly wholly foreign-owned copper industry, the chief source of foreign exchange for the country, is given fairly low priority by Petras' sample of bureaucrats (p. 326). Both full employment and controlling the inflation (typically issues which would be of primary interest to the middle class in general) were assigned more importance than the copper reform (pp. 326–27). While some 51 percent of the bureaucrats saw the peasantry as the class which must be improved first (p. 328), the higher bureaucrats tended to feel that workers and peasants were actually being favored as much as business and industrial groups (p. 320). While most bureaucrats identified overwhelmingly with the middle class (p. 321), they also, overwhelmingly, saw that class as the least favored by government policy under the Christian Democratic government (p. 320).

In view of the cartorial aspects of Chilean bureaucracy, strongly oriented toward job security and clientele politics, one cannot expect that strong support for development goals will arise out of the internal operation of the country's administrative system.

The capacity of the presidency to constrain the negative implications for development policy of the operation of the internal systems of the bureaucracies varies. Since most bureaucracies concerned with development policy are decentralized, direct executive control through hierarchical authority relationships is vitiated. If there is a strong presidential commitment to a particular development-policy objective, the president must manipulate his appointment and budgetary powers to obtain compliance from the bureaucracy. However, strong action against recalcitrant bureaucrats is difficult, since there is an elaborate system of civil service provisions which protect their jobs, and the bureaucrats can often count on the support of powerful clientele groups in the environment whose interests may be threatened by the policy being pushed. In many cases, as has happened in the agricultural area, the political costs to the president of giving very strong support to a policy, even though legally adopted by the congress, may be too great in relation to possible payoffs.

Conclusion

The foregoing pages represent a brief attempt to explore a range of bureaucratic obstacles to the achievement of development objectives in a democratic environment, relying on the Chilean case for evidence. Democratic procedures shape the operation of mutual partisan adjustment mechanisms in ways which give considerable weight to the best-organized political interests in a society. It is usually these interests which have the most social and economic resources which can be put to political purposes. To survive, public bureaucracies in such settings must devise strategies to deal with these interests. If these bureaucracies seriously attempt to achieve objectives which run counter to the interests of such powerful groups, then they must have ways to insulate themselves from the pressures that can be brought against them. Often this involves finding other forces in the environment to counter the influence of those opposed to the goals. Failing this, the alternative is to accommodate through redefining the bureaucratic objectives into objectives which do not threaten influential groups.

The elements in the Chilean situation which encourage co-optation as a bureaucratic strategy illustrate the problem. As Selznick points out:

Cooptation reflects a state of tension between formal authority and social power. The former is embodied in a particular structure and leadership, but the latter has to do with subjective and objective factors which control the loyalties and potential manipulability of the community. Where the formal authority is an expression of social power, its stability is assured. On the other hand, when it becomes divorced from the sources of social power its continued existence is threatened.[45]

Since development goals are often threats to those whose formidable social power is based on economic and social relationships which the policies are aimed at altering, formal authority supporting development policies is inevitably divorced to some degree from social power. It must be expected that the tension described by Selznick will exist in any political system attempting to achieve development goals. As a result, the tendency toward cooptation and other factors capable of diverting development policy must be accounted for and controlled if the development goals are to be served and the attempt is not to be turned to serving merely the interests of the best-organized political groups.

The problem of managing the tendencies of bureaucracy toward cooptation and other practices which threaten development goals becomes, in our formulation, a problem of structuring the environments of the development bureaucracies so that they provide support for development objectives.

In the controversy between disjointed incrementalism and comprehensive national planning, the "incrementalists" would logically seek to restructure environments so as to increase the number of people in the effective interest groups, i.e., in the groups that have their interests represented in the operation of the policy mechanisms. There is, however, a complication in this position for underdeveloped countries. In an underdeveloped country the rapid organization of large groups of economically and socially deprived people may well result in severe demands

45. Selznick, p. 289.

upon the capital resources of the system. If sustained economic development is to be achieved, the capacity must be present to save and invest in the sectors in which capital-output ratios promise a high rate of growth. The newly organized groups may well opt for raising consumption and so undermine saving capacity. Such an increase in demands on a system like that of Chile could lead to considerable political instability.

Despite the arguments ranged by Lindblom against central planning, arguments that make much of the limitations of human knowledge, it well may be that comprehensive national planning provides a useful force for breaking the sort of democratic deadlocks which the operation of disjointed incrementalism has produced in the Chilean case. It has been the commitment of national and international organizations to comprehensive planning which has provided much of the impetus for the achievement of development goals in Chile. The support of international as well as other multilateral and bilateral foreign organizations to comprehensive national planning provides considerable leverage for those interested in achieving national development goals. This is particularly true of organizations which have resources to devote to development, such as the Agency for International Development. In producing national plans which set development targets and attempt to suggest procedures for achieving them, an element is added to the policy process which counters the normal operation of the disjointed incrementalism that inevitably attends any policy-making effort. By pointing forcefully to the disparities between the goals pledged and goals actually achieved, national planning bodies can become an important element in the environment of the development bureaucracies and thus provide a counterforce to pressure-group structures based upon the organization of the interests of the middle and upper social and economic strata. In Chile there is an attempt to fill this function by the Office of Development Planning (Odeplan). Given the democratic nature of the environment in which the development bureaucracies must survive, the problem in Chile is not that comprehensive national planning is endangering a rational use of resources through setting inflexible programs based upon too little knowledge, but rather that Odeplan does not play a strong enough role in making development policy.

The major difficulty that emerges for development-policy making, from our viewpoint, is getting the relevant bureaucracies to adopt development goals as their own, rather than redefining them into other goals which serve other purposes. This problem is viewed as primarily one of structuring the environments and the internal systems of the bureaucracies in ways that encourage the dynamic process of goal definition to be consistent with development ends. The creation of national planning bodies with real power can be an important factor leading to this end. Whatever the validity of the arguments of those who criticize comprehensive national planning when studying the problems of the centrally planned economics of the socialist bloc, their reservations are not well taken for democratic countries such as Chile, which are attempting to shape development goals out of a highly unsettled policy-making environment.

Whatever the inadequacies of the analysis presented here, it is hoped that it will encourage further exploration of the applications of concepts drawn from organization theory to the problems of development-policy making. Our discussion has been largely devoid of the language and ideas of political-development theory. It is hoped that this divorcing of organizational concepts and political-development theory may be beneficial and may, if pursued, provide a greater understanding of the similarity of the problems presented by organizations in society, whether that society is a rich, industrialized one such as the United States or a relatively poor, industrializing one such as Chile. It strikes me that, for example, Selznick's analysis of cooptation in the TVA tells us more about the problems of development-policy making in Chile than any amount of speculation about the "prismatic" nature of Chilean society.[46]

46. The author would like to especially thank Jorge Tapia-Videla and Paul N. Rosenstein-Rodan for their criticisms of a draft of this study.

Chapter 10

Centralism and Political Elite Behavior in Mexico

William S. Tuohy

The Mexican political process is capped by a leadership apparatus under the guise of government in association with a single dominant political party (the PRI). One of that informal apparatus's key functions is control, in order to preserve the centralized national regime. Not only the general public but even members of the governing apparatus (elites themselves) find their political behavior closely regulated. The sources, nature, and consequences of that control are the immediate concern of this study. This type of analysis constitutes one approach to the question of government responses to national-development issues.

The study of elites is one of the most fruitful and efficient entrees to description and evaluation of government. The following generalizations focus on middle- and low-level political elites, specifically those associated with the government-party apparatus that rules Mexico. Numerically these elites constitute a large proportion of all government posts in Mexico's ostensibly federal system. They are not "the prime movers and models for the entire society," however, and thus not the "top influentials" or the "ruling elite."[1] Rather, the roles closest to our middle- and low-level category fit into the public side of what Robert Scott

1. These terms are taken from Suzanne Keller, "Elites," in the *International Encyclopedia of the Social Sciences*, vol. 5 (New York: Macmillan, 1968), p. 26. Her "ruling elite" concept approximates what Frank Brandenberg refers to as the top echelon of Mexico's Revolutionary Family, or what Robert Scott calls the "ruling class." See Brandenberg, *The Making of Modern Mexico* (Englewood Cliffs, N.J.: Prentice-Hall, 1964), pp. 2–7; and Scott, "Mexico: The Established Revolution," in *Political Culture and Political Development*, ed. Lucian Pye and Sidney Verba (Princeton, N.J.: Princeton Univ. Press, 1965), pp. 371 ff.

calls Mexico's "mediatory class" and partly overlap his "governing class" concept.[2] The majority of such politicians and politician-bureaucrats hardly qualify as politically "powerful," except perhaps in isolated transactions with persons of lower status, but collectively they perform essential functions. They also provide a valuable mirror for the political process: more intimately accessible for research than are the top national leaders, they are inevitably participants in the latter's policies.

Preservation of the existing regime has been a complex and difficult task, the magnitude of which undoubtedly contributes to preoccupation with its security. Whether or not this task is the national leadership's single most important political motivation, what might also be called organizational maintenance (of the regime and its arrangements among elites) definitely is a compelling force.[3] Analysis of the means used to pursue that goal will be facilitated if the pattern of political domination and organizational stability is seen as a function of (i) the kind(s) of social control used to maintain the organization and (ii) the reactions of the human groups involved.[4] The latter include not only middle- and low-level elites, but also their political superiors and publics. Thus, the assessment of human reactions requires information about both the general political culture and specific political role cultures. In the absence of adequate data much of the commentary about attitudes and culture is necessarily impressionistic; such topics nevertheless demand consideration.

The impetus for this report came from a study of political decision making in the city of Jalapa, capital of the state of Vera-

2. See Scott, pp. 380–81. The low- and middle-level political elite grouping corresponds roughly to the third, lowest level of the Revolutionary Family; see Brandenberg, p. 5.
3. Antonio Ugalde credibly argues that Mexican government is highly centralized in order to perpetuate the present regime and not primarily for reasons of economic and social development, as often claimed; see Ugalde, *Power and Conflict in a Mexican Community* (Albuquerque, Univ. of New Mexico Press, 1970), p. 181.
4. These two categories were suggested by Michel Crozier, *The Bureaucratic Phenomenon* (Chicago: Univ. of Chicago Press, 1964), p. 203. Much of that book about French bureaucracy is very relevant for Mexico—especially Crozier's consideration of bureaucracy as a cultural phenomenon, which points up the need to study a bureaucracy's relations with its social and cultural environments; and his view that bureaucracy is closely related to the problem of social control, and therefore eventually to legitimacy and consensus.

cruz. Interviews in the national capital, and examination of the literature about Mexican politics in general and of the few comparable community studies, amplified and partially tested the Jalapa experience.[5] While obviously one state capital can provide only partial answers to questions about national politics, certain structures and processes found in Jalapa and Veracruz represent much that is endemic throughout Mexican political life. Such a study therefore permits some extrapolation.

The Mexican Political Situation

For the fifty years or so since cessation of civil warfare, Mexican governments have claimed the democratic and developmental mantle of the Revolution. Even today, governments and the Partido Revolucionario Institucional or PRI (whose title translated is the Institutionalized Party of the Revolution) use the image of continuing Revolution to legitimize themselves and to promote their policies and aspirations. Postrevolutionary regimes have seen considerable progress, for example, in the critical areas of economic productivity, social welfare, and political stabilization and mobilization. Nevertheless, serious problems remain, many of them inherent in economic underdevelopment, and are surrounded by political controversy.

The issue is not usually whether basic problems remain or

5. For reports on Jalapa see Richard Fagen and William Tuohy, *Politics and Privilege in a Mexican City* (Stanford, Calif.: Stanford Univ. Press, 1972), and William Tuohy and Barry Ames, "Mexican University Students in Politics: Rebels Without Allies?" *Monograph Series in World Affairs*, Monograph no. 3, vol. 7 (Denver: Univ. of Colorado, 1970). Ugalde's study of Ensenada in Baja California offers very suggestive comparisons with leadership behavior in Jalapa. Other works especially relevant for insights into decisional processes are William D'Antonio and William Form, *Influentials in Two Border Cities: A Study in Community Decision-Making* (Notre Dame, Ind.: Univ. of Notre Dame Press, 1965)—their study included Ciudad Juárez in Chihuahua; Bo Anderson and James Cockroft, "Control and Co-optation in Mexican Politics," *International Journal of Comparative Sociology* 7, no. 1 (1966); Orrin Klapp and L. Vincent Padgett, "Power Structure and Decision-Making in a Mexican Border City [Tijuana, Baja California]," *American Journal of Sociology* 65, no. 4 (1960); Jorge Capriata, "Political Behavior in Two Mexican Communities" (Ph.D. diss., Stanford Univ., 1971), a study of San Cristóbal and Tuxtla Gutiérrez in Chiapas; and Lawrence S. Graham, "Politics in a Mexican Community," *University of Florida Monographs*, Social Sciences no. 35 (Gainesville: Univ. of Florida Press, 1968).

development is sufficient, but involves different interpretations of governmental performance and intentions. Is today's "institutionalized Revolution" compatible with real development, or at the most are we seeing growth without necessary structural alterations? Those leftist critics who dare speak out claim that the Revolutionary mystique has been captured and calcified and is now manipulated by a new capitalist or bourgeois establishment. They see little or no development today, and even regression into increasing class inequities.

Supporters of the government-PRI-led regime naturally tend to disagree with claims of continuing or increasing class exploitation with government connivance. (In private, however, some admit that such problems exist.) They generally assert that the rulers continue to pursue reformist and progressive goals, though recognizing that the Revolution's "institutional" phase requires great stress on maintenance of political stability and on increased industrial productivity. In practice, these latter concerns have brought a capitalist developmental policy orientation to Mexican government; that is, an essentially capitalist economy is governed with major federal controls or interventions in key industries and social services.

The governing elite is highly sensitive about its ties to the capitalist sector. In exchange for needed tax and investment resources, plus other forms of cooperation, government leaders realize that they are making important concessions to the affluent capitalist sector. These concessions sometimes threaten the mechanisms of government autonomy. Possibly an even greater threat confronts the regime in the long run, however. This is the strain on legitimacy induced by strict controls over popular political supporters and supposed beneficiaries of postrevolutionary regimes. Consequently, the rhetoric of Mexican government now fails to acknowledge fully the magnitude of the shift away from previous reformist and populist ideals. In the present policy context the already vague Revolutionary mystique becomes even more of an enigma.

The scarcity of strong opposition and major conflicts is a remarkable feature of recent Mexican political history, especially because problems and contradictions in the society and polity would seem to yield a great potential for discord. Electoral opposition remains moderately weak and is concentrated in certain regions and manifested largely in activities of a temperate conservative party, the Partido de Acción Nacional (PAN). Thus far, the PRI-linked regime has not permitted opposition victories in state gubernatorial elections. Extralegal resistance occurs regularly, but major incidents are sporadic and most commonly take the form of skirmishes with students and isolated peasant protests.[6] Even these latter two types usually have focused on specific local grievances and have not represented challenges to the incumbent federal leaders or to the regime itself. Overall, the authorities and certainly the regime have weathered these challenges very well, and without major policy concessions. How has this been possible?

The government and its PRI apparatus have not relied solely on the increasingly ambiguous legitimizing force of the Revolutionary mystique. Whatever intellectual and emotional support that belief pattern supplies is supplemented by more tangible political, police-military, and economic controls; these are evidenced throughout the polity and in crucial areas of the general society. Control mechanisms are an essential part of the authoritarian regime, obviously, and provide emotion-laden issues. Proponents tend to view the centralized control pattern as justified by threatened disorder and resistance to what they regard as a progressive government. In other words, the limitations on autonomous political participation serve the public interest. For critics these controls tend to be repressive and are used to suppress opposition and to stifle discussion of governmental failures

6. For additional information on peasant resistance see Pablo González Casanova, *La democracia en México* (Mexico City: Ediciones ERA, 1965); Anderson and Cockroft; Moisés González Navarro, *La Confederación Nacional Campesina* (Mexico City: Costa-Amic, 1968); and William Tuohy and David Ronfeldt, "Political Control and the Recruitment of Middle-Level Elites in Mexico: An Example from Agrarian Politics," *Western Political Quarterly* 22, no. 2 (1969). See also David Ronfeldt, *Atencingo: The Politics of Agrarian Struggle in a Mexican Ejido* (Stanford, Calif.: Stanford Univ. Press, 1972). Regarding students see Tuohy and Ames, "Mexican University Students in Politics," and citations there.

and duplicity. Left radicals share with right-wing reactionaries much of this last interpretation. However intended, the controls clearly operate, and the way in which Mexico's democratic norms coexist or otherwise interact with authoritarian rule is a basic issue.

Mexico's socioeconomic problems strike hardest at working-class citizens, whose plight and aspirations draw support from left-wing intellectuals; it is at both these groups that government directs extensive control measures. Leftists have been largely immobilized through censorship, bribery, character assassination, and threats to their livelihood and personal freedom. While the increasing number of middle-class citizens constitutes a growing political challenge to the regime's customary operations, neither that sector nor the extreme rightists have in recent years presented the government with ideological and organizational problems commensurate with those that emanate from the poor. The latter class has historically been much more of a political problem, for therein reside the Revolution's major unfulfilled promises and its key symbols of legitimacy. Nevertheless, the thrust of low-class dissent is mitigated considerably by its limited resources. One such deficiency is weakness in organizational capability, but the lack of strong and politically autonomous working class organizations also derives from government policy.

For a variety of reasons the governing elite concentrates political mobilization and organizational efforts on the working class. In one sense this focus merely reflects the status of the poor as supposed beneficiaries and a moral touchstone of Revolutionary development. Yet, feared reactions to continuing deprivations also prompt careful supervision of low-class politics. Other factors which enter are tied even more directly to current policies than to the ideological content of the Revolution. Thus, through its controls the government-PRI elite uses the extensive working-class organizations as counterweights in its bargaining with the wealthy capitalist sector. This practice in itself need not be detrimental to low-class interests, except to the degree that they are deliberately ignored or misjudged. More difficult to assess, finally, are the consequences of the government's interest in a compliant labor supply for the growing economy, and especially for industry; some controls probably derive from this goal too.

Outside the formal government hierarchy the PRI, often called Mexico's official party, is the chief organizing instrument in the political process.[7] Party efforts concentrate on the working class, for the reasons just mentioned. A key technique in the strategy of limiting political autonomy has been cooptation and, in line with the special concern over low-class resistance, particularly of the non-Communist left. Thus, many low-class leaders are enticed or pressured into PRI affiliations. More than just formal membership, however, affiliation in their cases usually involves considerable subservience to the incumbent government elite.

Widespread cooptation fits nicely with another control technique: to build support and a large corps of manipulable followers, sinecures are provided in an immense government and PRI patronage system. The combined patronage and cooptation structure is then used to suggest democratic representativeness both within the party and in government. That inclusiveness plus the existence of some interparty electoral competition thus supposedly serves a legitimizing function, without seriously impairing centralized control. Regardless of the regime's or the PRI's legitimacy in their eyes, however, the scarcity of alternative channels leaves would-be spokesmen of the working class little choice but to rely on (and therefore affiliate with) the PRI and its labor-union associates. Consequently, present PRI controls over the articulation of such political interests appear likely to continue and be successful unless underlying conditions change drastically.

A more imminent challenge nationally to this control through cooptation and patronage may come from the growing middle

7. Interpretations of the PRI's functions can be found in Robert Scott, *Mexican Government in Transition*, rev. ed. (Urbana: Univ. of Illinois Press, 1964), pp. 145 ff.; Brandenberg, pp. 3 ff. and 142 ff.; L. Vincent Padgett, *The Mexican Political System* (Boston: Houghton Mifflin, 1966), pp. 44 ff.; Ugalde, chaps. 6–7; and González Casanova, chap. 2; and also Roger Hansen, *The Politics of Mexican Development* (Baltimore: Johns Hopkins Press, 1971), esp. chap. 5. A useful review of studies of the national power structure is Carolyn Needleman and Martin Needleman, "Who Rules Mexico?" *Journal of Politics* 31, no. 4 (1969).

class. Though not yet either numerically preponderant or economically secure, that group of white-collar employees and professionals poses an eventual threat to the PRI's exclusive status and to the entire system of controlled participation. Many governmental and especially PRI services that are badly needed by working-class persons are less important to the middle class.[8] Whether the present, often indirectly coercive mainstays of centralism can be adapted to new and stronger mass interest groups, either to permit increased competition or to suppress it, is a critical question for the future of political stability and popular participation.

Though the government is very much on top, its relationship with the single dominant party has major elements of mutual dependency. In Mexican society today PRI needs are clear; its privileges in the political and governmental processes to a considerable extent require government protection, and the attractions of those privileges plus other government interventions appear vital for coherence within the PRI organization and at least a semblance of national party unity.[9] While often given less attention, or else valued for erroneous reasons (such as the idea that the PRI rules the nation), important benefits also accrue to the government. Of interest here are benefits at the core of the governmental process, not the whole range of functions, however necessary, which political parties generally perform.

The official party assumes important organizational and control duties which otherwise, under another authoritarian regime, would require direct governmental action. The party's roles relate particularly to political participation of the working class. In

8. Middle-class persons tend to reside in urban areas, and national voting patterns show that the PRI receives proportionately fewer votes as urbanization increases. See Barry Ames, "Bases of Support for Mexico's Dominant Party," *American Political Science Review* 64, no. 1 (1970), for a quantitative analysis of election data. Ames also summarizes various general hypotheses that have been offered to explain the existence of stronger electoral competition in urban or developed settings than in rural settings. On the same topic see González Casanova, chap. 7; and Ugalde, pp. 158–61.

9. Internally disruptive reactions to the 1965 experiment with primary elections (to select candidates for municipal offices) revealed the precariousness of PRI unity and also showed how central patronage concerns are. For studies of primaries in two municipalities see Ugalde, chap. 7; and William D'Antonio and Richard Suter, "Elecciones preliminares en un municipio mexicano," *Revista Mexicana de Sociología* 29 (enero 1967): 93–108.

another perspective, the PRI is a target for considerable popular discontent, a welcome buffer for government leaders. In the absence of such an arrangement many functions now lodged in the PRI would necessarily fall to government directly, increasing the latter's administrative burden and its already great policy-making load. Some optimistic commentators have also interpreted the government/party separation as evidence of democratic intentions, a portent of meaningful interparty competition. Whatever the many implications, the formally separate hierarchies do appear as more than mere organizational conveniences or camouflage. Separation allows government added flexibility in dealings with its publics (and important publics are not encompassed within the party framework) and bolsters an often strained democratic image. Such increments of adaptability may be vital and responsible for the regime's durability and strength.

Control from Above

The executive branch of the federal government (ultimately the president) controls basic policies and even numerous mundane aspects of the centralized political system. Within each state the governor is very powerful, but he owes his job to the federal executive and must defer to it. In effect, the governors have most latitude in controlling patronage and the normal administrative operations of their respective governments. These functions are important because of the number of jobs and other benefits involved. In contrast, the federal congress and state legislatures operate for the convenience of the executive branch; they offer patronage opportunities but are uniformly unconvincing as components of a democratic process. The so-called "free municipality" (*municipio libre*), at the lowest governmental level, is almost universally ineffective as a policy-making entity. Municipal governments perform minor administrative functions and provide low-level patronage opportunities.

Numerous formal mechanisms promote and sustain the centralization of political power. An abundance of laws and other formal enactments both establish controls and insure that these are monitored by the state and federal government. For example, each municipal government (*ayuntamiento*) is closely regulated by state laws, which even specify many of its administrative procedures. Financial supervision is a particularly significant form of intervention. In Veracruz annual budgets must receive prior approval from the state government, transactions must be reported monthly, and all revenue sources are closely regulated. Besides the lack of fiscal autonomy, municipalities have very limited revenues (this constraint, felt also by state governments, is partly due to government policy at the national level). Strong police and military forces help secure these control arrangements.

Less formal, extra and often technically illegal procedures supplement the controls just mentioned. Informal manipulation of personal interests has been highly successful and underlies the government's relatively infrequent reliance on overt force in recent Mexican political history. Patronage is at the core of many informal controls. Government monopolies over policy and recruitment to public office help the top-level political elite convince its publics (which include low- and middle-level elites). This process can occur through manipulation of job rewards, licenses, government and other politically controlled expenditures (including contracts with business concerns), and allocation of such miscellaneous benefits as bribes and other forms of corruption.

The macrostructures of centralism (both formal and informal) operate on individuals whose behavior and attitudes are more than simple, predetermined responses to the stimuli of the regime's control patterns. Personal traits also influence that behavior and even affect the macrostructures themselves.[10] Specifically, in Mexico the centralized political process limits most individuals' decisional power; all major decision-making capabilities are reserved for the highest levels of government. That centralist pat-

10. On politics and Mexican personality structures, see Scott, "Mexico," pp. 347 ff.; Raúl Béjar N., *El mito del mexicano*, 2d ed. (Mexico City: Editorial Orientación, 1971); Michael Maccoby, "On Mexican Machismo: Politics and Value Orientations," *Western Political Quarterly* 18 (Dec. 1965); and Joseph Kahl, *The Measurement of Modernism: A Study of Values in Brazil and Mexico* (Austin: Univ. of Texas Press, 1968). Octavio Paz comments at length on the identity problem in *The Labyrinth of Solitude*, Engl. trans. (New York: Grove Press, 1961); so do Brandenberg, pp. 171–76, and Samuel Ramos, *Profile of Man and Culture in Mexico*, Engl. trans. (Austin: Univ. of Texas Press, 1962).

tern is accentuated by personal traits, however. Throughout the politico-administrative hierarchies, officials feel the burden of much routine and trivial decision making that, in a more technical or expertise-oriented and less personal perspective, might be resolved by subordinates. But the officials act as they do partly because though the controls often are personally burdensome and socially inefficient, those controls and the deference associated with them are important.

Centralized political control finds important and necessary support in both the role culture of Mexican politicians and the general political culture. One type of fit between attitudes and the needs of centralism has just been mentioned. At a more basic level it states that a major psychocultural source of the fear of decisional responsibility seems to be a widely shared sense of personal insecurity. Thus, political centralism and compelling psychological need are complementary and result in the customary stress on subordination and the conspicuous communication of deference. The subordinate in each such transaction senses the dangers involved if he should appear to frustrate his superior's needs.

These forces contribute greatly to the prominence of service to superiors as the primary criterion of acceptable conduct in low- and (though not so exclusively) middle-level elite roles. That service tends to be conceived in terms of unquestioning response to the superior's wishes or, in the absence of detailed instructions, self-regulated behavior in a manner known to be satisfactory. Not surprisingly, under these circumstances decentralized decision making and innovative leadership are nearly inconceivable. Unlikely to produce immediate response is any situation in which an official is confronted with a need to decide an issue but is unsure of his superior's views on it.

Recruitment to Public Office

Centralized control, avoidance of decisional responsibility, and the typically personalist orientation in transactions help shape and in turn find support in the customs of political recruitment.[11] Patronage as a control-and-reward mechanism ties into continuous recruitment, whose impact on officials' behavior is considerable. Constitutional prescriptions require that state and federal administrations change at six-year intervals, while municipal governments do so every three years. While the law requires a complete turnover only of elected officeholders, in a related phenomenon a great many important and even unimportant posts in the bureaucracies rotate at least as frequently, much to the detriment of expert performance.[12]

Underlying the change of elected officials is a norm of the continuing Revolution: Effective Suffrage, No Reelection. That norm is widely acknowledged as a reaction to the self-perpetuation of prerevolutionary governments; now the public gets its electoral licks in regularly, and new or at least changed faces are guaranteed. This situation reflects continuing popular distrust of politicians and their instruments of rule (as illustrated in Table 10.1). Enforced turnover also serves the ruling elite, because ambitious subordinates and colleagues are constantly reminded of the need to conform to rules of the political process. Not surprisingly, job instability is a major preoccupation.

Politicians' careers hinge on what one informant called "an intricate network of alliances," about which two journalists observed when interviewed: "The only way to political success is through friends and contacts"; and "Politics here is men trying to gain the attention and favor of the governor. Some approach this by emphasizing good works; others rely more on maneuvering for friendships and other contacts, without demonstrating their qualifications in tangible works." At the state level the governor is the key to recruitment chances, but on the national level and even

11. The following impressions are based primarily on interviews with members of political elites; no life-history interviews were conducted, however. For additional information on recruitment structures see Brandenberg, chap. 6; Scott, *Mexican Government in Transition*, chap. 7; Padgett, pp. 79–85 and 136–43; Anderson and Cockroft; Tuohy and Ronfeldt; Ugalde; D'Antonio and Form, esp. pp. 161–78; Marvin Alisky, "The Governors of Mexico," *Southwestern Studies*, Monograph no. 12, vol. 3 (1965); and Karl Schmitt, "Congressional Campaigning in Mexico," *Journal of Inter-American Studies* 11, no. 1 (1969).

12. In Ensenada the system of fast rotation in the bureaucracy "seems to be imposed by the need to increase the possibilities for political patronage"; a consequence is common bureaucratic inefficiency. Ugalde, p. 98.

Table 10.1. *Attitudes toward government and politicians in Jalapa*

Test statement		Jalapa adults[a] (N = 399)	Sample of university students in Jalapa[b] (N = 97)
A. Are the majority of public officials in Jalapa trying to help the community in general, or to advance their personal interests?	Help	38%	27%
	Serve selves	62	73
B. It is useless to vote in municipal elections because our leaders are pre-selected by the Party.	True	76%	70%
	Partly true	7	22
	Not true	18	8
C. Every politician is a crook.	Agree completely	35%	27%
	More or less agree	23	43
	More or less disagree	11	10
	Disagree completely	20	14
	Don't know or no answer	11	5
D. It is said that certain persons or groups have a lot of influence in running the government, influence that they use to their own advantage while forgetting the well-being of the city.	True	60%	78%
	Partly true	24	19
	Not true	10	1
	Don't know or no answer	6	2
E. All the candidates make beautiful speeches, but one never knows what they will do after they come to power.	True	82%	81%
	Partly true	10	15
	Not true	5	1
	Don't know or no answer	3	2

a. Data from Fagen and Tuohy survey; see note 5. Due to rounding, some totals may not be exactly 100 percent.
b. Data from Tuohy and Ames; see note 5.

more important are the president (who selects each governor) and certain other members at the top of the Revolutionary family.

The recruitment process can fruitfully be viewed as a political career game, which is both a major preoccupation and a favorite diversion in Mexican political circles. Definite movement patterns exist, along the following lines. With necessarily frequent shifting of offices, success is defined as the consistent holding of desirable posts. High-level government offices are best; some national and even the one or two top state PRI offices definitely count; but other party jobs tend to be less prestigious than even middle-level state government posts. Both luck and skill are necessary to choose and then to cultivate good political contacts in a process that might be regarded as a political lottery. Ambitious men repeatedly stake their careers on the success of certain politicians they judge to be more prominent and likely to succeed. Everybody then waits to see where the chips will fall. Success brings a post to be held for as long as the individual satisfies his political patron, but for no longer than one term of a given elective office. Thereafter, "Effective Suffrage, No Reelection" again shuffles the incumbents.

Some insurance exists, however, in the form of sinecures which the immense government and PRI bureaucracies provide for large numbers of the less fortunate PRI office seekers. The extent of the dependence on the government and party apparatuses for some post, even if of low status, becomes more comprehensible in view of the fact that there is no such large-scale government-to-business job mobility (and vice versa) as is common in the United States. In Mexico the public, political realm and the private, business spheres are generally quite separate, both socially and ideologically. The personal economic dependence of most politicians is compounded, moreover, by the normal scarcities in an economically underdeveloped society.

The following rules outline standard tactics used to "make it" in Mexican politics; they have been distilled from observation of career patterns. In these norms lie additional reasons why the recruitment process is so distracting and among most public officials conducive to minimal attention to substantive policy questions. "So you want to be a politician? Well, Juan Fulano, you must act on these rules."

RULE 1. Choose your political allies carefully. Know whom to please, but take care not to antagonize other important leaders; an ability to divine the futures of higher-status politicians is obviously crucial.

RULE 2. Adhere to the regime's basic rules of political life. These are mostly procedural norms which guide the fray; for example, at least nominally support the PRI's official candidates, especially for the presidency and for state governor.

RULE 3. Avoid entrapment in stands on specific issues of major concern to the state and federal governments; you need to keep open channels of political alliance and minimize unintentional offenses to other politicians.

RULE 4. Avoid situations where public protests are directed at your personal exercise of authority; especially scandalous and therefore threatening are protests that verge on or include overt violence.[13] It is dangerous for an official to appear so arbitrary that sectors of the public energetically protest in ways that cannot be ignored by his political superiors, who also fear for their own careers. In part this is true because of great concern over demonstrations which call widespread attention to the regime's many arbitrary characteristics and thus cast doubt on its legitimacy. The personal risk inherent in such a situation was described as follows by one Veracruz politician-informant: "Politicians have a strong aversion to widespread controversy; entanglement in such controversy can easily ruin a political career." Similarly, Ugalde discovered that "the misuse of force is the road to political obscurity."[14]

RULE 5. Whenever possible demonstrate political and/or administrative competence, but not necessarily initiative. Hard work or the appearance of it constitutes a good start, but best of all are tangible accomplishments that attract commendation from the public and the attention and approval of political superiors. Unfortunately, an all too familiar consequence of this norm is *plazismo,* a "fountain syndrome" affecting many officials, who seek prominence through public works which are quickly implemented and highly visible but of little or no developmental utility.

---

13. The link which exists between popular participation and the recruitment of government officials is an important control, however partial and occasional, over those officials. James Payne found similarly important extra and illegal tactics in the political articulations of organized labor in Peru; see his *Labor and Politics in Peru* (New Haven: Yale Univ. Press, 1965).
14. Ugalde, p. 78.

Pressures from Below:
The Public and Government

For many years the Mexican regime has been at least tolerated by the bulk of the politically aware public. However reluctantly, the public still generally accepts constrained and largely covert political competition, under what Marvin Alisky has called a governmental system based on "authoritarian executivism." He touches on a key facet of the regime when he writes:

> The framework of authoritarian executivism . . . is desired and respected by most Mexicans even as they criticize it . . . Both the ruled and the rulers of Mexico value highly governmental stability and the growing consumer markets of the urban and semi-urban areas. The impoverished peasants are not in general as articulate as the relatively few noisy demonstrators and squatters seem to indicate.[15]

Attitudes in Jalapa fit this pattern. Considerable informal grumbling notwithstanding, it seemed to be a common view that some form of modified authoritarianism is still needed in order to develop the country economically and socially and to avoid bitter political conflict. The latter, it is feared, would throw Mexico into chaos. Here we see the classic tension between civil and political liberties, and other societal values.

Acceptance of the regime entails considerable ambivalence for most Mexicans, however. Along with their diffuse approval for the general goals and many of the institutions built in the name of the Revolution, they are extremely skeptical about the motives and behavior of politicians and other public officials.[16] One hypothesis concerning this ambivalence is this. In view of the obvious social improvements brought about by postrevolutionary

15. Alisky, pp. 27–28.
16. For comments about ambivalence and pertinent survey data from Mexico see Tuohy and Ames, "Mexican University Students in Politics," pp. 15–24; Kahl, especially pp. 114–16; Scott, "Mexico," and Gabriel Almond and Sidney Verba, *The Civic Culture* (Princeton, N.J.: Princeton Univ. Press, 1963), especially pp. 414–28 and 495–96.

governments the populace's authoritarian personality traits facilitate acceptance of "authoritarian executivism"; concurrently, however, widespread lack of interpersonal trust casts suspicion on individual officeholders.[17] Not only can incumbents be blamed for the government's mistakes and failures, but they are also suspect because of their power capabilities and the demands for deference they make on the public.

On a psychological level political ambivalence almost certainly interacts with attitudes about personal commitment and finds a parallel in them. Michel Crozier's findings in France are highly suggestive in this regard:

> On the one hand, people would like very much to participate in order to control their own environment. On the other hand, they fear that if and when they participate, their own behavior will be controlled by their coparticipants. It is far easier to preserve one's independence and integrity if one does not participate in decision-making. By refusing to be involved in policy determination [or implementation] one remains much more free from outside pressures.[18]

The Mexican government's elaborate measures of cooptation and control certainly give cause for skepticism about opportunities for political participation. In addition to the deterrent of elite-imposed penalties for certain types of participation, however, politically conscious Mexicans may find psychological relief by allowing government to cope with problems where they lack direct interest or self-confidence.

In Mexico, more tangible political and social factors also shape the behavior of those who undertake to articulate their interests. Not surprisingly, under an authoritarian regime and in an economically poor society, if an ordinary citizen is even to be heard by government, he must give careful attention to what the elites

17. This hypothesis is offered only for illustration. In fact, use of concepts such as psychological insecurity, identity, and authoritarianism in analyses of national-level politics generally is of dubious validity. For comments, largely critical, about the literature on Mexicans see William Tuohy, "Psychology in Social Science: The Case of Mexican Politics," paper presented at the annual meeting of the Latin American Studies Association, Madison, Wis., May 1973.
18. Crozier, p. 204.

consider acceptable content and appropriate style of articulation. The style had best be deferential, and increasingly so as citizens look farther up the official hierarchy. The need for caution is compounded by the vagueness of the distinction made by many public officials between legitimate articulation and personal or political attack. This problem can be seen in the following comments by two politically prominent Jalapa residents:

> It is possible to exchange impressions with political leaders, but unless you personally have a secure economic position it is risky to criticize government actions in front of some officials. This is true because to point out errors often is regarded as an attack on the political regime or on the administrative system within which they operate. . . . There is a tendency, still present but diminishing with the increasing competence of government leaders, to regard all criticism as destructive. . . .
>
> Criticism of the political establishment is greatly tempered, not because of fear of physical violence but more in order to defend one's other interests.

Hypersensitivity and mutual suspicions within the Mexican public itself accompany presentation of political demands. People often seem to view their own articulation differently from similar attempts by others. Their own efforts to influence government are seen as legitimate, validated by formally accepted democratic norms; other interests and alien groups are less trustworthy, however, and therefore suspect when they seek political influence. This differentiation may relate to a common rationalization about influence. Many of the Jalapa informants denied that they themselves try to influence government; they preferred the expression "cooperating with" rather than "influencing" public decision making. Efforts to cooperate are also less likely to offend status-conscious public officials. For some citizens, finally, this semantic distinction may derive from a realistic appraisal of what they can and what they cannot accomplish.

Despite some inhibitions on articulation, this economically poor society with large-scale government intervention inevitably defines a wide variety of interests as political. Each is then articulated as high up in the decisional hierarchy as its proponents can reach. For example, in Jalapa the state government is besieged with unaggregated requests about local affairs which have been articulated immediately to that body. Similar patterns occur throughout Mexico, including up through the national level. Both the political structures of centralism, including its psychological supports, and the nature of the interests themselves force the aggregation function—that is, the conversion of demands into general policy alternatives—close to centers of decisional power. To add to the leadership burden, an immense share of the demands and requests are highly particularistic and therefore almost impossible to aggregate; such interests can only be dealt with by decisions that in each case have little utility as general policy statements.

Conclusion: Administered Politics and the Fate of Development

Broad areas of national development lie beyond the empirical scope of this study. It would thus be imprudent to venture beyond previous, largely tangential references to topics such as investment priorities and the details of administrative organization. Important structures and processes have been treated in detail, however; these illuminate vital elements of Mexican government and also suggest the utility of applying similar analytic approaches elsewhere in Latin America.

Vital consequences for governmental performance are associated with the patterns of centralized control and political recruitment, and the attitudes that have been described. In the behavioral realm, public officials are encouraged toward conservatism and detachment from the content of public policy. They tend to be conservative in the sense that maintaining the existing political structures and the status quo of socioeconomic stratification is the safest goal. In that context the "good" politician or administrator is a manager of hierarchically delegated responsibilities and a manipulator of the public environment; he is not a responsible or responsive public servant in the classical democratic sense.

Detachment from the content of public policy follows partly from the nature of political and administrative careers. Within the government and PRI organizations competition and decisional activities must focus on the distribution of personal rewards or patronage; the ruling elite does not welcome and rarely tolerates open political competition over policy matters or the regime's chief procedural arrangements. Administrative performance clearly suffers, but the emphasis on officials' personal rewards and conformity to established procedures is valued in the name of stable political control.

A second type of consequence is in the realm of institutional capabilities, where Mexican government exhibits a devaluation of skill and planning. Over the past decades the level of professional skill and the devotion to the planning ideal have grown in Mexican public life.[19] Nevertheless, the system of rapid rotation in office, combined with the use of thousands of positions in the government-party apparatus as a patronage structure designed to stabilize and maintain existing political arrangements, is extremely corrosive of a continuing and creative focus on problems of public policy. In fact, it can be argued that whatever benefits accrue to rationalization and coordination of policy through the centralized organizational forms are lost owing to the corruption, inefficiencies, and careerism that are the other side of Mexican centralism. Thus, developmental planning gets sacrificed to system maintenance, and patronage takes precedence over expert performance.

The contemporary Mexican Revolution appears at least middle-aged as well as middle-class in orientation. In an epoch where "middle of the road" has become a rallying cry for many of the complacent but a curse for others in United States politics, Mexico too faces urgent dilemmas in defining policy moderation. For years Mexican governments have effectively controlled their

19. See Robert Shafer, *Mexico: Mutual Adjustment Planning* (Syracuse, N.Y.: Syracuse Univ. Press, 1966).

political competition, at times with notable results for development. The sought-after stability and governmental strength have been accompanied by increasingly dubious responsiveness to the needs of much of the population, however, and therein lie both the challenge and many ominous signs for the future. The political system may well be approaching the empirical realization that administration or controlled politics cannot forever and so extensively be substituted for political bargaining which includes all major sectors of the population. Thus, a basic question today is whether the dominant elites will move toward accommodating dissatisfied publics or will confront discontent with additional controls; cooptation as a control technique becomes repressive when dissidents will not be bought off. In any case, the fate of Mexican development is eminently a political question.

Chapter 11

Cuba: Fourteen Years of Revolutionary Government

James F. Petras

Social and Economic Development

The Cuban economy today stands at the crossroads. Up till the middle 1960's the Cuban revolutionary process was largely concerned with redistributing wealth rather than focusing on the problems of production.[1] The first years of the revolution involved two agrarian reforms, 1959, and then later in 1962, which broke the power of the foreign and Cuban entrepreneurs who owned and controlled most of the land and transportation system.[2] Large farms were nationalized or distributed to peasants. Cooperatives and individual landholdings were followed by the establishment of state farms. In the urban areas rents were cut, houses were built, and educational and health programs were instituted on a massive scale. Illiteracy was practically eliminated. The first five years of the Cuban Revolution largely involved the destruction of the old ruling class and the redistribution of goods and property. In the process of reordering society a number of costs were incurred. One major cost was the hostility of the U.S. government which responded by instituting an economic blockade. This seriously limited the ability of the Cubans to obtain spare parts. As a result, many of their industries and machinery

1. On the early phase of the revolution see Leo Huberman and Paul Sweezy, *Socialism in Cuba* (New York: Monthly Review, 1969); James O'Connor, *The Origins of Socialism in Cuba* (Ithaca, N.Y.: Cornell Univ. Press, 1970); Dudley Seers, ed., *Cuba, the Economic and Social Revolution* (Chapel Hill: Univ. of North Carolina Press, 1964).
2. Edward Boorstein, *The Economic Transformation of Cuba* (New York: Monthly Review Press, 1968); and O'Connor.

were incapacitated despite the great ingenuity which the Cubans have shown in repairing and maintaining their machinery.[3]

The period from 1959 to 1964 and the whole period prior to the revolution created an ambiance in which productivity was a secondary consideration. Top priority was given to breaking the power of the ruling class and to providing social benefits for the population. In a sense this was necessary in order to consolidate revolutionary power. The real social benefits that accrued to the working class and the peasantry during the redistributive phase provided the motivation and the enthusiasm which were to sustain the revolution during the development drive.[4] The specific measures were concrete manifestation of the popular program which the government was embracing and reinforced the allegiance of the lower class to the revolution and its leadership. The ability of that leadership to call on the people to make the enormous efforts necessary for economic development was rooted in the fundamental changes which took place in the period from 1959 to 1964.

On the other hand certain negative features carried over into the development phase. One was the concern with the shortages of consumer goods, found especially among urbanites. Prior to the revolution Cuban society experienced lopsided development.[5] The heavy emphasis was on consumer import from the United States. Though this was concentrated among a small sector of the population, especially an urban population, nevertheless the emphasis was on values of consumption as opposed to production. Cuba was not an industrial society and lacked a factory culture.[6] It was largely a marketplace for American-made manufactured goods. In addition, because Cuba was a major tourist center, as well as an agricultural exporting society, there was considerable emphasis on the values of consumption at the expense of industrial activity. Prior to 1959 the Cuban population experienced

3. Boorstein, chap. 4.
4. Maurice Zeitlin, *Revolutionary Politics and the Cuban Working Class* (Princeton, N.J.: Princeton Univ. Press, 1967), chap. 11.
5. O'Connor.
6. United Nations Social and Economic Council, Symposium on Latin American Industrialization, *El desarrollo industrial de Cuba* (ECLA/conf. 23,1.63 Marzo, 1966).

deprivation within a consumer-oriented society; this was followed by a revolution which was largely involved in redistributing consumer items. Subsequently the Cuban leadership initiated a development program which demanded sacrifices from the population—a change that did not appeal to all segments of the urban population. In 1969 the most important factor about Cuba was not the benefits which the population was getting from the government or from society, but the involvement of large numbers of people in economic activity which had very little immediate payoff. This sense of working for the larger good over a long period of time has been characteristic of Cuba since. The conversion from consumptionism to productionism remains a very important element in understanding much that goes on in Cuba today. The long lines in the cities, the lack of consumer items, the deprivation that Cubans put up with in their day-to-day life, are all part and parcel of the same society which can elicit extraordinary effort, by average citizens, to overcome serious economic bottlenecks.[7]

The Cuban economy has gone through a series of changes which have crystallized in the effort to maximize agricultural production. Today the Cuban economy is largely agricultural, as it was 14 years ago; yet there are very significant differences. Mechanized agricultural production on the basis of nationalized property and smallholdings are the major features of the Cuban countryside. Most of the investments that are made in Cuba today are going into the agricultural sector and within the agricultural sector into the purchase of machinery. The developmental revolution is largely rooted in the countryside.[8] The most dynamic aspect of agriculture is located in the sugarcane fields. The population in the countryside continues to receive a disproportionate share of the benefits; the government inputs into the economy continue to favor agriculture and workers in the countryside. Most new construction and welfare programs are located in rural

7. For a detailed account of political mobilization see Richard Fagen, *The Transformation of Political Culture in Cuba* (Stanford, Calif.: Stanford Univ. Press, 1969).

8. Martin Kenner and James Petras, eds., *Fidel Castro Speaks* (New York: Grove Press, 1969).

areas, while on the other hand very little new housing is being constructed in the cities.

The symbols of socialist Cuba are largely agricultural implements or agricultural figures (the machete and the cane cutter). The whole society is mobilized to develop the agricultural sector, with resulting sacrifice of the urban population, industrial activity, and urban services, which even show the signs of disinvestment. The urban population is being ruralized through large-scale mobilizations of voluntary labor.[9] Cuban education is more and more oriented toward agricultural production. New power and light facilities are concentrated in the countryside.

Contrary to the experience in eastern Europe, the urban population is being squeezed for the peasantry. The peasant is a relatively privileged fellow, receiving subsidies and a higher proportion of government funds than many of his urban brothers. Children of peasants receive scholarships and attend live-in schools, beginning at the primary level through the secondary, and many go on to higher education. Unlike eastern Europe and the Soviet Union, Cuba has no "peasant problem," because the peasantry is being bought off. Their children are being educated and will become skilled agricultural workers or go into other activities related to agriculture or into nonagricultural work. Very few of them, if any, will go back and work on their parent's little plot of land.[10]

Cuba's development strategy is based on mechanized agriculture. Industrial development revolves around the production of machine products directly related to agricultural growth. On the input side, factories will produce farm machinery, while on the output side industries will be built that process and transform agricultural products.

The production of ten million tons of sugar was to be very

9. Fagen, esp. chap. 3.
10. Twelve thousand fincas were sold to the state between 1967 and 1969. However, only 5,000 small farmers (less than 5 percent) are members of the Communist Party. Interview with Pepe Ramirez, president of the National Association of Small Farmers (ANAP) 15 July 1969. Observations and interviews in Oriente province among peasants confirmed the assertion that children of smallholders were abandoning the small farms, as they graduated from high school and technical schools.

important in solidifying Cuba's international financial standing. It would allow Cuba to pay back its debts to the eastern European countries and reestablish on a much sounder basis its credit with the noncommunist countries. Cuba's ability to obtain machinery and other goods on credit depended upon improvement of its international financial status. The production of the 10,000,-000 tons was intended not only to serve to substantially benefit the consumer public, but to also provide the basis for further development. The development effort of 1970 was meant to be only the first of several very intense efforts in subsequent years.[11]

Cuban Economic Development and the Latin American Revolution

Sometime between the defeat of Che Guevara's guerrilla movement in Bolivia and the mobilization of Cuban society to produce ten million tons of sugar, there was a shift in Cuba's policy away from supporting revolutionary movements in Latin America. Cuba's policy gradually began to shift from moral and material aid to revolutionary movements to largely propagandistic support. Beginning in 1968, and throughout 1969 and 1970, the major direction of Cuba's political efforts was in the area of internal economic development.

Five major factors appear to have converged and strongly influenced this shift in Cuban political priorities: (i) the death of Che Guevara, the main architect of continental revolutionary struggle and a major influence in shaping Cuba's efforts in support of the indigenous guerrilla movements; (ii) the failures, defections, and fragmentation of the guerrilla groups leading to their diminished political significance, reduced size, and isolation from sources of political power; (iii) persistent stagnation in the economy, resulting in serious internal problems, a weak international trading position, and increased dependence on the USSR; (iv) emergence in Latin America of nationalist developmentalist

11. Fidel Castro's speech "We are determined not to lose this battle," *Granma* (English weekly supplement, Havana), 15 Feb. 1970, p. 5.

regimes pursuing policies which conflict with U.S. policies and interests in a number of areas. As a consequence of these factors, the Cubans have turned from revolutionary internationalism toward internal development as a means of breaking out of isolation. The change was visible to anyone present in Cuba in 1969.

Each year Cuba celebrates a particular theme. In 1968 it was the Year of the Heroic Guerrilla. In 1969 it was the Year of Decisive Effort—referring to the proposed production of ten million tons of sugar. In those two contrasting themes one gets an idea of where Cuba's priorities are today. Cuba is still interested in and supports the struggle of liberation movements in Latin America. But the overwhelming effort is being directed toward internal development and the practical problems concerning sugar production.

Cuba's international politics are pragmatic. The Cubans do not initiate or organize revolutionary activities in Latin America. They have maintained ties and fraternal relationships with ongoing revolutionary movements. They have supported those movements which have shown themselves capable of initiating serious struggles for power in Latin America. At the same time the Cubans do not commit themselves to movements that hardly exist or to tiny grouplets incapable of engaging in serious political warfare. Where Communist parties have large popular followings, they are parties which are basically integrated into the legal political structures of their country.[12] The Cubans are not interested in subsidizing reformers whose intent is to ameliorate political and social situations, within a capitalist context.

Because the international situation is not very promising, because of their commitments to their own population and because of their international financial obligations, the Cubans have turned toward building their economy. Currently the Cubans are not offering prescriptions for Latin American revolution. They have shown a considerable amount of flexibility in giving support to the "revolutionary measures" (as they characterize them) of

12. Latin America's largest legal Communist Party is found in Chile. For a discussion see James Petras, *Politics and Social Forces in Chilean Development* (Berkeley: Univ. of California Press, 1969).

the Peruvian military junta; they are conscious of important changes within the Catholic church and in general show a willingness to consider new revolutionary developments as they occur.

Concomitant with the ebbing of the revolutionary movements in Latin America, Cuba has experienced a period of extended economic stagnation. Despite high investment rates and moral exhortations the Cuban economy continued to flounder. Administrative inefficiency, poor planning, and labor indiscipline coupled with leadership preoccupation with noneconomic problems produced an economy whose performance was less than adequate. In 1968 and thereafter the Cuban leadership "discovered" the seriousness of Cuba's internal and external economic situation. The cumulative effect of a series of poor years, resulting in excessive external debts, generated a dependence and vulnerability which could threaten Cuba's sovereignty if not its survival. Lacking any basis for expecting a Latin American revolution to occur in the near future which might justify emphasizing international revolution at the expense of internal development and perceiving that a continuation of the downward trend could lead to political disaster within Cuba, the leadership decided, in typical Fidelista fashion, to promote all-out mobilization for internal development.[13] The original rationale for internal development was that current investment of energy and time in it would lead to even greater support for revolution—later. In the meantime the Cubans in effect told the guerrilla groups that as of 1968–69, they were on their own: Cuba was going to be strictly occupied with the struggle against internal underdevelopment—the problems of work, organization, technical innovation and, above all, increasing production. In more ways than one Cuba was coming to adopt the strategy of building socialism in one country.

The shift toward "building socialism in one island" has apparently had two interrelated consequences: a tendency for the Cubans to reach out toward the new elite nationalists in Latin America while minimizing ties with the guerrillas, the latter being

13. Fidel Castro: "This harvest begins today and it will not be stopped until we have ground the last bag of the 10 million" *Granma* (Cuban edition), 15 July 1969, p. 4.

a condition for the former. Cuba remains a sanctuary where indigenous revolutionaries can take refuge, as occurred in 1969 with the Brazilian political prisoners exchanged for the U.S. ambassador.[14] The focus on consolidation of the Cuban economy is part of normalization of relations with as many existing Latin regimes as possible. In sum, international revolution is being subordinated to internal economic development.

While the Cubans may be changing their policy, there are several factors limiting this change:

(1) Continued U.S. hostility—the economic blockade and the opposition of pro-U.S. governments in most of Latin America. Expressions of the intransigent opposition of the United States can best be seen in the Rockefeller Report and in Nixon's policy speeches.

(2) The Vietnam War expresses the willingness of United States to invade and massively occupy a country to shape its internal politics. Cuba cannot rule out the possibility of a similar occurrence in this hemisphere.

(3) Ideological bonds link Cuba's politics to those of revolutionaries in the Third World. Past and present ties have taken on a reality apart from the particular circumstances in which they arose.

While the priorities and dominant tone of Cuban politics may have shifted from internationalism to nationalism, from guerrilla struggle to agricultural work, the commitment to support revolutionary struggle elsewhere is still strong.[15] Cuba is far from accepting U.S. hegemony in the hemisphere—let alone seeking out a negotiated settlement on the basis of the existing established order in Latin America. Given the degree of U.S. penetration and the conservative nature of the political regimes in almost all Latin countries, a general accord appears unlikely. Nevertheless

14. "Brazilian revolutionaries arrive in Cuba," *Granma,* 5 Oct. 1969, p. 1.
15. On the priority of the politics of production in Cuba in 1970 the following quote clearly indicates the policy view of the Cuban leaders: "Because, in the first analysis politics in its new context is no more than this: how to organize production and social life in general, insuring an ever more conscientous, an ever more enthusiastic and an ever more effective participation of the masses of the people in that production and in that social life." Speech by Armando Hart, Organizational Secretary and member of the Political Bureau of the Cuban Communist Party. *Granma,* 5 Oct. 1969, p. 4.

the Cubans have opened the door to new currents in Latin America—the development of new nationalist formations from previously status-quo-oriented institutions—while continuing to support, as in the past, revolutionary groups in the countries still following U.S. leadership. Cubans have adopted a pragmatic attitude, supporting specific measures or positions adopted by the newly emerging forces without giving blanket support to any one group or government.

Administration in a Revolutionary Setting

Mobilization, military organization, and egalitarianism are major features of contemporary Cuban politics. The organization, the structure of Cuban politics, is one in which the leadership sets policy. Policy has been supported by the majority of the population. Within that majority one can see a very substantial proportion of the population which is very enthusiastic and deeply committed to realizing the tasks set forth by the leadership. Parallel with the command structure of political life is the mass participation in the tasks set forth. The masses participate in carrying out the specific duties which are outlined: they discuss, on the local level, implementation, not policy making. Decisions are made at the top and carried out on the bottom. Discussion, where it exists, is largely over methods. The command-mass participation syndrome in Cuba is based on and is successful to the degree that the commands are obeyed with enthusiasm and voluntarily by the population. For the population few avenues exist for expressing disagreement over basic policies.

Among the political actors in Cuba one finds more and more the merger of the politician and the administrator. Politics in Cuba today is largely the administration of work, the allocation of manpower, and the organization of production. To a considerable degree the politician and the administrator are one. The administrator is a politician and the politician is an administrator. There is very little functional specialization: politician bureaucrats administer farms, organize communities, participate in policy meetings, direct the distribution of welfare, organize production, direct security and vigilance, and the like. They have a multitude of tasks, some of which are delegated to subordinates who are responsible to them. The bureaucrat in Cuba is largely ambulating. The ambulating bureaucrat is the characteristic feature of the Cuban bureaucracy. In the field, visiting projects, discussing with subordinates, workers, employees, peasants, the bureaucrat communicates with his home base by a two-way radio. He is constantly on the move attempting to locate problems and to solve them on the spot. Thus, while the politico-administrative chief maintains control over decision making, the system is flexible and responsive to problems. Most bureaucratic activity focuses on specific problems encountered in specific areas. Attention is concentrated in an attempt to correct and rectify particular problems as they occur.

Most bureaucrats are "generalists": officials quite often change positions from one area of political-administrative life to another. Few stay in one position for very long. Administrators can be found who have been in education, agriculture, industry, security, and the military. Very few are concerned with a career in one particular administrative area.

Another characteristic of the bureaucracy is that very few were prepared for their administrative careers. Many of the administrators are from lower-income or lower-status occupation groups. Many of them were previously industrial workers and in some cases agricultural workers. One can find many examples of administrators of large plants who once were skilled machine operators.

Foremost among the criteria in recruiting personnel for the Cuban bureaucracy is political reliability. Cubans allege that during the first years of the revolution hostile administrators attempted to sabotage many of their social and economic projects. The overwhelming majority of trained managerial personnel fled to the United States after the revolution. As a result the bureaucracy has not been efficient in terms of the norms usually associated with bureaucratic organizations. The average educational level of a party member is a sixth-grade primary education. The politically reliable and technically efficient bureaucrat is the administrative ideal that Cuba is aiming to achieve. In recent years there has been an increasing flow of technically trained and politically reliable administrators from the universities. Nevertheless, there is still a very acute shortage of managerial personnel capable of organizing production and rationally allocating labor in most Cuban enterprises. But the current administrative inadequacies are assumed to be transitory. The Cubans are training administrators who are politically attuned to the revolution. The difficult period is passing; the administrators who were politically reliable but lacking in technical and managerial skills are being replaced. The most acute shortages can be found on the middle and lower levels of the bureaucracy, for the most competent officials usually go to the top quite rapidly.

In overall administrative performance there are very serious problems of finding personnel capable of taking the initiative in decision making. There has been a tendency to avoid making decisions which might turn out to be "mistakes." This lack of initiative has had its own ill effects on the Cuban development process.

One of the key areas where the Cuban development efforts have suffered greatly is in the area of information collection. Prerevolutionary Cuba was not very well developed in the area of systematic collection and transmission of information to policy-makers. This problem was exacerbated by the emigration of managerial personnel. Especially with the emergence of a planned economy based on nationalized enterprises, information collection became crucial. During the last few years many faulty decisions have been made because the information necessary to make rational decisions was lacking or was erroneous. During the 1970 sugar harvest, when ten million tons was the goal, a key development was the establishment of a day-to-day information-collecting apparatus functioning down to the very smallest unit of production. Information was collected and transmitted to regional and then to national information bureaus, and decisions affecting the particular unit were then transmitted back to the local levels.

It appears that substantial progress has been made in creating channels for the upward flow of information. This progress is largely confined to administrative channels having to do with economic matters—performance, and production reports—and is not related to political and social matters. The Cubans have been very much involved in creating an efficient administrative apparatus, which they consider critical to their economic efforts. Administrative weaknesses have been pointed to repeatedly as the source of many of the ills which currently afflict Cuban economics. To the extent that this is so, the efforts of recent years in this direction, both in education and organization, should improve the situation, though it is difficult to judge at this time.

In conclusion, then, one can say that Cuba has gone through three revolutions. The first was the political revolution that overthrew Batista and ended in 1959 with his flight out of the country. The second revolution, the social revolution, was between 1959 and 1964 and largely demolished the old ruling elite and the social structure upon which it was based. The establishment of public ownership over the means of production, agrarian reform, and egalitarian norms characterized the second revolution. The redistribution of goods in general was the major feature of the social revolutionary phase. The third revolution beginning in 1964–65 initiated the drive for economic development. During this period a serious effort is being made to organize the population and to maximize the production of goods, services, and new productive facilities. In each revolution a conversion process occurs. During the social revolution a diffuse kind of "oppositionist" political militant is converted into a cadre concerned with social problems and economic redistribution. Political rebels are converted into social revolutionaries. In Cuba this meant the conversion of guerrilla fighters into mass political organizers. This conversion was very successfully carried out in the process of consolidating the revolution. There were serious conflicts and defections along the way, first from the right-wing anti-Communists who opposed the social revolution, and then by the old communists around Anibal Escalante, who attempted to replace the leadership and reorient the revolution around different political and social criteria. The process of conversion was successful and Cuba's transformation from a political to a social revolution was carried out and the new cadre created. The third revolution, the development revolution, required the conversion of social revolutionaries into technical and administrative cadre. This change has been much more difficult than the previous changes; rather than a shift from one type of politics to another, it required a totally new set of qualifications: technical and administrative skills. The development revolution and the conversion of cadre was not as successful as the prior efforts. Many of the political leaders could not develop the proper skills to manage economic enterprises and as a result, serious errors have been made along the way. The future Cuban development effort will depend more on creating new cadre rather than conversion. In fact a new technical intelligentsia is developing which is taking over many of the managerial functions of economic enterprises. The growth of a technical intelligentsia, however, raises new problems: whether the technical cadre, and those social revolutionaries who were successfully converted, can maintain their political identity and the revolutionary élan that propels the revolution. Can they maintain the values of the earlier revolutionary phase, or will they be oriented toward a less egalitarian society, a society more closely geared to social differences and a differential reward system such as is found in the USSR? The Cuban leadership is acutely aware of this problem, hence the intense effort to inculcate the idea of collective and productive work in the technical personnel as they are being trained for their technical or their professional careers.[16]

16. A longer version of this paper was commissioned for the Austin conference. It was subsequently published without the last section, "Administration in a Revolutionary Setting," in *Politics and Society* 1 (Nov. 1970) as "Cuba: A Decade of Revolutionary Government." Because this material is available elsewhere, the editors have removed major parts of the already published sections, "Social and Economic Development" and "Cuban Economic Development and the Latin American Revolution," which provide further detail on Cuban policy in socio-economic development and foreign affairs and which are not directly related to development administration. The information on Cuban bureaucrats has not been published elsewhere.

Chapter 12

The Military and Government in Peru

Luigi R. Einaudi

The subject of this paper is the nature of relations between two public bureaucracies: military and civilian. Though there are a number of other bureaucracies in Peru, notably those of the Catholic church and of various private economic enterprises, the public bureaucracies, their characteristics and skills, are most important in defining the resources available for state-directed innovation, particularly of the type apparently under way since the revolution of October 1968. If the process begun with the overthrow of President Belaunde by the military forces under General Juan Velasco Alvarado is to be more than a coup transferring elite power from one group to another, much will depend on the capacity of the Peruvian state to administer expanding economic programs.

Unfortunately relatively little is known about either the military or the civilian bureaucracies. Although this situation is largely due to the relative underdevelopment of social science knowledge about Peru generally, in the case of the military, general ignorance derives also from a policy of positive secrecy on the part of the Peruvian military establishment. This policy, in force since the Peru-Ecuador conflict of 1941–42, denies even other Peruvian public agencies, not to mention academic researchers, information of a kind often readily available in the United States or in other Latin American countries. Information on civilian bureaucracies in Peru is further limited by lack of development of uniform professional standards among public employees, who function under separate regulations depending on the agency of employment.

Although several separate bureaucracies fall within each of the "military" and "civilian" categories, taken as a whole, Peruvian public employees in the senior administrative positions (as studied, for example, by Hopkins[1]) are probably roughly comparable in numbers to the approximately 5,000 men in the officer corps of the three military services. However, there is probably a significant imbalance between the two bureaucracies based on the military's greater internal cohesion and education, as well as on their greater access to the means of coercion.

Peruvian officers have traditionally striven to make up in quality of professionalism for what they have often lacked in operational capacity and military matériel. All Air Force and Navy officers and more than 90 percent of Army officers are graduates of university-level military academies. Specialized training is provided routinely for all branches beginning shortly after academic graduation. A competitive-entrance two-year General Staff course has functioned continuously since 1902 and has become a prerequisite for line promotion to general officer.

Since the turn of the century, military training available in Peru has been supplemented by attendance at foreign military schools, until World War II largely in France and since then more frequently in the United States. In 1960, nearly half of Peruvian general officers had received foreign training, and from nearly a dozen foreign countries.

Since World War II the training available to military officers has included increasing emphasis on nonmilitary elements related to national defense, including public administration, economic planning, and political studies. Since 1950 much of this has been concentrated at the Center for Higher Military Studies (CAEM). During the past decade, however, it has with increasing frequency also included attendance at civilian universities and international training institutes both in Peru and abroad. Peruvian officers, for example, have attended both MIT and the training courses offered in Chile by the U.N. Economic Commission for Latin America.

1. Jack W. Hopkins, *The Government Executive of Modern Peru* (Gainesville: Univ. of Florida Press, 1967).

By relating this advanced system of military education to career promotion the Peruvian military leadership made of it the cornerstone of a rationalized bureaucratic structure. The career significance of education is without parallel even in the major military powers where combat performance contributes to lower correlations between training and promotion. It is impossible to predict, on a statistical basis, the future of a West Point graduate. In Peru, 80 percent of the division generals serving between 1940 and 1965 were in the top 25 percent of their academy's graduating class.

The structure of skills represented by this military bureaucracy has gradually evolved in the direction of the more technical services. Infantry officers and cavalry officers predominated during the nineteenth century; artillery became an important service after the turn of the century. Engineering and other traditional support services, including veterinary medicine, became accepted military subspecialties, followed more recently by economics and public administration. By 1960 the Peruvian Army had more engineers than cavalrymen as officers.

In sum, although he operates within a largely underdeveloped society, often with inferior and dangerous equipment, the Peruvian officer considers himself a modern professional. Indeed, one of his greatest frustrations is that he has often been trained to be a professional in matters beyond the military capacity or interests of his country. He often believes himself better equipped than most civilians to deal with the problems of development.

This imbalance between military and civilian bureaucracies in a country where the military has often intervened to assume direct control of the state, together with the deficiencies of the public civil service, has led some observers to comment that in a country as underdeveloped as Peru the military are virtually the only real bureaucracy. Yet the suspicion persists that such a statement serves largely to underscore the weakness of the Peruvian state.

The successful consummation of the reforms introduced by the current military government depends ultimately on Peru's overall administrative capacity. The military, no matter how greatly expanded its roles or how competent its officers, cannot overlook the rest of Peru's state apparatus. If reforms are introduced in a way to alienate the civilian bureaucracy or if the civilian and military bureaucracies are for other reasons unable to cooperate, then clearly the prognosis for the Peruvian revolution must be dubious in the short run, even with major efforts to recruit additional administrative personnel.

Officers as Politicians and Public Officeholders Before 1968

Military men have held virtually every major office in Peruvian political and administrative life, from the presidency to minor administrative posts at national and provincial levels. The Army is overwhelmingly the most important service in this regard. Table 12.1 provides an indication of the Army's absolute and relative dominance in providing officers who engage in major political activities. The only exception to Army dominance is the understandable fact that Navy and Air Force officers have a relatively greater likelihood of becoming ministers of the Navy or Air respectively than do Army officers of becoming ministers of War. This is logical, since each service provides a senior officer to fill its respective ministerial post and the Air Force and Navy have smaller officer corps than the Army. In all other categories, however, Army officers are more politically active than their service brethren. In fact, in some areas the provision of officeholders is not an adequate indication of relative power. The "civilian" ministries (Table 12.1, line 3) include several cases in which Navy and Air Force officers were included in cabinets out of institutional solidarity and deference to juridical equality rather than because of individual influence or the political power of a branch of the service.

Political but nongovernmental activities of military officers are discussed elsewhere. In the nineteenth century, before the military career became a full-time profession not routinely combined with private activities, military officers sometimes shuttled be-

Table 12.1. *Number of officers engaging in specified political activity, 1900–1965, by service*

Activity	Army	Navy	Air Force	Police	Total
1. President	8	0	0	0	8
2. "Military" minister[a]	42	22	11	0	75
3. "Nonmilitary" minister	45	10	7	1	63
4. Senator	28	4	0	0	32
5. Ambassador	7	1	1	0	9
6. Deputy	14	3	0	0	17
7. Prefect	39	7	0	0	46
8. Participant in political party affairs	44	3	3	1	51
9. Participant in military coup attempt	109	11	5	7	132
10. Internal pacification[b]	18	2	0	0	20
Totals[c]	354	63	27	9	453
Approximate number of officers serving in period 1900–1965[d]	7300	1600	1000	3000	

Categories 1–4 account for all officers holding these positions in this period. Categories 5–10 are totals only for officers included in coded biographies, and are thus illustrative only.

 a. "Military" ministry = Air, Army, or Navy.
 b. Excludes 1965 counterinsurgency campaign.
 c. Some officers engaged in more than one activity.
 d. Estimated.
Source: Coded biographies.

tween a variety of careers. Their access to public office then could as easily derive from their personal wealth, or the activities of civilian political organizations, as from their military roles. Today access is normally dependent on the military career itself, with public positions open to the promoters of a successful coup as in 1962, or, as after 1950, to the followers of a general who had successfully imposed his "legal" election to the presidency.

Despite their frequent prominence, then, and with the general exception of the Ministries of War, Navy, and Air (with rare exceptions occupied by military men throughout the past fifty years) and the Ministry of Government and Police (often held by a military man), military officers have held political office less frequently than civilians. This is even true of the presidency, although more Army officers have been president than have members of any other single profession.

Some indication of the relative status of military personnel within the political class as a whole a generation ago is provided by an occupational analysis of the 1943 membership of the Club de la Unión. Unlike the Club Nacional, which tends to be socially restrictive (except in time of political turmoil, when it coopts military members for protection), the Club de la Unión is broadly open to prominent public personalities. In 1943, military officers, with about 12 percent of the membership (about three-fourths from the Army) made up the fourth largest occupational category. A comparison with the 1940 census listing of those actively practicing their professions further reveals that the military were well behind the more prestigeful professions of engineer, lawyer, and even doctor in their rate of access even to the Club de la Unión. Civil servants, with the exception of employees of the Foreign Ministry, had even lower status, it would appear: while 200 of the club's 1701 members were military officers, only 8 were listed as "public functionaries."

Military officers also participate in a number of nongovernmental activities of a semipolitical nature with some consequences for public administration. Important among these are leadership in the provincial associations and clubs of Lima. Officers are often among the most successful sons of given provinces. This, together with their leadership capacity and their presumed private influence, frequently projects retired officers into the presidency of these clubs, which often form important links between the capital and the provinces.

Table 12.2 suggests that although the absolute number of generals engaging in specified political activities has remained constant or increased only slightly during the past fifty years, those politically rewarded in this fashion have tended to decline as a proportion of all general officers. The decline in relative opportunity for political activities during the last fifty years could be interpreted as a decrease in political involvement by officers except for the steadiness of the absolute figures and the absence

Table 12.2. *Army general officers on active duty in selected years engaging in specified political and military activities at some point in their careers*

Activity	1916	1929	1940	1950	1960–65[a]
President	33%	7%	10%	7%	2%
	(1)	(1)	(1)	(2)	(2)
Minister	67%	36%	60%	50%	24%
	(2)	(5)	(6)	(15)	(20)
Senator	33%	29%	30%	7%	0%
	(1)	(4)	(3)	(2)	(0)
Other "legal" political	67%	50%	40%	23%	7%
	(2)	(7)	(4)	(7)	(6)
Coups	67%	43%	40%	23%	23%
	(2)	(6)	(4)	(7)	(19)
Internal pacification	33%	50%	30%	10%	1%
	(1)	(7)	(3)	(3)	(1)
Combat	67%	14%	10%	23%	4%
	(2)	(2)	(1)	(7)	(3)
Total	(3)	(14)	(10)	(30)	(84)

Definitions

President: Includes presidents of juntas.

Minister: Includes all ministries.

Other "legal" political: Includes deputies, prefects, unsuccessful senatorial and presidential candidates and party leaders.

Coups: Includes participating in unsuccessful as well as successful attempts.

Internal pacification: Troop command in controlling internal rebellions and disorders.

Combat: Against foreign troops (Chile, 1879–83; Ecuador, 1941; Colombia, 1912, 1932, etc.).

Source: Coded biographies.

a. Since men in this category have in some cases not completed their careers, the figures here may still increase somewhat.

of comparable data on the number of civilians engaging in such activities in similar periods. What does emerge, however, is that, among all activities of all general officers, individual involvement in public affairs plays a less prominent part.

Areas of Permanent Institutional Concern
Before 1968

Although we see (Table 12.2) that political activities have played a decreasingly prominent part over time in the personal lives of most general officers, the areas of continuing institutional military concern and interest have steadily expanded in both breadth and detail to encompass most areas of public life to some degree.

Preservation of Institutional Autonomy

The major continuing concern of the military, as of any major bureaucracy, is institutional preservation and solidarity. In Peru this has largely taken the form of attempts to insulate the military from external interference. In essence, this policy began with the attempt to professionalize the Army after 1895, with the policy of "no tocar al ejército." Beginning with the presidency of General Oscar Benavides in 1914, this was extended to include the habitual naming of a military officer as service minister. Benavides continued the policy of military autonomy during his second presidency, 1933–38, and it was further strengthened by the imposition of broad secrecy regulations in 1941. These have been maintained since, and with the further development in the 1950's of the view of the minister as senior service officer, virtually independent of civilian selection or control, the military have succeeded in steadily enlarging the areas of institutional autonomy and freedom from external control. This remains the predominant concern of the Peruvian military today, although a greater social awareness on the part of most officers in the 1960's has led to a rather ambiguous attempt to combine the "survival through autonomy" strategy with one of "survival through leadership of change," which may lead to considerably greater involvement than military conservatives would like.

Control and Development of Remote Areas

Frontier provinces where the possibility of border conflicts arises have traditionally been another important military concern. The northern province of Tumbes and the Amazonian province of Iquitos, for example, were initially administered largely by the military, who provided health, sanitation, and other facilities incidental to the stationing of troops and to the consolidation of national territory. In these remote and under-

populated areas, these were the first such facilities to be provided
for the local population.

Since the 1920's the doctrine of the frontier has been expanded
and amended to include all remote areas. Military topographers
and engineers worked in the 1930's and 40's to plan roads which
were initially justified as demanded by strategic need of communications for external defense, but which are now viewed, and
were built during the 1960's, largely as means of access and development for areas where conditions of labor supply, security, or
health are such that private enterprise could not operate efficiently.

National Planning and Development

Military government of remote areas set the precedent for
greater military participation in studies and projects on national
development which began in the mid-1950's. The CAEM as-
signs the primary responsibility for national development to the
state, strongly implying the need for extensive military participation.

When the CAEM published its study of the development of
the Central Selva, in 1958, it was the first effort to develop cost
estimates for a specific Peruvian development program. More
important, it was a proposal that the Central Selva be put under
military administration for the purpose of conducting a controlled
experiment in agricultural and industrial development. This proposal was successfully sidetracked by Pedro Beltrán with a substitute less dangerous to established patterns, the Peru-VIA
project reported on by A. D. Little.

By 1962, however, the military junta had founded the National
Planning Institute, with a highly competent colonel at its head.
In the mid-1960's, most groups in the military were chary of civic
action and development programs in general, but Peru has sent
ten officers to study agricultural cooperatives in Israel, and it was
rare to find a committee or a commission traveling to inspect an
area that did not include at least one military officer.

Education

The Ministry of Education was founded as a separate ministry by General Benavides in 1936 with his close associate General Ernesto Montagne Marckholz as the first minister of public education. Since then a number of officers have held the ministry, including General Juan Mendoza Rodríguez during the presidency of General Manuel A. Odría (1948–56), and General Ernesto Montagne Sánchez (son of the original minister) under President Belaunde in 1964–65.

The military interest in education is thus of long standing. It derives partly from an often personally based appreciation of education's importance to social advancement, and partly from recognition of the utility of the educational system to the development of a broad base of instruction for national defense and nationalist affirmation.

Under the senior General Montagne a number of basic reforms were introduced to control and "Peruvianize" private secondary education by establishing curriculum requirements, such as minimal standards for the study of Peruvian history, and controlling nationality of teachers and language of instruction. In 1939 Montagne reorganized and extended the program of "Pre-Military Instruction," designed to provide secondary and university students with basic military education, and largely reoriented it toward the study of Peruvian history, geography, and the "defense of nationalism."

When General Mendoza became minister of education in 1948, he had already participated with Generals Marín and Romero Pardo in the creation of a militarized secondary school, the Colegio Militar Leoncio Prado, dedicated not only to providing an opportunity for young men to become acquainted early with the military vocation, but as Romero Pardo put it in an interview, to "transmit military values of honor, duty, and discipline to future civilian leaders." General Mendoza, reflecting the experience of most military men in the difficulty of acquiring a secondary education, concentrated largely on modernizing technical equipment, building new schools, and otherwise easing the bottleneck in

secondary education. This choice of priorities was roundly de-
nounced by university students whose educational needs Mendoza's policies largely ignored.

Foreign Policy

Although foreign policy has been a traditional concern of the
military because of its closeness to its national defense mission,
the military have had little to do with either the formulation or
execution of foreign policy. Only six officers had by 1965 held the
portfolio of foreign affairs, a smaller number than for any other
long-established ministry.

This limited role probably reflects not only the limited latitude
of Peru in foreign policy but also the self-consciousness and sense
of inferiority of most army officers in the face of the complexities
and aristocratic pomp of diplomacy. The most important military
foreign ministers have been Navy men: Admiral Federico Díaz
Dulanto and Admiral Luís Enrique Llosa G.P., who were well-
connected in cosmopolitan social and political circles.

Military nationalism, traditionally rather narrowly frontier-
minded, began to be more broadly concerned with issues of national sovereignty and development. To the traditional defense of
territorial waters petroleum was added in the late 1950's. Until
1968, however, military conservatism and ambivalence toward its
political tormentor, but military benefactor—the United States—
forestalled action.

Support of Government Administration

The armed services have traditionally supplied an important
number of aides to the president of the republic and to the Senate
and Chamber of Deputies, as well as occasionally loaning officers
to work in the civilian ministries. These positions, not infrequently
going to outstanding junior and field-grade officers, have sometimes served as means of coordination between the agencies concerned, but with individual exceptions seem largely to be political
communication channels between the military services and the
specific office to which the officer is assigned.

Roles of the Military in Public Administration
Before 1968

The Military as Expediters

Military power and autonomy are such that often the military can undertake new programs rapidly, minimizing or simply ignoring standard civilian procedures. Since this usually implies poor coordination, the results may in the long run prove inefficient, though useful as stopgap measures. Given the difficulties of obtaining action in Peru, however crippling the drawback when considered theoretically, such action is resorted to frequently on matters ranging from water for slums to oil and agrarian reform.

The Military as Buffer Between Government and Opposition

The prestige and power of the military and the fear inspired by it are often invoked by presidents in political difficulties as a buffer against criticism and an appeal to national unity. This was the path chosen by Bustamente after the Graña assassination in 1947 and by Odría after the Merino revolt in 1956. The two presidents, one civilian, the other military, but both serving under the constitution, dismissed their civilian cabinets, replacing them with entirely military cabinets which they hoped would appear above politics and thus give them respite from political critics.

The method may be used also in piecemeal fashion. When President Belaunde was faced with censure of his minister of government early in 1964, he replaced him with a naval officer. When, later that year, his minister of education was censured, he replaced him with General Montagne. Although neither of the appointments was objectionable—both men were known as good professionals, moderate progressives in the Belaunde fashion, honest men who lived within their salaries—the purpose was clear: to exploit traditional civil military tensions, and particularly the civilian politicians' fear of antagonizing the military, by naming military ministers who symbolized military support and who might be treated carefully by the opposition during interpellations.

In Lima, when Montagne's appointment brought the number of military officers serving as ministers to five of twelve, the wags put their finger on the difficulty inherent in the military as buffer. It was said that Peru, having already produced the novelty of the "institutional coup" in 1962, was now introducing the latest refinement in military politics: the "coup by ministry." As events turned out, of course, this was not the immediate prelude to a coup, although it probably did further undermine civilian authority among some officers. How often can civilian rulers interpose military men as buffers to their own political conflicts without convincing the military that the "incompetent political hacks" are proving incapable of running the country and need to be replaced by others, yet unnamed, but "more competent, more patriotic, more disciplined"?

The Military as Rulers

A military man usually attains power by virtue of military qualities; to remain in office, however, even if ruling "by force," the officer must turn politician. Only if the officer-turned-politician is equal to or better than his civilian contemporaries can he expect to retain power on more than a temporary basis.

But to succeed, the officer-turned-politician must also face the question of his relationship to the military institutions from which he originated. Meanwhile, however, the military institutions themselves are confronting the same problems as the officer-turned-politician, but with large and possibly greater consequences. If the military are to govern as an institution, they must also develop new skills and links to the civilian population. Can such a transformation take place without imperiling military discipline and efficiency? Until 1968 the answer provided by experience to this dilemma was unclear because there had never before been an exclusively military government for more than a brief transitional period.

The five successful coups of modern Peru before 1968 produced two transitional governments, two lasting governments headed by military officers, and one government, the longest in Peruvian history, with a civilian very much in control. The latter case, the outcome of the revolution of 1919 which put Augusto B. Leguía, who had already been president once, from 1908 to 1912, back into office, this time for eleven years until 1930, was in no way a military government and need not concern us, except as evidence that a military coup need not necessarily lead to greater military participation in government.

The two coups which produced transitional governments were the anti-Bollinghurst coup of 1914, which put Benavides in power for sixteen months, and the 1962 coup, which led to a caretaker military government which lasted a year and ten days.

In 1914 the coup was essentially negative or preventive in nature. Bollinghurst was deposed, and the objective was achieved. Benavides, who had been chief of the nascent general staff, but not commander in chief, merely acted as chief of state until a convention of political parties could be convened to agree on a new civilian president. He did not bring military officers into the administration and made no effort to become a politician. This first Benavides government is a prototype for civilian manipulation of power behind a military façade.

In 1962, although the situation was similar in that the coup had a specific immediate goal—annulment of the elections—the military institutions took over the government as such, in strict accordance with the formal military chain of command. There were also a number of indications that some officers were dissatisfied with the limited caretaker function assumed by the military junta. The president of the junta and a few military ministers allowed themselves a number of statements indicating policy preferences which went beyond even the most broadly defined caretaker role. In the end, however, the officers who had shown signs of becoming politicians were shunted aside, and the junta, after a cautious term, returned power to a civilian and retreated into obscurity.

The 1930 revolution (which after the Sánchez Cerro–Apra feud ultimately brought Benavides to power again, this time from 1933 to 1939) and the 1948 revolution (which began an eight-year rule by General Odría) were very different, though both resulted in lengthy military rule.

Benavides became enough of a politician the second time to

remain in office, but not enough of one to lose his military allegiances. In a country where government was still relatively limited, and in which the politically articulate were largely agreed on a breathing spell from violent partisan strife, Benavides behaved like a conservative autocrat, managing government with an occasional technocratic touch, and placing strong emphasis on rationalized promotion procedures as the basis of military professionalism. Benavides' political skill is amply demonstrated by the fact that Peruvians still disagree on whether he ever really wanted to be president—this, of a man whose stays in the Casa de Pizarro lasted nearly eight years on two occasions spanning more than a quarter of a century.

Odría, on the other hand, rapidly opted for the conversion to politician. Unlike Benavides, who had had the reputation of being the best soldier of his generation, Odría was known more for his personal courage (which was unquestioned) than for his intellect. After his break with his initial civilian allies, moreover, Odría, managed to stay in power only through extensive use of the police combined with large-scale public works made possible by the rising foreign-exchange revenues received in the wake of the Korean War. Not until after military pressures provoked by the corruption of his regime forced him to step down and a new election approached in 1962 was it realized that the public-works prosperity of his regime had bought him considerable political capital among the urban working class and the slumdwellers.

The evidence from this rapid review of the consequences of military interventions prior to 1968 suggests that the military was not particularly well qualified or able to govern on its own for more than a brief caretaker period, but that it played an important mediation role between factions, whether in or out of power, while making a limited contribution to development. Do the events of 1968 and since suggest changes in this assessment?

The Revolutionary Experiment in Military Government Since 1968

A number of commentators, including Fidel Castro as well as President Juan Velasco Alvarado, have taken to referring to the political process under way since the military coup which deposed Fernando Belaunde in October of 1968 as a revolution. Although it is not my intent to discuss the politics of the current Peruvian government in this chapter, I will briefly discuss some general considerations about this most recent form of political activity by the military.

In my view the internal political diversity of the Peruvian armed forces will continue to prevent the adoption of consistent development policies by the military institutions as such over any extended period of time. The current military regime may, as it did with the nationalization of the IPC petroleum complex at Talara, briefly take dramatic steps of considerable symbolic significance for overall development policies, particularly in instances which are amenable to executive action. Such acts may even be called for by radical elements of left and right who see the military as a means of outmaneuvering conservative and liberal democratic political opponents. Policies adopted under such circumstances may thus be the result of the development strategy of a specific political group, but they are most decidedly not the strategies of the military as an institution.

As permanently established bureaucracies, the military forces are likely to continue to behave in the long run in accordance with their historic institutional policy concerns. These include, as we have seen and in order of importance: (i) institutional autonomy and survival, (ii) public order and the control of remote areas, (iii) foreign policy and boundary questions, and (iv) more recently, national development, including under that rubric education, industrialization, control of strategic materials (petroleum, telecommunications), and general national planning and support for central government authority and administration.

The possibility that the military might adopt some form of revolutionary strategy has been fed in recent years by increased military concern over the need for modernization of society as a whole as a prerequisite to survival of the military as a modern institution. Likewise, the possibility that the military might adopt a strategy with anti-imperialist overtones has been fed in recent years by increased military suspicion of U.S. security and economic policies.

Taken as a whole, however, it is unlikely that the military institutions as such will be able to resolve what they are likely to see as a contradiction between military discipline and the partisan political activity required for the organization of development. Nonetheless, just as it is unlikely that the military can be bureaucratically controlled for long by any single partisan clique, so also it is possible that the military officer corps may produce individual politicians who may under certain conditions lead the struggle for development. But such men will in practice cease to be military officers.

A second reason for skepticism about the military's capacity for revolutionary innovation derives from the nature of Peruvian society rather than from the nature of the military itself. I suspect that revolution from above by the military is likely to fail in Peru for reasons similar to those for the failure of guerrillas to lead revolution from below. One of the most important of these common reasons is the unmanageability of Peru, whether it be measured in social, political, or administrative terms. Peru has nearly twice the population of Cuba spread out over an area more than ten times as large, but with less than one-fifth as many television sets per capita. With neither a charismatic leader nor an overwhelming external enemy against which to unite, how can a Peruvian revolution hope to find and communicate the emotional cement necessary to hold a revolutionary effort together?

Shortly after the self-styled revolutionary military government assumed power, it became apparent that there were a number of serious internal difficulties over the program to be followed. To maintain momentum while debates raged over internal policy, the military turned to its traditional interest in public morality.

There is undoubtedly a great deal to be said for making trains run on time. Few things are more demoralizing than public displays of habitual ineptitude and corruption. In addition, a major public scandal over smuggling, with deep implications for members of the military as well as for highly placed civilian friends of President Belaunde Terry, had contributed in the spring of 1968 to the atmosphere that later led to the military intervention. One of the first acts of the new revolutionary government, therefore, was to proclaim the need to eliminate graft and corruption. The moralization campaign which ensued included a series of measures to increase efficiency, including a reform of the basic structure of government, creating three additional ministries.

The attempt to improve public administration services included the unheard-of introduction of time clocks for all public employees (to be punched by supervisors and employees alike) and the slogan 'hora exacta, hora Peruana" to replace the traditional Peruvian habit of tardiness accompanied by the statement that the nobody who was on time was operating on "hora inglesa."

The incoming military ministers made a largely unprecedented (except for some members of the 1962 junta) public accounting of their wealth upon assuming office, and there can be no doubt that the regime as a whole has good intentions. Some ministers appear to be incorruptible to the point of fanaticism. In fact, one of the concerns raised by the present regime is its ability to retain the question of corruption in some perspective.

Harsh and immediate legal proceedings were instituted in the spring of 1969 against those officials of the Ministry of Finance and of the Central Bank, military as well as civilian, who could be charged with corruption or incompetence in the granting of an export license permitting the International Petroleum Company to withdraw funds from Peru. So severe and sharp was the military government's reaction that it sent a shudder of fear throughout the civilian bureaucracy, extending also to many private citizens with the technical competence needed if Peru is to enlist intelligence and knowledge in public service.

Excessive zeal in the eradication of corruption and ineptitude can heighten the deficiencies of public administration. This irony is perhaps most evident in an underdeveloped country with a large marginal population. In such a society, any educated man has means disproportionate to the environment as a whole. A sensitive member of the middle or upper classes from which senior public officials must of necessity be drawn finds it almost impossible to live in Peru without somehow feeling corrupt, if only because he lives well while others subsist in a near-animal state.

To offset the shortages in administrative personnel automatically imposed by the adoption of new government programs such as agrarian reform, the government has attempted to turn to retired officers and to church personnel. Again, a quick consideration of the numbers involved reveals the poverty of Peru's resources compared to the magnitude of the task. There are fewer than 2500 priests in all of Peru. Even assuming that church resistance over cooperation with the authoritarian military can be overcome in the common cause of development, this is simply not a very large pool from which to draw. Finally, the limits on this form of expansion of the bureaucracy are underscored by the fact that there are even fewer retired officers than priests.

Since the revolution also, increasing numbers of officers have been assigned to the nonmilitary ministries, often occupying senior and even middle-level posts previously occupied by civilians. This proliferation of military officers in what would normally be considered civilian functions can be explained partially as attempts at reform and partially as a method of political control.

The assignment of officers to these functions may create tensions within the military itself. Officers holding administrative posts draw extra basic pay allotments denied to those remaining on line duty in the barracks. This irritant may act as a catalyst for morale and other issues contrasting military politicians unfavorably with military professionals.

Of greater immediate concern is the possibility for demoralization of the senior civilian element of the bureaucracy. Many of these men have long practical experience in day-to-day management of affairs in areas only vaguely understood by the military men who now not only block their chances for promotions, but seem, with their insistent demands for revision and change, to imply that previous efforts were incompetent. Bureaucrats know too well the difficulties of innovation.

One of the political functions of the military in Peru has traditionally been to act as a means by which ambitious and talented civilian leaders could take office without having to undertake the messy business of organizing or currying the favor of political parties. As a means of bypassing the party system, which certainly has not always been a paradigm of statesmanship, the military has enabled the nation to draw in more or less routine fashion upon the intelligence of some of its more intelligent and competent civilians.

Whatever the merits of such a pattern (and to one brought up in the United States they appear dubious), the current military intervention, with its insistence upon military decision making and military control of key positions, suggests that the Peruvian military, under the leadership of the Army, is attempting to erect itself as a superbureaucracy dominating the state in its search for a modern nation. This attempt to run a purely military government is an exception to previous military policies, and a marked change even with regard to contemporary military regimes in other Latin American countries, such as Brazil and Argentina, where civilians have continued to exercise key policy-making functions.

The ultimate problem is that Peru's strength may not be in its bureaucrats, military or civilian (both of whom are generally looked down upon by social, economic, and intellectual elites), but in the private sector. The tragedy is that this private sector has until now acted in such a private manner as to discredit itself by appearing to deny the national goals to which the military, more than any other group in Peru, is dedicated. Military dictatorship and perhaps even ultimately stagnation may thus be the price of the antinationalism of past Peruvian elites. The magnitude of that price will be determined by the political wisdom and flexibility of the military as they seek to lead Peru—and so save themselves—to an improved accommodation with the pressures of modernity.[2]

2. This chapter draws on materials contained in Chapter 7 of the author's RAND Corporation-sponsored draft, "The Peruvian Military." The views contained herein are not necessarily those of the RAND Corporation or of public or private sponsors of its research. As published here, this chapter is an almost verbatim reproduction of the paper presented by the author at the Austin Conference in April 1970. Only slight editorial changes have been made in the original draft. Dr. Einaudi has since published more detailed and fully documented accounts in *U.S. Foreign Policy and Peru*, ed. Daniel A. Sharp (Austin: Univ. of Texas Press, 1972), under the title "United States Relations with the Peruvian Military as Military and as Government," and in a Rand document prepared jointly with Alfred C. Stepan III, *Latin American Institutional Development: Changing Military Perspectives in Peru and Brazil*, Report no. R–586–DOS prepared for the Office of External Research, Dept. of State (Santa Monica. Calif.: Rand Corporation, 1971).

Chapter 13

Bureaucracy During a Period of Social Change: The Case of Guatemala

Jerry L. Weaver

Even if the city folded up, the sky split asunder, and men deserted the earth, the government offices would open at their appointed time to administer nothingness. I am eternal, and my paradise is furnished with archives and desk blotters.
                    The Chief Bureaucrat in CAMUS, *L'Etat de siège*

The recent history of Guatemala illustrates the profound impact on a society of the interaction of social upheaval and political change. Since 1944 Guatemala has been racked by revolution and counterrevolution, insurgency and counterinsurgency. New political structures have arisen, have flourished, and have been replaced. Social and economic institutions have been drastically modified. However, basic patterns of social, economic, and political behavior dating from the seventeenth and eighteenth century remain virtually unmodified. This chapter will examine the role of the Guatemalan bureaucracy as a force for orderly, rational change during the post-World War II era. Special attention will be paid to the decade of the 1960's, which for Guatemala as for much of Latin America was marked by dramatic population growth, industrialization, violence, and a failure of democratic reforms.

Latin American Bureaucracy

There are few empirical studies of the composition, behavior, or impact of either Latin American bureaucrats or bureaucracies. The study of Latin American public administration, to paraphrase

Kling's biting observation, resembles the area itself: underdeveloped and traditional.[1] From the handful of monographs available comes a picture of extreme centralization of authority and unwillingness to delegate decision-making competence, rigid reliance on written regulations rather than encouragement for situational initiative and innovation, involvement by both clients and public officials of politicians or high executives in the resolution of all manner of requests, duplication of services, and absence of coordination of complementary, often interdependent programs. Patronage appointment and promotion, high personnel turnover, low level of technical training or occupational experience, and absence of commitment to public service are often-mentioned characteristics.[2]

Little systematic research has been reported on the political behavior or attitudes of bureaucrats as a specific social group. A basis for speculating about the bureaucrats' political role is offered by studies of the middle class. But while writers agree that the Latin American bureaucracy is a major element of the middle class, there is little consensus about middle-class political norms, attitudes, and behavior. Several observers see the middle class as supporting social change, economic development, and political democracy.[3] Others argue that the middle class supports only

1. Merle Kling, "The State of Research on Latin America: Political Science," in *Social Science Research on Latin America,* ed. Charles Wagley (New York: Columbia Univ. Press, 1964), p. 168. It is noteworthy that of the 36 concrete research proposals Kling lists to help correct the deficiencies in the state of political science research on Latin America, none refers to bureaucracy or public administration. Cf. Kling, pp. 192–94.

2. See Robert T. Daland, "Development Administration and the Brazilian Political System," *Western Political Quarterly* 21, no. 2 (June 1968): 325–39; Lawrence S. Graham, *Civil Service Reform in Brazil* (Austin: Univ. of Texas Press, 1968); James Petras, *Political and Social Forces in Chilean Development* (Berkeley and Los Angeles: Univ. of California Press, 1969); Jack W. Hopkins, *The Government Executive of Modern Peru* (Gainesville: Univ. of Florida Press, 1967); Freeman J. Wright, *The Upper Level Public Administrator in Ecuador* (Quito: Editorial Fray Jodoco Ricke, 1968).

3. John J. Johnson, *Political Change in Latin America: The Emergence of the Middle Sector* (Stanford, Calif.: Stanford Univ. Press, 1958); Robert J. Alexander, *Today's Latin America* (Garden City, N.Y.: Anchor Books, 1968), pp. 110–12; Victor Alba, "The Latin American Style and the New Social Forces," in *Latin American Issues: Essays and Comments,* ed. Albert O. Hirschman (New York: Twentieth Century Fund, 1961), pp. 43–51; Joseph A. Kahl, *The Measurement of Modernism: A Study of Values in Brazil and Mexico* (Austin: Univ. of Texas Press, 1968); Albert Lauterbach, *Enterprise in Latin America: Business Attitudes in a Developing Economy* (Ithaca, N.Y.: Cornell Univ. Press, 1966).

changes that secure and assure its political hegemony; once in power, the middle class is statusquo-ish, unwilling to share economic rewards or political power with the popular sector, and supports authoritarian military takeovers when threatened by under-class political mobilization.[4]

Thus the available data and interpretations offer little guidance in researching the impact of the Guatemalan bureaucracy on the complex political, social, and economic processes that have shaped the society during the post-World War II period. Does centralization facilitate or confound rapid economic expansion? What are the consequences of non-civil-service personnel practices for political stability? Do bureaucrats readily accommodate to pressures for procedural innovation? In order to answer these and other questions about bureaucracy's role in social change we must collect information and make evaluations. But how can we be sure that our data are reliable and valid—that we have asked the right questions? And against what standards do we assess the characteristics?

Bureaucracy and Political Development

In the absence of competent empirical research that might serve as a guide for the analysis of the Guatemalan bureaucracy, I have turned to a formal model of bureaucracy's role in social change. Weber's model of rational society offers an explicit set of variables and hypotheses relating bureaucratic characteristics to particular social and economic structures. For example, although the emergence of an organized, complex, law-based (ra-

4. Luis Ratinoff, "The New Urban Groups: The Middle Classes," in *Elites in Latin America,* ed. Seymour Martin Lipset and Aldo Solari (New York: Oxford Univ. Press, 1964), pp. 61–93; Rodolfo Stavenhagen, "Seven Fallacies About Latin America," in *Latin America: Reform or Revolution? A Reader,* ed. James Petras and Maurice Zeitlin (Greenwich, Conn.: Fawcett Publications, 1968), pp. 23–26; José Nun, "The Middle-Class Military Coup," in *The Politics of Conformity in Latin America,* ed. Claudio Veliz (New York: Oxford Univ. Press, 1967), pp. 66–118; James Malloy, "Revolution and Development in Bolivia," in *Constructive Change in Latin America,* ed. S. Cole Blasier (Pittsburgh: Univ. of Pittsburgh Press, 1968), pp. 177–232; Dale L. Johnson, "The National and Progressive Bourgeoisie in Chile," *Studies in Comparative International Development,* 4, no. 4 (1968–69): 63–86; Petras, *Political and Social Forces,* pp. 114–57; Jerry L. Weaver, "The Political Elite of a Military-Dominated Regime: The Guatemalan Example," *Journal of Developing Areas* 3, no. 3 (April 1969): 373–88; Richard Newbold Adams, *The Second Sowing: Power and Secondary Development in Latin America* (San Francisco: Chandler, 1967).

tional) society is the consequence of the creation of complex economic and political institutions, the engine of rationalism is bureaucratic administration.[5] Weber's bureaucratic administration is characterized by impersonalism, hierarchy, merit, tenure, and the like. Treating rational society as a dependent variable and bureaucratic administration as an independent variable, we have the research hypothesis that post-1944 social change in Guatemala is a consequence of the rationalization of the Guatemalan administrative system. Since Weber offers indices of both main variables (law-based, complex society, hierarchy, impersonal administration), we have specific operational criteria to research. Moreover, we have a frame of reference against which to evaluate the functionality/dysfunctionality of specific bureaucratic characteristics.

What variables affect the course of administrative action? The traits of bureaucratic administration do not simply appear: they are introduced by some force or forces. To guide us through the universe of variables impinging on the performance of the bureaucracy, I have formulated the following corollary to the research hypothesis: The extent to which the bureaucracy is an agent of rationalization is a consequence of the interaction of three variables—elite ideology, system of administration, and bureaucratic values.

Weber's model forms the basis for our work by offering definitions and suggesting research strategies. I have selected it because it is a formal theory, is well known, and is reducible to hypotheses and indices. It must not be assumed, however, that Weber's bureaucratic administration and rational society is a goal which either Guatemalans or I consciously seek. I share Weber's pessimism about the survival of meaningful personal freedom and individuality in rational society;[6] many Guatemalans are tolerant of, if they do not fully approve, the continuation of nonrational institutions and behavior throughout their society. I regret the distortion of our comprehension of Guatemala through the use of abstract ordering devices, yet I realize the necessity of this prac-

5. Max Weber, *The Theory of Social and Economic Organization*, trans. Talcott Parsons and A. M. Henderson (Glencoe, Ill.: Free Press, 1947), p. 337.
6. See Wolfgang Mommsen, "Max Weber's Political Sociology and His Philosophy of World History," *International Social Science Journal* 17 (1965): 45.

tice because of our inability to fashion a theory of administrative behavior based on Latin experience.

Elite Ideology

Until 1944 Guatemala was ruled by a classic Latin American political elite: plantation owners, senior military officers, social and economic notables, and representatives of major foreign commercial interests. Authority was exercised by the traditional strong man, whose rule was paternalistic, arbitrary, and predicated on his ability to hold the confidence (or keep alive the fear) of garrison commanders and other key military officers. Guatemala's last *caudillo*, General Jorge Ubico (1930–44), ruled the nation with, as his admirers fondly remember it, an iron hand. The *caudillo* insisted on punctuality, Calvinist comportment, and absolute rectitude. Primitive capitalism, the sanctity of private property, and classic Latin American liberalism were dominant elements of official ideology.[7]

The middle-class-based and-led revolt which forced Ubico from power in 1944 ushered in a decade of reform and innovation that succeeded in establishing Guatemala's small middle class of managers, technicians, entrepreneurs, professionals, and commercial farmers firmly in political power.[8] When the Arbenz regime

7. On prerevolutionary Guatemala, see Chester L. Jones, *Guatemala, Past and Present* (Minneapolis: Univ. of Minnesota Press, 1940); Mario Rodríguez, *Central America* (Englewood Cliffs, N.J.: Prentice-Hall, 1965). For an analysis of the ruling elite, see Mario Monteforte Toledo, *Guatemala: monografía sociológica* (Mexico City: Instituto de Investigaciones Sociales, 1965), pp. 251–70. On the bureaucracy and Ubico, see Russel H. Fitzgibbon, "Guatemala's 'Ley de Probidad,'" *Pacific Historical Review* 8, no. 1 (March 1939): 75–80; Elías Herrera Ayala, "A Study of and Recommended Personnel Administration for the National Government of Guatemala" (master's thesis, Brigham Young University, 1962). Best overall source is Nathan L. Whetten, *Guatemala: The Land and the People* (New Haven, Conn.: Yale Univ. Press, 1961).

8. Kalman H. Silvert, *A Study in Government: Guatemala* (New Orleans: Tulane Univ. Press, 1954); Robert L. Peterson, "Social Structure and the Political Process in Central America" (Ph.D. diss., Pennsylvania State Univ., 1962); Leo A. Suslow, "Aspects of Social Reform in Guatemala, 1944–1949," *Latin American Seminar Report 1* (Colgate, N.Y.: Colgate Univ. Area Studies, 1949); G. E. Britnell, "Problems of Economic and Social Change in Guatemala," *Canadian Journal of Economics and Political Science* 17 (1951): 468–81; Archer C. Bush, "Organized Labor in Guatemala, 1944–1949," *Latin American Seminar Report 2* (Colgate, N.Y.: Colgate Univ. Area Studies, 1950).

(1951–54) began to mobilize *campesinos,* workers, and traditional Indians, and to flirt with agrarian reform and workers-and-peasants militia,[9] the middle class grew progressively more alienated until the regime was overthrown by a U.S.-supported "liberation army" of 300-odd Guatemalan exiles invading from Honduras.[10]

The counterrevolutionary governments of Castillo Armas (1954–57) and General Miguel Ydígoras Fuentes (1958–63) destroyed the experiment in popular mobilization and social reform and returned Guatemala to a firm anticommunist, pro-U.S. foreign policy.[11] Domestically this meant welcoming foreign investment, assurances that agrarian and tax reform would not reduce indus-

9. A well-documented review of the mobilization of the popular sector is found in Ronald M. Schneider, *Communism in Guatemala, 1944–1954* (New York: Praeger, 1959). Various points of view about the revolution are found in Robert J. Alexander, "Guatemala's Communists," *Canadian Forum,* 1 April 1954, pp. 5–7; Oscar René Cruz, "La Reforma Agraria de Guatemala," *Revista de Economía* (Mexico), Dec. 1958, pp. 326–28; Charles C. Cumberland, "Guatemala: Labor and the Communists," *Current History* 24 (March 1953): 143–48; A. Fuentes-Mohr, "Land Settlement and Agrarian Reform in Guatemala," *International Journal of Agrarian Affairs* 2, no. 1 (Jan. 1955): 26–36; D. S. Scern, "Guatemalan Agrarian Reform," *American Journal of Comparative Law* 2, no. 2 (Spring 1953): 235–38; Whetten, *Guatemala,* pp. 152–66; José Luis Paredes Moreira, *Reform agraria: una experiencia en Guatemala* (Guatemala City: Imprenta Universitaria, 1963); Stokes Newbold, "Receptivity to Communist Fomented Agitation in Rural Guatemala," *Economic Development and Cultural Change* 5, no. 4 (1957): 338–61.

10. There is a voluminous literature on the events of 1954. For differing views, see Juan José Arévalo, *The Shark and the Sardines* (New York: Lyle Stuart, 1961); Guillermo Torjello, *La Batalla de Guatemala* (Mexico City: Ediciones Cuadernos Americanos, 1954); Manuel Galich, *Por qué lucha Guatemala: Arévalo y Arbenz: dos hombres contra un imperio* (Buenos Aires: Elmer Editor, 1956); Daniel James, *Red Design for the Americas: Guatemalan Prelude* (New York: John Day, 1954); Norman A. La Charité, *Case Study in Insurgency and Revolutionary Warfare: Guatemala, 1944–1954* (Washington, D.C.: American Univ., 1964); John D. Martz, *Central America: The Crisis and the Challenge* (Chapel Hill: Univ. of North Carolina Press, 1959); Stokes Newbold, "Receptivity"; John Gillin and K. H. Silvert, "Ambiguities in Guatemala," *Foreign Affairs* 34, no. 3 (April 1956): 469–82; Philip B. Taylor, "The Guatemalan Affair: A Critique of United States Foreign Policy," *American Political Science Review* 50, no. 3 (Sept. 1956): 787–806; United States, Department of State, *A Case History of Communist Penetration in Guatemala* (Washington: Inter-American Series 52, 1957); Julio Adolfo Rey, "Revolution and Liberation: A Review of Recent Literature on the Guatemalan Situation," *Hispanic American Historical Review* 38, no. 2 (May 1958): 239–55.

11. Newbold, "Receptivity"; Whetten, *Guatemala,* p. 338; John Gillin, "San Luis Jilotepeque," in *Political Changes in Guatemalan Indian Communities,* ed. Richard N. Adams (New Orleans: Middle America Research Institute, Tulane Univ., 1957), p. 27; Richard N. Adams, "Changing Political Relationships in Guatemala," in Adams, *Political Changes,* pp. 48–52; Richard N. Adams, "Social Change in Guatemala: Its Implications for United States Policy," in *Social Change in Latin America Today: Its Implications for United States Policy,* ed. Richard N. Adams et al. (New York: Vintage Books, 1960).

trial or agricultural profits, and priority for public investments in roads, electrification, and commercial credit. Service bureaucracies were reduced or redirected within the areas of education, agricultural extension to *campesinos*, public health, and other popular-sector programs. Political activity in the popular sector was strictly controlled with both official and vigilante organizations assigned to guard against the reappearance of labor organizers, builders of cooperatives, and representatives of similar "communistic" movements.[12]

Where the pre-1944 elite had been content to rule through a system of delegates who were directly responsible to the *caudillo*, the revolutionary elite attempted to penetrate the society with formal organizational structures, both governmental and unofficial, which they themselves controlled. The inability of the would-be revolutionaries to mobilize supporters in the popular sector is indicative of the failure of their mass-elite relationship. The pattern of expectations and social roles that wove the popular sector together with the *patrones* on the plantations and in the factories, and the *caciques* and *jefes politicos* in the villages and towns was simply too strongly established to be displaced, especially by a regime whose only abundant resource to induce new patterns of behavior and commitments was enthusiasm.

Although a nascent national political elite sought to consolidate channels of mobilization and control in its hands during the 1950's, this process was not completed until the 1960's.[13] During the Military Government (1963–66) and continuing through the Mendez Montenegro (1966–70) and Arana Osorio (1970–74) regimes, Guatemala passed into the hands of a political elite drawn from commercial, manufacturing, and agricultural enterprises, representing diverse regional and business interests and seeking to control the society directly through bureaucratic struc-

12. Kalman H. Silvert, *The Conflict Society: Reaction and Revolution in Latin America* (New York: American Universities Field Staff, 1966), pp. 66–67; Adams, "Social Change"; Rafael Piedra-Santa A., "La mala distribución de la tierra como un obstáculo para la industrialización de Guatemala," *Guatemala Indígena*, 1, nos. 3–4 (July–Dec. 1961): 5–14.

13. For an account of the shifts in power relations, see Richard N. Adams, *Crucifixion by Power: Essays on Guatemalan National Social Structure 1944–1966* (Austin: Univ. of Texas Press, 1970), especially chap. 3, "The Organization of Power, 1944–1966," pp. 174–237.

tures (political parties, police, service bureaucracies, the army, and the church). Thanks to the industrial and commercial policies of the revolution, this new elite and the groups from which it comes and from which it draws support (managerial, professional, and commercial) is far larger than was that of the 1950's. In part because of its size, in part because of its experience in politics during the 1950's and early 1960's, and in part because of the emergence of a professional military officer corps which seems less willing to interfere directly in politics, the civilian elite seem to have grown from a junior partner to coequal or even dominant partnership with the senior officers in running the country. The willingness of the Military Government (which contained a large number of civilians among its elite) to pass authority at this time to a moderately progressive civilian government in 1966 and the unwillingness of the officers to overthrow it in the face of severe provocations from both leftist insurgents and rightist thugs suggest a penchant on the part of some officers for supporting civilian rule as well as the ability of civilian elites to mobilize sufficient power to offset the *golpeistas*.

If there is any notion that the elite which rules Guatemala is an ideological monolith or that it commands a well-oiled, efficient, and effective political machine along the Mexican model, we need only look into the administrative system to see ample evidence to the contrary. Here important programs and agencies duplicate each other's efforts, act toward each other in a manner that stretches the concept of autonomy, and follow contradictory policies and procedures. While this independence and disintegration in part may be put down to the nature of bureaucracy, the strength and ubiquity of these characteristics is indicative of the competition for power and the battle for survival among factions of the elite and their followers. I believe that the lack of effective control and absence of indoctrinated followers of elite ideology reported below continue to characterize the Arana Osorio regime also, even though this government has surpassed its predecessors in its use of public-opinion-building techniques and its employment of official and vigilante terrorists.

While the Military Government was largely a holding operation during which a new generation of civilian and military elites completed their replacement of the pre-1944 elite that had returned to share power in 1954, the Mendez Montenegro and Arana Osorio governments represent the two wings of the national elite. Each has attempted to implement its own vision of Guatemalan development. Both have relied heavily on client-centered and public-service bureaucracies such as agrarian extension, education, and (in the case of the latter), public health. Thus in their own ways, both extended the mobilization process initiated by the revolutionary elite.[14] But as yet no elite has successfully surmounted the barriers to a viable political mobilization of Guatemalan society; no elite has succeeded in promoting ideological indoctrination of the population, perhaps least of all the bureaucracy. Intraelite rivalry and competition are embodied in continuing efforts to implement rival doctrines, to support special interests, and to build personalistic followings through specific action programs.[15]

System of Administration

"System of administration" refers to the way things are done—the practices and procedures, formal and informal, that characterize the day-to-day operation of a bureaucracy. In seeking these characteristics, I have looked to Weber's model of rational administration. The fact that the Guatemalans themselves do not consciously strive to implement this model does not detract from its utility; however, we must be on guard when evaluating our findings that we do not piously cite the variation from the model as proof that what is being done is inefficient or ineffective. But does the employment of Weber's model cause us to overlook prac-

14. This is reflected in the continued expansion of the national bureaucracy. It seems that the increase in permanent positions (salaried rather than hourly) is this: 1944, 8,000; 1950, 15,500; 1954, 22,300; 1957, 27,900; 1963, 37,900; 1966, 40,000; 1970, 43,000—exclusive of military personnel and computed from national salary budgets.

15. This competition is discussed more fully in Jerry L. Weaver, "Political Style of the Guatemalan Military Elite," *Studies in Comparative International Development* 5, no. 4 (1969–70): 63–81.

tices and procedures that have a major bearing on the how and the why of things? With this question in mind I try to report not only what my research frame of reference directed me to but also what it did not. Remaining alert for variables not included in the research hypotheses is, it seems to me, a crucial if little noticed element in the gathering of data and building of middle-range theory.

What are the dominant characteristics that affect the implementation of public policy and the satisfaction of demands? Weber's model of rational administration points to impersonal official obligations, hierarchy of office, clearly defined spheres of competence, recruitment based on technical qualifications, fixed salary based on rank, career service with promotion based on seniority or achievement, and systematic, strict discipline and control in the office. At the center of rational administration is the official who exercises his office on the basis of his expertise and knowledge, an official whose selection is largely based on education. These characteristics provide us the paradigm against which we shall order our observations of the internal operations of the Guatemalan bureaucracy.

Research Procedure

The data reported below were systematically gathered in 1965–66 from an intensively analyzed sample of agencies. The actual selection of agencies studied involved a double-stage, stratified random-sampling, proportional-allocation technique.[16] This formidable terminology masks a simple procedure. Initially we determined that 25 agencies would be an optimum sample, given the resources at our disposal. After determining the total number of operational program agencies (units) within the Guatemalan bureaucracy, the number of units within each ministry was divided by the system total to give us the percent of the total found in each ministry. This percent served as the basis for

16. Frederick F. Stephen and Philip J. McCarthy, *Sampling Opinions: An Analysis of Survey Procedure* (New York: Wiley, 1958), pp. 403–17. For a discussion of variance tests and the utility of "proportional stratified random selection," see Leslie Kish, "Selection of the Sample," in *Research Methods in the Behavioral Sciences*, ed. Leon Festinger and Daniel Katz (New York: Holt, Rinehart and Winston, 1953), pp. 193–213.

allocating units within the total sample. For example, the Ministry of Agriculture's 24 units represented approximately 12 percent of the bureaucracy's total of 230 units. When we apportioned our sample of 25 units among the ministries, Agriculture received 12 percent of the 25, or 3 units in the sample. Three units from among the 24 described by Agriculture's organization chart were selected at random. Each unit on the chart was assigned a sequential number, 1 through 24, so each had an equal probability of selection. Next, three numbers between 00 and 25 were drawn from a book of random numbers. The corresponding agencies were included in the study sample.

The sample agencies were evenly divided between line units and staff units.[17] The size of the units varied considerably ranging from 3 to 433 full-time contract employees.[18] Table 13.1 presents a

Table 13.1. *Size and function of units in office practices survey*

Number of employees	Line	Staff	Total
1–25	2	6	8
26–75	4	3	7
76–150	2	2	4
Over 150	3	1	4

Source: 1965 Program Budget of the Government of Guatemala.

breakdown of the sample by function and size. What these data do not demonstrate is the vast diversity of programs and activities found within the sample. In fact, our sample encompassed nearly all types of occupations and programs found throughout the bureaucracy.

One source of data concerning administrative practices was a

17. The chiefs of the 25 units selected in the sample all agreed to permit interviewing and observation, but when field work began two of them changed their minds. Consequently, we completed the work with a sample of 23 units.
18. These figures refer to salaried employees, those whose positions are covered in the national budget. The term "contract" simply means that the employee's position is a continuing one: no Guatemalan public employee holds anything like a tenure contract. "Contract" is used to distinguish this segment of the work force from those working on an hourly basis. The latter include day laborers on public works and the like who come and go as the work, budget, and mood strike them. In overall size and scope of activity, two of the sample units are among the half-dozen largest employers of hourly-rate laborers.

brief questionnaire administered to the supervisory personnel of each sample unit: unit chiefs and assistant chiefs, administrative assistants, auditors, accountants, and section supervisors. Along with questions concerning office practices, each respondent was asked his length of tenure in public service and in his present position. This tenure item allows us to test the widely reported notion that middle- and upper-level bureaucrats are often fired when there is a change of government.

Supervisory Instability

Table 13.2 reports the startling contrast between average over-all service and average tenure in present position. This datum

Table 13.2. *Tenure of administrative officers*

Position	(N)	Present position (average, years)	With government (average, years)
Unit chief	(23)	1.9	22.0
Assistant chief	(8)	1.5	19.5
Section chief	(7)	2.1	15.0
Auditor	(6)	2.0	16.0
Accountant	(5)	1.7	9.0
Administrative assistant	(17)	5.6	21.8

Source: Office Practices Survey.

suggests that middle-level supervisory personnel bear the brunt of reorganizations and personnel shuffling. Frank Tannenbaum suggests that such instability is directly related to the emphasis given demonstrable personal loyalty: "Each incoming minister brings in his own band of loyal followers, for the minister like the president [of Mexico], has to fall back upon absolute loyalty. And, as I have often seen, when the Minister of Agriculture moves to Foreign Relations, almost everyone—in one case even the door-man—moves with him."[19] We shall explore below the alleged emphasis on personal loyalty as well as the general phenomenon of personnel turnover.

19. "The Influences of Social Conditions," in *Public Administration in Developing Countries*, ed. Martin Kriesberg (Washington: Brookings Institution, 1965), p. 38.

Though middle-level supervisory personnel typically bring many years of experience to their positions, rapid turnover at this level adversely influences administrative performance in several ways. No matter how many years of experience an administrator has had, he requires weeks or even months to adjust to the particular routine, procedures, and clientele of a new agency. The high turnover of supervisory personnel suggests that men unfamiliar with the ways and means of their agencies occupy key decision-making positions. Consequently, rapid turnover may be accompanied by procedural confusion and malintegration because of the idiosyncratic preferences of each new individual. And while directors are adjusting to new offices, subordinates and office routines must adjust to new directors. Necessarily, perhaps, the confusion which surrounds the changing of supervisory personnel comes to affect the bureaucracy's clients. Thus constant change fosters indecision, reduces the possibility of building rapport between demands of clients and requirements of office routine, and encourages clients to "go to the top." In Guatemala, everything seems to rise to the top.

Centralization of Authority

Several writers have suggested that Guatemalan public administration is characterized by a high degree of centralization of authority, or conversely, a low level of effective delegation of decision-making competence.[20] In order to test this hypothesis, an index for measuring centralization was constructed of four questions concerning task planning and office routine decision making. On the basis of interviews with supervisory personnel and extensive observations, a unit coefficient of decisional centralization was determined for each agency within the sample.

QUESTION 1. What person or persons has the duty of determining the long-range goals of this unit?

20. See the International Bank for Reconstruction and Development, *The Economic Development of Guatemala* (Washington: International Bank for Reconstruction and Development, 1951), p. 75; Whetten, *Guatemala*, p. 331; Herrera Ayala, "Recommended Personnel Administration," p. 14; Rafael Armando Tellez Garcia, *La función pública: necesidad de una ley de servicio civil en Guatemala* (Guatemala City: Facultad de Ciencas Jurídicas y Sociales, Universidad de San Carlos de Guatemala, 1965).

Unit chief and/or his superiors   (19)
Unit chief and/or his superiors in consultation
    with section chiefs   (4)

(The number in parentheses is the number of units within the sample.)

Our investigation found that very little control over long-range planning is delegated to agency supervisors. Nearly every decision, even to the hiring and firing of clerks and janitors, requires consultation with and approval from the minister (or in the case of autonomous agencies, the board of directors). When supervisors were asked, What types of decisions require the permission of your supervisors?, eleven replied that they lacked final authority over personnel matters, seven indicated that they did not establish the salaries of their own personnel, and one candid individual stated: "I don't do anything until I check with the minister." If we project from these indications of restricted decision-making competence, it seems reasonable to conclude that determining annual performance targets, establishing operational programs, and other unit-level planning functions are well removed from operational-level control.

We found that unit chiefs worked closely with their superiors but did not include section chiefs and other subordinate supervisory personnel in decision making. Section chiefs reported that they were briefed by the unit director on what was expected of their sections in the coming month or year and that section chiefs were occasionally required to submit cost estimates; but not one of the units reported a planning and review procedure that effectively integrated and coordinated the responsibilities of the entire operation, that maintained adequate reporting and data analysis procedures, or that drew section chiefs into the planning and evaluation routine.

QUESTION 2. Who established the sections' weekly and monthly priorities?

    Unit chief and/or his superiors   (10)
    Unit chief and/or his superiors in consultation

with section chiefs   (10)
Section chiefs (or operational supervisor)   (3)

QUESTION 3. Who determines the sections' daily work sched-
ules?
Unit chief and/or his superior   (7)
Unit chief and/or his superior in consultation
   with section chiefs   (9)
Section chiefs (or operational supervisor)   (7)

QUESTION 4. What type of decisions do section chiefs normally
make without obtaining specific permission from their supervisor?
None   (3)
Those dealing with technical matters or
   involving only the daily routine of the
   section members   (16)
As outlined in the written rules of the unit   (4)

Responses to questions 2, 3, and 4 indicate that little delegation
of effective authority was typically allowed. Several unit chiefs
reported that because of chronic indecision there was such a
logjam of petitions and reports from subordinates that it was impossible to provide rapid decisions on important matters: minutiae made it impossible to set aside sufficient time for dealing with
major policy issues. One minister expressed the fear that the
volume of administrative business would increase with social and
economic development until the bureaucracy would become more
and more ineffective and unable to meet the society's need for
quick and clear-cut decisions.

Legalism

The tendency to centralize control is reinforced by legalism,
the practice of attempting to provide codified responses for every
administrative contigency. Laurin L. Henry suggests that legalism
in Latin American bureaucracy stems from the Roman-law basis
of government. He argues that legalism is stimulated by the practice of recruiting administrative personnel from the graduates of

law faculties. Henry qualifies his criticism of legalism by pointing out that the practice at times protects individuals against arbitrary decisions and that the lack of qualified personnel in most bureaucracies necessitates detailed directives and regulations to control operations.[21]

In Guatemala legalism takes the form of consulting innumerable statutes, executive and legislative decrees, *circulares* (bulletins), and specific ministerial orders. These documents specify administrative purpose, organization, and day-to-day procedures in great detail. Since field administration is held strictly accountable to the letter of the law, bureaucrats seek solutions to their problems in their file boxes.

Guatemala's code fetish is related to the widespread phenomenon of legislated procedural rigidity. For example, the director of one large agency readily admitted that no effective delegation of authority existed and that he personally checked and approved every petition, letter, and memorandum. To explain this situation the director read from the agency's organic law that no document was considered legal unless personally signed by the director. In another case, an agency employing over 250 employees and operating on an annual budget of nearly a million dollars possessed an organic law stipulating that the director must sign every purchase order, even orders involving only a few cents.

Confronted with this emphasis on formal legal procedures, it is not surprising that bureaucrats seem to be endlessly searching code books and seeking legal counsel. Where existing rules and regulations do not apply, long delays are incurred while a new circular or decree is prepared or a written opinion is obtained from the minister's office. Consultants to the government of Guatemala have produced studies demonstrating that thousands of revenue dollars are lost each year because of spoilage, theft,

21. In a sample of 243 randomly selected bureaucrats discussed below, we found that 46 percent of those with university education reported attending the faculty of law. Economics and engineering divided almost all of the remainder. Henry's observation probably is more valid for highest civil servants, most of whom were older and were recruited into service prior to the recent emphasis on technical preparation. See Laurin L. Henry, "Public Administration and Civil Service," in *Government and Politics in Latin America*, ed. Harold E. Davis (New York: Ronald Press, 1958), p. 485.

and destruction of goods held by Customs while awaiting rulings on tariff rates. Similarly, all manner of development programs are delayed, clients angered and rebuffed, and business opportunities lost while bureaucrats search the code books or await rulings from their superiors.

Inadequate Communication

Given the vast amount of paperwork moving through the administrative system, it is paradoxical that little meaningful information is received by decisionmakers, especially on a regular basis. Yet this is certainly the case. The explanation lies in the fact that form, not substance, characterizes much of the paperwork.

In the Guatemalan administrative system there exists no uniform procedure for collecting, integrating, and reporting management information. Examination of reports shows that they reach executive personnel with little or no accompanying analysis and often without reference to major obstacles or program shortcomings. Subordinates seem loath to point out their own difficulties or to mention mistakes committed by superiors. Consequently, reports are often either misleading or outright fabrications. On other occasions, errors in computation grossly distort reports: pounds reported as tons, columns of figures incorrectly totaled, charts and graphs inaccurately reproduced.[22]

QUESTION 5. How often is written information and data concerning unit operations distributed?

Daily	(1)
Weekly	(4)
Biweekly	(0)
Monthly	(17)
Irregularly	(4)
Never	(1)

22. The writer discovered computation inaccuracies in many official documents, including the national budget. These spurious statistics found their way into subsequent reports and served to further detach decisionmakers from reality. For example, a report by the National Institute of Agrarian Transformation, which is widely used as a standard reference for data concerning acreage and numbers of plots distributed to landless peasants since 1954, was found to contain major errors in computation: columns incorrectly summed, graphs distorted, numbers transposed. See Rony S. Alvarado Pinetta, *La transformación agraria en Guatemala* (Guatemala City: n.p., n.d.).

(Several units are listed in two or more categories because financial, operational or statistical reports are presented separately.)

QUESTION 6. At what intervals are reports submitted by subordinates on the activities of their sections?

Daily	(2)
Weekly	(3)
Biweekly	(1)
Monthly	(12)
Irregularly	(1)
Never	(5)

While frequency of reporting is no measure of quality, it is worth noting that even the most comprehensive and sophisticated reports delivered on a monthly basis remain insensitive to the dynamic nature of development administration. Such an extensive delay between reports drastically curtails the ability of decision-makers to detect problems and revise programs accordingly. Witness that when a wave of kidnaping and extortion struck Guatemala City in November and December 1965 and brought with it an unusual decline in retail sales and a run on foreign reserves as fearful citizens sent money abroad, government officials remained unaware of the extent of the business slump and dollar drain and were therefore kept from taking corrective action until a serious financial crisis had developed.

QUESTION 7. At what intervals are meetings of administrative officers held to discuss the operations and problems of the unit?

Daily	(0)
Weekly	(5)
Biweekly	(0)
Monthly	(3)
Irregularly	(7)
Never	(8)

Aside from written reports, conferences of supervisory personnel allow the exchange of information, as well as the exploration of individual problems. Responses to question 7 indicate that regular administrative conferences are rarely held. Not only are conferences infrequently held at the unit level, they are seldom convened by ministers and other higher executives. One unit director remarked that while he and three other directors were responsible for mutually interdependent programs, the four colleagues had met only once with their minister. The informant said that each director attempted to maintain private contact with the minister in order to assert his own importance. It was considered a measure of status, according to the informant, to be able to see the minister privately. The directors seemed to feel that group conference would be interpreted by their subordinates and peers in other ministries as a reduction of their status.

Incomplete Staff Management

QUESTION 8. Is there a person or persons in this unit who is assigned the duty of supervising organization and work methods?

Yes	(4)
No	(19)

QUESTION 9. Are there written descriptions and qualifications for all positions within this unit?

Yes	(10)
No	(13)

(Of the ten units with some type of written job description, no more than four presented comprehensive documents, and it is doubtful if even in these cases standards were rigorously enforced.)

QUESTION 10. Does the unit have an internal auditor?

Yes	(9)
No	(14)

QUESTION 11. Are there orientation programs for new employees?

Yes	(3)
No	(20)

QUESTION 12. Does the unit offer or sponsor in-service training for its employees?

Yes (7)

No (16)

QUESTION 13. Does the unit draw its supplies from a central supply service?

Yes (4)

No (19)

Responses to questions 8 through 13 point up the absence of effective staff-management procedures. Little if any provision is made for introducing new employees to existing routines or for upgrading the skills of veterans; yet complex new equipment and procedures were widely introduced in the Guatemalan administrative system during the 1960's. Because of the lack of a uniform job-classification system, employees received unequal pay for equivalent work, a situation drawing much unfavorable comment from bureaucrats and one which was cited as a major reason for a civil service law—a law not enacted, however. In another sphere the absence of internal auditors places strain on the understaffed Comptroller General's Office and nullifies effective financial control at the operational level. Consequently, tedious hours are spent on special audits called to unravel the status of accounts and to determine budgetary reserves.

Perhaps no administrative deficiency weighs more heavily on the performance of the bureaucracy than the prevailing system of property control. According to an ancient Guatemalan law, each public employee is personally liable for all office equipment and supplies assigned him—desk, chair, paper, pencils, and the like. But the cards on which accounts are maintained are often incomplete and rarely current. In no way does this system effectively check pilferage. It does cause great confusion, however, when the annual inventory is conducted.

But the disruption of the inventory is overshadowed by the impact of the property-control system on public equipment. Since the physical presence of an item satisfies the letter of the law, there seems to be little concern about preventive maintenance or stockpiling spare parts; countless pieces of equipment sit idle for lack of minor repairs or insignificant replacement parts. One of the complaints most commonly heard from engineers and supervisors of construction projects was that subordinates, and particularly property clerks, seemed unable to grasp the importance of preventive maintenance and adequate stores of spare parts.

From the preceding account of typical office routine, we draw a picture of an iceberg-like authority structure: only a tiny fraction of the total bureaucracy above the decision-making water level. Comments by middle-level supervisory personnel indicate that consultation with top officials takes place on nearly every matter. Delegation of authority in the form of Weber's hierarchical functioning pyramid seems practically nonexistent.

Presumably the statutory attribution of responsibility for all acts of subordinates, coupled with severe financial-liability laws making each level of supervisors responsible for losses or mismanagement by subordinates, militates against delegation. So, too, does the absence of formal career protections: a mistake by a subordinate, an incautious action that offends an important personage, may result in instant dismissal or transfer. And undoubtedly tradition plays a major part in office routine. In a small bureaucracy located almost exclusively in the national capital, until two decades ago, there was little pressure to decentralize, since top officials were physically close at hand. Going to the top, especially when the top wished to remain in charge of daily activities, became the routine.

The data point to a pattern of deferring decisions to the highest executive (cabinet or ministry) level, and this pattern supports the conventional view that there is an extreme centralization grinding away the efficiency and effectiveness of Latin bureaucracies. It is paradoxical, therefore, that an official government of Guatemala review of obstacles to national development should cite administrative decentralization as both a prevailing condition and a major liability to the effective deployment of the bureaucracy as an instrument of action.[23] Yet, there are substantial grounds for the plausibility of this hypothesis.

What we have seen in our study of decision making is a process

23. Government of Guatemala, Secretaria General del Consejo Nacional de Planificación Económica, *Situación del desarrollo económico y social de Guatemala* (Guatemala City: n.p., 1965), p. 232.

of constant referral to higher authority; we have not yet examined the consequences for field administrators of the phenomenon of going to the top. We noted that top executives complain of being overcome by minutiae, of being unable to devote time to major policy questions. We found that intraministry communications are infrequent and often misleading, erroneous, and without analytical commentary. We discovered that the average tenure for middle-level supervisors is two years—a condition, we surmised, likely to be detrimental to effective middle-level control and management. We have a picture of top executives seated behind mounds of petitions, memos, and requests for rulings; besieged by clients, friends, and subordinates begging assistance or opinions; and occasionally and hastily scanning a report which is probably largely fictitious and almost inevitably devoid of critical analysis. But a basic condition of centralization—control—seems to be absent from this picture. How does the minister or director general insure compliance with his orders? In fact, there is no means available to the Guatemalan executive to insure compliance, to actually achieve direct control over day-to-day operations. The all-important middle level of the bureaucracy, the unit supervisors, are not effective managers, in part because of personnel turnover in this rank, in part because they constantly seek higher approval for each case with which they are confronted.

Through the habit of deferring decisions (or as a result of the inability of executives to delegate decisional competence), middle levels of the bureaucracy are stripped of responsibility for their actions. Knowing that their superiors have little information about actual operating practices other than that which they themselves provide and recognizing that there are no staff management procedures to integrate effectively operational units through span-of-control techniques, the office, agency, section, or bureau is able to behave as if it were autonomous. In colonial Latin America the bureaucracy devised a formula for dealing with royal orders which conflicted with local interests: the contemporary condition might fairly be described by this ancient formula—"We obey but do not execute."

We found a suggestion of this axiom in the structural reforms imposed on several ministries. In the Budget Office a reorganization was undertaken to make accounting of public funds more efficient and effective: a program budget structure was designed in order, among other things, to facilitate control over administrative operations through the designation of specific programmatic goals. To this end the minister of public finance decreed the reorganization of the Budget Office. The order was obeyed: a new section was created; but in reality the spirit of the order was ignored, since the new section was merely added to the existing structure of the office, thus vitiating the desired procedural reform.

I am not arguing that in this particular case, or as a general rule, the power of the bureaucracy to insulate itself from its masters is solely responsible for the failure of the government to manage effectively the administrative system. Factionalism within the elite, the salience of traditional organizational patterns, and the desire to maintain and expand personal empires all support the operational autonomy of the bureaucracy. One factor which strengthens the freedom of the bureaucracy is its habit of displaying deference to its executives through a conscious display of rectitude, humility, loyalty, and respect. With cabinet changes or new governments, the new executives are met with what seem submissive and compliant subordinates—the idealized attributes of the bureaucracy. The fact is, however, that the Guatemalan bureaucracy is centralized only from the point of view of a client who presents a request for a particular service and finds that a month or six weeks is consumed while the paperwork receives the necessary approval. This client-eye view, perhaps, has given rise to the characterization of centralism. But viewed as a dynamic system, seeing the ability *not* to make a decision as a significant index of power, the absence of interagency and interministry planning and review boards, the absence of effective personnel control, and the absence of indices of performance at the operational level—these factors bespeak the absence of effective executive control and direction. Seen in the perspective of the actual deployment of the bureaucracy as a vehicle responsive to both elite and client, operational autonomy, not centralization, is the *bête noire.*

Composition of the Bureaucracy

A major consequence of the revolution of 1944 was the recruitment into the bureaucracy of a number of individuals who were committed to social, economic, and political change. These individuals, we thought, because many were university-trained and some had lived or studied abroad, also differed in their definition of proper bureaucratic practices. Moreover, the post-1954 recruits, many of whom were recruited to staff new technical services and programs begun by Castillo Armas, while not subscribing to a revolutionary doctrine, nevertheless were different by education, experience, and outlook from their pre-1944 colleagues. These speculations suggest that the Guatemalan bureaucracy of the 1960's contained a combination of values—modern and traditional—stemming from the differing social, educational, and political milieu from which its membership was drawn. In this section we shall examine the attitudes of bureaucrats towards their jobs, their superiors, and their profession. In particular we shall examine the extent of Weber's professional norms throughout the bureaucracy and treat these data as an index of the rational model. Our data are drawn from interviews with randomly selected middle- and lower-range bureaucrats drawn proportionately from the office practices units. (See Table 13.3 for a breakdown of the sample by occupational category.)

We have already noted that supervisory personnel tend to be men of long service but fairly new to their current posts. More than half of the supervisory-level respondents reported having entered the bureaucracy before the revolution. Most of these individuals had grown up in Guatemala City; they are sons of laborers or marginal business and commercial families; and they have received limited education and in-service training (see Tables 13.4, 13.5, 13.6, and 13.7). These men have survived and prospered: they represent the traditional middle class of Guatemala—families that have used the bureaucracy as a means of social mobility. There is a suggestion that these men have been faithful to their families: in a society in which middle-class status and considerable economic reward may be derived from govern-

Table 13.3. *Composition of the public employees sample by occupational category*

Occupational category	Guatemalan bureaucracy	Sample
Supervisor (unit and section chiefs, foremen, directors of agencies, bureaus, etc.)	6.1	7.5 (18)
Professional (lawyers, engineers, doctors, economists, etc.)	5.3	5.4 (13)
Technician (agronomists, laboratory analysts, medical assistants, etc.)	30.0	35.4 (88)
Office worker (clerks, bookkeepers, secretaries, etc.)	26.4	26.6 (64)
Service and security (messengers, janitors, drivers, prison guards, etc.)	29.8	23.9 (57)
Artisan	2.4	1.2 (3)
Total	100.0 (N = 20,677)	100.0 (N = 243)

Source: Figures on overall work force were computed from Government of Guatemala, *Numero de puestos permanentes por categoría ejercicio fiscal 1965*, Table 5.

Table 13.4. *"Where have you lived the majority of your life?"*

Locale	Supervisor	Professional	Technician	Office worker	Service and security
Guatemala City	83.3	76.9	62.1	64.1	35.1
Secondary city	5.6	15.4	11.5	14.1	7.0
Village	11.1	0	23.0	18.8	31.6
Countryside	0	0	1.1	1.6	22.8
Other	0	7.7	2.3	1.4	3.5
(N)	(18)	(13)	(88)	(64)	(57)

Source: Employees Survey. Goodman-Kruskal Gamma, .316. The artisan category (N = 3) has been eliminated from this and subsequent tables.

ment service, but where there is great competition for government jobs, 72 percent of the supervisors report one or more members of their family working for the government—and no fewer than 50 percent report two or more kinfolk in government service (Table 13.8).

The professionals and technicians in our sample diverge significantly in social and economic status patterns from supervisory personnel. A quarter of the *técnicos* come from rural Guatemala;

Table 13.5. *Percent of occupational category by occupation of parent or head of household*

Occupation of parent	Supervisor	Professional	Technician	Office worker	Service and security
Professional	23.5	41.7	12.8	14.1	3.7
Managerial, technical	11.8	0	5.8	17.2	3.7
Skilled worker	11.8	8.3	9.3	6.3	7.4
Semiskilled worker	17.6	0	22.1	26.6	5.5
Unskilled worker	35.3	50.0	50.0	35.9	79.7
(N)	(18)	(13)	(88)	(64)	(57)

Source: Employees Survey. Goodman-Kruskal Gamma, .177.

Table 13.6. *Percent of occupational category by principal employer of parent or head of household*

Employer of parent	Supervisor	Professional	Technician	Office worker	Service and security
Government	11.1	38.5	27.4	32.8	12.7
Private firm or plantation	16.7	23.1	16.7	25.0	7.3
Sole proprietor or farmer	72.2	38.5	55.9	42.2	80.0
(N)	(18)	(13)	(88)	(64)	(57)

Source: Employees Survey.

half are sons of *campesinos* or small shopkeepers; a quarter come from families whose head worked for the government, usually in service or clerical capacity; they tend to have completed secondary school and at least one in-service training course. Technicians and professionals also are members of bureaucratic families, although not as often as supervisors.

The *técnicos* represent a new stratum of the middle class. They are younger as a group than supervisors and have arisen from lower-class families, ostensibly through obtaining specialized education or training. Since most either entered the bureaucracy or matured during the revolution (Tables 13.9 and 13.10), we can speculate that their adult values and political culture reflect the more complex ideologies of the post-1944 period. At the same time *técnicos* manifest a higher commitment to public service as a career than do supervisors. Sixty-nine percent of the former as

Table 13.7. *Percent of occupational category by educational attainment*

Educational attainment	Supervisor	Professional	Technician	Office worker	Service and security
Secondary					
None	17.7	0	23.0	22.3	87.5
Technical vocational	47.0	20.0	35.6	33.3	3.6
Liberal arts	35.3	80.0	41.4	44.4	8.9
University					
None	61.2	0	76.8	81.3	100.0
Law	27.8	30.8	7.0	14.0	0
Economics	5.5	7.6	9.3	1.6	0
Engineering	5.5	30.8	4.6	0	0
Other	0	30.8	2.3	3.1	0
In-Service					
None	66.7	76.9	40.7	68.8	89.1
One course	11.1	15.4	25.6	14.0	9.1
Two or more courses	22.2	7.7	33.7	17.2	1.8

Goodman-Kruskal Gamma, −.449

Source: Employee Survey.

Table 13.8. *Percent of occupational category reporting other members of family employed by the government*

Number of other members	Supervisor	Professional	Technician	Office worker	Service and security
None	27.8	53.8	37.9	40.6	61.4
One	22.2	38.5	29.9	29.7	19.3
Two, three, or four	38.9	7.7	26.4	26.6	14.0
Five or more	11.1	0	5.8	3.1	5.3
(N)	(18)	(13)	(88)	(64)	(54)

Source: Employees Survey. Goodman-Kruskal Gamma, −.096.

compared with 50 percent of the latter indicated that they plan to make government work their career.

Lower levels of the bureaucracy, especially service and security personnel, represent Guatemala's marginal middle class. They are drawn from rural laboring and *campesino* (often Indian) families, have little education, and are young. Table 13.10 shows that 49 percent of the service and security workers were thirty

Table 13.9. *Seniority of respondents by regime at date of entry into the bureaucracy: percent by occupational category*

Regime	Supervisor	Professional	Technician	Office worker	Service and security
Military Government (1963–66)	5.6	23.1	11.5	25.1	36.8
Ydígoras (1957–63)[a]	5.6	30.7	14.9	15.6	15.8
Castillo Armas (1954–57)[a]	11.1	15.4	16.1	20.3	24.6
Arbenz (1951–54)	22.2	23.1	17.2	15.6	7.0
Arevalo (1944–51)[a]	0	0	14.9	12.5	7.0
Ubico (1930–44)[a]	55.5	7.7	25.4	10.9	8.8
(N)	(18)	(13)	(88)	(64)	(57)

Source: Employees Survey. Goodman-Kruskal Gamma, −.287.
  a. Includes interim governments.

Table 13.10. *Percent of occupational group by age level*

Age level	Supervisor	Professional	Technician	Office worker	Service and security
25 years or less	0	0	12.6	17.2	24.6
26 to 30	11.1	23.1	18.4	21.9	24.6
31 to 35	11.1	23.1	21.8	25	7.0
36 to 40	11.1	30.8	16.1	15.6	10.5
41 to 50	27.8	7.7	17.2	6.3	19.3
51 and older	38.9	15.4	13.8	12.7	14.0
(N)	(18)	(13)	(88)	(64)	(57)

Source: Employees Survey. Goodman-Kruskal Gamma, −.180.

years of age or younger. Although clerical and service and security positions constitute a large and long-established segment of the bureaucracy, incumbents in these posts report short tenure. Twenty percent of the office workers and 32 percent of the service and security employees interviewed report less than one year in their present positions. Twenty-five percent and 37 percent, respectively, had entered the bureaucracy since the 1963 overthrow of Ydígoras. This phenomenon of short tenure may be related to a number of factors, including youthful job dissatisfaction and experimentation, high turnover due to women getting married or pregnant, personnel leaving government to enter Guatemala's expanding industrial and commercial private bureaucracy. High turnover in lower-level positions may also be related to specific recruitment and promotion policies.

Since 1944 the growth pattern of the Guatemalan bureaucracy reflects a pattern of creating new bureaus and autonomous agencies rather than adding functions to existing organizations. This practice was introduced by Arévalo to keep his new programs out of the hands of prerevolutionary officials and to find high-level employment for friends and supporters. The practice, followed by succeeding governments, places a premium on finding established middle- and upper-level supervisory personnel to assist the politician or spoilsman put in charge of a newly formed agency. A look at the service records of supervisory and professional personnel supports the notion that established employees are transferred in order to form a managerial cadre for new agencies: over half the supervisors interviewed reported having worked in three or more ministries or autonomous agencies before their present assignment.

The tradition of creating new agencies and promoting established employees allows a new government to build important political support. Friends and supporters are brought into newly created positions of prestige and power. Surely the newly promoted bureaucrats are aware of their benefactors and recognize the necessity for (and the proper forms of) reciprocation. At the same time students and other younger middle-class individuals are recruited to fill the slots left open by promotions and transfers. Consequently, while some waste is involved, new agencies certainly pay handsome short-term political dividends.

The notion that occupational mobility in Guatemalan public service is tied to political considerations is reinforced by data concerning the career patterns of lower bureaucrats: clerks, typists, service personnel, and the like. Among these respondents little horizontal (interagency) mobility is noted. Rather, individuals tend to move vertically (if at all) within the organization into which they are first hired. This pattern seems to involve an admixture of administrative and political considerations.

Since Guatemalan schools produce an oversupply of office

workers, there is no demand to transfer semiskilled and unskilled personnel to new agencies. Nor would marked political advantage accrue from such transfers. At these lower levels leverage is almost totally with the political elite. For every typist or clerk there are dozens of potential replacements. Consequently, withdrawal of support by clerical or service personnel has only slight effect on the government: low-level employees are easily replaced. This is not the case with professionals and technicians: here there is a shortage. During the 1950's and 1960's the commercial and manufacturing sector of the local economy grew to provide seasoned, high-quality technocrats and professionals with acceptable alternatives to public employment. Clerical and service personnel, on the other hand, find themselves in a buyer's market, a situation that places their superiors in a decidedly advantageous position.

No attempt was made in the public employees survey to ascertain the ethnic composition of the Guatemalan bureaucracy. While Guatemala is considered to be approximately 50 percent Indian, operationally this term defies measurement. The generally accepted local definition of an Indian is any person who speaks an Indian language, dresses in Indian costume, and is considered by himself and his neighbors to be an Indian. The designation of Indian or Ladino, therefore, refers far more to conditions of mind or culture than to biological criteria. This situation facilitates social integration because a change of clothes and language is sufficient for passing into Ladino society. By the same token it becomes impossible to determine—if it is not volunteered—whether or not a respondent is (or was) an Indian.

Suffice it to say that no Indians were identified within the sample. This is not to say that no former Indians were interviewed; indeed, the educated guess of the interviewers put the number of former Indians at about 15 percent. Typically these respondents were found in service and security positions. It would seem, then, that the Guatemalan administrative system begets a high level of ladinoization, acceptance of European culture, with renunciation of traditional Indian culture, as a concomitant of recruitment. Here the bureaucracy reflects the widespread Ladino belief that to be an Indian is to be inferior, that

Indian culture contains nothing worthy of respect. Indians may enter "proper society" if they are willing to accept the standards of society, which means giving up everything that makes an individual an Indian.

During 1965 and 1966 a lively public debate transpired in the mass media of Guatemala City concerning the equality of the sexes. Polls were conducted on such questions as: "Should women participate in politics?" "Should women follow a profession or occupation?" "Should women attend school?" The collective answer was a firm no. In the same vein, the enlightened architects of the Constitution of 1966 prescribed separate (delimiting) voting conditions for women.

It is not surprising, therefore, to discover a disproportionate underrepresentation of females in the public employees sample—only 11 percent—and these were found exclusively in the office worker and technician strata. While the head of the Military Government made a chivalrous gesture towards the fair sex by appointing one of their number to the directorship of Bienestar Social, it is doubtful whether this was anything more than recognition of the lady's personal prestige and political support within the government.

From the standpoint of regional integration the Guatemalan administrative system is surprisingly effective. While 59 percent of the sample reported having lived the major part of their lives in Guatemala City, 10 percent had lived in one of the secondary cities: Quezaltenango, Puerto Barrios, Escuintla, Cobán, Jutiapa, Retalhuleu, and Antigua. But more noteworthy is the datum that 29 percent of the respondents represent small towns (less than 2,500 inhabitants) and farmdwellers. Members of this group come from all regions of the republic. Since Guatemala's Indian communities are scattered about the country, diverse regional recruitment also suggests ethnic integration.[24]

This breadth of recruitment brings about a problematic situation in the bureaucracy. Guatemala's urban-dominated social

24. Nevertheless the Guatemalan bureaucracy is disproportionately urban in origin. The national census of 1964 indicates that 66 percent of the population live in rural areas, principally in the country's approximately 7,000 *aldeas* (hamlets) of less than 1,000 inhabitants. Government of Guatemala, *La situación,* pp. 93–95.

pecking order considers rural people inferior and treats them with disdain. Those on the receiving end of this cultural discrimination may well attempt to protect their sense of self-worth and dignity by retreating behind such defenses as formality, legalism, and, where pressure is severe and the apparent threat grave, indecision. Thus the bureaucrat from the rural region, with his basic unfamiliarity with technology and poor scholastic preparation compounded by social and psychological problems, is handicapped in the fulfillment of administrative expertise in a way his urban cousin is not.

This hypothesis points to a basic contradiction in development theory. On the one hand the theory recognizes the necessity of integrating diverse social, regional, and cultural segments of the population in order to create a stable society and growing economy. National bureaucracy is cited as one of the most accessible vehicles for this task. On the other hand, development theory emphasizes the importance of effective and efficient performance of administrative programs. Such performance is directly related to administrative expertise. In a country such as Guatemala where rural and urban people are divided by a cultural barrier as profound as the differences between the sixteenth and twentieth centuries, how can the demands of integration and expertise be reconciled? During the 1960's there was little pressure by the nascent rural *campesino* organizations or existing political parties to staff rural service agencies with local people. But given a more mass-based regime, rural and other lower-class interests will become more effective in advancing their claims to the loaves and fishes of political patronage. By what formula should administrative expertise be sacrificed for national integration?

The middle level of the Guatemalan bureaucracy is stable, seasoned, formally (if not effectively) subordinated to the political elite. Supervisors are men of long and varied experience. Presumably they are placed in positions of responsibility because they have demonstrated their reliability—personal and political if not necessarily administrative. Most of them are not highly educated nor are they familiar with modern technical and administrative procedures. The supervisory stratum contrasts sharply with the professional and technician strata which represent a new element in the bureaucracy. The latter are more highly educated and trained and younger and, we have speculated, are generally of a more progressive bent—and probably restless at being supervised by older, premodern types.

While we see the bureaucracy as composed of three distinct subsystems (supervisors; *técnicos* and professionals; clerical, service, and security personnel), we suspect that the three share a commitment to the existing social order. The bureaucracy has been a vehicle for upward mobility for nearly every respondent in the survey. Through education, family or political connection, or through dogged perseverance, many bureaucrats have risen from the marginal middle or lower classes. They have prestige, wealth, and life style far above their parents. It is the existing system that brought them this success and it is in the existing system that they are able to enjoy power and privilege.[25]

Bureaucratic Values

Aside from gathering biographic data, our survey sought to examine the attitude patterns of Guatemalan bureaucrats regarding social, economic, and political change as well as their attitudes toward and relative priorities attached to public service as a career. We planned to determine the extent to which bureaucrats used family, political, or professional connections to gain employment and to win promotions. And we wanted to ask our respondents to identify shortcomings and problems in their offices and agencies.

Unfortunately, little of this work was possible. In 1965–66 Guatemala was suffering terrorist attacks, counterinsurgency, a presidential campaign, and the aftermath of the disclosure of Project Camelot. Pretesting of the instruments was just begun when the research became the subject of widespread public comment: *"Cuestionario Inquieta a los Burócratas"* proclaimed one headline.[26] Consequently, questions which appeared par-

25. Cf. Robert E. Scott, "The Government Bureaucrats and Political Change in Latin America," *Journal of International Affairs* 20, no. 2 (1966): 297.
26. *Prensa Libre,* 9 Nov. 1965.

ticularly controversial were eliminated from the final survey instruments.

Careerism

When asked if they planned to make government service a career, 67 percent of the respondents replied affirmatively. Surprisingly, however, careerism varied inversely with occupational status: professionals and supervisors reported a lower percent of affirmative replies than clerical and service personnel. This may reflect the advanced age of many supervisors: many had already completed twenty or more years of service and were contemplating retirement, not a career. But the lower rate among supervisors may also indicate a feeling that since individuals at their level are often moved around or demoted, the question of a career, at least one acceptable to them, is beyond their control. An additional factor related to lower career orientation may be inferred from the findings that 46 percent of the professionals and 33 percent of the supervisors report other sources of income such as private practices, offices, business ventures, and farms. Thus upper-level bureaucrats have other activities which may lead them to be less dependent on public employment and less committed to it.

The desire of two out of three respondents to remain in public service is certainly understandable given the paucity of alternative employers of clerical, service, and liberal arts/law-trained personnel. But careerism in no way implies a rational, professional behavior. Careerism in the Guatemalan context suggests a dependence on those who direct the bureaucracy as well as an openness to manipulation by superiors, because of an absence of commitment to ethical norms and performance standards. In assessing the implications of careerism it becomes crucial to determine the controlling operational values of the bureaucracy.

"How Does One Get Ahead in This Office?"

In order to analyze the system of values of which careerism is part, a number of questions, both directed and open-ended, were planned. When this part of the study was aborted, rather than forgo completely the exploration of bureaucratic values, several questions were used which were designed to probe respondents' perception of recruitment and promotion criteria. While the data generated by these questions in no way define the actual procedures involved in recruiting and promoting bureaucrats, they are presented here as suggestive of what in fact happens. At the same time the very fact that the findings support the commonly advanced claim that favoritism and personal nonachievement criteria are controlling should alert us to the need for further study.[27]

When asked "What are the most important qualities an employee must possess in order to get ahead in this office?" only 19 percent of all respondents mention specific skills, technical or occupational education and training, or specific on-the-job experience. Another 21 percent suggest that seniority or some general (unspecified) skill or education is important. Honesty, respect, and integrity, often mentioned in combination with *capaz* (competence—knowing one's way around), were the most commonly cited criteria for advancement (Table 13.11).

Table 13.11. *"How does one get ahead in this office?"*

Means of advancement	Supervisor	Pro-fessional	Technician	Office worker	Service and security
Specific skill, experience, or training	11.1	30.8	31.8	15.6	3.5
General skill, basic education, seniority	11.1	15.4	22.7	17.2	28.1
"Capaz," competence	33.3	15.4	14.8	17.2	21.1
Honesty, respect, loyalty	33.3	30.8	23.9	45.2	45.5
Influential friends	0	0	3.4	1.6	1.8
No response	11.1	7.6	3.4	3.2	0
(N)	(18)	(13)	(88)	(64)	(57)

Source: Employees Survey.

27. Cf. the study of the Chilean bureaucracy by Bertilio J. Nery Rios, "Estudio de un instituto burocrático en Chile," *Ciencias Sociales* (Venezuela) 1, no. 2 (June 1964): 183–224. Nery Rios employs formal hypotheses and data to analyze the operational values of supervisors and subordinates. A nonquantitative study of Guyana bureaucrats is found in M. Kazin Bacchus, "Relationship Between Professional and Administrative Officers in a Government Department During a Period of Administrative Change," *Sociological Review* 15, no. 2 (July 1967): 155–78.

Recruitment Criteria

The emphasis on attributes of character or personality is repeated in responses to another question: "What are the most important qualities that a good public employee ought to possess?" Nearly half of the respondents stressed loyalty, respect, and honesty. A quarter of the sample mentioned *capaz*. Only 25 percent referred to a high school diploma, some sort of training, or a desire to serve the public.

Nearly nine in ten of the supervisors and professionals agreed with the majority emphasis on strong character. Technicians, however, again demonstrated a basic difference of priority. Twenty-six percent (as opposed to 6 and 7 percent of supervisors and professionals) replied that general education or familiarity with administrative procedures is important. In this judgment technicians are joined by a nearly identical percent of office workers. Service and security personnel, however, are even more concerned with rectitude than their supervisors. Seventy-three percent of the lowest-level personnel picked honesty, loyalty, and respect as the most important characteristics (Table 13.12).

Table 13.12. *"Most important quality of a good public employee"*

Quality	Supervisor	Pro-fessional	Technician	Office worker	Service and security
Specific skill, education	5.6	0	7.0	6.3	3.9
General education, familiarity with office routine	5.6	7.7	26.4	23.4	11.5
"Capaz," competence	61.0	30.8	24.1	28.1	11.5
Honesty, loyalty, respect	27.8	61.5	41.5	42.2	73.1
(N)	(18)	(13)	(88)	(64)	(57)

Source: Employees Survey.

Tannenbaum calls our attention to the heavy emphasis on demonstrable personal loyalty in the Mexican bureaucracy. According to him, when a minister moves to another post, almost everyone moves with him. Tannenbaum's observation apparently is just that—an observation unsupported by survey data. Perhaps many Mexican bureaucrats do migrate with their *patrón*—

tribal fashion—from location to location. There is evidence that this is not the case in the Guatemalan bureaucracy. Technicians, office workers, and service personnel tend to remain in the agency of initial recruitment. Middle-level supervisors, on the other hand, do move from agency to agency, ministry to ministry; but whether this is largely tribalism or a product of prevailing organization-building practices has not been determined. Since, in contrast to Mexico, the past three decades have been marked by at least three major upheavals and replacements of Guatemalan governments, there is cause to discount the effect of tribalism on personnel mobility.

Why, then, the emphasis on loyalty, honesty, and respect? Certainly Hispanic tradition is not unimportant. From the colonial era through the twentieth century, appointments at all levels of administration have been based on patronage, with office seen as a temporary means of self-enrichment.[28] But unlike Great Britain or the United States, in Guatemala administrative patronage stems less from purely partisan or political considerations than from a general cultural phenomenon: *patronismo*. The *patrón* relationship is essentially a reciprocal arrangement tying members of various social (and in the present case, administrative) strata together—not merely for momentary political or economic advantage, but rather in a web of social, political, economic, and even familial obligations. Gillin sees the *patrón* as taking a personal interest in the welfare of his subordinates and their families. This system of obligation, according to Gillin, permeates most of the middle class from which the bureaucracy is drawn. Small *patrones* usually have *patrones* of their own—bigger and more powerful men upon whom the lesser *patrones* rely for protection; individuals to whom the lesser men provide support, information, and the other obligations of followership.[29]

While we have reservations about the extent and viability of

28. Stanley J. Stein and Barbara H. Stein, *The Colonial Heritage of Latin America* (New York: Oxford Univ. Press, 1970), p. 70; John Leddy Phelan, *The Kingdom of Quito in the Seventeenth Century* (Madison: Univ. of Wisconsin Press, 1967); José María Ots Capdequí, *El estado español en las Indias* (Mexico City: Fondo de Cultura Económica, 1957).
29. John P. Gillin, "Some Signposts for Policy," in Adams, *Social Change*, pp. 36–37.

patronismo in the Guatemalan bureaucracy, we cannot overlook this cultural norm as an important dimension of the emphasis on loyalty, respect, and rectitude. However, at least two other factors besides *patronismo* seem likely to contribute to the extreme caution of many respondents. We have already alluded to one factor—the absence of institutional safeguards against capricious treatment by superiors. In Guatemala the public servant has no tenure or merit protection, no uniform wage scale, no public employees' union or interest group to protect him. While the bureaucracy in general is well insulated and protected from molestation from above, individuals who perchance come under attack are essentially defenseless. Consequently, manifesting loyalty and respect to superiors seems obligatory if one wishes to have a friend at court.

Finally, deference and demonstrating rectitude is reinforced by a society-wide norm of being respectful and respectworthy. For the subordinate this emphasis on giving and winning recognition is played out by referring to one's superiors in the *usted* form of address (formal—"you, sir"), speaking with peers in the *tu* form (familiar—"you"), and addressing social inferiors as *vos* (demeaning—"hey you"). Thus language patterns hint of the broader social norms of formally respectful deportment that is obligatory in Guatemala and impinges on interactions of members of the administrative hierarchy.

If we accept the operation of *patronismo*, social formality, and the absence of institutional protections as largely responsible for the heavy emphasis on loyalty, honesty, and respect, to what should we attribute the deviation from this norm among professionals, technicians, and office workers reported in Tables 13.11 and 13.12? In part their greater emphasis on achievement criteria may stem from the demands of their work routines. In typing letters, completing blueprints, recording experimental results, and similar work there is a concrete index of performance—a finished piece of work that can be examined. A good man may not be a good employee. Perhaps this is more readily apparent to individuals who themselves operate against tangible performance standards.

At the same time it is likely that Tables 13.11 and 13.12 reflect the interaction of two conflicting roles: that of member of a particular sociocultural milieu and that of member of a particular occupation or profession. The former role demands deference, loyalty, and rectitude and is firmly reinforced throughout Guatemalan society. Individuals from occupational categories with diffuse or nonexistent professional reference groups are most likely to reflect general social norms of evaluation: supervisors, office workers, and service and security personnel. For professionals and technicians, however, the existence of reference groups below the most general (i.e., society) level may well exert pressure to conform to other expectations. The faculties of law, economics, and medicine and the professional associations affiliated with these occupations provide and enforce specific norms and sanctions. Thus it is not surprising that 31 percent of the professionals identified themselves as a professional or member of a specific profession (such as lawyer, engineer, or other) while only 11 percent of the supervisors and 18 percent of the technicians produced an occupationally specific self-identification.

To draw on role theory for insight into the variations in emphasis on promotion and recruitment criteria,[30] the hypothesis appears that the Guatemalan bureaucracy has in large measure resolved the conflicting and contradictory demands of the several roles its individual members are asked to perform by ignoring or being ignorant of the expectations of "bureaucrat," "clerk," or "supervisor." But as education, retirement, and the evolution of functionally specific associations change the character of the bureaucracy, the impact of newer reference groups, such as the economic reformers among the national political elite,[31] should be reflected in the increased recognition given profession-based achievement criteria for recruitment and promotion. Typists, engineers, and auditors will continue to disagree over specific criteria for recruitment and promotion, but there will be less

30. See Jerry L. Weaver, "Role Expectations of Latin American Bureaucrats," *Journal of Comparative Administration* 4, no. 2 (1972): 133–66.
    31. Weaver, "Political Elite."

emphasis on *capaz* and rectitude and more emphasis on education, training, experience, and performance.[32]

Uncritical Responses

In the research design it was decided to probe the attitudes of respondents towards their work situations. First, we thought that answers to questions like "What do you like least about your work?" would lead us to problems and shortcomings of administrative procedure. We expected bureaucrats to reply, "I dislike filling out so many reports"; or "I don't get paid enough for the work I do"; or "He and I do the same job but he gets more money than I do." Thus employee identifications would augment observations and other questionnaires seeking to characterize administrative procedures. Second, we thought that responses to the question "What do you like best about your work?" would provide insights into the level of professional identification of bureaucrats: "I like the opportunity to serve the nation"; "the biggest problem confronting people who do the same work as I do is the absence of a strong civil service system." Responses such as these would assist in determining operational value patterns.

But actual replies to several questions did little to highlight procedural problems or professional identification. For example, the question "If you were to become the chief of this office, what changes would you make around here?" produced a 10 percent refusal-to-reply rate. Twenty-four percent replied that they would make no changes at all. Another 9 percent said that offhand they couldn't think of anything they would change, but when they became chief they would give the question closer attention. In sum, nearly half of the sample refused to indicate anything concerning their work situation that should be changed.

---

32. The greater weight given attributes of character versus education and experience by younger members of the bureaucracy is seen in the comparison of responses of 40-and-younger and 41-and-older employees. Younger respondents cited competence, honesty, and loyalty as major criteria for recruitment seven times in ten compared with 78 percent for the older group; as major criteria for promotion, 51 percent of the former and 62 percent of the latter cited similar traits of character.

Eight percent refused to answer the question "What is the major problem confronting the people who do the same kind of work as you do?," and 37 percent of the sample replied that there was no major problem.

Asked what they liked least and what they liked most about their present work, 31 percent of the sample replied that they liked everything. Nearly 50 percent replied that they did not dislike anything about their present position. Only 7 percent reported that what they liked best was the opportunity to serve people or the state.

Why did so many bureaucrats fail to speak out and to identify areas of personal dissatisfaction? Once we dispose of the hypothesis that this segment of the sample believes they worked in the best of all possible worlds, lack of confidence in the integrity of the interview comes to mind. Possibly some respondents did not believe the declaration that all replies were absolutely confidential and that no one outside of the survey staff would see the questionnaires. This lack-of-confidence hypothesis makes a good deal of sense, since survey research is practically unknown in Guatemala. As one bureaucrat put it: "Only three types of persons come around here asking questions: missionaries, tax collectors, and spies from the police."

Perhaps respondents believed that they would get into difficulty if they indicated personal dissatisfaction. These individuals may have thought, "Maybe the interviewer works for the minister, or the secret police, and these questions are meant to test my loyalty"; or "The boss will find out that I criticized the low pay or complained about his mismanagement. . . ." Although it may be difficult to understand this timidity, we must remember that Guatemalan bureaucrats have no civil service protection and that many lack alternative sources of employment. And note the prevailing belief that a good public employee must be loyal and respectful. Would it be loyal and respectful to criticize the system and, by extension, the men who supervise and direct it? Perhaps more important, would the boss think it loyal and respectful?

Following this line of reasoning, we are led to suggest that the selective refusal to respond may indicate unfamiliarity with the questions or mental fatigue or lack of an active imagination, but most probably it indicates the calculation that to offer a personal and critical opinion would lead to trouble—some sort of negative sanction, possibly dismissal, by superiors. This hypothesis is based on the assumption that the respondents were aware of the absence of institutional safeguards from capricious manipulation by superiors and that employees sought to avoid what many considered to be an unacceptable risk involved in expressing dissatisfaction. Many bureaucrats may have been unsure of the response required of them, and being without formal means of protection in what amounted to a crisis situation, remained noncommittal.

A close look at the data reveals that the noncommittal syndrome is not evenly distributed throughout the sample. While 52 percent of the male respondents were found in the noncommittal class, a disproportionate 63 percent of women were included. Perhaps the prevailing antifeminism referred to above has brought women to be more discreet than men. A more likely explanation, however, is found in the fact that women are almost exclusively employed in service and clerical positions, positions having little status but many competitors. Moreover, since women have entered the Guatemalan bureaucracy in any number at all only during the 1960's, most female respondents have only limited experience and familiarity with their work environment.

Analyzing the variables associated with uncritical responses, we found that occupational status is strongly related to willingness to criticize. As the final column of Table 13.13 illustrates, supervisors and professionals are significantly more willing to offer critical opinions than are office workers and service and security personnel. (The correlation between occupational status and willingness to criticize is Gamma, .398.) Many professionals and supervisors have alternative sources of employment or other sources of income; and since they are members of the established middle sector, they have family, professional, and political *patrones*. Both employment and social leverage contribute to a higher tolerance for risk taking among upper-status employees.

The notion that length of tenure is related to willingness to

Table 13.13. *Comparison of frequency of uncritical responses by occupation and length of tenure.*

Length of tenure in bureacracy	Supervisor	Pro-fessional	Technician	Office worker	Service and security	Seniority group
Less than 3 years	0[a]	33.3	40.0	62.5	71.4	58.8
3 to 7 years	100.0	0	46.1	60.0	77.8	53.8
7 to 10 years	0	0	42.8	53.8	78.6	53.2
10 to 15 years	50.0	33.3	33.3	50.0	75.0	47.2
15 to 20 years	0	0	38.4	62.5	50.0	48.0
More than 20 years	30.0	100.0	54.7	85.7	80.0	57.8
Occupational category	33.3	23.1	43.2	60.9	77.2	53.9

Source: Employees Survey. Goodman-Kruskal Gamma, −.355.

[a] Percent of total cell frequency classified as providing an uncritical, noncommital response. In this instance the entire cell (1) was critical, i.e., 0 percent uncritical.

criticize reflects the assumption that any new environment appears hostile; that newer bureaucrats perceive themselves powerless to control their situations, as being dependent on their superiors for survival; and that these junior men will avoid taking risks, especially expressions of opinion that might be interpreted as disrespectful or disloyal to their seemingly all-powerful superiors. Conversely, men with ten to fifteen years of service have had ample time to adjust to the demands of the bureaucracy; such senior employees have survived several changes of government—experience likely to increase one's self-confidence and sense of security.

Contrary to our expectation, when we look at the relationship between seniority and willingness to criticize we find no correlation (Gamma, .044). Table 13.13 reveals that while there is a slight trend towards greater critical expression with increase in seniority, this slight trend is firmly reversed by the most senior respondents, those with more than twenty years of service. Among office workers with less than three years seniority, 62 percent were uncritical; among those with ten to fifteen years, 50 percent were uncritical; but among those with more than twenty years, 85 percent. Similar U-shaped trend lines may be observed in the other occupational categories. In each column, the upswing that breaks the trend occurs with the more-than-twenty-years segment.

Why should twenty years of service be a watershed for uncritical, noncommittal responses? This group contains a large proportion of older bureaucrats, men fifty, sixty, seventy years of age. Can it be that age, not twenty years service per se, is responsible for the reversal of the trend? "As we grow older, we become more conservative." In the survey situation, withholding critical comment might well be considered the prudent, cautious, conservative response.

Interestingly, the hypothesis that age is the main factor is not supported by the data: the correlation between increased age and uncritical responses is Gamma, $-.036$. If anything, the data suggest that older respondents may be slightly more willing to be critical. Thus seniority, not age, seems to be at the heart of the anomalous reversal of the trend toward increasing criticism. The watershed effect in the more-than-twenty-years column clearly has its origins beyond the fact of the group's containing many older respondents.

A possible explanation rests in the reference date of those with more than twenty years seniority. Counting back from the date of the survey, we find that all members of this group joined the bureaucracy prior to the revolution. The most-senior bureaucrats received their early training and prerecruitment socialization during the Ubico regime.

General Ubico stressed strict discipline, formal deportment, and absolute loyalty. Calvinist in his own life style, the *caudillo* tolerated no deviation from his personal code; at any rate, so he is remembered by veteran bureaucrats who once served him. Sitting at his desk amidst coatless, coffee-drinking colleagues, a crusty veteran of forty-three years' service sadly remarked that there was no longer any discipline or pride in the bureaucracy. He recalled the prerevolutionary era when "everyone knew his place; there was respect then." The remnants of this era consisted of men socialized in a small bureaucracy which was personally scrutinized by the *caudillo*, which stressed Victorian-like behavior and attire, and in which service was a family tradition to be preserved and passed along. Ubico typically began each day by visiting the offices in the National Palace; bureaucrats who were absent from their seats when the work bell rang were

summarily dismissed. These respondents have not grown more
conservative as they have grown older; rather, they merely expressed to the interviewers the reserve and caution which was so
much a part of the bureaucratic response during the Ubico
period. My guess is that had these respondents been interviewed
in 1940 or 1950, their refusals to reply and noncommittal responses would have been substantially the same as found in 1966.

What Table 13.13 illustrates is another dimension of the dis-
similarities found throughout Guatemalan society. The world
and one's way in it have changed significantly for many Ladinos
since the revolution; subsequent events have allowed and encouraged new attitudes, perceptions and values to flourish in
Guatemala. But the bureaucracy, one of the social institutions
most firmly in the grasp of the pre-1944 power structure, continues to provide protective shade for glacierlike traditional
mores; death rather than the machinery of reform will reduce
the chilling effect of senior bureaucrats.

Summary and Conclusions

By employing Weber's model of social change we have ascer-
tained that Guatemala's political processes and institutions have
undergone basic transformations since 1944. The traditional
Ubico gave way to the dynamic personalism of the revolution,
which in turn was replaced by an institutionalized, bureaucratic
authority structure. The latter is characterized by a complex national elite composed of competing economic, social, and ideological groups. The outline of the rational legal authority structure
is clearly visible in Guatemala, although Weber's model conceals
and distorts even while illuminating. Equally significant changes
have transformed economic and social systems.

Weber posits bureaucracy as the driving engine of rationalization, but Guatemala's experience violates this expectation. Indeed,
while the economy and polity increasingly manifest the forms of
modernity, the contemporary bureaucracy seems progressively
less able to meet the demands of its rulers and clients, especially

when compared with the performance of the revolutionary period when the elite used the bureaucracy to stimulate greater demands by actively encouraging peasants, Indians, and laborers to seek goods and services. The Ubico bureaucracy was effective and efficient; the revolutionary bureaucracy, though often disorganized, was typically active and more than able to serve the needs of the middle and lower sectors; but the contemporary bureaucracy is neither effective and efficient nor active and innovative.

Many current political elite seek the reorganization of the bureaucracy and the expansion of infrastructure, public health, public credit, agriculture extension, and similar programs. Yet disorganization, waste, and underachievement characterize bureaucratic programs. To a high degree this failure reflects the fact that the elite has changed drastically both in composition and ideology during the past three decades. Ubico built bridges; in 1944 a social revolution was launched; since 1954 infrastructure and social-control programs have been the chief concerns. Yet none of the post-1944 governments have successfully reorganized the bureaucracy. Consequently, a hodgepodge of agencies compete with each other, duplicate existing efforts, and manifest little skill for and less commitment to national development. The bureaucracy has not had firm direction, either ideological or managerial, from recent governments.

The failure to gain control over and to integrate the various programs and levels of the bureaucracy permits the continuation of traditional procedures. But more than simply reflecting the weakness of the rulers, the present state of affairs stands witness to the power of bureaucracy to resist subordination. While individual bureaucrats are defenseless, they are rarely attacked. Everything rises to the top; the top does not delegate and thus cannot fix responsibility; the operational level exercises effective control by refusing to take action; *patrones* protect; subordinates express deference and rectitude; compliance, not performance, is the standard for evaluation.

The ability of the bureaucracy to isolate itself from executive control, to defy fixing of responsibility, is as much a consequence of tradition, the unwillingness of men like Ubico to delegate authority, and the relative smallness of the system, as it is the product of the inherent power of middle-range bureaucrats. Moreover the prevailing system serves a number of interests fairly well. The benefit to the bureaucrat is obvious: protection through inaction. The bureaucrat's superior deals with requests largely in order of the client's political significance. Since the social, economic, and political elite constitute only a tiny fraction of the national population, and since they are well known to him, the superior is able to avoid being identified with a subordinate's mistakes by directly serving the elite himself—a service likely to enhance his social status, intrasystem prestige, and quite possibly his bank account as well. Finally, the elite find their business made easy through dealing with an established routine with well-defined points of contact and a long existing etiquette.

Our study suggests that this system of relationships is breaking apart, perhaps more rapidly than might be apparent. We have seen that the values and perceptions of the bureaucracy, as well as its work routines, are changing under the impact of public education, in-service training, and new clientele. The economic elite has greatly diversified interests and their demands are often highly technical; moreover, new elements have entered the elite who either are not familiar with or refuse to accept traditional relations between elite and bureaucracy. Finally, urban labor, service and clerical personnel, middle- and small-scale businessmen, and even peasant groups are beginning to make demands. This growing work load is in part a legacy of the revolutionary period, in part a product of efforts by the post-1954 elite to extend control throughout society by incorporating all sectors into a national system. Civic action and literacy programs, both of which have as a consequence the transformation of rural peasants into consumers of bureaucratic services, are examples of the latter effect.

The Guatemalan bureaucracy has not been a sturdy vehicle for national development and has not made any but minimal adaptive changes, because it has not been effectively directed or controlled, has not been infused with achievement values, and has not been taxed beyond its capacities by the demands of its clients. The fact that societal values, elite control, and level of demand are changing does not necessarily portend major structural and procedural modifications within the bureaucracy. The content of ideology, rather than mere potential for control, and internalization of achievement norms, rather than mere change in value systems, appear as major determinants of the bureaucracy's development role. To assert this is not to ignore the significance of the level of popular demands as a determinant of bureaucratic behavior; but in Guatemala 60 to 70 percent of the population are so completely without political and economic strength as to have little if any real leverage. No, the key factor is not Juan Chapín. The key to the role of the Guatemalan bureaucracy in a changing society is the configuration of values, attitudes, and perceptions held by bureaucrats and the political elite.[33]

33. I wish to express my appreciation to the Henry L. and Grace Doherty Foundation for support and to Professor Richard N. Adams of the University of Texas at Austin for encouragement and guidance for undertaking the research herein reported. Ms. Barbara DePaola provided valuable assistance in the preparation of this chapter.

Chapter 14

Brazil: Diffusion and Centralization of Power

Gilbert B. Siegel

At every level, national and local, Brazil's government is beset by demands for change to face ever-mounting problems. Unfortunately, the responses that government has been making do not seem to meet the demands nor solve the problems. In fact, these responses often inhibit movements in the direction of innovations that are vital if there is to be political development. How this situation has come about is the topic of this chapter.

The Synergism of Power Centralization and Power Diffusion

It is not surprising that so huge a country as Brazil should suffer both from centralization and from diffusion of political power—features which might be expected to offset each other, but in fact exacerbate each other's bad effects, since they require of the government diametrically opposed courses and thus inhibit movement in any direction. Even if power diffusion is favored as bringing a cure for the ills of centralization, the cure and its aftereffects may be worse than the disease.

The principal legacy of imperial Brazil was unity: the country maintained itself as one nation, instead of fragmenting like Spanish America. But between the date of the establishment of the independent Brazilian monarchy in 1882 and today, political power and influence have come to be widely dispersed and decentralized. Certainly, the diffusion in Brazil's political system is still what strikes the observer first. The bases of political power are varied and numerous; there is little consensus on the basic goals of society; few institutions force political groups to coalesce. On the other hand, the stage is set for the development of a leadership vacuum, and into it move elements that are impatient with the endless bickering and intransigence of the system, eager to forestall others who they fear will seize power first. Such situations not infrequently eventuate in authoritarian regimes with strong centralizing drives. But no matter whether the government is marked by a diffusion of power or by its centralization, there is one sort of project that is sure to suffer, the sort that development administration finds most vital for strengthening the resources of public policy. The eternal victim is initiative toward planned change.

Political parties in Brazil typically represent disparate interests, which vary along many dimensions. From his reading of history Guerreiro-Ramos[1] has abstracted five ideal types of politics still extant there. These are (i) clan-style politics, which were characteristic of colonial Brazil and focused on patriarchal families; (ii) oligarchical politics, most typical of the period 1822–1930, which revolved around regional political bosses; (iii) populist politics exemplified by the Brazilian Labor Party (PTB), and representing a larger concentration of political support than the first two political styles; (iv) pressure-group politics, which appeared only in more recent years and gathered specific economic interests; and (v) ideological politics, which reached maximum development during the Quadros and Goulart governments. Each type has been predominantly characteristic of a particular historical period, but, as Guerreiro-Ramos observes, a type does not disappear with the emergence of a new phase; instead all types continue as residual styles of the Brazilian polity. Accordingly, we may expect to encounter clan and oligarchical styles today, and the behavior implicit in older types may carry forward to more recent ones, at least psychologically. For example, Brazilian populist-style politics seems to involve a translation of the much older arrangement which was characteristic of the

1. Alberto Guerreiro-Ramos, *A crise do poder no Brasil* (Rio de Janeiro: Zahar Editôres, 1961), pp. 49–67.

oligarchical and clan styles of colonial days and the First Republic, when an individual depended on a *patrón* who was typically a landowner. The big-city politician can often manipulate the economic insecurity of the citydweller by trading votes for favors. In any case, Brazil is a mosaic of these political styles, mirroring its national diversity.

The diffusion of power bases carries through into legislative bodies such as the Brazilian Congress. In the absence of institutions which promote coalescence and compromise, parties tend to be regional and local coalitions of convenience; most representatives behave as individuals on most issues. Naturally, this promotes legislation concentrating on special details and interests. The example of 1957[2] bears this out; of 274 laws and 41 legislative decrees, more than two-thirds are each concerned with one specific subject. Examples are laws which cover the opening of additional credits, provide approval of international agreements or acts of the Tribunal of Accounts, grant specific customs exceptions and pensions, and create individual positions, subventions, assistance, and grants. The remaining third of the acts of Congress also cover narrow legislative subjects. For example, there are those that clarify budgetary rules, alter administrative nomenclature, assign the names of illustrious Brazilians to roads, bridges, and airports, authorize the issuance of commemorative stamps, and federalize specific schools.

While several Brazilian state governments are formidable power centers, the problems which characterize the central government also plague the states. At the bottom of the pile are the municipalities. Not only are local governments weak decision-makers; they are also the least capable purveyors of services, except for the largest of cities. States and municipalities lack financial resources, for revenue, both as to amounts and sources, has been systematically denied to local governments. Thus getting anything of significance accomplished in a state, and especially in a municipal government, requires intercession with the federal government, for the latter is where resources of all kinds are concentrated. This situation naturally intensifies the diffuse character

2. Oswaldo Trigueiro, "A crise legislativa e o regime presidencial," *Revista Brasileira de Estudos Políticos*, Nov. 1959, pp. 40–53.

of the political system. As Sherwood points out, "these imperatives in the Brazilian environment . . . place great pressure on the political leader of a community to exercise influence upward. A positive relationship with the governor and/or the President has been perhaps the most important qualification for a position of community leadership in the eyes of the electorate."[3]

In the face of this situation, the one focus in the Brazilian system where power is concentrated in a single individual more than anywhere else is the Presidency of the Republic. This is evidenced by the gradual accretion of presidential power by constitutional means over time.[4] Under the Constitution of 1891, the President was authorized to sanction, promulgate, and publish laws and resolutions of Congress. His legislative initiative was limited to the annual message in which he outlined needed legislation. With the advent of the 1934 Constitution, the President gained authority to present bills. By 1946, the President constitutionally assumed the role of colegislator. He had exclusive authority to initiate legislative action to create positions in existing services, to increase salaries, and to modify existing laws relative to the armed forces during a legislative session. He also shared the responsibility for all financial laws and laws relative to the armed forces with the Chamber of Deputies. Other significant powers of the President under the 1946 Constitution were his veto power (including an item veto), which Congress frequently found difficult to override by the necessary two-thirds majority; the decree power, limited to authority to execute laws of Congress, but frequently applied in excess of this limitation; and the power to intervene in the affairs of the states under certain conditions.

Accordingly, we see that even under conditions of openness in the political system that prevailed between 1946 and 1964, operating under constitutionalism and with competitive politics holding sway, a movement towards centralization of power in the chief executive resulted. This form of centralization, which might be called executive aggrandizement, contrasts with out-and-out seizure of power. Before 1930, political power was so diffused in Brazil that the states were virtually independent entities, their

---

3. Frank P. Sherwood, *Institutionalizing the Grass Roots in Brazil: A Study in Comparative Local Government* (San Francisco: Chandler, 1967), p. 74.
4. Trigueiro.

political behavior being more characteristic of international than federal relations. In 1930 Vargas gained power following a revolution against this situation, among other things. Probably inspired by the successes of European dictators of the day, he proceeded to dismantle the somewhat formalistic federalism and to centralize, ultimately through a dictatorship. Without doubt Vargas had a popular following and the system needed changing. However, to bring about change he chose to centralize and monopolize power through an authoritarian regime.

During the period of the open political system (1945–64) the military intervened on several occasions to maintain the "democratic order" as they saw the need: to depose Vargas in 1945 because of the demand for popular elections; to remove him again in 1954 for corruption. And it almost intervened again in 1961, after the resignation of Jânio Quadros, to prevent the presidential succession of João Goulart (this intervention lost momentum because of division within the army). In 1964 the military ultimately deposed Goulart, alleging a total breakdown of the economy and government apparatus and his leftist political orientation. Most recently (1969) they intervened to preclude presidential succession of the Vice-President upon physical incapacitation of President Costa e Silva. Ultimately the military placed General Médici in the presidency, the government proceeding without either constitution or congress. Thus we see that two kinds of centralization have taken place in Brazil since 1930: (i) executive aggrandizement, under an open political system, and (ii) outright seizure of power by the military, with the military actually running the government in recent years. In both cases what has been described as the characteristic of diffused political power unchecked by governmental institutions helps us to understand the countervailing reaction of centralization.

Vignettes of Organizational Consequences

We will now turn to three capsule descriptions of planned change efforts undertaken to directly or indirectly better public policy making and implementation.

DASP

When Getúlio Vargas was swept into power in 1930, he had various commitments to urban populations to provide new services and programs. The corrupt and inefficient nature of the administrative machinery he inherited was a formidable obstacle to such programs. He also had power maintenance needs in order to break with the pattern of the past. Initial efforts which were directed at standardizing government purchasing and reorganizing the civil service, its status, pay, and the like, largely failed. Other actors appeared on the scene, particularly Luis Simões Lopes. Simões Lopes was able to secure passage of legislation in 1936 which established the basis for a federal personnel system consisting of both a central personnel agency and ministerial units. Eventually, this arrangement was abandoned because personnel controls were being neutralized by budgetary execution decisions under control of the Ministry of Finance. Also, Simões Lopes saw the need for coordinated efforts in other areas; the personnel function was too narrow in scope.

By late 1937 Vargas had proclaimed his New State, and with it the Administrative Department of the Public Service (DASP).[5] As originally conceived, DASP as an arm of the President was to control all organizational matters in the government; to prepare the national budget and audit its execution; to select, develop, and control civil servants; to inspect the public service; to develop and control material systems and specifications; and to operate a legislative reference service for the President. Administrative staff and housekeeping services along with governmental reform activities were to be centralized. These powers, and more, were implemented throughout the seven years of the New State. In part, overexpansion of activities during the agency's first seven years in conjunction with the emphasis on centralizing control set the stage for many of the difficulties DASP was to experience later on. Special emphasis was placed upon the personnel

5. Summarized from Gilbert B. Siegel, *The Vicissitudes of Governmental Reform in Brazil: A Study of the DASP* (Los Angeles: School of Public Administration, Univ. of Southern California, 1966). See also Siegel, "The Strategy of Public Administration Reform: The Case of Brazil," *Public Administration Review* 26 (March 1966): 45–55.

function, particularly control of ingress to public service appointments.

Because controls were emphasized so heavily, the more positive benefits of organizational studies were little realized. Structural analyses, the formal aspects of organization, and the control of official organization patterns received great attention. The need for central approval of organization structure resulted in much formalism in government organization.

One of the most interesting organizational improvisations of the DASP was the concept of the "coordinative system" which apparently grew out of the early administrative ideas of organizational separation of ends and means, and F. W. Taylor's functional management principle. On the matters of organization, budget, personnel, and material, DASP established a direct channel to the staff agencies in the ministries for purposes of obtaining information on administrative operations and to facilitate the performance of auxiliary staff functions. These staff agencies were responsible to their ministerial chain of command on general administrative matters and responsible to DASP on technical affairs. Real power rested with DASP. Most employees of the ministerial staff sections were selected by DASP, and being concerned with the means and not the ends of government administration, they were naturally oriented toward DASP. This so-called coordinative system was abolished with the end of the Vargas dictatorship; but over time thereafter, it has been formally reestablished. However, these staffs have been little used by the ministries, which never accepted the ends-means dichotomy.

During the dictatorship, DASP also reproduced itself in the states which were under the supervision of administrators, an administrative department, and the State's Affairs Commission appointed by Vargas to replace the state governors and to give overall coordination to the system.

With the fall of the dictatorship in 1945, DASP, which had been thoroughly identified with the regime, was "reformed" by having its powers vastly curtailed, especially the so-called coordination, control, and auditing powers. DASP's lines of control into the ministries were broken, and only central overhead controls on such functions as personnel administration remained. The agency's budget was curtailed, matériel management was completely removed from the organization, and the agency's status was lowered by downgrading the title of the organizational head from president to director general.

DASP limped through the Dutra presidency engaging in minor skirmishes; it did what it could to survive. By 1950, with Vargas again in the presidency, DASP began to rearm. A major undertaking of the period was the previously untried technology of position classification. Congress did not actually consider the DASP classification bill until 1956, under the Kubitschek presidency. When the law finally emerged in 1960, Congress had so amended it to favor special interests, especially subaltern-level employees, that its logic and premises were gutted.

President Kubitschek tolerated DASP as far as his interests did not conflict with those of the agency. Thus, he removed control of public buildings from DASP in order to expedite construction of Brasilia. He made thousands of spoils appointments and restrained DASP from holding competitive examinations.

While the volatile and unpredictable Jânio Quadros seriously intended to utilize DASP as it had not been employed since the dictatorship, his short tenure in office prevented materialization of this goal.

Under the presidency of João Goulart, the problem of patronage appointments which had been made to pay off Brazilian Labor Party electoral support of Kubitschek came to a head. Most of these appointments were made as temporaries, and were retained as such through presidential restraint of the competitive examinations. Goulart eventually backed down on his attempt to blanket the temporaries into the civil service after high drama and the creation of a national *cause célèbre*. Ultimately, and with the exception of the personnel function, DASP lost its remaining powers, such as control of the budget.

It appears that selection of the strategy of control and centralization led to the failure of administrative reforms and to the downfall of DASP, which was conceived to be the vehicle of reform. The agency became a target for hostility and frustrations, both political and administrative. Considerable conflict with other governmental units resulted, especially with the Ministry of Finance. The more positive functions either were not performed or were transformed into controls. The entire DASP strategy ceased to be efficacious in the open political system where diffused political forces were at play. On the other hand, when operational under a closed system, its reform goals were displaced by the power-maintenance needs of the leader.[6]

Institutionalizing Planning in an Unstable Political System

Is it possible to institutionalize planning, especially central national planning, in an unstable political system—one with a high level of dissensus, and one in which it is the rules of the system themselves that are in question?[7]

We know the manifest function of planning is to produce change in the direction of economic development. This is as true in Brazil as in the rest of the developing world. What is the Brazilian theory of how planning is expected to produce more rapid economic development? There are two elements. First, it is held that the proper allocation of economic resources will speed economic development. Second, it is held that the proper allocation of resources can be achieved through the use of appropriate governmental policies as administered by the bureaucracy.

The planner in Brazil is the economist—the expert. In the early stages of planning engineers were used, but for the past fifteen years the people who have made plans have been economists, up to and including the Minister of Planning. With the aid of commissions of experts, economists have increasingly based their plans on the performance of the Brazilian economy. "The plan" has been an economically comprehensive effort to alter economic behavior to improve overall economic structure. The role of the planner has been to advise the political authorities on what remedies to apply at any given time.

6. In addition to the two Siegel references already cited, see Lawrence S. Graham, *Civil Service Reform in Brazil: Principles versus Practice* (Austin: Univ. of Texas Press, 1968).

7. Edited and abridged from Robert T. Daland, *Brazilian Planning: Development Politics and Administration* (Chapel Hill: Univ. of North Carolina Press, 1967), pp. 203–12.

The second assumption—that planning decisions will be implemented by the bureaucracy—is intimately related to the first. The Brazilian experience clearly shows the growth of the idea of a permanent central planning staff at the summit of the bureaucracy. During the Goulart regime this staff became a ministry, and plans were made to convert it into a control organ. During the Branco regime such plans were revived in somewhat different form, and the first steps were taken to make the Ministry of Planning an actual organ of coordination and control. This approach to planning organizations stems from the Weberian ideal type of rational, professional bureaucracy and from the scientific-management ideas of Frederick W. Taylor with his "one best way." The planning experience of the post-Vargas era mirrors the movement toward administrative centralization of the Vargas regime through the mechanism of DASP. The relation between the two is emphasized in that DASP was the home of the early Brazilian plans.

The reality is that the Brazilian bureaucracy resembles the Weberian ideal type only on paper. In this respect Brazil seems to conform to the situation in many transitional countries. Fred Riggs accounts for this type of bureaucracy in his theory of prismatic society.

The style of Brazilian planning has varied as between recent Brazilian regimes, but one factor is strikingly constant: the amount of governmental participation in the economy, in the name of planning for development, has increased with every recent administration. Both governmental controls of private enterprise and direct participation through public or mixed corporations have increased. To what may we attribute this increased governmental activity, whether by the regimes of right or left? Certainly the answer is not to be found in the strong institutionalization of the planning process in a centralized bureaucracy. Rather we may look to the centers of political power. The goals of the traditional landed elite, the new industrial elite, and the omnipresent military elite were not in conflict over industrialization and over the planning which sought to control it. Thus the elites of Brazil have not remained polarized around distant interests as has been the case in some countries. The political battle is preeminently a struggle for access to power rather than for ideology, policy, or protection of a particular interest. Therefore *policies* have found general acceptance among Brazil's ruling elites. We must be careful to distinguish between the functions of development policies and the functions of a central planning *institution*. The latter, represented by the central planning organ and its embodiment of a plan, has not always been received with enthusiasm by all elements of the elite. Before considering the sources of conflict over planning, however, let us review the functions of the planning institution for the regime.

The central and presumably comprehensive plan has a number of values not related directly to the attainment of the goals stated in the plan itself. The first of these is the public-relations benefits of the plan. The plan asserts that the regime knows where it is going and that it is working for the common good. These sentiments are contained in the plan itself, but they are strongly repeated in the vast number of speeches and other contacts with groups of the citizenry incident to presentation and defense of the plan. The Kubitschek, Furtado, and Campos plans in particular served important public relations purposes. It has been repeatedly pointed out that the Castelo Branco government in particular justified its political existence on the crucial need for planning of the "right" kind.

A second and more subtle function of Brazilian plans has been to provide a specific technique for focusing the effort to arrive at consensus on policy. The technique worked for Kubitschek. It did not work for Goulart, for consensus was never achieved among his own supporters. With the use of Cosplan (an advisory planning council created in 1965 under the Branco regime), the Campos plan appears to have achieved this purpose to a considerable degree. The controversial aspects of the Castelo Branco regime reflect differences over political institutions rather than planning goals. When, as in the Goulart case, the planning institution did not achieve its consensus-building purpose, it served an alternative function as a sacrificial goat, leaving the regime itself intact.

Third, the exigencies of the struggle for foreign aid, especially under the Alliance for Progress, required the existence both of a plan and of planners commanding the respect of experts in the organs of international financing.

A fourth and most important function of the planning institution is related to all the others. The Brazilian plans have represented deliberate and calculated effort on the part of the regimes in power to increase the powers of both the incumbent President and of the presidency as an institution. Assembling sufficient power to govern has been the crucial problem of Brazilian governments. The plan, like the creation of DASP under Vargas, is intended to establish new centralized control over administrative hierarchy. The first plans were located within DASP itself. Later they were attached directly to the President's office. The Plano Trienal was timed to boost the vote for a return to presidentialism under Goulart, from the 1961–62 interregnum of parliamentary government. Later proposals for organizing the Ministry of Planning were based on central implementation of plans with varying degrees of compulsion. Even with the firm support of victorious military forces at his back, President Castelo Branco saw the need to initiate a plan and justified the revolution as necessary to carry it out. Much of the rationale for the Institutional Acts (under which he governed during a suspension of the Constitution) was to provide powers necessary to implement the plan. These powers were notably of a political character, establishing a more centralized government. Among other things political parties were abolished in favor of two political groupings to replace fourteen parties, presidents and governors were to be chosen by the legislative bodies rather than by election, and even the mayors of the state capitals were no longer to be elected.

Returning for the moment to the subject of Brazilian bureaucracy, we find that it performs several important social functions; these are (i) to provide a channel for upward mobility for the educated middle class, (ii) to provide permanent incomes for that portion of the middle class which furnishes support for the regime, (iii) to provide a low level of certain services, and (iv) to provide opportunities for private entrepreneurship based on the powers attaching to certain offices. These functions are essentially political in nature. Broadly stated, the purpose of the bureaucracy is to provide patronage, while maintaining a certain level of services. It would be a mistake, however, to regard the bureaucracy as dependent on the political elite in power at a particular time. The bureaucracy has succeeded in insulating itself from all but the most drastic changes of political direction.

The essence of rational planning in a developing country involves sacrifices in the short run to achieve long-run gains, the reallocation of existing resources, and the modification of the processes by which allocation decisions for the society are made. All three of these effects of planning run counter to the self-perceived interests of a bureaucracy of the kind described above.

In the Brazilian case, civil and military personnel have been most reluctant to accept the restrictions on salary increases envisioned in the last two plans. Restriction on the addition of new positions and budget containment generally have been opposed. The imposition of controls over old agencies by new planning and coordinating agencies has been stoutly fought in the political arena. A forecast of things to come was the controversy between the old Department of Construction Works Against Drought in the Northeast (DNOCS) within the Ministry of Public Works and the new Superintendency for Development of the Northeast (Sudene) during the Kubitschek and Goulart regimes.

The fate of proposals to create a ministry of planning and implementation machinery under Furtado and Campos represents the opposition of powerful elements of the bureaucracy through its highly politicized elements.

To orient administrative programs toward achievement and performance, rather than patronage, would strike at the roots of the political balance of power which exists. Even with the control of the country firmly in the hands of the military, efforts to centrally coordinate and coerce the bureaucracy have been difficult, though intensive efforts to do so were made. The natural reaction to this situation is to create new entities to carry the programs needed by the plan. This course has been taken through the establishment of additional government corporations. However, this is also a dangerous road. The proliferation of new agencies merely creates more jobs, a larger payroll, and an increase in the governmental budget. These trends run counter to the purpose of the plans. Moreover, the new agencies, born into a highly politicized bureaucratic environment, may take on the characteristics of the old agencies. The notorious histories of Sudene and Petrobras (the national gasoline monopoly) are indications of this phenomenon. The Brazilian experience thus seems to show that implementation of central plans is dysfunctional from the point of view of the bureaucracy. This conclusion is further supported by Pinto's institution-building analysis of the Brazilian National Bank for Development (BNDE).[8] His findings suggest that the capacity of the bank to accomplish its developmental goals is inversely related to its political functionality. Thus, the accomplishment of developmental goals and the maintenance of the political regime remain incompatible.

Tax Administration Reform and the Decline of Brazilian Municipal Government

U.S. technical assistance in the area of taxation in Brazil has focused on income-tax collection.[9] Largely through these efforts Brazilian federal tax revenues increased (after adjustment for inflation) 40 percent from 1961 to 1967. In 1961 federal tax revenue collected represented 10.6 percent of gross domestic product; in 1967 it rose to 12.4 percent, and it was estimated that it would rise to 13.9 percent in 1968.

These results have been produced by improvements in five areas. First, a conversion to modern computing equipment was introduced, with major facilities established in large population

8. Rogério R. S. Pinto, *The Political Ecology of the Brazilian National Bank for Development (BNDE)* (Washington: Organization of American States, 1969).
9. See U.S., Congress, House, *USAID Operations in Latin America Under the Alliance for Progress,* 90th Cong., 2d sess., Jan.–Feb. 1968, pp. 745–52, on tax administration reform. Information related to municipal government is based on Ivan L. Richardson, "Municipal Government in Brazil: The Financial Dimension," *Journal of Comparative Administration* 1 (Nov. 1969): 321–43.

centers throughout the country. Before, equipment had been used only for billing and printing; tax accounts in the true sense of the word had not been kept. The second area of improvement was the institution of a program to identify people who do not file returns. The third area was that of auditing returns. Shortages of accounting personnel and other problems originally led Brazilian tax authorities to examine each tax return, at least superficially, to determine whether technical errors appeared on the face of the return or if supporting proofs were omitted. An annual planned audit program was substituted for this procedure, whereby returns are selected for audit on the basis of their potential for producing revenue. A fourth area of improvement involved long-range planning and coordination of different departments and bureaus of the Ministry of Finance to preclude working at counterpurposes. The fifth area is the training of personnel. The Finance Ministry was persuaded by U.S. AID advisors to establish a training center to upgrade its personnel. As of 1968 the training target was 5,000 clerical and administrative employees each year when the training center is in full operation.

Three laws passed by the Brazilian government have also assisted tax collection. A 1964 law subjected tax arrears and fines to monetary correction for the effects of inflation. In 1965 another law made systematic tax evasion a criminal offense, with penalties up to two years in prison. Still another law passed in 1965 established pay withholding.

Thus we see that truly significant inroads have been made in the area of revenue production. A combination of circumstances, including this increased revenue as well as its distribution under the 1967 Constitution, has set in motion events which may serve to emasculate many Brazilian municipalities, especially the smaller, less developed ones. Under the 1946 Constitution municipalities could spend their own money as well as grants and shared tax revenues virtually without federal and state controls. Such expenditure autonomy appeared to be more a product of neglect than a result of deliberate efforts to develop home rule, for much corruption and misuse of funds resulted.

In an attempt to remove many defects in the shared-revenue system of the 1946 Constitution, new concepts were introduced in the 1967 Constitution. Many objects of local taxation were eliminated, especially by development of a Municipal Participation Fund through which municipalities were allotted federal monies. The twenty-two state capitals and Brasilia were allocated 10 percent of the fund by a formula. The quota for the noncapital cities and the three federal territories was computed on a scale in proportion to population. Expenditures under the Municipal Participation Fund were to be controlled in great detail. In particular, the Federal Tribunal of Accounts was to preaudit and could postaudit expenditures and ultimately suspend payments for failure to comply with legal requirements imposed by the federal government.

As the effects of new tax-collection procedures began to be felt in 1967 and 1968

> the improved income tax and the new industrial tax were producing in such amounts that the problem for many municipalities appeared . . . to be how to utilize the flow in a rational manner.
>
> One of the greatest municipal complaints, the unpredictability and nonpayment of shared revenues was apparently solved. The municipal share of the income and industrial taxes did not become part of the federal budget; quotas were calculated by the nonpolitical Tribunal of Accounts; payments were made automatically by the Bank of Brazil; and partisan politics was removed from the process. Municipalities could budget and plan with certainty.[10]

For Brazilian municipalities such a windfall was too good to last. On 13 December 1968 the new constitution was suspended and the nation's executive was given authority to rule by decree. Meanwhile the Federal Tribunal of Accounts found it impossible to do anything but cursorily audit municipal records because of budget and personnel deficiencies. The federal government also charged municipalities with misuse of the money from the Mu-

10. Richardson, p. 336.

nicipal Participation Fund, especially in regard to "simple political maintenance" expenditures versus development investment. Finally, the tax-collection system was producing so much more revenue than expected that the national government cast a covetous eye towards the share earmarked for the cities. Thus, by 1969 the state and local governments' share was reduced, first to 7 percent and later to 5 percent of the Municipal Participation Fund. Naturally the effect of these reductions was to curtail the income of many municipalities drastically. Accompanying the cuts in the Municipal Participation Fund was establishment of a Two Percent of Revenue Fund, allocations from which are totally under the control of the federal government, and which may be used to coerce "appropriate" behavior on the part of municipalities.

Thus we see an interesting chain of events produced by a successful application of technical assistance at the cupola of government. The development of a new constitution which removed previously reserved sources of taxation from municipalities substituted a near total dependence upon the central government. However an unanticipated consequence was production of quantitatively significant and predictable income for municipalities in a situation in which monetary starvation has been the general rule. Further, inattentiveness to system-wide consequences were seen in (i) the overloading of the Tribunal of Accounts, the audits of which (required by the new constitution) were reduced to a formality, and (ii) the inability of municipalities to allocate newfound resources for development-oriented projects (since no action had been taken to enhance this capability over the years). In the final analysis these outcomes resulted in aggrandizement of the central government's power at the expense of the periphery.

Concluding Comments

We have described two pervading themes of Brazilian politics —power centralization versus power diffusion—as synergisms because their combined effects tend to exaggerate and exacerbate political phenomena. Two points on power diffusion have been discussed: (i) the older condition of political reality was one of decentralized and diffused power; as modern styles of politics have developed, power diffusion continues as a characteristic of the Brazilian polyarchy; (ii) Brazil apparently has had little success in developing governmental and societal institutions which soften the impact of diffused power by causing coalescence among political groups.

Power centralization appears to be causally related to power diffusion in several ways. (i) Over the years of living with these antitheses Brazilians have tended to concentrate constitutional authority in the hands of the President of the Republic in order to facilitate the functioning of governmental institutions. (ii) This has happened, among other reasons, because a highly pluralistic atmosphere prevails in Congress, a branch of government preoccupied with details and with individual and special interests; as a result, Presidents occupy the broader decision field in many areas. (iii) Finally, the preceding factors, combined with what is perceived by some as an undesirable direction of national drift, not infrequently cause a seizure of power often succeeded by an authoritarian regime; elected governments which follow such regimes, in turn, apparently never totally eradicate the advances of power centralization which preceded.

The following generalizations accrue from our analysis. First, the behavior of the bureaucracy, the local governments, and Congress, is more typical of the diffused power situation than of the centralizing one. The Chief Executive is counterposed to them, using whatever special resources he possesses.

The second generalization is that the diffused power situation causes the Executive to rely heavily on control institutions. The third generalization is a corollary: Brazilian Presidents tend to use central agencies for regime maintenance. In the case of DASP, regime maintenance and controlism were blended. For central planning agencies, regime maintenance involves consensus building on developmental goals.

A fourth generalization is that basic organizational goals of central agencies concerned with change tend to become displaced, suboptimized, or not pursued by the agencies. While the bureaucratic reform goals of DASP are our best example, central planning agencies appear to have had problems in carrying out their programs as well. A subset of this generalization is a reason for goal displacement—the system overload effect. The case of financial controls on municipalities demonstrates the overload principle which can produce formalism. DASP has had this difficulty as well.

The fifth generalization derived from our analysis is concerned with a kind of vicious circle effect. Little attention and few resources are applied to increasing the municipal capability for deciding and acting politically and administratively. Naturally, this produces poor performance, which then becomes the rationale for tightened control and centralization. This was demonstrated when local governments squandered and misallocated resources newly assigned under the Constitution of 1967, and the situation was used as justification for reducing autonomy and the total amount of these resources. Administrative incompetence, among other difficulties, had been a problem of municipalities for years; what changed was freedom and magnitude of expenditures.

In closing let me make a statement about global strategy for strengthening public policy making in Brazil. We can represent the dilemma of this paper in the following formula:

Diffused power $>$ consensus-building institutions $\rightarrow$ centralization and control

The global strategy which has been applied has placed emphasis on the yield side of this formula—centralization and control—as a strategy of overcoming diffused power. As we have seen, centralization-and-control solutions, from authoritarian intervention in particular, tend to be short-lived, to have undesirable and repercussive consequences, and generally to inhibit societal change during the period in which they are in force.

For amelioratives which require the least overall intervention, an alternative is to focus on strategies which seek to modify basic aspects of society such as culture-based behavior. The payoff here is long-run; change in the present is highly valued because things allowed to proceed as they are may produce undesirable outcomes. Then retreat is difficult or impossible.

Perhaps tinkering with the middle part of the formula—consensus-building institutions—will be more productive. Any institution that promotes coalescence and discourages divisiveness would come in here. For an example of an institution of the opposite tendency, one which probably exacerbated divisive tendencies in the society, consider proportional representation in the election of Congress under the 1946 Constitution. On the other hand, national plan development has been a consensus-building institution, though the same cannot be said for plan execution. Perhaps we should focus upon consensus-building strategies for reducing the effects of power diffusion and thus restraining the tendency toward centralizing and control behavior through authoritarian intervention or executive aggrandizement.

Finally, would it not be efficacious to attempt to break the pattern of controlism? This strategy suggests eschewing involvement of the public bureaucracy as much as possible, because the behavioral goals of the Brazilian civil service appear to be incompatible with developmental aspirations, and its programs deteriorate into controls for regime-support purposes. Direct doing, overseeing, and regulating are only three approaches among many available to an administration. Perhaps activities such as development of important economic and social infrastructure projects should be turned over to private hands. President Kubitschek did this when Oscar Niemeyer was given *carte blanche* authority for development and construction of Brasilia. The President saw this as the only way to guarantee persistence of the project after his term in office expired. He did accomplish what he wanted, for the investment already sunk in Brasilia is too great to ignore or abandon.

Chapter 15

The New Ignorance and the Future of Public Administration in Latin America

Alberto Guerreiro-Ramos

The approaches available in public administration in general, and those in particular which are reflected in this volume, make a flagrant display of conceptual dissensus. Sometimes the authors may coincide in pointing out the same problems, but nevertheless their theoretical trends are multifarious. This is certainly a result not necessarily of weaknesses of the scholars, but rather of the historical crisis in which mankind is living. A reformulation of the theoretical framework of public administration in Latin America has to be undertaken without losing sight of the fact that if the discipline is to be scientific, it has to rely on a set of basic assumptions that are the same everywhere. Such assumptions have never been clearly articulated. The task of this chapter is to try to express some of them and to present some speculations about the future of our academic field.

Throughout history there have been successive different terms of theoretical consensus, successive different models or paradigms of science;[1] and in the transition from one to another a high degree of confusion and uncertainty necessarily obtain. In each of those transitions what was tacit or unconscious in the behavior of the practitioners became explicit and conscious. But this improvement in awareness did not enable them automatically to perceive the new paradigm; it rather made them aware of the extent of their ignorance in relation to the new challenges they wanted to face and diagnose. Thus each of those transitional mo-

---

1. On the history of models of science, see Thomas S. Kuhn, *The Structure of Scientific Revolutions* (Chicago: Univ. of Chicago Press, 1966).

ments is characterized by a new ignorance.[2] Such ignorance is not overcome until a basic framework of inquiry is structured abreast of the new historical trends. Thoughts are not suprahistoric; they are produced by minds of men shaped in their motivations and urgencies by concrete circumstances which vary from period to period. We cannot make ourselves clear in our conceptualizations when the trends of our daily doings and vicissitudes are still inchoate, or do not show their pattern. These are the times when our ignorance becomes striking.

Let me distinguish between two kinds of ignorance. There is the unguessed ignorance of the man who does not realize the obsolescence of his intellectual schemes and structures in relation to new circumstances and who tries unsuccessfully to marshal them, resorting to extrapolation. His overcommitment to an episodical frame of reference makes him insensitive to the uniqueness of unprecedented situations. The causes of this form of schizophrenia are diverse—among them, vested interests in acquired positions, lack of psychological strength necessary for self-renewal, fear of facing uncertainty and ambiguity, psychic closing-off, which, according to Lifton, is a total desensitization to unexpected incidents of life.[3] On the other hand there is the self-conscious ignorance which deserves to be called, in line with the classical expression of Nicholas of Cusa, learned ignorance (*docta ignorantia*). This is the ignorance we must not be ashamed to recognize as ours at this point in the history of our field.

The "New Public Administration"

A debate about what the "new public administration" is goes on in many circles of our professional community. The question is undoubtedly timely. It seems, however, too soon to try to find the conceptual cosmos that the question begs for. At this point in the history of our field, the "new public administration" is

2. I take this expression from Gardner Murphy. See his *Human Potentialities* (New York: Basic Books, 1958), pp. 9–14.
3. R. J. Lifton, *History and Human Survival* (New York: Random House, 1970).

defined less by conclusive statements than by the attitude of learned ignorance. That is to say, the "new public administration" is characterized by the perception of the gap between what we know and what we must know to fulfill the specific duties of our profession. To the extent that we realize how far we are from knowing what we must, in other words, that we qualify our eventual ignorance, we will reach the threshold of the "new public administration."

The learned ignorance is paradoxical if one considers its phenomenological flavor. It is structurally intentional, in the sense that it results somehow from the perception that there are questions that we must answer, although our available knowledge is of little avail. It is a qualified self-conscious ignorance of something. At least it indicates that there is something there to be known. It places, therefore, its subject in a position of getting the new knowledge he needs, if he has enough courage and strength to unlearn his usual schemes and learn by acting, or, if you prefer, through action-research.

The "new public administration" is essentially nonprescriptive. It substitutes the attitude of learned ignorance for the normative approaches of the traditional public administration. That is why Kurt Lewin's idea of action-research has achieved such momentum these days. In fact, if we develop thoroughly the idea, we find ourselves tackling the problem of reconceptualization of science and of its practice. Action-research may be considered a revival of the Hegel-Marxian notion of *praxis*. In general terms, the Hegel-Marxian meaning of *praxis* entails the indissoluble unity of theory and practice, a dialectical integration of the speculative and the empirical. After the death of Hegel, the Polish philosopher August von Cieszkowski undertook the task of updating Hegel's doctrine. He worked out the consequences of Hegel's contention that will is a specific mode of thought. From this it follows, according to Cieszkowski, that ordinary human action can have a philosophical or theoretical content. Cieszkowski concluded that man could expel chance and necessity from the realm of history and become a "conscious master builder"[4] of his

4. See Nicholas Lobkowicz, *Theory and Practice* (Notre Dame, Ind.; Univ. of Notre Dame Press, 1967), p. 198.

own future. But for man to attain the stature of a conscious change agent, his thinking has to "descend from the heights of theory to the open country of *praxis*."[5] Later on, Marx echoed Cieszkowski in his *Theses on Feuerbach*, where *praxis* is presented as "practical-critical activity," or action pervaded by thinking. Accusing the traditional philosophers of being *scholastic*, he states: "The philosophers have only *interpreted* the world; the point is to *change* it."[6]

Putting aside the dogmatic elements of the Hegel-Marxian conception of history, today's action-research-oriented practitioners in the field of administration (R. Chin, W. Bennis, Kotarbinski, Kaufman, and others) have points in common with those who in the past century were trying to rehabilitate practice by bestowing a theoretical content upon it, such as the quest for a new model of science and thinking where theory and action were inseparable, and a concern for conscious invention of the future. The notion of learned ignorance gives to the contemporary model of action-research its specificity in relation to the Hegel-Marxian conception of *praxis*, in the sense that today's action-research-oriented practitioners no longer support the idea, as the Hegel-Marxians did, of a unilinear social development.

One can see present action-research-oriented practitioners as experts in learned ignorance. They are neither optimists nor pessimists regarding the future course of history, but stress the requirement of engagement, commitment, and responsibility in the decision-making process in all levels of the social system.

5. Ibid., p. 202.
6. There is a need in our field for a systematic study of the problem of unity of theory and practice. The issue is implicit in Bennis's quest for "theories of changing" and Robert Biller's integration of thinking and acting. The German representatives of the Hegelian Left were particularly concerned with this question, long before Karl Marx. For instance, Ludwig Feuerbach wrote: "In speculative philosophy I miss the element of empiricism and in empiricism the element of speculation. My method therefore is to unite both not as two different materials but as different principles, i.e., empirical *activity* and speculative activity." See Sidney Hook, *From Hegel to Marx* (Ann Arbor: Univ. of Michigan Press, 1966), p. 224. William James' pragmatism has points in common with the Hegel-Marxian theory of *praxis*. The following statement by James would be subscribed to by Marx: "The center of gravity of philosophy must alter its place. The earth of things, long thrown into shadow by the glories of the upper ether, must resume its rights. . . . It will be an alteration in the 'seat of authority' that reminds one almost of the Protestant Reformation." See, "What Pragmatism Means by Practical," in John Dewey, *Essays in Experimental Logic* (1916; New York: Dover, n.d.), p. 306.

The following statement seems to be representative of the new public administration.

> We are in increasing danger of acting as if we knew what we were doing when we don't, and then not being able to bear the consequences of having erred. Such a situation would continue to erode the credibility of organizations and the change strategies they employ, and the legitimacy accorded to a government and the political process which produces it. To respond to such a situation by trying harder to make those procedures work which have contributed to the emergence of the problem may be to risk a serious spiral of political and organizational bankruptcy. Something different is called for.[7] . . . An alternative would attempt to fuse knowledge and action. It would recognize that to have different people thinking and acting, or the same people thinking and acting at different points in time, is unlikely simply to make thought impractical and action uninformed. To have some people planning, thinking, acting, accepting risks, and experiencing outcomes, would be recognized by an alternative model as inane at best. Acting would be recognized as the basis of planning.[8]

The "new public administration" tends to be nonprescriptive, antischolastic, action-research oriented. In the following paragraphs, an effort will be made to validate this characterization more consistently.

From Blind to Conscious and Systematic Commitments

The problem of reorienting the study of public administration in Latin America is not different from the same problem in other areas, regarding some fundamentals of the discipline. In each

7. Robert P. Biller, "Combining Knowledge and Action: Toward a Post-Reform Society," in *Blueprint*, Working Papers, School of Public Administration, University of Southern California, 1969, p. 20.
8. Ibid., p. 23.

stage of its evolution, public administration is part of a larger historical context. And maybe what today we think is a crisis of public administration consists largely in the fact that we have been abiding by a model of the discipline that is not pertinent today. A new historical context has emerged whose implications are probably ahead of our thinking and acting. This feeling pervades our professional community. Fred Riggs, for instance, expresses it in these words: "Our changing world compels us to raise . . . questions. How shall we deal with them?"[9] And he answers: "I am afraid that we can never face up to them honestly and intelligibly until we change some of our implicit assumptions about the meaning of public administration. We are handicapped by some fundamental ambiguities which block clear thinking."[10] To overcome this situation, it may be useful to explicate what seem to be some of the assumptions of the new public administration. They will be called commitments, because in fact they are value premises of our professional behavior. It is our contention that a clear and systematic consciousness of the nature of these commitments will rid our thinking of the ambiguities Fred Riggs refers to.

Commitment to the World

"The world" has at present in the field of social sciences at least two important connotations: it is a category of analysis and an object of ethical cathexis.

The world as a category of thinking has a long historical tradition, but only in the last decades has it become a matter of critical concern among the scholars of various scientific fields. In the past the world was a fiction of philosophical speculation. The classical thinkers did not face a situation of technological and economic development and interdependence such as we face today. In their circumstances, the different societies were rather segregated from each other and the world had only a speculative interest. Today, however, technology has made the world a con-

9. Fred Riggs, "Administration and a Changing World Environment," *Public Administration Review*, July–Aug. 1968, p. 350.
10. Ibid.

crete single system. There is no isolated place in the planet. World problems exist now without solution, unless an effort of institution building is systematically undertaken on a planetary scale; at the same time, available and potential resources seem to exist capable of freeing all mankind from poverty; if there are still great disparities in the standards of living of different people, they must be an outcome of institutions rather than of scarce means. The main drawback, the thing that according to some precludes the universalization of welfare and the exorcising of threats of a widespread thermonuclear catastrophe, is the nation-state.

The position is seriously taken by scholars that knowledge, mainly in the form of technology, is taking on the role that capital once had in economic development. "Any invention man can imagine may eventually be realized,"[11] one futurologist says. Emmanuel Mesthene, director of Harvard Programs in Science and Technology, states: "We have now, or know how to acquire the technical capacity to do very nearly anything we want."[12] Consequently, progress, at least theoretically, could be unlimited in the present days. Thus wealth has a new meaning. It is no longer exclusively nature-made. It is essentially man-made. One can create wealth through adequate management, i.e., applied knowledge. We have reached, at this point, an unprecedented modality of political economy. The circumstances are ripe for a new Adam Smith whose assignment would be to write, not *The Wealth of Nations,* but *The Wealth of the World.* In fact, indications are that such treatises are being written by several people. Individual authorities and organizations like the United Nations and the World Bank are already relying on the assumption that a world economy exists and that it can be managed as whole, and the notion of a gross world product is becoming an analytical tool. It is not accidental that President Nixon launched his first message on *The State of the World.*

These are positive signs that the world has increasingly become

11. Richard Kostelanetz, ed., *Beyond Left and Right* (New York: Morrow, 1968), p. xxv.
12. Quoted in Victor C. Ferkiss, *Technological Man: The Myth and Reality* (New York: Braziller, 1969), p. 20.

a mandatory category of inquiry. The age of world development has come. This fact, although largely unrealized by the average man everywhere,[13] has enormous consequences in the scientific community in general. It certainly has a revolutionary impact in the very disciplinary field this book is particularly concerned with: development administration.

Indeed, if development administration, as a discipline and profession, makes sense, its business is to study issues and problems of world development, what its conditions and limits are, how to approach it, how to promote it. Such business demands an effort of conceptual creativity, ingenuity in the designing of adequate strategies of resources allocation, and last but not least, a formulation of goals to be attained. There is, however, a danger that the notion of world development may become captive to criteria alien to its intrinsic nature. A brief reflection about what conception of world development is more cogent for our profession is in order here. It is possible to differentiate three conceptions of world development.

World development can first be approached from a utopian standpoint. There are, of course, people who wish a world better than the present: religious authorities, visionaries, pacifists, artists, idealists. Their method of creating such a world is ordinarily exhortation or appeal to the generosity of those who are wealthy and powerful or the example of their own life, in which they incarnate the ideal of universal fraternity. One could include among the supporters of this idea people of varied orientation; churchmen of several denominations, a missionary writer like Albert Schweitzer, popular idols like the Beatles, and even many of the so-called hippies. However, although agencies of this sort may perform an important pedagogic role by making visible the misery of conformism, nevertheless, their actions have remote effects, if any. They count too much on the demonstrative effects of their attitudes and lose sight of the fact that social systems can hardly be changed by simple exhortation.

A second approach deserves to be labeled "sectarian." For

13. About perception of the world see several articles in H. C. Kelman, ed., *International Behavior* (New York: Holt, Rinehart and Winston).

instance, hegemonic powers conceive the ideal world according to their own conveniences. The so-called "socialist world" and "free world" are illustrations of this approach. In each of these political fields, external aid, economic aid, and technical assistance are given by centric to peripheral nations, primarily for hegemonic reasons. It is true that international transactions within each of these fields are not necessarily exploitative. Effective aid has been given by the United States and the Soviet Union to their respective allies. Hegemonies have been a chronic fact of mankind's history and perhaps the main trait of the utopian character is impatience and inability to deal with facts and to understand what has been called the "ruse of history." There are always latent processes in history that sometimes deceive hegemonic intents. Very often, these are the processes which paradoxically turn hegemonies into blind agents of progress. One has to face hegemonies *sine ira ac studio*, without reifying them either as intrinsically good or bad. Such reification is typical of many who employ the term imperialism without sociological expertise. The expression "third world" is also misleading and sectarian. It is an alienated way of legitimizing the two other worlds. This poor metaphor is serviceable rather to vested interests of politicians and is therefore questionable from the standpoint of comparative social science. There are muckrakers in our field and often Machiavellian designs are disguised under generous pleas. It is certainly true that "in our era, as never before, every intellectual revolution" has created "its own conservative class"[14] or establishment. In these circumstances, the critical challenge of development administration, as well as of social science in general, is to find an approach to world development "beyond left and right,"[15] i.e., transcending any conservative vested interest.

The possibilistic[16] approach to world development is our next concern. The task of the scientific community towards world

14. Kostelanetz, p. xxi.
15. Ibid.
16. About the possibilistic approach see Guerreiro-Ramos, "Modernization: Towards a Possibility Model," in *Developing Nations: Quest for a Model*, ed. Beling and Totten (New York: Van Nostrand Reinhold, 1970).

development is to convert concrete possibilities into action. Those are possibilities within our immediate reach, not abstract ones. If one reads the present accurately and sensitively, he realizes that mankind as a whole has already passed the stage of necessity. As R. Buckminster Fuller has observed, although now the capability exists "of providing 100 per cent of living humanity with all the basic materials of life, only about one-half are now so fortunate."[17] In these circumstances, our capacity to contribute as public or development administrators to governmental policies is narrowly limited by our conformity to the prevailing institutionalized interests.

Public administration and particularly development administration has been historically associated with the nation-state. It now faces a dilemma: although the nation-state may still have a viable role to play, it is nevertheless very often a handicap to world development. A choice has to be made. The world is not only a category of scientific analysis, but also, as we have pointed out, an object of ethical cathexis. The traditional association of public administration with the nation-state exposes the practitioners to ambiguities. Ambiguity is a permanent dimension of the human condition. But the way one gets rid of ambiguity may occasionally damage the ethos of science and scholarship.

An incident in the contemporary history of social science nicely illustrates the thorny dilemma. During the discussion of the Camelot project, Kalman H. Silvert took a position stating that "American social science is in a crisis of ethics,"[18] explaining that such a crisis had long been recognized "as latent by sensitive observers."[19] Of course, the closure of the Camelot case does not indicate that the profession of social scientist in this country will no longer face ethical dilemmas. But what the Camelot case made clear is that no scholar can be indifferent to the ethical require-

17. Cited in Kostelanetz, p. xxv.
18. Kalman H. Silvert, "American Academic Ethics and Social Research Abroad: The Lesson of Project Camelot," in *The Rise and Fall of Camelot Project,* ed. I. L. Horowitz (Cambridge, Mass.: M.I.T. Press, 1967), p. 80. On ethical implications of development administration, see Dail Neugarten, "A Critical Review of the Role of Social Scientists Within the Field of Development Administration," mimeographed, School of Public Administration, Univ. of Southern California, May, 1969.
19. Ibid.

ments of science, whatever it may be. Silvert's position is exemplary to the extent that it shows that the profession of social science entails an ethical engagement. He writes, "I . . . am an engaged scholar. By 'engaged' I mean that I am personally concerned with the course of social events; by 'scholar' I mean that I attempt not only to use objective procedures but also to take care that the specific questions I ask are theoretically determined and not the fruit of passion."[20] Such an engagement is more than an individual characteristic. It is rather an essential qualification of the scientist in general.

World development tends these days to become the ultimate goal of the scientific community, a point effectively demonstrated by the results of a recent survey undertaken by Daniel Lerner and Albert H. Tech among scientists working at CERN—the cooperative twelve-nation European Organization for Nuclear Research, in Geneva, Switzerland. It is not appropriate to review in this paper the revealing quantitative results of the survey. What it is important to stress is the conclusion that there is among scientists "a trend toward transnational solutions,"[21] and "the frame of reference within which they evaluate nations and world problems and policies is certainly much larger than their own national origins and loyalties."[22] In other words, they tend to refuse to behave as what Marshall Sahlins calls "scholastics of cold war theology."[23] One would assume that social scientists have no specific reason to behave differently.

Some pertinent considerations could be addressed to those who think that the possibility approach to world development is impractical. One could argue: How can a scientist put his world commitment ahead of his duties as citizen of a given nation? This is, indeed, a thorny question. No general conclusive answer can be given.

One can counterargue, though, that above the level of mundane problems of everyday life, the nature of the citizen's duties

20. Ibid., p. 82.
21. Daniel Lerner and Albert H. Tech, "Internationalism and World Politics Among CERN Scientists," *Bulletin of the Atomic Scientists,* Feb. 1970, p. 4.
22. Ibid., p. 10.
23. Marshall Sahlins, "The Established Order: Do Not Fold, Spindle or Mutilate," in Horowitz, p. 78.

and national interests is far from being clear. Who or what categories or groups would be in the best position to formulate the interests of a nation? What are the criteria according to which they are determined? Buckminster Fuller pointed out that "to ask a politician to lead [the scientist] is to ask the tail of a dog to lead the dog."[24] This may sound arrogant. It would be, if Fuller meant that the scientists have been given the privilege of leading the rest of the citizens, which is not the case. The greatest threat mankind would face in these days would be the political conformism of the scientific communities in the hegemonic countries.

In pursuing the goal of world development scientists have to consider the political feasibility of their policies. This term is taken from Dror, who defines political feasibility as "the probability that it will be sufficiently acceptable to the various secondary decisionmakers, executors, interest groups, and publics whose participation or acquiescence is needed, that it can be translated into action."[25] Scientists are not above the polity. But they may feel a duty of trying to influence public policy making toward world development, within the constraints of political feasibility. Sometimes such constraints are too narrow, in which case they may be exposed to an ethical dilemma. How to cope with such a dilemma is a matter that cannot be treated with a univocal prescription.

Commitment to Human Growth

The affluent context has been making us increasingly aware of the exploitative character of existing public bureaucracies. The capacity of thinking affluent thoughts is becoming widespread over the world, even in areas usually called underdeveloped. This trend undermines the legitimacy of prevailing administrative systems. The abolition of the fundamental scarcities that have thwarted human development throughout history is now a concrete possibility. To the extent that people, mainly intellectuals, live always a step ahead of their immediate present, they are asking for new forms of organizations, designed according to

24. Cited in Kostelanetz, p. xxxvi.
25. Yehezkel Dror, *Public Policymaking Reexamined* (San Francisco: Chandler, 1968), p. 35.

requirements that never in the past have obtained. The fact is that the anachronism of the existing formats of public bureaucracies is stunningly visible. We are reaching a point in history where the prediction of Saint-Simon can be accomplished, i.e., the stage in which the administration of things makes unnecessary the administration of persons. Management today tends to be rather an art of creating wealth than a technique of maximizing and manipulating scarce resources.[26] In the present era of research and development, organizations can be designed as complex systems in which the exploitation of machines brings a much higher rate of return than the exploitation of the human labor force. In the last two decades, new types of machinery have been conceived, and already implemented on a limited scale, which change the nature of management in our times. In fact, from the vantage point of the available technology, what most of us are teaching in classes and writing in books is rather folk management than scientific management. The so-called "knowledge industry" tends to become a commanding sector of the productive structure, and every society in the world will be affected by this trend.

The postindustrial machine already in existence is so different from the machine ordinarily known that one wonders if the same word is appropriate to designate both of them. It is an intelligent, flexible, and purposive robot whose activities can be programed by tape to attack assignments as they arise. It works with its own control system and eliminates the need of directly productive human labor. One can foresee, resulting from the widespread utilization of new machines, an increasing "ephemeralization"[27] of the environment, i.e., the shrinkage in size and weight of the productive devices, with, however, a progressive increase of outputs per unit of energy and raw material. A concrete example of the new machine is the one available now to make automobile tailpipes.[28] It is no longer constituted of jigs, dies, fixtures, and settings. Instead, it is less costly and smaller than its predecessor

26. Kostelanetz, pp. xvii–xli.
27. "Efficiency = doing more with less. Efficiency ephemeralizes." See R. Buckminster Fuller, *Nine Chains to the Moon* (Carbondale: Southern Illinois Univ. Press, 1963), p. 279.
28. Bernard J. Muller-Thym, "The Meaning of Automation," in Kostelanetz, p. 53.

and functions as a purposive servomechanism, with its activities programed by tape. Instead of only one kind of tailpipe, as in earlier manufacture, it can produce, in successive steps, eighty different types of tailpipes at the same speed and cost as eighty machines of the old type.[29] Ephemeralization, as visualized by Fuller, is becoming pervasive; the whole social system is to be changed, and what Robert M. Maynard has pointed out is not unrealistic:

> Of the pillars of our society, property and work, the first has now been transformed; it has changed from visible goods into a series of claims, and the second is certain to disappear. We are going to have to live in a world without work, a world without want, a world without disease, and if we are to live at all, in a world without war.[30]

These concrete trends constitute the background of our speculative efforts about the nature of what has been called the "new public administration." It is time now for us to start all over again. The impact of these trends or possibilities is generating unrest, impatience, rebelliousness. The new generations, particularly, feel that organizations and bureaucracies, and even social systems as they predominantly exist, are prisons. They do not have the perspective of many of us who are older and have been around during the transition from the old to the new. They want the future now, as Margaret Mead[31] has stressed. Dwight Waldo equates this urgency with revolution and wisely points out: "Raised in the midst of affluence, our children can afford altruism in a way we couldn't—or thought we couldn't. Bitter irony: the 'Square World' that they reject is what made it possible for them to reject the 'Square World.' "[32] Indeed present organizations and public bureaucracies were designed to be effective in scarcity complexes. And they have proved to be very successful, but at

29. Ibid.
30. Quoted in John R. Platt, *The Step to Man*, (New York: Wiley, 1966), p. 158.
31. Margaret Mead, *Culture and Commitment* (New York: Doubleday, 1970).
32. Dwight Waldo, "Public Administration in a Time of Revolutions," *Public Administration Review*, July–Aug. 1968, p. 365.

the very moment when they have accomplished their goals, because of such efficiency, they are no longer needed. The emerging values of affluence make them intolerable, and if they do not change or are not replaced by more expendable sociotechnical structures, present human problems will reach a threatening criticality.

The bureaucratic model which Max Weber synthesized in his famous ideal-type still dominates our prevailing management practice.[33] Consciously or unconsciously the captives of vested interests, many practitioners are trying to solve today's questions with yesterday's solutions. Therefore another kind of dilemma is challenging our discipline and profession. We are caught between powerful pressures of maintenance of the status quo and the imperative of social renewal on a large scale. The extant model of organization and bureaucracy meets neither the imperatives of human growth nor the requirement of revamping the macrosocial system—this at a time when the "interval between a problem's emergence and its potential criticality"[34] is shorter than ever.

We have been relatively successful in demolishing the hierarchical model in the field of theory. Pioneering investigators— like Whyte, Argyris, Maslow, Warren Bennis, McGregor, Presthus, Likert, Mouton and Blake, Herbert Shepard, and others— have demonstrated the obsolescence of that model from the standpoint of human needs. The general contention of these authors is that such a model works at high psychological costs, since it is based on a type of repressive socialization of participants in the organization. It "gives rise to practices and relationships that duplicate childhood to a considerable extent."[35] A careful examination of the psychological implications of such a model supports the conclusion that it is largely a refinement of the master-slave relationship.

33. "Under the influence of the primitive monistic ideal, modern organizations are modeled more on the parent-child relationship than on the adult relationships of equals and colleagues. Attempts to maintain the legitimacy of the ideal lead to a great deal of hypocrisy and pretense and to the creation of myths, such as the 'ignorance of the masses,' the 'indispensability of leadership' and the 'magical power of fear.'" Victor A. Thompson, *Modern Organization* (New York: Knopf, 1966), p. 20.

34. Biller, p. 19.

35. Thompson, p. 95.

The master-slave relationship may have been effective in its historical setting. What makes us today aware of its alienated character is our commitment to a value system that is becoming a normative standard for social systems. Thus one cannot agree with Victor Thompson's statement that "organization theory is not concerned with personality," nor when he writes: "Fortunately, the very general standard personality assumed by organization theory fits most people, otherwise, organizations would have to be managed from top to bottom by psychiatrists."[36] Evaluative criteria of human behavior have changed throughout history. They are today in rapid transition. The master-slave relationship prevailing in ancient societies was also one in which most people fit; it may even be considered healthy in its specific context. However, later historical developments engendered ethical imperatives that made that type of relationship untenable. On the other hand, what has been precisely demonstrated today is the fact that the people who best fit the "modern" organization are sick. Whyte's *The Organization Man* is an indictment. In Presthus's *The Organizational Society,* all patterns of accommodations described as typical of the "modern" bureaucracy are conducive to pathological behavior. Thompson's argument is statistical, quantitative. But the statistical normality he relies on does not reflect fundamental proclivities of the human being. Conformity is not synonymous with health and, as pointed out by Eric Fromm, there is a pathology of normality:

> What is so deceptive about the state of mind of the members of a society is the "consensual validation" of their concepts. It is naively assumed that the fact that the majority of the people share certain ideas or feelings proves the validity of these ideas and feelings. Nothing is further from the truth. Consensual validation as such has no bearing whatsoever on reason or mental health. Just as there is a "folie à deux" there is a "folie à millions." The fact that millions of people share the same vices does not make these vices virtues, the fact that they share so many errors does not make the errors

36. Thompson, pp. 8–9.

to be truths, and the fact that millions of people share the same forms of mental pathology does not make these people sane.[37]

Dropouts and hippies are today living critics of the modern organization. They express in acute terms the general malaise disguised under the conformity of those who apparently fit the modern organization. Thus organization theory must be subsumed under a theory of human development, with the healthy personality as one of its paramount concerns.

At the level of macrosocial systems, identical reservations are being voiced against the effectiveness on the existing model of bureaucracy. As Dwight Waldo points out, "The twentieth century . . . we know was hardly the goal of Elizabeth, of Louis XIV, of the Great Elector; the administrative instruments sharpened and wielded by them were not directed toward achievement of the late twentieth century's definition of development."[38] In other words, the Weberian bureaucratic model has today become an anachronism. We need, in centric as well as in peripheral nations, a new model of development organizational systems. Victor Thompson has remarked: "Development administration is in the crisis period; it desperately needs new ideas."[39] Thompson seems to assume that development administration is for export only; he does not see it as also required if problems are to be solved in centric countries like the United States. But development administration begins at home. Keeping in mind this objection, the following statement by Thompson seems perfectly true.

Administrative practice and principles of the West have derived from preoccupation with control and therefore have little value for development administration in underde-

---

37. Erich Fromm, *The Sane Society* (New York: Fawcett World Library, 1967), p. 23.
38. D. Waldo, "Development in the West: The Administrative Framework," paper prepared in connection with a seminar on Development: The Western View, held at the State University of New York, Albany, 24 Sept.–4 Oct. 1968 (unpublished manuscript), p. 33.
39. V. Thompson, "Administrative Objectives for Development Administration," *Administrative Science Quarterly* 9 (June, 1964): 108. Cited by Berton H. Kaplan, "Notes on a Non-Weberian Model of Bureaucracy: The Case of Development Bureaucracy," *Administrative Science Quarterly*, Dec. 1968, p. 479.

veloped countries where the need is for an adaptive admin- istration, one that can incorporate constant change. How- ever, adaptive administrative principles can be derived from the researches and theories of the behavioral sciences, and these should become the administrative objectives of de- velopment administrators. Illustrative of such objects are the following: an innovative atmosphere; the operationalizing and sharing of goals; the combining of planning (thinking) and acting (doing); the minimization of parochialism; the diffusion of influence; the increasing of toleration of inter- dependence; and the avoidance of bureaupathology.[40]

Without a commitment to humanistic values, social science, and therefore administrative science, is meaningless. Since its birth, social science has been a useful tool for reorienting the his- torical process to the extent that its value content has enabled us to transcend the present and to design countersystem models. An ethical project for the future has always been at the root of the most influential classical social scientists. Saint-Simon's and Comte's positive stage, Spencer's postindustrial society, and Marx's communism were value-loaded images of the future, from whose vantage point the remains of the *ancien régime* could be criticized and practically overcome. The very Weberian model of bureaucracy has accomplished a revolutionary function. Its full implementation was functionally required to speed up social and economic development in capitalistic terms, when feudalistic drawbacks still thwarted such development. It was thus an in- strument of socialization, or incorporation of the ascending mid- dle class into the existing social systems. Today, however, the intimate association of the bureaucracy with the values and culture of the middle classes is a drawback to the developmental process. Social scientists now face the task of designing counter- systems according to new images of the future.

Today's objective of development, in centric as well as per- ipheral nations, is well-being for all citizens.[41] Classically con-

40. Cited in Kaplan, pp. 478–79.
41. See Eric Trist, "The Relation of Welfare and Development in the Tran- sition to Post-Industrialism," paper prepared for the Canadian Center for Com-

ceived as occasional outcomes of charity and philanthropy, well-being of all citizens today is a systematic goal of the state everywhere and a universal right. Development policies are oriented to the distribution of wealth rather than its concentration in a few hands. Thus, while in today's so-called advanced countries, the GNP per capita developed at a rate of less than 1.5 percent during the period 1890–1950, at least 3 percent is considered the minimum today in the peripheral countries.[42] Within the centric countries, distributive policies are identically considered from the standpoint of similar criterion. To achieve this intent, there is a need to resocialize organizational systems.

In this perspective, the organization-client relationships tend to become a central issue. It has been correctly observed that classical bureaucracy has been "a key medium through which the middle class maintains its advantaged position vis-à-vis the lower class."[43] Under present conditions it is losing its original role of facilitating upward mobility and becoming a factor of rigidity in the social structures. The poor in advanced nations and the masses in the peripheral countries are unable to influence existing bureaucratic structures. Middle-class bureaucrats hardly understand the "culture of poverty," and abiding by impersonal rules, aggravate the powerlessness and alienation of the underprivileged in face of governmental services. On the other hand, the impersonal rationale that is congenial to middle-class clients gives them an advantage in dealing with governmental services. As has been pointed out, "Just as is the case of children and adults in actuality, where parents enforce the rules of behavior on their children which they violate themselves, 'childlike' lower class clients are forced to conform to rules and to patterns of treatment

munity Studies, Ottawa Seminar, Nov. 1967 (mimeographed publication of Socio-Technical Systems Division, Western Management Science Institute, Univ. of California, Los Angeles, Feb. 1968), p. 4.

42. See Bertram M. Gross, "The State of the Nation: Social Systems Accounting," in *Social Indicators*, ed. Raymond A. Bauer (Cambridge, Mass.: M.I.T. Press, 1966), p. 253.

43. Gideon Sjoberg, Richard A. Brymer, and Buford Farris, "Bureaucracy and the Lower Class," *Sociology and Social Research* 50, no. 3 (April 1966): 325. See also Gideon Sjoberg, M. Donald Hancock, and Orion White, Jr., *Politics in the Post-Welfare State: A Comparison of the United States and Sweden* (Carnegie Seminar, Department of Government, Univ. of Indiana, 1967).

which 'adult' middle-class clients are able to avoid."[44] No wonder programs such as Federal Job Corps and the War on Poverty so often fail, since their design and practice are oriented by criteria in conflict with the behavioral patterns of their clients. Plagued by a distorted perception of clients' needs and orientations, the conventional public policies often accentuate the problems they are supposed to cope with. A case in point is the "law and order" campaign. Because of middle-class bias, the more it is pursued, the more the curve of crimes and unrest rises.

In peripheral countries, the role of classical bureaucracy deserves some qualifications. Those countries are dual.[45] In each of them the modern is emerging in some spots and the rest of the territory is premodern. In such conditions bureaucracies accomplish contradictory functions. On one hand, they are a medium through which "middle sectors" are formed or subsidized and so facilitate upward social mobility; on the other hand, just as in centric nations, they perform custodial functions[46] the results of which are the alienation of most of their clients, who are usually underprivileged people and "account for events in the social sphere in terms of spiritual forces, chance, luck, and the like" and "have little or no sense of control of their own destiny."[47] Thus, nonprescriptive approaches are most indicated to design organizational systems in peripheral nations. In these countries, as pointed out by Sjoberg, one "must pay special attention to the whole resocialization process and the development of structures through which this process can effectively be carried out."[48] Developmental programs, with or without external support, when implemented through conventional bureaucratic services are very often coopted by the traditional manipulators of the social system

---

44. Orion F. White, Jr., "The Dialectical Organization: An Alternative to Bureaucracy," *PAR*, Jan.–Feb. 1969, p. 34.
45. The duality of peripheral countries is dialectical. On this subject, see Guerreiro-Ramos, *Administração e estratégia do desenvolvimento* (Rio de Janeiro: Fundação Getúlio Vargas, 1966), pp. 414–19.
46. See Sjoberg, Hancock, and White, p. 18.
47. Sjoberg, Brymer, and Farris, p. 331.
48. Gideon Sjoberg, "Ideology and Social Organization in Rapidly Developing Societies," *CAG Occasional Papers* (Bloomington, Ind.: American Society for Public Administration, Dec. 1966), p. 27.

and are consequently frustrated in their intentions. To eliminate this situation, resocializing organizations have to be created.

Commitment to Legitimacy

Social systems throughout the world today are, in different degrees, in a crisis of legitimacy. The Rousseaus and Lockes of contemporary times, so sorely needed, have not yet appeared. Public administration goes astray in circumstances where the requirements of legitimacy are confused. And ours is precisely such a time.

Max Weber was perhaps the first to realize that public administration meets its optimal conditions of effectiveness in legitimate polities. He also pointed out that the bases of legitimacy have changed historically. After distinguishing four ways of ascribing legitimacy to the social order, he observed: "Today the most usual basis of legitimacy is the belief in legality, the readiness to conform with rules which are formally correct and have been imposed by accepted procedure. The distinction between an order derived from voluntary agreement and one which has been imposed is only relative." And making the issue still more elusive, he adds: "So far as it is not derived merely from fear or from motives of expediency, a willingness to submit to an order imposed by one man or a small group, always in some sense implies a belief in the legitimate *authority* of the source imposing it."[49] However, many questions are left without answer. How can one detect the citizen's willingness to submit to an imposed order or belief? What is "formally correct"? How can one operationally evaluate an "accepted procedure"? Is a policy decision which is "formally correct" necessarily legitimate in all cases? Is an action which is not "formally correct" necessarily illegitimate in all cases? These are questions that probably will never have definitive answers. Nevertheless in the vagaries of the issue one certainty seems to be perceptible: public administration loses ethical ground when reduced to an expediency of naked force.

Fred Riggs has given profound thought to the subject of

49. Max Weber, "Legitimate Order and Types of Authority," in *Theories of Society,* ed. Parsons, Shils, Naegele, and Pitts (New York: Free Press, 1965), p. 233.

legitimacy as a meaningful issue in public administration. In Athens he met some civil servants of the Greek government who were in ethical stress. One of them, considering irresponsible and illegitimate the demands of the military government upon him, asked for advice: "What can I do?" And Riggs wonders if there is, in public administration, any clear guideline to apply to such a case. On the other hand, another civil servant, who holds a degree in public administration from a North American university, saw the military government as oriented to eliminating corruption and incompetence. This Greek civil servant and some others expressed their interest in inviting North American experts to help them. The situation is depicted by Riggs in order to highlight its perplexing nature.[50]

Indeed, definitive principles of public administration for dealing with controversial cases of legitimacy do not exist now, and maybe will never exist. But a serious concern with the matter is in itself a subjective factor of improvement of the quality of public administration. To ignore such a matter is certainly worse than to make it the objective of specific, continuous and systematic concern of public administrators. Acting in this way, at least one hopes to contribute to enforcing the effectiveness of the ethical deterrents to the use and abuse of naked force.

Furthermore, legitimacy is more than a matter of pure principle; it is a requirement of development to the extent that it makes the political and administrative system more responsive and responsible toward citizens' needs. "Developed systems," Leonard Binder observes, "tend to be more efficient in that the probability of a prolonged discrepancy between power and legitimacy is less likely."[51] When politicians and administrators obey the governmental commands only because they are threatened or are afraid of arbitrary sanctions against their decisions, the whole social system blocks its channels of feedback, without which maximization or optimization of human and nonhuman resources is hardly possible.

Arbitrary power is always prone to secrecy. It always reacts to

50. Riggs, *op. cit.*
51. Leonard Binder, *Iran: Political Development in a Changing Society* (Berkeley: Univ. of California Press, 1962), p. 47.

free flow of information as to a threat. Therefore it invariably begets distortive forms and rates of corruption, negative development, deterioration of the citizen's social behavior. Evidently, arbitrary power is not necessarily synonymous with a nondemocratic regime. There are nondemocratic and even dictatorial polities which are somehow legitimate, since they recognize themselves as limited by a set of norms, directly or indirectly accepted by the citizens. As Max Weber prudently remarked, the door is always open for the arbitrary power to legitimize itself by giving a consistent normative structure to the willingness of the citizens, when it really exists, to submit even to an imposed order. Without this "ethical minimum,"[52] the social fabric is led to a climate of confusion and disorder where public administration is no longer operative. Yet, arbitrary power, paradoxically, is intrinsically weak and unstable. Unwilling to establish the normative patterns necessary to transform force into authority, arbitrary power exists in a context where insurgency necessarily happens according to the logic of the self-fulfilling prophecy. The following statement of Riggs is in order here.

> We must know when to say that our administrative principles can no longer help because the context is one in which they cease to be relevant. If we saw insurgency movements as a natural consequence of the illegitimacy of governments rather than as the result of international subversion, and if we saw American aid to illegitimate governments as a sure way to undermine further whatever shreds of legitimacy they still have, our own policies might be dramatically revised.[53]

One can see that for obvious reasons there is a Siamese link between a centric country like the United States and Latin Amer-

---

52. "Law, the first and essential condition of the life of the groups, large and small, has aptly been called the 'ethical minimum.' As a matter of fact, the norms adequate to secure the continuation of the group (even if only precariously) constitute a bare minimum for the external existence of the individual as a social being." Georg Simmel, *The Sociology of Georg Simmel,* trans. Kurt H. Wolf (New York: Free Press, 1964), pp. 27–28.

53. Riggs, p. 361.

ica. One cannot say all that should be said about the study and practice of public administration in one of those countries without considering the state of the discipline in the United States.

As suggested before, legitimacy is also an essential condition for the improvement of the social intelligence of the policy. Although he relied on a dynamic and historical viewpoint, Max Weber did not visualize in modern times a legitimacy based on anything other than the belief in legality. Legality itself derives, however, from the aspiration to equality. Legality has been the most feasible equality in the industrial stage. But in the perspective of the postindustrial age, in which well-being tends to become a universal right, different equalities are to be institutionalized other than the equality before the law. One can address to legality the same criticisms that were applied above to the existing public bureaucracies and organizational systems. In contexts still plagued by extreme disparities in the social level of citizens' existence, legality accomplishes, rather, the role of system maintenance. Contemporary times are ripe for a redefinition of legitimacy. In a stage of development in which the well-being of all is feasible, governments enforce their legitimacy by showing their willingness or readiness to design public policies oriented to minimize social inequalities. Legality has been a strategy for minimizing social inequalities in the nineteenth century. In the late twentieth century a new sensibility to the problem has emerged. One realizes now that within the framework of legality, economic injustice can be institutionalized, i.e., economic development can take place without increasing participation in the GNP by the "bottommost groups."[54] The essential duty of the state now is to implement "inequality-reduction"[55] public policies. And even from the viewpoint of new currents in economics, the traditional GNP per capita is a very precarious measure of development. What essentially matters is the pattern according to which the income is distributed. Thus inequality, i.e., "the greater

54. See S. M. Miller, Martin Rein, Pamela Roby, and Bertram M. Gross, "Poverty, Inequality, and Conflict," in *Social Intelligence for America's Future,* ed. Bertram M. Gross (Boston: Allyn and Bacon, 1969), p. 284.

55. Ibid., p. 327.

accumulation of benefits and powers in one sector of society than another," is "a universal loss," since it violates one fundamental "human need . . . in all members of society, oppressors and oppressed alike; the need of men for each other."[56] This may sound facetious. However, the meaning of what economics is has changed. In fact, what has been called economics is a didactic fiction. There has never existed such a thing as the economic. The economic is the most salient feature of the social total phenomenon in situations of scarcity. Economics, as known and practiced up until recently, is a discipline valid only in a stage where no feasible alternative to gross inequalities between human beings and groups is discernible. In such conditions, development can take place only at a high price in human deprivation. But at the present level of productive forces, widespread well-being and development are no longer mutually exclusive. To the contrary, they are interdependent. Factors of production that the traditional economist used to overlook become relevant. Inequality as "income insufficiency" as well as "differential distribution of positive feelings"[57] is a loss for the global social system. Social accounting procedures are now necessary to assess the rates of idle productive capacity disguised under relative deprivation of human beings and groups.

Although these viewpoints have been generated in affluent societies, particularly in the United States, they can be applied, with adaptations in other contexts. More than that, the conformity to these approaches tends to become universal, since they express a social awareness that transcends national frontiers. It is probably true that complete equality will never be possible, that minimization of inequality is a continuing process. The new beliefs that constitute the basis of legitimacy today "must be translated into the choices and decisions that guide our individual and group living."[58] The issue of social indicators of progress seems to be of paramount importance for engaged social scientists and public administrators in particular. There is no science without

56. Perry Anderson, "Sweden: A Study in Social Democracy," *New Left Review*, May 1961. Cited in Gross, p. 328.
57. Miller et al., pp. 329, 326.
58. Lawrence K. Frank, cited in Trist, p. 50.

standards of measure. To assess the effectiveness of public administrative systems from the standpoint of well-being as a universal right is one of our compelling tasks today.

Some Selected Issues and Problems of Public Administration in Latin America

The three primary commitments described constitute the backdrop against which an effort will be made in the following paragraphs to examine the present situation of public administration in Latin America. One could argue that these commitments are different facets of a single thing—the *Zeitgeist*, the spirit of the times. What matters is to make clear that without these value premises, any search for a new theoretical framework in our academic field would be in vain.

Although systematic studies about public administration in Latin America are scarce, the consciousness of its main features and problems is widespread among learned citizens and scholars of various concerns. Publications are rare which have the panoramic scope of *Toward Strategies for Public Administration Development in Latin America*, edited by John C. Honey. One hopes that efforts of the same intent will be undertaken by other scholars and by institutions like the United Nations, the Organization of American States, and the Interamerican Development Bank. On the other hand, there is a great need for specific analysis of public-administration issues in the different countries of Latin America—for example, Lawrence Graham's *Civil Service Reform in Brazil*, Robert Daland's *Brazilian Planning*, Frank Sherwood's *Institutionalizing the Grass Roots in Brazil*.

In the following paragraphs, an intermediary line between the panoramic and the specifically national will be adopted, i.e., selected Latin American issues and problems of public administration will be discussed from a theoretical standpoint. A preference will be given to neglected aspects of such issues and problems.

Linkage Framework of Public Administration in Latin America

Let us now face an important question: What are the theoretical consequences of the emergence of the world as a single system for the students of public administration in Latin America? One of the most current theoretical deficiencies of the studies on public administration in the region is the neglect of the world system or a distorted view of its impingement on the different Latin American countries. In general, the authors, natives or foreigners, tend to take for granted that each of the Latin American nations is a closed system. This assumption is likewise pervasive of studies in fields other than public administration.[59] Social scientists, natives or foreigners, concerned with the Latin American countries have not been sufficiently aware of the fact that the nation is rapidly becoming an inadequate unit of analysis.[60] What is happening now to this concept is much like what happened to the concept of race, which was once an anthropological category and today has been largely expelled from science. Boulding has observed that today a social scientist cannot be a nationalist for the same reasons that a biologist cannot be a racist.[61]

Because the world is no longer a conglomerate of segregated societies, but is already a single system, a global social science[62] is needed. No national society today can be understood on the basis of its internal processes and conditions alone. Nations are penetrated systems[63] in the sense that the allocation of their

59. See Lucian Pye, "The Formation of New States," in *Contemporary Political Science,* ed. Ithiel de Sola Pool (New York: McGraw-Hill, 1967), pp. 182–203.

60. See Karl Deutsch, "Nation and World," in de Sola Pool, pp. 204–27. In this chapter, Deutsch points out that "the nation-state has failed" (p. 217) and "is . . . becoming for its people a cognitive trap in times of peace and a death trap in the event of war" (p. 218).

61. See Kenneth Boulding, "Dare We Take the Social Sciences Seriously?" *American Behavorial Science* 10, no. 10 (June 1967): 15.

62. The term "global" has been employed with equivalent meaning by Wilbert Moore in his *Order and Change* (New York: Wiley, 1967). In the chapter "Global Sociology: The World as a Singular System," he writes: "By global sociology I shall mean sociology of the globe, of mankind" (p. 266).

63. On the concept of nations as penetrated systems, see James N. Rosenau, "Pre-theories and Theories of Foreign Policy," in *Approaches to Comparative and International Politics,* ed. Barry Farrel (Evanston, Ill.: Northwestern Univ. Press, 1966), pp. 27–92. Rosenau's definition is: "A penetrated political system

resources and values results considerably from their need to cope with pressures from the international environment. Societies are continuously reacting and accommodating to the world system. Operational procedures have been recently designed[64] to focus on such transactions. For instance, the concept of linkage enables us to have a better understanding of phenomena that have been examined ordinarily from the standpoint of reified or metaphysical categories. Through linkages, penetrative processes take place normally throughout and across the world of nations. Such linkages are defined as recurrent patterns of behavior that originate in one system and generate correlative behavior in another.[65]

Studies about public administration in Latin American countries invariably underline phenomena like formalism, corruption, discontinuity in the policy-making process. However, the explanations of these phenomena have been largely impressionistic and often confuse cause and effect. Formalism cannot be explained with the psychological terms of imitation or demonstration effect. Formalism in Latin America is the outcome of pressures exerted by external and internal linkage groups, such as foreign governmental authorities granting credits, loans, or assistance; institutions like foreign banks, the International Monetary Fund, and so forth. Latin American countries are compelled to meet the terms of such agencies in order to get support for proposed policies. The institutional arrangements resulting from such transactions lead to formalism. Similar pressures are exerted by foreign investors and business groups to protect their interests. Thus, formalism in Latin America is quite largely a reaction to penetrative linkage processes. Moreover, formalistic administrative structures are not always a feature of administrative pathology. Sometimes they are part of a highly positive strategy of

---

is one in which nonmembers of a national society participate directly and authoritatively, through actions taken jointly with the society's members, in either the allocation of its values or the mobilization of support on behalf of its goals" (p. 65).

64. Mainly by Rosenau and his associates. See James N. Rosenau, ed., *Linkage Politics*, (New York: Free Press 1969).

65. This is a slight modification of Rosenau's definition, which reads as follows: ". . . any recurrent sequence of behavior that originates in one system and is reacted to in another." *Linkage Politics*, p. 45.

institution building and modernization.[66] Although the gap often exists between the normative content of such structures and concrete general social behavior, they nevertheless become factors of change in the middle or long range. The study of formalism in Latin America is still inaccurate. An analysis of this phenomenon from the standpoint of linkage agents, external and internal, is needed.

Similarly, corruption in Latin America has been overstated or misstated. First of all, corruption is chronic in all polities, centric and peripheral. One has the impression that the emphasis on the presence of corruption in Latin American polities is sometimes made for the sake of the picturesque color rather than for the sake of scientific rigor. Rigorous functional analyses of corruption in Latin American public bureaucracies is also needed. Besides its obvious dysfunctional roles, corruption has been a positive contextual strategy of development in the area. One has indications that corruption in Latin American countries may perform the "valuable function of a 'hedge' and safeguard against the full losses of a bad economic policy."[67] Again, an exact picture and evaluation of this phenomenon cannot be obtained without considering the role of external linkage groups. To what extent is corruption in Latin American bureaucracies an outcome of a vague complex of paternalism or of persistent cultural and psychological characteristics? Is there a Latin American "character," responsible for administrative corruption, or is such so-called "character" largely a persistent recurrence in the transactions of the area with its external linkages? To what extent, for instance, is the *quick buck*[68] of the foreign entrepreneurs investing in the area, in specific cases, a precipitating factor of corruption?[69] Answers to these questions are of great academic and practical interest.

66. On formalism from the standpoint of the world system, see Guerreiro-Ramos, *Administração e estratégia do desenvolvimento*, pp. 331–422.
67. See Nathaniel H. Leff in his "Economic Development Through Bureaucratic Corruption," *American Behavioral Scientist* 8, no. 3 (Nov. 1964): 11. See also Leff, *Economic Policy-Making and Development in Brazil, 1947–1964* (New York: Wiley, 1968); and J. S. Nye, "Corruption and Political Development: A Cost Analysis," *American Political Science Review* 61, no. 2 (June 1967).
68. See Moore, p. 165.
69. See Douglas Chalmers, "Developing on the Periphery: External Factors in Latin America," in Rosenau, *Linkage Politics*, p. 89; also W. Baer and M. H. Simonson, "American Capital and Brazilian Nationalism," in *Foreign Investment in Latin America*, ed. Marvin D. Bernstein (New York: Knopf, 1968), p. 279.

Another point deserving attention is the cognitive orientations of scholars toward the penetrative processes taking place in the area. A certain ideological fundamentalism is pervasive in some studies and reports according to which penetrative processes are intrinsically exploitative or detrimental to the area, which obviously is not true. In the present conditions of the world, penetrative processes are irreversible, and one certainly agrees with Douglas Chalmers that the desire to eliminate the influence of the foreigner on Latin American countries seems quixotic.[70] This influence has been examined by some writers who still work with a nineteenth-century concept of imperialism. A country like the United States is sometimes reified as an agency intrinsically imperialistic, and North American investors in the region are globally viewed with suspicion. This approach is not only scientifically inaccurate, it is detrimental to the improvement of the international capabilities of Latin American countries. There is no place in this chapter to discuss the notion of imperialism, in all its ramifications, but its application in the analysis of Latin American problems in the fashion some scholars still adopt is undoubtedly outdated.[71] Of course hegemonic influences are exerted on Latin American countries. However, to declare exploitative all external penetration into Latin American countries is far from factual. For example, a Brazilian historian of economics, a militant communist, has said in polemic against some of his companions in ideology: "In no other period of the Brazilian history has the [Brazilian] bourgeoisie improved its business and enriched itself so much as during the past twenty-five years in which imperialist capital literally submerged our economy. And it improved and enriched itself largely due to the enforcement, impulse, and example which the imperialist undertakings and initiative brought."[72] If imperialism has had such effects on the Brazilian economy, then it could be more appropriately called by another name, since the traditional one is heavily loaded with ideology. Nevertheless, a similar remark is made by an economist

70. Chalmers, p. 93.
71. On this issue, see J. Galtung, "A Structural Theory of Imperialism," *Journal of Peace Research* 8, no. 2 (1971).
72. Caio Prado Junior, *A Revolução Brasileira* (São Paulo: Editôra Brasiliense, 1966), pp. 188–89.

of ECLA, who points out that "imperialist exploitation, as depicted in the Latin American 'social' novel, is, generally speaking, a thing of the past. Today the enterprises with the highest wages and the best working conditions are often precisely those belonging to the great foreign consortiums."[73] One may say that the international environment of Latin America has changed and is changing, although the agencies of public policy do not seem to be fully equipped to deal with the new world configuration.

Public policy making promises to become a key issue for Latin American countries in the coming years. Economic development in Latin America has scarcely been a result of deliberate and systematic public policies. Although traditionally the state has always interfered decisively in economic development, middle- and long-range public policy making has scarcely been institutionalized in the public administrative systems of the area.[74] Developmental policies have been adopted and implemented by governmental authorities, but largely under the urgency of taking advantage of contingencies originated outside the area.[75] In the present international environment, the possibilities are narrowing for Latin America to continue to finance its development by taking advantage, through improvised policies, of eventual "breakthroughs in price or market" for its traditional exports, as Charles Anderson has observed.[76] Indications exist that in the new international environment such a traditional Latin American model of policy making no longer works.

In the present world system conditions are emerging which require an innovative effort from Latin American policymakers— new forms of trading and banking and multinational corporations. This writer is not competent to examine financial and economic implications of this transition, and only intends to stress that

73. Anibal Pinto, "Political Aspects of Economic Development," in *Obstacles to Change in Latin America*, ed. Claudio Veliz (New York: Oxford Univ. Press, 1969), pp. 15–16.

74. On the economic background within which public administration operates in Latin America, see Roberto de Oliveira Campos, "Public Administration in Latin America," in *Public Administration, A Key to Development*, ed. Burton A. Baker (Washington: The Graduate School, U.S. Dept. of Agriculture, 1964).

75. Pinto, p. 10.

76. Charles W. Anderson, "The Changing International Environment of Development and Latin America in the 1970's," mimeographed (Univ. of Wisconsin, Madison, Jan. 1970).

these events have significant impact in the field of public administration. It is estimated that by the year 2000 probably more than 50 percent of the world market will be internationalized,[77] which means, in the words of Servan-Schreiber, that business everywhere will have outgrown national boundaries. To meet this situation, the Latin American countries need to have administrative capabilities enabling them not only to draw resources from the international arena but also to build within their frontiers a sound and rational business environment.

Problems of Optimizing Administrative Models for Latin America

The needs people are aware of are basically the same everywhere. The feeling that the existing organizational systems are, in general, inadequate to fulfill these needs is ubiquitous in centric as well as in peripheral nations. From the standpoint of its value system, the world is already unified. However, the gap is striking between values and facts. In academic circles, to the extent that management and administration tend to be subsumed to a general theory of human needs, we trust we are inventing possible futures rather than accommodating students to "reality." We discover now that the traditional principles of our discipline have been designed for a "square world"; they are declared to be rules of thumb, "proverbs." The trend is toward McGregor's theory Y, 9, 9 managerial style, which Blake and Mouton see as a conciliation of a high level of production with high self-actualization of the workers; and toward Maslow's eupsychian

77. Judd Polk, "The Rise of World Corporations," *Saturday Review*, 22 Nov. 1969, pp. 32–33. On international business management, see John Fayerweather, *International Business Management: A Conceptual Framework* (New York: McGraw-Hill, 1969); Yain Aharon, *The Foreign Investment Process* (Cambridge, Mass.: Harvard Univ. Press, 1966); Richard N. Farmer, Hans Schollhammer, and Robert W. Stevens, eds., *Readings in International Business* (Bloomington: Graduate School of Business, Indiana Univ., 1967); S. Benjamin Prasad, *Management in International Perspective* (New York: Appleton-Century-Crofts, 1967); for a critical appraisal, see Hans Schollhammer, "The Comparative Management Theory Jungle," *Academy of Management Journal* 12, no. 1 (1969); Frank Brandenberg, *The Development of Latin American Private Enterprise* (Washington: National Planning Association, 1964); Theodore Geiger, *The General Electric Company in Brazil*, (Washington: National Planning Association, 1961); John Friedmann, "The Institutional Context," in *Action Under Planning*, ed. Bertram Gross (New York: McGraw-Hill, 1967).

management, nonhierarchical organization. John Stuart Mill said it is better to be Socrates unhappy than to be a contented pig. Many of us are certainly unhappy Socrateses.

The value of management and administration theory exposes the practitioner to cognitive dissonance when he has to give workable solutions to problems of the "real" world. If he is in an area like Latin America, his difficulties in keeping his work consistent with his values are particularly great. Are we expected to apply theory Y in affluent contexts, and theory X where scarcity prevails? If it is a fact that even in the United States the existing organization is far from the managerial styles which we think meet criteria of excellence, should we resign ourselves to implementing coercive and authoritarian organizational designs in peripheral countries?

These are relevant questions when we try to orient ourselves for tasks and duties in peripheral areas. There are no satisfactory answers. Nevertheless some tentative guidelines can be formulated.

First, what matters most is to live in a manner consistent with the value premises of our discipline. One can presume that a context is never so backward but it contains some concrete possibility of improvement. The workers in poor countries realize that organizations function within constraints. As a part of the global system, the organization cannot do much better than the global system can possibly do. However, the attitude of administrators on matters of resource allocation is a decisive factor in optimizing human energies. A healthy attitude enables the administrator to discover optimizing strategies even in poor countries. Such an attitude, in practice, generates positive participation of the workers when coercive procedures cannot achieve this.

In short, humanistic administrative styles require from the practitioner the skill to discover, through action-research, ad hoc procedures of resource optimization. Thus, the more we work to develop action-research models, the more we improve our skill to develop peripheral areas.[78]

78. See Richard N. Farmer and Barry M. Richman, *Comparative Management and Economic Progress* (Homewood, Ill.: Irwin, 1965). See C. West Churchman and F. E. Emery. "On Various Approaches to the Study of Organizations," *Proceedings,* International Conference on Operational Research and Social Sciences,

The pragmatic prospects of such models in Latin America have already been demonstrated. For instance, one of the most successful programs of development administration undertaken in Latin America, on the basis of an action-research model, has been the Vicos case. Only some of its main aspects need to be reported here. In January 1952 Cornell University in collaboration with the Peruvian Indigenist Institute started an integrated effort with the objective of modernizing Vicos, a Peruvian manor or large estate, which had a population of 1,703 monolingual Quechua-speaking Indians who since colonial times had been serfs and peons. The Hacienda Vicos, situated in an intermountain valley about 250 miles from the capital city of Lima, until 1952 had a typical oligarchical property regime and power structure. Within five years Vicos had been transformed: a democratic land reform was executed and power devolution to the peasants was achieved through the implementation of new political and administrative institutions, as well as a significant improvement in social and economic standards of the community. A detailed study of this experiment is recommended to those who are interested in contextual models of development administration. The Vicos project is a demonstration that humanistic client-oriented organizations can be implemented successfully in the most precarious environment of the poor regions of the world.[79]

Similar, though of less magnitude than Vicos, is the regional development project led by Morris Asimov in the Cairi Valley of the state of Ceará, Brazil. This project is a pertinent example of how to design ad hoc strategies and policies to mobilize and pool resources in poor areas and initiate its middle circles in rational technique of management of small enterprises.[80]

Cambridge, England, 14–18 Sept. 1964; F. E. Emery and E. L. Trist, "The Casual Texture of Organizational Environments," *Human Relations* 18, no. 1 (1965); F. E. Emery, "The Next Thirty Years: Concepts, Methods, and Anticipations, *Human Relations* 20, no. 3 (1967); Berton H. Kaplan, "Notes on a Non-Weberian Model of Bureaucracy: The Case of Development Bureaucracy," *Administrative Science Quarterly* 13, no. 3 (Dec. 1968); and William Foote Whyte, "Imitation or Innovation: Reflections on the Institutional Development in Peru," *Administrative Science Quarterly* 13, no. 3 (Dec. 1968).

79. See *The American Behavioral Scientist* 8, no. 7 (March 1965), special issue, "The Vicos Case," with articles by A. R. Holmberg, M. C. Vasquez, P. L. Doughty, J. O. Alers, H. F. Dobyns, and H. D. Lasswell.

80. See Morris Asimov, "Project Identification, Selection and Implementation on the Local Level: Experience Realized and Lessons Learned in N.E. Brazil," paper presented to the Second Session of the Conference of African Planners,

Other systematic efforts which are relevant but less pragmatic may eventually result in the improvement of the management of resources of the area. These efforts are addressed to the preparation of practitioners with a trained sensitivity to the specific theoretical and operational requirements of policy making in the area. In this case, reference has to be made to research program in execution in Venezuela, undertaken by the Centro de Estudios de Desarrollo (Cendes) of the Central University of Venezuela and the Center for International Studies of Massachusetts Institute of Technology;[81] and the survey of twenty-six Peruvian villages coordinated by the Instituto de Estudios Peruanos and Cornell University.[82] Both of these endeavors rely in part on contextual approaches to the problems of the region. In both programs, public policy-making issues are studied from an interdisciplinary standpoint. Sometimes Latin American universities have been advised to establish departments equivalent to those of advanced countries. This bureaucratic viewpoint has led foreign observers to say that in Latin countries there is no political science,[83] simply because chairs of political science, as conceived in advanced centers, are not often found in the universities of the area. Nevertheless, Venezuelan and Peruvian programs have a sound view of scientific institution building. One of the participants in the Peruvian survey observes that a "strategy of imitation" is detrimental to Peru and recommends interdisciplinary integration rather than emphasis on specialized fields such as political science, anthropology, sociology, psychology.[84] Whyte writes:

> The present content of these disciplines in the United States can be explained historically but cannot be justified on any logical basis. . . . It is my thesis that this very separation

Addis Ababa, 4–15 Dec. 1967 (U.N. Economic and Social Council E/CN.14/CAP/20, 29 Aug. 1967).

81. See Frank Bonilla and José A. Silva Michelena, *A Strategy for Research on Social Policy* (Cambridge, Mass.: M.I.T. Press, 1967).

82. See Whyte.

83. On this questionable viewpoint, see José Nun, "Notes on the Social Sciences in Latin America," in *Social Science in Latin America*, ed. M. Dieges Jr., and Bryce Wood (New York: Columbia Univ. Press, 1967).

84. Whyte, p. 380.

of methods among the fields is holding back the advance of knowledge in the United States.[85]

If we want to contribute to problem solving in the field of human and social development in peripheral areas, we have to be contextual also in disciplinary designs. This question cannot be examined here, although it is central in the reformulation of development administration.

Finally, we want to observe that a widespread effort to build client-centered microorganizations is highly needed in Latin America. The pioneering researches of Gideon Sjoberg and Orion White, Jr., are particularly indicative of what can be done within the framework of Latin American public administration.

The Problem of Legitimacy in Latin America

What are the main effects of Latin American standards of legitimacy on public administration? What should public administration practitioners do to improve such standards? These seem to be rather neglected issues. Certainly many authors have belabored the theme of political instability in Latin America and suggested that illegitimacy has been the persistent characteristic of its polities.[86] However, more accurate analysis of these subjects is needed.[87] Specific features of Latin American systems, one

85. Whyte, pp. 381–82.
86. See, for instance, Irving L. Horowitz, "Introduction: The Norm of Illegitimacy: The Political Sociology of Latin America," in *Latin American Radicalism*, ed. I. L. Horowitz, J. de Castro, and J. Gerassi (New York: Random House, 1969). Also Gilbert W. Merkx, "Legalidad, cambio político e impacto social en los cambios de los presidentes latinoamericanos, 1930–1965," *Revista Latinoamericano de Sociología* 4, no. 3 (Nov. 1968); Martin C. Needler, *Political Development in Latin America: Instability, Violence, and Evolutionary Change* (New York: Random House, 1968). On the political situation of Latin American countries, see Jorge Graciarena, *Poder y clases sociales en el desarrollo de América Latina* (Buenos Aires: Paidos, 1967); José Luis de Imaz, *Los que mandan* (Buenos Aires: Editorial Universitaria de Buenos Aires, 1964); Douglas A. Chalmers, "Parties and Society in Latin America," mimeographed (paper delivered at the Annual Meeting of the American Political Science Association, Washington, 2–7 Sept. 1968); *Social Research* 36, no. 2 (Summer 1969), special issue, "The Future of Latin America," with articles by R. M. Glassman, James F. Petras, D. E. Mutchler, C. T. Oliver, David Felix, Julius Rivera; Claudio Veliz, ed., *The Politics of Conformity in Latin America* (New York: Oxford Univ. Press, 1967).
87. In some recent studies there is a significant improvement. See Alfred Stepan, *The Military in Politics: Changing Patterns in Brazil* (Princeton: Princeton Univ. Press, 1971). This is, in my view, the most accurate and intelligent analysis

realizes now, can hardly be detected through the usual categories and assumptions of social scientists of centric countries. For instance, the validity of studies that posit the existence of true social classes in Latin American polities, such as dominant class, industrial bourgeoisie, land bourgeoisie, proletariat, and even middle class, is highly questionable. Chimerical situations have been presented as the "reality" of Latin American countries by authors rigidly committed to the class approach. Latin American polities seem to be more intelligible when explained in terms of "power contenders" or "actors" rather than in terms of reified classes. Likewise, a number of authors take for granted that Latin American countries are already societies, that in each Latin American country the dichotomy of state versus society exists in the same terms as in the centric countries.[88] A satisfactory theory of the nature of the state in Latin America is still to be formulated.

Some writers suggest that the state in Latin American countries exists in a sort of inchoate environment, of colloidal suspension, so to speak.[89] In Latin American countries societies are still amorphous to the extent that a society means a minimum of order, i.e., a minimum of enduring and consistent rules of associated life. Samuel Huntington stresses correctly this point. Evoking Tocqueville, he comments:

> Among the laws that rule human societies, de Tocqueville observed, there is one which seems to be more precise and clear than all others. If men are to remain civilized or to

of the 1964 Brazilian coup d'état. Also Luigi R. Einaudi, *The Peruvian Military: A Summary Political Analysis* (Santa Monica, Calif.: RAND Corp., 1969); Claudio Veliz, "Centralism and Nationalism in Latin America," *Foreign Affairs* 47, no. 1 (Oct. 1968).

88. I employ the word "society" here in the sense that Lorenz von Stein made classic in the field of western European political theory, i.e., as an autonomous sphere of movements, independent of the state. See Lorenz von Stein, *The History of the Social Movement in France, 1789–1850* (Totowa, N.J.: Bedminster Press, 1964).

89. See Raymundo Faoro, *Os donos do poder: formação do patronato político brasileiro* (Pôrto Alegre: Editôra Globo, 1958). See also Guerreiro-Ramos, *A crise do poder no Brasil* (Rio de Janeiro: Zahar Editôres, 1961). See also Charles W. Anderson, *Politics and Economic Change in Latin America* (Princeton, N.J.: Van Nostrand, 1967); and Merle Kling, "Towards a Theory of Power and Political Instability in Latin America," in *Political Changes in Underdeveloped Countries*, ed. John H. Kautsky (New York: Wiley, 1966), and "Violence and Politics in Latin America," in Horowitz.

become so, the art of associating together must grow and improve in the same ratio in which equality of conditions is increased. The political instability in . . . Latin America derives precisely from the failure to meet this condition: equality of participation is growing much more rapidly than the art of associating together.[90]

The tenuous character of associated life in Latin America has been pointed out by several native observers of the area. For Alberto Tôrres, society in Brazil is not yet constituted. He pointed out that a true society cannot be equivalent to a collectivity of individuals subject to "whims of chance"[91] or lottery-like events. Bolívar wrote more dramatically: "There is no good faith in America, either among men or among nations. Treaties are paper, constitutions books, elections battles, liberty anarchy, and life a torment. The only thing one can do in America is emigrate."[92] Without Bolívar's emotional flavor, numerous scholars have also conveyed the view that Latin America has not yet overcome the Hobbesian stage of chronic disorder, that the problem of social order has not yet been solved there and a situation of permanent disguised martial law obtains. Thus, Merle Kling points out:

The legal and formal aspects of Latin American political systems . . . serve to maintain and perpetuate violence. For overt acts of violence yield an output of constitutional instability, disregard for prescribed legal norms, conducting government through executive orders, and the institutionalization of procedures for exile and asylum. In turn, these legal and formal concomitants feed back into the system and contribute to the perpetuation of violence, since constitutions do not inspire respect, prescribed legal rules do not impose effective restraints, decision making by the executive is customary, and the rule of asylum, by protecting the loser in a

90. Samuel Huntington, *Political Order in Changing Societies* (New Haven, Conn.: Yale Univ. Press, 1968), pp. 4–5.
91. Alberto Tôrres, *O Problema nacional brasileiro* (São Paulo: Cia Editôra Nacional, 1938), p. 112.
92. Cited in Huntington, p. 29.

violent political struggle, does not discourage revolutionary conspiracies.[93]

In such circumstances the legitimizing process of Latin American polities is very special and certainly cannot be fully understood from the standpoint of the classic criteria prevalent in centric countries. The obscure character of such a legitimizing process is a serious drawback to the effectiveness of public administration. In the words of Riggs, "the effectiveness of public administration varies with the degree of legitimacy of government. The maintenance of a high level of legitimacy is the least costly way of securing effective government performance."[94] A recent study empirically supports Riggs' view. Utilizing quantitative indexes of military expenditures, political instability, economic development, developmental tensions, social structure, and social decision in Latin America, Alaor Passos indirectly indicated that the higher the percentages of expenditures for coercive apparatus, the smaller the average rate of economic growth.[95]

The political environment of public administration has probably been neglected by those who emphasize what is apparently bureaucratic pathology in Latin American countries. In fact, public administrators cannot do much more than the polity allows. It is time for the practitioners to systematically raise the issue of legitimacy versus administrative effectiveness in Latin America, and to search and find sound guidelines for the public administrators of the area. Furthermore, we must ask what, within the

93. Merle Kling, "Violence and Politics in Latin America," in Horowitz, pp. 201–2. One can assume that the high degree of uncertainty resulting from these circumstances explains, partially at least, why gambling is so popular in Latin America. Games such as *quiniela* and *jôgo do bicho* (animal game) are widespread in the region. According to an estimate of *Time* magazine, 25 March 1966, pp. 31–32, the *jôgo do bicho* in Brazil is a $500-million-a-year business and employs roughly 1 percent of the nation's labor force. Roger Caillois reports estimates indicating that 60 to 70 percent of the Brazilians spend each day about 1 percent of their income in playing the game. He observes that this amount of money could represent considerable reserves for investments. Although the accuracy of such estimates is highly questionable, the fact is that gambling is a very salient feature of social life in Latin America. In 1931, according to R. Caillois, a governmental Department of Social Assistance of the State of São Paulo (Brazil) was financed with resources drawn from the *jôgo do bicho*. See Roger Caillois, *Quatre essais de sociologie contemporaine* (Paris: Olivier Perrin, 1951), pp. 41–42.
94. Riggs, p. 358.
95. Alaor Passos, "Developmental Tensions and Instability," *Journal of Peace Research* 5, no. 1 (1968): 70–86.

reach of public administration, can be done to improve the legitimacy requirements of Latin American politics. In this line, at least, two final remarks seem to be in order. First, more attention has to be given in the area to institution-building theory and practice. Institutionalization is, in the last analysis, a corrective of illegitimacy. Thus, presumably, there is some room left in Latin American countries where public administrators can be agents of institutionalization. In Brazil, for instance, the Instituto Brasileiro de Administração Municipal has played a positive role, becoming a factor of what Frank Sherwood calls the "institutionalization of grass roots," that is, of local agencies of government. This strategy of counter-illegitimacy probably can be implemented in other areas of government. It is an auspicious sign that the Escola Brasileira de Administração Pública (EBAP) in Brazil has given special attention to the study of institution building. Four of its professors wrote their doctoral dissertations on this issue.[96] Expertise in institution building, given the prevalent circumstances of Latin American polities, is certainly a functional and desirable qualification for practitioners.

Second, the further development of social indicators of administrative effectiveness may enlighten the publics about how their needs are being met and may lead indirectly to more legitimate standards of associated life. In fact, the development of such social indicators may increase the capability of the different groups in expressing their interests. Indexes of the cost of living have been useful to workers' associations in Latin America in justifying their demands, and for this reason governmental actors often try to influence their evaluation in order to minimize criticism among citizens. Thus, the difficulties that will be found in the further development of social indicators in peripheral coun-

96. See Kleber Nascimento, *Change Strategy and Client System: Administrative Reform in Brazil* (Los Angeles: School of Public Administration, Univ. of Southern California, Feb. 1966); Paulo Vieira, *Toward a Theory of Decentralization: A Comparative View on Forty-Five Countries* (Los Angeles: School of Public Administration, Univ. of Southern California, Feb. 1967); José Silva de Carvalho, *EBAP: An Experiment in Institution Building* (Los Angeles: School of Public Administration, Univ. of Southern California, June 1967); Aluízio Pinto, *The Brazilian Institute of Municipal Administration: A Case Study of Institution Building* (Los Angeles: School of Public Administration, Univ. of Southern California, 1967).

tries are not to be overlooked. However, this is not sufficient reason for practitioners not to try such a line of action. Great progress has been made in recent years in the technique of designing indicators, and they are available for Latin American policymakers.[97] An attempt to launch such indicators is in process in Brazil, under the sponsorship of the Escola Brasileira de Administração Pública (EBAP).

In today's Latin America, public administration faces new challenges. The time has come for us to reassess our concepts, methods, and assumptions. It may be pretentious to assume that we can now begin to move toward a solution of the specific issues and problems of public administration in Latin America within the context of a new paradigm, but if we are to progress as a discipline and a global society we dare do no less.

97. On the design of social indicators, see B. M. Gross, ed., *Social Intelligence;* see also Philippe C. Schmitter "New Strategies for the Comparative Analysis of Latin American Politics," paper prepared for delivery at the Latin American Studies Association Meeting, New York City, 7–9 Nov. 1968; and *Annals of the Academy of Political and Social Science* 388 (March 1970), special issue, "Political Intelligence for America's Future."

Part IV

Conclusions

Chapter 16

Evaluations and Recommendations

Lawrence S. Graham

In evaluating the chapters assembled in this volume as a single block of material, there are two perspectives that warrant consideration: the degree to which they give us insight into the current status of knowledge on Latin American development administration and the extent to which they permit us to make projections about future directions for research and the application of these ideas in practice. The configuration of public administration in Latin America offered by this group of authors constitutes a multifaceted view of problems, issues, experiences, and recommendations emerging from attempts at transforming governmental organizations and bureaucrats into instruments of change beginning in the mid-1950's and extending through the 1960's. Their analysis has continually shifted from one level of discourse to another—from specific problems and concerns in development administration peculiar to Latin America, to the examination of distinctive national experiences, to the identification of regional approaches to training, to the elaboration of change-oriented strategies mirroring wider patterns and processes characteristic of public administration as a field of endeavor independent of any one nation-state.

In joining together this body of experience one cannot help but be reminded of the imagery developed by Fred Riggs in his attempts at conceptualizing public administration in countries confronting and undergoing rapid change.[1] Variation within the Latin American region, even within the framework of a spe-

---

1. Fred W. Riggs, *Administration in Developing Countries: The Theory of Prismatic Society* (Boston: Houghton Mifflin, 1964).

cialized subject matter such as the present one, is so great that perhaps we would do better to begin with the disjunctures inherent in Riggs' model of transitional societies as a premise, rather than attempt to construct a single integrated, composite picture linking together what is by definition a series of incompatible elements.

Many of the dilemmas presented here are old ones for public administration, although with a flavor distinctive to the environment surrounding and interacting with public bureaucracies throughout Latin America. The preceding chapters in this book reflect the nature of the dialogue and offer a sample of the discussion which has gone on within the LADAC framework over the past seven years. There is scarcely an issue raised in them that has not led at some stage to a revival of the debate between practitioner and academician, between North American bureaucrat or scholar and his Latin American counterpart. On one side stand those involved in the implementation of public administration programs throughout the region. They have maintained consistently that academic public administration has not been of much assistance in helping them confront the day-to-day problems raised by attempting to improve performance in the bureaucratic sector. In the final analysis, they have argued, because agency personnel can find little to draw on in the new literature on public administration, safe but proven strategies and approaches continue to be employed, even though it is known that their results will at best be limited. On the other side stand members of the academic community, committed to the accrual of greater amounts of information on bureaucratic behavior in Latin America. Among them, one group has been concerned more with the analysis of what is, rather than what should be, while another has been involved essentially in normative questions. In between stand a limited number of individuals who have attempted to span the gap between those participating in ongoing programs and those analyzing general patterns and processes as observers on the scene.

Rather than deplore this state of affairs the editors of this book have taken the stance that this conflict among opposing viewpoints is inevitable. All that we have asked is that the debate continue to move in fruitful directions as we grapple with the issues of how to conceptualize and respond to change in the public sector in Latin America. Hence this volume's heterogeneity in subject matter, its overlapping themes, and its awareness of the divergence between theory and practice.

As a volume designed to provide an overview of the work on public administration in Latin America produced by our committee, it is important at this point to attempt to synthesize the views offered in the preceding pages. One way of accomplishing this is to make a group of evaluative questions the center of our discussion and attempt to build from them a series of propositions. In so doing our aim will be to bring into focus knowledge regarding development administration in Latin America and present deficiencies. Following the guidelines set out by Warren Ilchman as a means of evaluating the CAG effort as a whole, there are six questions which can be raised. In an academic perspective the relevant ones are these: How do the chapters of this book compare with what we already know about public administration in Latin America? Do they confirm conventional wisdom, revise it, or challenge it? To what extent do they add significantly to our empirical knowledge of public bureaucracies in Latin America? From the standpoint of the practitioner, equally valid questions include these: Do the chapters offer a greater understanding of the problems of development and the role of public bureaucracies in responding to change and hence make it possible to identify more clearly some of the alternatives? Do they increase the likelihood of successful action in the public sector? Do they take into account the cost of replicating these ideas in the world of politics and the constraints imposed by time, resources, and alternative purposes?[2]

2. These questions are paraphrased from a paper by Warren Ilchman evaluating the efforts of the Comparative Administration Group. See Warren R. Ilchman, "Comparative Wisdom and Conventional Administration: The Comparative Administration Group and Its Contributions," paper presented to the National Conference on Comparative Administration, Syracuse, New York, 2–3 April 1971, p. 50, and later published as *Sage Professional Papers in Comparative Politics*, 01-020, vol. 2 (1971).

Development Administration Strategies

In the discussion of development administration strategies the first proposition advanced is as follows: Given previous difficulties in implementing comprehensive national plans in Latin America, the "micro" or project approach to inducing change in public bureaucracy supplies a more feasible short-term strategy. This is because it is more comprehensible and more adaptable in developing an action orientation that can function in the Latin American environment, it can come to terms more quickly with human and organizational problems, and it provides a way to reduce the complexities of administrative change to a manageable size. Closely tied to this proposition, abstracted from Thurber (Chapter 1), are three conditions which can also be stated in proposition form: In order to function as an innovating center from which further development can proceed, a public organization must possess leadership characterized by "bureaucratic entrepreneurship," the capability for organizational development and "institutional transformation," and the capacity for establishing viable links with other like-minded institutions and their publics which share developmental goals. Within this context it becomes the responsibility of the development administrator to identify "islands for development"—the organizations within the public sector approximating these conditions, from which and through which change agents can act.[3]

None of the authors suggests that the improvement of performance by public bureaucracies in Latin America can be achieved exclusively at the "micro" or project level. Closely tied to their concern with program performance is the issue of how to engineer change at the top, among national decisionmakers, which will lead to greater policy integration and coordination among the multitude of independent public organizations to be found in the Latin American republics. In moving from the level of agency operations, where specific clientele groups are involved, to the policy level, where issues of coordination are para-

3. Thurber, pp. 45–46 above.

mount, the two Venezuelan case studies (Chapters 2 and 3) suggest a number of related propositions. First, where programs of general reform or change in administration are involved, continued executive support in both the formal and practical sense is essential. Second, such reform proposals must be based upon a careful study of the prevailing situation—i.e., identifying feasible strategies and alternatives, isolating areas where little or no progress can be expected, and focusing attention not on the structural components of organization but on the behavior of civil servants. Third, government-wide administrative reform programs devoid of a sense of practical politics are destined to failure. The difficulties of the Public Administration Commission, when compared with the relative successes of the Planning Commission, underscore the saliency of this point. Fourth, any government-wide strategy of change must contain a sense of the feasible; it must identify those areas, those organizations, those agencies which are the most critical and which provide the greatest opportunity for change. Otherwise, little can be expected except increased formalism.

When viewed from a standpoint external to the region and in the terms Guerreiro-Ramos (Ch. 15) suggests the theoretical contribution of this block of material to general knowledge is not particularly impressive. It presents few explicit propositions that are new and summarizes little more than conventional wisdom. But, within the context of the Latin American republics, where normative and formalistic administrative doctrine continues to predominate, these chapters offer Latin American data suggesting why the less institutional the model of change, the more flexible the strategy pursued, the greater the awareness of the political constraints present, and the greater the possibility of cooperation among change-oriented individuals and organizations, the greater is the likelihood of success in implementing development programs in the public sector.

In contrast to the project or program perspective adopted by Thurber, Groves, and Levy (Chapters 1 through 3), Jaguaribe (Chapter 4) takes as his unit of analysis the total national setting. He argues that unless one is careful to consider the influence exercised by the external political, social, and economic system on public bureaucracy, the chances of success in implementing developmental strategies are slight. Jaguaribe drives home with unrelenting logic the argument that unless a national government itself is willing to support the human sacrifices required to modernize, there is little that outside assistance can achieve except to accelerate the societal disintegration. He holds individual governments responsible for the lack of success in achieving development-oriented goals. For him the issue is twofold: how to redirect the application of external resources so that those national governments committed to modernization will receive the necessary assistance and, at the same time, how to insure that these external resources will be utilized in such a way that they contribute to the greater success of national programs focused on fundamental change. He takes past technical assistance efforts in Latin America to task for having made what is in his opinion a greater contribution to dissolving national social systems and to increasing their external dependency on world economic centers than to helping this group of states confront the issues of change and establish a basis for self-sustaining innovation. Rather than increased economic performance he sees cultural alienation, social alienation, and national alienation as the consequence.

Where U.S. technical assistance has had its greatest impact, Jaguaribe associates it with the reinforcement of the means of coercion practiced by status-quo-oriented governments. Nevertheless, for him, the influence exercised by the United States, as a technologically advanced society, on underdeveloped Latin American republics is not so much a case of intent or design. He views it more as a consequence of narrowly conceived policies, based on fallacious assumptions, and the failure to understand the national context into which developmental change must be channeled. This last point is an important one, for the polemics focused on U.S. aid in Latin America have frequently centered on the question of whether or not dependency relations have been fostered by intent, and the wider issues raised by "nationalistdevelopmentalists," such as Jaguaribe, have been minimized or overlooked.

Training Civil Servants for Development

One of the oldest concerns in public administration has been the nature and the role of training in the preparation of persons for public-service careers. Recognizing the importance of the governmental bureaucrat as a critical link between public policies designed to bring about change and specific programs intended to implement change, such a topic is of particular interest to anyone involved in development administration. Repeatedly in Part III the authors identify bureaucratic obstacles to change as a consequence of attitudes and values held by middle-range civil servants who—contrary to conventional expectations— demonstrate not frequent and wide-scale job turnover but a tenacity that survives regime fluctuations. As long as the public service is viewed essentially in terms of sinecures and as a major source of employment, and where promotions on the basis of merit are often uncommon, innovative behavior is difficult to achieve. Still, an essential premise behind existing development administration training programs is that these situations can be altered and bureaucratic behavior transformed in such a way that occupants of bureaucratic roles will become more supportive of policies and programs oriented toward transforming national societies.

Cannon (Chapter 6), Boeninger (Chapter 7), and Sherwood (Chapter 8) are all quite cognizant of this situation, and each attacks the training problem in a different way. Cannon would resolve the problem by changing the input going into training courses throughout Latin America. Boeninger would alter the institutional framework within which executive-level bureaucrats are trained by moving such programs out of training institutes into a university setting where professional preparation can be offered at a level equal to that provided by other professional schools. Sherwood stresses the importance of linking training efforts with institution-building strategies adapted to the particular needs of individual countries.

Of the chapters included in Part II, Sherwood's is the only one to examine in depth the record left by an existing binational program, one that was designed to have an impact on a national civil service by preparing more qualified personnel to occupy positions at the middle range and upper levels. This case is significant on several counts. Brazil has been one of the largest recipients of U.S. technical assistance, both in general and in the specific area of public administration. It constitutes the Latin American country with the longest established administrative tradition and the most comprehensive experience in public administration. In fact, outside France, none of the "Latin" countries has experimented with administrative reform programs more frequently and over a longer period of time. Brazil has also come to be recognized as a center for public administration training in Latin America; consequently, its influence in this area extends far beyond its national borders.

From the experience of the University of Southern California's School of Public Administration contract in Brazil, Sherwood singles out three lessons to be kept in mind in handling technical assistance in public-administration education. First, the teaching of administration cannot be handled as a generic process. In a developmental setting, business and public administration must be separated because of the distinctive political environment surrounding and interacting with public organizations. Second, the only strategy feasible in a developing country is an intensive one focused on institutional development; an extensive one emphasizing national administrative programs with wide-scale impact within a limited time span simply cannot be made operational in complex societies. Third, an institution-building strategy must center on identifying organizations in the host country whose viability is already established or which offer the potential of being able to extract resources from the national environment on a continuing basis. If the organization cannot demonstrate such a capability, the provision of foreign resources will mean little over the long run. In this manner Sherwood provides specialized country data supporting Jaguaribe's point that the national context is the critical element in engineering change and Thurber's contention[4] that an "islands for development" strategy has a greater chance of success than a "macro" approach.

Sherwood makes no pretense of formulating general guidelines for future training programs or for cooperative cross-national efforts in like cases. Nor does he provide data from which any generalizing propositions can be constructed. His is largely an impressionistic account of the complexities involved in a bi-national attempt at inducing change in programs preparing persons for the public service. Yet, in the absence of more extensive material, his chapter does suggest the richness of the experience in previous programs in technical assistance in the Americas remaining to be tapped. For those involved in similar programs it identifies some of the ecological factors which must be taken into account in planning training programs and attempting to generate action-oriented research, and how these factors interact with project implementation at every stage.

In the training field there is a great need for a comprehensive survey of existing programs and for inquiry into previous attempts at institution building. Sherwood suggests the experience to be drawn on, the need to handle such experience systematically, and the importance of abstracting from it general propositions regarding the successes and failures of training programs. At present even a coherent body of conventional wisdom in this area is lacking.

In the absence of systematic cross-national empirical data on public-administration training in the Americas, the two chapters concerned with the need for more dynamic training programs throughout Latin America—those by Cannon (Chapter 6) and Boeninger (Chapter 7)—of necessity deal with the problem largely in the abstract, although each writer draws upon the experience he has had personally within Latin America. Cannon argues for the necessity of infusing current programs with a heavy dose of participant training and suggests how group dis-

4. Chapter 1, above.

cussion, case studies, supervised internships, role playing, simulation exercises, and human-relations laboratories offer a host of possibilities in creating more dynamic training. Generally speaking, the training methods used throughout the region continue to focus on passive methods of learning clustering around the lecture. Recognizing the demand for improving on-the-job performance at all levels, Cannon outlines a number of possibilities of how such training might be converted into a more active learning experience. While Boeninger shares Cannon's interest in preparing executive-level personnel, he sees such programs as closely linked with university education.

The issues raised here cannot be confined solely to public administration education, for they are part of the wider problem of allocating and utilizing skilled manpower for developmental purposes. For this reason Shearer's chapter (Chapter 5) has been placed at the opening of Part II, to direct attention first to the general problem encountered in the shortage of high-level human resources in Latin America before examining specialized public-administration needs. Shearer underscores the necessity of trained, competent personnel to implement national development plans. Yet, he states, far too often plans drawn up for expanded productivity in industry and in agriculture give inadequate attention to this critical factor. He also points to the fallacy of assuming that the presence of modern organizations—in the form of foreign corporations—will necessarily serve to modify this problem or will entail the utilization and maximization of the skilled personnel of the country. Finally, he leaves the impression that unless public-administration training can be tied more consciously to general problems of national development and conceptualized as part of the difficulty in allocating human resources adequately, there is little hope for progress in this area.

Generating Empirical Data on Bureaucratic Behavior in Latin America

In recognition of the relative lack of data on public bureaucracies in Latin America at all levels, the chapters in Part III explore various approaches to the study of bureaucratic behavior and attempt to link the analysis of bureaucratic phenomena to the more general concerns of the social sciences. As a means of directing attention to the role of public administration in situations of rapid social, political, and economic change, a common theme was set for the Austin conference (this is the origin of Chapters 9 through 15). Six countries were selected as a sample of the variety of political and administrative systems available in Latin America, and papers were commissioned in advance. Each participant was asked to consider a common set of questions in preparing his paper. These included such topics as the role of public bureaucracy in generating change as well as in responding to pressures for change from the surrounding environment, organizational responses to change (whether or not innovating patterns of behavior had resulted), and interaction within specific national contexts between politics and bureaucracy as developmental aspirations have been articulated. As might be expected, the results were quite varied and not all the papers followed the same general guidelines. But seen as a group these chapters provide insight into the dynamics of public bureaucracy in Latin America, an element hitherto neglected in much of the writing on public administration and comparative politics in this region. As a general rule—except for specific cases cited by Weaver (13) and Guerreiro-Ramos (15)—the public-administration literature on Latin America has been largely descriptive, prescriptive, and formalistic.

In handling questions related to the interaction between public organizations and their environment, the first conclusion emerging from this body of material is the need to link organization theory, which has developed largely from data drawn from U.S. experience, with comparative public administration, which to a great extent is centered on developing areas. Utilizing the concept of cooptation, Parrish (Chapter 9) demonstrates how public bureaucracy has been shaped in Chile in such a way that it presents a major obstacle to the achievement of development objectives in a democratic environment. He goes on to establish the middle-class character of the Chilean bureaucracy, the predominance of employment criteria over developmental values, and the stalemate which had emerged, prior to Allende's coming to power, in a policy process characterized by "disjointed incrementalism" and strategies of "reformmongering." Generally speaking, the comparative analysis of complex organizations in the public sector throughout Latin America and a precise delineation of the variables affecting organizational behavior in this area of the world remain unexplored territory.

Equally important with the need to establish a clear-cut organizational focus for future work in public administration in Latin America is the emphasis in Tuohy's and Petras's chapters (10 and 11) on approaching government as an integral process involving both political and bureaucratic actors. In neither Cuba nor Mexico can the dynamics of the administrative process be understood without recourse to the larger political system. In fact, both cases provide strong arguments for the view that the very concepts "administration" and "politics" direct attention away from the composite policy process which has appeared in each instance. In Cuba, Petras cites the merger of the roles of the politician and the administrator and points out that in the context of postrevolutionary Cuba, where developmental goals predominate, little functional specialization in government can be noted. Related to this pattern is the shift inward in public policy in Cuba, away from internationalism to the building of socialism "in one island" as the present governing elite has sought to consolidate the political, the social, and the economic revolutions experienced by Cuba.

In Tuohy's chapter there is little public-administration language employed, yet the author is immersed in the analysis of a public-policy process that is highly bureaucratized. Tuohy uses the term "administered politics" to define his area of concern and focuses his remarks on middle- and low-level elites in Mexico, on those associated with government-party apparatuses. A mechanism central to the maintenance or preservation of the centralized national regime is the extensive use of cooptation in the hierarchy of the formal government and the official party (the PRI). As characteristic of "administered politics" in Mexico, Tuohy singles out four phenomena for attention: centralized control and political recruitment, encouragement of public officials to take conservative stances, prevalence of the concept of the "good" politician and administrator as managers of hierarchically delegated responsibilities and as manipulators of the public environment, and detachment of government officials from the content of public policy.[5] For all the work by political scientists on Mexico, we still have little available that goes beyond Tuohy's analysis to provide an insight into the interaction between politician and bureaucrat in the policy process. This situation, however, is not unique to Mexico; rather, it is endemic to the status of political-science research on Latin America as a whole, where far greater attention has been devoted to interest groups, political parties, and the inputs into the political process than to the policy outputs of governments or the role of public bureaucracies as a relevant part of national politics.

The public-policy focus inherent in the chapters by Petras and Tuohy and the interest in the chapter by Parrish in utilizing organization-theory concepts to better understand problems of development policy making meet in present-day Peru (Chapter 12). There the central issue has become whether or not the present regime and the public bureaucracy under its jurisdiction have the capacity to administer and implement the developmental policies to which they have become committed. Einaudi, the author of this chapter, calls attention to the importance of examining the relations between the two major public bureaucracies in Peru, the military and the civilian. Although he does not actually follow through on this task, he does proceed to develop a profile of the military bureaucracy governing the country since October 1968. Again, to generalize, in the work on Latin America we encounter a great deal of writing on the military, but few attempts at handling the military as a public bureaucracy, as Einaudi handles it, or at analyzing the interaction between military and civilian bureaucrats. Yet, to understand the policy process in Peru since 1968 and in Brazil since 1964—two of the cases under consideration in Part III—such knowledge becomes essential.

5. Touhy, pp. 278–79 above.

While Einaudi directs attention to the military bureaucracy as a political force in Peru, Weaver in Chapter 13 supplies complementary material for the Guatemalan case in his analysis of the role of the civilian bureaucracy in political change. Within this section of the book, his is the only chapter which actually generates clearly defined propositions for testing. His central hypothesis can be paraphrased thus: The extent to which the bureaucracy is an agent of rationalization is a function of the interaction of the factors: political elite, bureaucratic values, and system of administration.[6] Regardless of the political upheavals experienced by Guatemala over the past thirty years, Weaver concludes, there is a large degree of bureaucratic autonomy and resistance to change which have developed within the present administrative system. He indicates that the key to understanding the role of the Guatemalan civilian bureaucracy is "the configuration of values, attitudes and perceptions held by bureaucrats and the political elite."[7] Both Weaver and Parrish identify the problem of bureaucratic change with the salience of societal norms over organizational norms as determinants of bureaucratic behavior.

Underlying this discussion is the issue of centralization versus decentralization as a factor affecting developmental policies. Weaver and Parrish call attention to the diffusion of power among numerous public bureaucracies in Chile and Guatemala, in the midst of political systems whose formal characteristics lead one to expect a high degree of centralization. While Tuohy and Einaudi do not develop these dimensions in their chapters, in Mexico and Peru the same anomalies are present, if one examines the independent operations of the central ministries and the prevalence of literally hundreds of autonomous agencies in the public sector in each country. This particular theme—the interplay between centralization and decentralization forces—is made more explicit by Siegel (Chapter 14) in his analysis of three efforts at planned change in Brazil: the creation of a central administrative reform and control agency called DASP, the

6. Weaver, p. 317 above.
7. Weaver, p. 361 above.

development of an elaborate planning system, and the symbiotic relationship between tax administration reform and the decline of municipal government under the regime in power since 1964.

The last chapter in Part III (Chapter 15), by Guerreiro-Ramos, shifts attention away from consideration of the distinctive patterns of bureaucracy to be found in these six countries to general issues and problems which cut across the region and link public administration in Latin America to cross-national or global phenomena. He accounts for the great variety in approaches to administrative phenomena in terms of a wider process affecting the world as a whole. Within the field of public administration he believes this to be the consequence of a shift from one paradigm or world-view to another. Part of the change under way is reflected in the emergence of a "new" public administration. For him, this "new" public administration must not be limited just to North American experience; instead, it has to be related to public administration universally. This leads him to attempt to specify the content of the "new" public administration. Those identified with this movement, he writes, share an awareness of the gap between what we know and what must be accomplished and a commitment to "praxis"—the wedding of theory and action. He thus characterizes the writing produced by the "new" public administration as being nonprescriptive, antischolastic, and action-research oriented.

For Guerreiro-Ramos, reorienting the study of public administration in Latin America is no different from the problem in other areas. He views the search for a new theoretical framework in public administration as everywhere based upon three value premises. First, public administration, particularly development administration, must address itself to issues and problems of world development and break with the historical tradition of associating public administration primarily with the nation-state. The discipline must be cognizant of the growing movement toward transnational solutions and the emergence of transnational organizational phenomena, such as the multinational corporation. Second, the "new" public administration is premised upon a particular concern with human growth, with the search for new organizational forms which will replace the exploitative character of existing public bureaucracies, and with the development of client-focused organizations which will face up to the problems created by widespread alienation in contemporary society. Third, the present crisis is a crisis of legitimacy; consequently, says Guerreiro-Ramos, we must search for a new basis of legitimacy for public organizations.

When transferred into the Latin American setting, he states that these issues and problems require us to think in new terms. In the future, he says, we must examine linkage problems intra-nationally as well as internationally and analyze those external variables which affect administrative behavior throughout Latin America. One of the consequences of this world or penetrative linkage process is the prevalence of administrative formalism. Equally important, in his view, is the belief that we cannot contribute to problem solving in peripheral areas, such as Latin America, unless we are contextual in our approach and concerned with the development of client-centered micro-organizations. Finally, he maintains that unresolved problems of legitimacy raise the issue of political environment as a preeminent factor in determining bureaucratic behavior in the region.

Prospect

Acknowledging the case-study character of these chapters, as explorations in the unique, this final chapter has attempted to take a "nomothetic"[8] approach to the analysis of development administration within Latin America. In contrast to earlier treatments of public administration in the region, the editors of this volume have aimed their sights on escaping from the single-

---

8. Riggs uses the term "idiographic" to refer to studies of the unique in general, such as a case study or focus on a historical event, single organization, individual country, or culture area. In contrast "nomothetic" refers to studies which seek "generalizations, 'laws,' hypotheses that assert regularities of behavior, correlations between variables." See Fred W. Riggs, "Convergences in the Study of Comparative Public Administration and Local Government," *Studies in Public Administration* no. 23 (Gainesville: Public Administration Clearing Service, Univ. of Florida, 1962), p. 9.

country monograph as well as from global treatments of the region, which demonstrate little sensitivity for the specific problems and issues to be found in the various countries represented or which ignore topics of concern to development administration. It has been our intent to treat public administration in Latin America in greater depth and comprehensiveness than has occurred previously.

As an initial effort, pulling together and consolidating a good part of what we know about Latin American public administration, this body of writing does not so much confirm, revise, or challenge conventional wisdom about administration within this group of nation-states as represent a first step in simply supplying an overview of the material. Its greatest departure from earlier administrative writing on the region has been its attempt to avoid prescriptive, normative judgments about how public administration in the region ought to function according to standards and values alien to the area—although, certainly, individual chapters are based on value judgments as to what actions should be followed on the basis of the author's experience and knowledge of different components of Latin American administrative reality.

Hopefully, this volume will add to our empirical knowledge about public bureaucracies in Latin America—not so much through having exhausted the material available as through opening up for the reader the possibilities for more meaningful and more action-oriented research in the region. The individual country studies and the review of program and project experience are based by and large on an effort to appraise what is, before passing judgment on what should be.

From an academic point of view, the major problem with this material has been the absence of a common unifying framework. Consequently it has not been possible to engage in greater in-depth comparative analysis across national lines nor to specify more precisely within-nation differences. Still, by focusing on change or development as a common theme, the reader can obtain from these pages an idea as to the variety of governmental actions and the bureaucratic responses made to developmental pressures.

In terms of identifying more clearly the alternatives open to development administration in Latin America, and in providing guidelines for the practitioner, this material has been less than successful, for there is little systematic macro and micro theory-building to be found in these pages. It is in confronting the issues of program implementation and how to initiate changes in bureaucratic behavior in Latin America that go beyond the commonplace that this volume has been most deficient. There is a call for action-oriented research and a number of discrete case studies are provided, but there is little else of a concrete nature.

By identifying some of the problems encountered in our joint efforts in Latin American development administration over the past seven years and by attempting a mid-term appraisal of our efforts at this point, it becomes possible for us to underscore more clearly our accomplishments and failures as we look towards what is needed.

We would like to see future research in public administration in Latin America move along lines which will increase our knowledge substantially about the dynamics of public bureaucracy, within the context of changing environments, and which will allow us to bridge more effectively the gap between knowledge of what is and what has to be done by the policymaker. Within this framework there is a need both for a comprehensive review of the whole approach to education and training of civil servants in the region and for a systematic collaborative research effort among North Americans and Latin Americans to generate comparative empirical data on bureaucratic behavior. If these two tasks could be realized, those of us working from a Latin American data base might then be in a better position to make a distinctive contribution to the general understanding of public administration as a universal phenomenon.

Index